Religious Freedom

16 September 2013
Dear Michael
with best wishes
[signature]

Religious Freedom

Did Vatican II Contradict Traditional Catholic Doctrine?
A Debate

Arnold T. Guminski & Brian W. Harrison, O.S.

Preface by Gerard V. Bradley

ST. AUGUSTINE'S PRESS
South Bend, Indiana

Manufactured in the United States of America

1 2 3 4 5 6   19 18 17 16 15 14 13

Library of Congress Cataloging in Publication Data
Guminski, Arnold T., 1932–
Religious freedom:
did Vatican II contradict traditional Catholic doctrine?: a debate /
Arnold T. Guminski and Brian W. Harrison, o.s. – 1st [edition].
pages cm
Includes bibliographical references (pages   ).
ISBN 978-1-58731-698-2 (paperbound: alk. paper)
1. Vatican Council (2nd: 1962–1965). Declaratio de libertate religiosa.
2. Freedom of religion. 3. Catholic Church – Doctrines.
I. Harrison, Brian W. II. Title.
BX8301962.A45 D54 2013
261.7'2088282 – dc23   2012039822

∞The paper used in this publication meets the minimum requirements of the American National Standard for Information Sciences Permanence of Paper for Printed Materials, ANSI Z39.481984.

St. Augustine's Press
www.staugustine.net

TABLE OF CONTENTS

Preface
by Gerard V. Bradley

Dialectic is a reliable pathway to sound understanding, and to truth. Plato's dialogues are classics of disciplined inquiry. Aquinas famously worked towards enlightenment by sympathetically stating, and then refuting, objections. Some (mostly, older) law professors continue to teach according to the Socratic method. Lawyers engage in structured oral argument before the bench. Presidential debates roll around every fourth autumn.

Unfortunately, dialectic today is often a caricature of the real thing. Political debate tends to be theater. Judges joust with lawyers more than they try to learn from them. Scholarly "exchanges" (nee: debates) are typically sequences of set speeches, not fluid, critical discussions. "Socratic dialogue" was once the norm of law school teaching. But it is fast disappearing, and today's law students do not miss it. They scarcely know what they are missing: they were passive learners in college, and it is two generations since "forensics" was a staple of high-school and collegiate life. The scholastic "debate" team (if there is one) is now just for geeks.

Dialectic may be a vanishing art. But its decline owes not to any lost prowess as a pathway to truth. Its decline owes instead to reduced interest in the possibility of truth, and to lethargy about pursuing it. Dialectic is *still* the best way to reconnoiter certain questions. When expertly practiced it can *still* illumine as no other method of inquiry can. In the right hands, a spirited adversarial presentation *still* outperforms other ways of seeking the truth of a disputed question, or the right meaning of a subtle text.

Dignitatis humanae – the Second Vatican Council's *Declaration on Religious Liberty* – is ripe for dialectical investigation. Nearly fifty years out, the meaning of parts of this hugely important text remains controversial, and even obscure. What are the legitimate grounds for civil society's suppression of religious activity? Are they compressed into something called "public order"? What does that term encompass? Does *DH* teach that the recognition of a religion as the state's "establishment" is never just? Or is it sometimes just, but only so long as Catholicism is recognized by public authority as uniquely true?

1

Perhaps most important: what *is* "the traditional Catholic teaching on the moral obligation of individuals and societies towards the true religion and the one Church of Christ" which the Council Fathers expressly left "intact"? Is this a question only about an important norm around which *DH* detours? Or is it the hermeneutical key to the whole document, as if the Fathers said: interpret *DH* throughout so that its meaning in each case is consistent with "traditional teaching" about the "moral obligation of individuals and societies to the truth"? If so, then the precise meaning of that tradition is of paramount importance.

In this book Arnold Guminski and Fr. Brian Harrison take up this most difficult of all the questions about *DH*, namely its compatibility with traditional Church teaching on religious liberty. Each author possesses expert knowledge and they explore the subject via a sustained and disciplined dialectical exchange.

Quite simply, it works.

Religious Freedom: . . . A Debate is not a primer. It is not a comprehensive treatment of *DH*. Nor is it a full-dress narrative of *DH*'s genesis and evolution at the Council. Father Harrison and Mr. Guminski relentlessly pursue the question of doctrinal continuity, especially with regard to what the Church has taught – up to and including *DH* – about the liberties of non-Catholics, about public manifestations of their faiths and their proselytizing. In so doing, however, the authors take readers on a tour of *DH* and of the world (of Scripture, Church teaching, and theological opining) from which it emerged. *Religious Freedom: . . . A Debate* turns out to be a sound albeit select introduction to the history of Church teaching on religious liberty.

The authors affirm some points (concerning *DH*) which other commentators deny. The most important example is Mr. Guminski's and Father Harrison's agreement that *DH* teaches that civil authorities *may* without injustice recognize the Catholic faith as uniquely true, so long as everyone's right to religious freedom is respected. (One might call this a very mild "establishment.") They also agree (in effect) that way too many scholarly treatments of *DH* have read way too much of John Courtney Murray into that document.

A Debate also includes extensive treatments of matters wholly ignored by other scholars. Chief among these (and the presentation of it in Appendix A is largely a joint one) is the nature and scope of the Church's inherent coercive power pertaining to religious activities. By "inherent coercive power" the authors do *not* mean those penalties which we associate with public authority. Rather, they have in mind mainly spiritual penalties, such as excommunication and the like, which have contingent temporal effects and preconditions (such as concrete acts as a condition of absolution from sin or cessation of interdict). Mr. Guminski and Fr. Harrison affirm that *DH* teaches the truth that the act of faith must be free. This means that no one may be coerced into professing religious faith, nor may anyone be coerced to remain in a household of faith once freely chosen. Thus they affirm (and say that *DH* affirms) the immunity from coercion of apostates, schismatics, and heretics. But the Church possesses "inherent coercive power" nonetheless. In all cases, however, exercises of this power must be within the limits of a just public order.

Mr. Guminski and Fr. Harrison focus chiefly in *Religious Freedom: . . .A Debate* on that part of *DH* which pertains to the "right" of individuals and religious communities "*not to be prevented* from publicly teaching and bearing witness to their beliefs by the spoken or written word." [My added emphasis] Persons and communities have concomitant "right[s]" to manifest their beliefs in "public worship," "in erecting buildings for religious purposes," and to "hold meetings or establish educational, cultural charitable or social organizations." All these "rights" pertain to non-Catholic religions. The precise meaning of this teaching, as well as its compatibility with prior authoritative Church doctrine, is the main focus of the book.

The authors agree that, according to *DH*, there is no circumstance in today's world wherein suppression of non-Catholic propaganda or worship *as such* could be justified by the requirements of the common good. The authors disagree, however, about the status (if you will) of that teaching and – more so – about its relationship to the tradition prior to Vatican II. They agree that the prior doctrine was that such repression could be, and was, sometimes justified. Then they part company.

Fr. Harrison argues that *DH* is compatible with that prior doctrine insofar as it does not affirm or imply that the repression in question has *always and everywhere* been unjust. In Fr. Harrison's view, the innovative feature of *DH* is its clearly implied prudential policy judgment, or norm of ecclesiastical public law, to the effect that *in the modern world* – so very different from old Christendom – such repression can no longer be justified, even in Catholic countries, by the requirements of the common good.

Mr. Guminski argues, on the other hand, that *DH* teaches that there is (and always has been) a natural right not to be prevented from propagating non-Catholic religions *just as such,* subject to the exigencies of a just public order understood not to presuppose the truth of natural or of any positive religion (including Catholicism), or any other supernatural consid-erations. This teaching of *DH* implies, then, the injustice of preconciliar doctrine incompatible with it. And here I take Mr. Guminski to be talking about authoritative, but not infallible, Church doctrine.

The importance of a sound understanding of *DH* is great, and grow-ing. For Catholics, coming to a sound understanding of such terms in *DH* as "public morality," "public order" and the "common good" – as well as to the more precise matters debated by our authors – contributes strategi-cally to understanding what the Church teaches about political life in gen-eral. *DH* treats authoritatively the first freedom, that of religion. In doing so it constitutes itself as a primer on political society. *Religious Freedom: . . . A Debate* is therefore helpful to comprehending the Church's whole political theology.

Anyone can see that questions about the scope and foundations of reli-gious liberty are in every day's news. The nature and bases of Church teaching on religious liberty are thus, in light of the Church's influence upon human rights' thinking, important well beyond the Church's confines. The congruence of Catholic teaching with authoritative secular teachings, such as *The Universal Declaration of Human Rights,* magnifies the impor-tance of Church teaching, too. *Religious Freedom: . . . A Debate* is there-fore potentially valuable reading for anyone who wishes to bring Church teaching to bear upon our world's affairs.

Part I:

Contra Harrison in re Libertate Religiosa: On the Meaning of *Dignitatis Humanae**

Arnold T. Guminski

1. Father Brian W. Harrison, O.S., well-known to readers of *Faith & Reason* and other journals, has been widely noticed for his efforts directed toward showing that there is no inconsistency, and that there is indeed a legitimate continuity, between the doctrine of the Second Vatican Council concerning religious liberty, as set forth in *Dignitatis Humanae* (hereafter "*DH*"), and that of the preconciliar Church. Fr. Harrison's views are to be found in his book *Religious Liberty and Contraception*[1] (hereafter "RLC"), and as modified or augmented in several articles or book reviews.[2]

---

*   The title of this essay is abbreviated throughout this book as "CH."

1   Brian W. Harrison, O.S., Religious Liberty and Contraception (Melbourne: John XXIII Fellowship Co-Op. Ltd, 1988). Fr. Harrison's book, as its title indicates, is very much concerned with the status of the Church's doctrine on contraception. He wishes to show that DH, which does not define infallible doctrine, does not somehow constitute a precedent for relaxing the Church's teaching on contraception (assuming for the sake of argument its doctrinal status as being fallible) because DH's doctrine is not inconsistent with preconciliar doctrine on religious liberty (see RLC, 133–140). Nevertheless, Fr. Harrison contends that the Church's doctrine on contraception is indeed infallible, by virtue of both the exercise of the Church's ordinary and extraordinary magisterium (ibid., 138n17, 163–181). He thoroughly discusses the status of the doctrine concerning contraception as being infallible in his article, "The Ex Cathedra Status of the Encyclical Humanae Vitae," in Faith & Reason, vol. XIX, no. 1. Spring 1993, 25–78.

2   "Vatican II and Religious Liberty: Contradiction or Continuity?" Social Justice Review, July/August 1989, 104–112 (hereafter "SJR89"); "The Church, Archbishop Lefebvre, and Religious Tolerance," Fidelity, October 1989, 38–44 (hereafter "F89"); "The Second Vatican Council and Religious Liberty by Michael Davies," Living Tradition, No. 44, January 1993, 4–12 (hereafter "LT93"); "Roma Locuta Est, Causa Finita Est," in For the Glory of God and the Salvation of the World (Proceedings of the 26th Annual National Wanderer Forum September

5

2. In a lengthy article such as this, I do not propose to discuss exhaustively all the many issues, doctrinal and historical, upon which I find myself in agreement or disagreement, as the case may be, with Fr. Harrison. However, I shall here focus upon what he holds to be a legitimate interpretation of *DH*'s doctrine, and how he undertakes to demonstrate that this interpretation is consistent with what he understands to be preconciliar doctrine. What I hope to illustrate is that Fr. Harrison's interpretation of the doctrine of *DH* on religious liberty is unjustified, and that his thesis as to how that doctrine can be reconciled with preconciliar doctrine is fundamentally flawed.

A. An Analysis of *Religious Liberty and Contraception* on Preconciliar Doctrine and Practice

3. We first turn to his book. Fr. Harrison has rightly noted that the doctrine of *DH* concerning religious liberty, albeit authoritative, is not an instance of the exercise of the infallible magisterium.[3] Given this starting point, it is remarkable that in his book: (1) Fr. Harrison assumes, for the sake of argument only, that preconciliar doctrine on religious liberty is fallible, although authoritative.[4] (2) He limits his discussion of preconciliar doctrine respecting religious liberty to papal declarations – and thus without any reference to the relevant teaching (whether infallible or fallible), if any, of the ordinary universal magisterium. (3) He makes no reliance upon any real or purported *practical* infallibility with respect to the Church's legislation or policy, as distinguished from doctrine, bearing on religious liberty.[5]

24th–26th, 1993) (The Wanderer Forum Foundation), 39–48 (hereafter "Roma . . . Est"). His article, "John Courtney Murray: A Reliable Interpreter of Dignitatis Humanae?" in We Hold These Truths and More: Further Reflections on the American Proposition, eds. Donald J. D'Elia & Stephen M. Krason (Steubenville: Franciscan Univ. Press, 1993), is the published version of his paper read at a conference held 8–11 November 1990. This very ably written article, however, is expressly limited to a discussion of church-state issues other than those pertaining to matters of religious liberty.

3   *RLC*, 102.
4   Ibid., 138–139; but see 102.
5   The Church is *practically infallible* if it has that divinely endowed property whereby it is impossible for her, when she makes and imposes general disciplinary laws on all the faithful, to command what is contrary to evangelical law, prescribe what is intrinsically evil, or to proscribe what is intrinsically good. That such practical infallibility exists had been commonly maintained by approved theologians before

4. With the foregoing in mind, we may examine how Fr. Harrison summarizes preconciliar papal teaching. He does so as follows:[6]

> 1. The *Civitas* – the civic community as such – has a duty to honour God, and to recognize as uniquely true the religion entrusted by Christ to the Catholic Church.
>
> 2. Civil authority therefore has the duty to protect the true religion and the Catholic Church by restricting (to the extent that the common good requires) the free propagation of doctrinal error – both that which opposes reason or the natural law and that which opposes revealed truth. (It then pertains to ecclesiastical and civil law, mutable according to circumstances, to propose norms governing *how much* restriction the common good does in fact require in particular cases.)
>
> 3. In a well-constituted society, the common good will always require some degree of restriction over and above that which is necessary merely for the maintenance of public peace.
>
> 4. Civil authority can and should tolerate the diffusion of error to the extent that the common good requires, but may never give positive approval or authorization to that error, since nobody has an objective right to believe or propagate what is false, or to do what is wrong.
>
> 5. Nobody may ever be coerced into embracing the Catholic faith, since the act of faith must be free.

the Second Vatican Council, with some differences of opinion as to its scope and limits, and as to its doctrinal status. I do not mean to imply that Fr. Harrison denies this doctrine; he certainly does not do so, as we shall see. Rather, I simply point out that he has merely seen fit to ignore it in his book, together with the two other points also mentioned in the accompanying paragraph in the text. Fr. Harrison mentions in his book "the realm of Church policy, law or discipline – in which field she [the Church] does not enjoy any guarantee of infallibility." Ibid., 87 (see 26). However, I understand Fr. Harrison to be referring in this cited passage to doctrinal infallibility.

6   Ibid., 60–61. Notes omitted. The preconciliar papal pronouncements upon which Fr. Harrison focuses are: Pope Gregory XVI's encyclical, *Mirari Vos* (1832), Pope Pius IX's encyclical, *Quanta Cura* and the accompanying *Syllabus* (1864), Pope Leo XIII's encyclicals, *Immortale Dei* (1885) and *Libertas Praestantissimum* (1888), and Pope Pius XII's allocution, *Ci Riesce* (1953). I sharply disagree with some of Fr. Harrison's opinions concerning the interpretation of these papal documents. However, I assume (for the purposes of this article) the substantial accuracy of his account of preconciliar papal doctrine. Hence I shall not discuss these documents in this article, which focuses upon the proper interpretation of the doctrine of *DH* on religious liberty.

5. The foregoing can be safely assumed for the purposes of our discussion as substantially accurate, as far as it goes.[7] The term "common good" is used to refer to the natural and the supernatural good of the community, the latter good including the salvation of souls.[8] The common good endows, as it were, civil authority with coercive power to repress some violations of revealed truth or divine positive law, and not only of natural law.[9]

6. For Fr. Harrison, the distinction between policy and doctrine is critical. It is essential, for our purposes, to notice especially that he states:

> In the realm of policy – the practical assessment of what means are in fact necessary for upholding the common good – the Church traditionally judged that, at least in an already Catholic country, the public diffusion of ideas and practices opposed to Catholicism is *ipso facto* a sufficiently serious threat to the common good to outweigh other factors (such as the dignity or good conscience of erring individual persons) which might incline towards tolerance: and that therefore such activity should be legally restricted even when it does not in itself violate commonly held truths of reason or the natural moral law.[10]

7   Michael Davies, in his *The Second Vatican Council and Religious Liberty* (Long Prairie: Neumann Press, 1992), 168, rightly points out that the first point should be amplified to include: "In a predominantly Catholic society this will be achieved by the union of Church and State in which false religions will not be granted the same rights as the true religion." But see Harrison, *RLC*, 70, 76–82. I do not propose to discuss in this article doctrinal issues pertaining to an establishment of religion provided that full religious liberty is constitutionally guaranteed. As to the second point in the summary, I do not see why Fr. Harrison, by the use of "therefore," holds that a duty to restrict the free propagation of any doctrinal error flows from the duty postulated in the first point.

8   *RLC*, 55, 93, 135.

9   Ibid., 83–84, 100–101. By *coercive power*, as used in this essay, I mean the power to impose penalties of the kind typically imposed by civil authorities only (and thus involving the use, or the threat of the use, of physical force by an agent of that authority), as distinguished from the kind typically imposed by ecclesiastical authority, i.e., spiritual and such temporal penalties as are not typical of civil authorities only. [N.B. This note has been changed from that in the original text in *Faith & Reason* in the interest of clarity.]

10 Ibid., 83–84. The same point is essentially made in many other places. See, for example, ibid., 59, 87, 108, 141. The other references make it clear that Fr. Harrison is referring to overwhelmingly Catholic countries, and his use of "should" is to be understood in the sense of what is ideal but which is to be realized only to the extent it is prudent or expedient to do so. Fr. Harrison refers fre-

7. It should also be noted that Fr. Harrison, in his explanation of the relevant preconciliar papal documents concerning religious liberty (as distinguished from papal public ecclesiastical law or policy), insists that what was condemned was the following proposition: *"All* peaceful non-Catholic propaganda has a right to immunity from civil prohibition."[11] He means by this that a person has a natural right to be immune from civil prohibition as to *any* peaceful non-Catholic propaganda.[12] What was not condemned, according to Fr. Harrison, was the following proposition: a person has the natural right to be immune from civil prohibition as to *some* peaceful non-Catholic propaganda.[13] According to him, "Vatican II . . . was thus eventually able to affirm [that *some* peaceful non-Catholic propaganda has a right to immunity from civil prohibition] without contradicting earlier Catholic doctrine."[14] On the other hand, Fr. Harrison claims that *DH* "leaves open the possibility that at least *some* activity which violates revealed truth, but not naturally knowable truth,

quently to this public ecclesiastical policy as "law," which I suggest is perhaps too strong a term.

The term "public," with reference to the manifestation, exercise, or diffusion of religion, is ambiguous. Fr. Harrison usually uses "public" as synonymous with "external" or "exterior" and thus to refer to what only occurs, or is open to the view of those in public places, such as streets, parks, squares, and the like – and not to what occurs within buildings open to the public, such as churches and temples. See ibid., 51n46, 56–59, 86n4; but see also 125–26. The term "public" as used in the relevant Church documents in connection with the public exercise of religion, however, appears ordinarily intended to refer to what occurs within or without buildings open to the public.

11 Ibid., 44.
12 Ibid., 44. He explains that he uses the quoted expression "merely for economy of expression."
13 Ibid. I do not accept Fr. Harrison's analysis as accurate, but will assume its accuracy for the purpose of our discussion. Briefly, my opinion is: (1) according to preconciliar papal doctrine (most probably up to John XXIII's encyclical, *Pacem in Terris* (1963), there is no natural right *whatsoever* to freely (i.e., to be immune from coercion by civil authority) engage in the public manifestation or propagation of any non-Catholic religion; (2) that this doctrine, although authoritative at the time, should be held as not having been promulgated in the infallible exercise of the papal magisterium.

Unless otherwise indicated, the term "definitively taught" as used in this article refers only to those doctrines which have been taught by the Church in the exercise of its infallible magisterium.

I shall generally use terms "natural right to be free to" or "natural right to freely" in place of "natural right to be immune from coercion by civil authority."
14 *RLC,* 44. 15 Ibid., 100.

might endanger the 'public order,' and hence be subject to civil restrictions."[15]

8. Thus, a fair reading of Fr. Harrison's discussion of the matter justifies the conclusion that the objective meaning of what he has written is that preconciliar papal teaching did not condemn the proposition: in a predominantly Catholic country there is a natural right to be free (i.e., immune from coercion by civil authority) to publicly manifest and propagate (peacefully) *some* non-Catholic religions, and that *DH* affirms this right.[16] Indeed, when discussing the "fairly constant (though unfortunately far from invariable) practice" in medieval Catholic states of tolerating the public exercise of non-Christian cults of those never baptized, he writes:[17]

> But it does seem fair to say that such an elevation [from a permissive to a mandatory toleration], carried out explicitly by *Dignitatis Humanae* when it teaches that at least some false religious practices can have a right to religious liberty, is an harmonious bringing to the surface of something which good Catholics had traditionally observed in practice, and perhaps recognized theoretically in an obscure or partially formulated way.

B. Fr. Harrison on the Meaning of *Dignitatis Humanae*

9. Turning now to the doctrine of *Dignitatis Humanae*, Fr. Harrison summarizes it as follows in his book:[18]

> C1. The "traditional Catholic doctrine" concerning the "moral duty of men and societies towards the true religion and the one Church or Christ" remains "intact."
>
> C2. The human person, by virtue of his innate dignity, has a right to immunity from human coercion in religious matters both individually and collectively, in public and in private, so that

---

15 Ibid., 100.
16 See ibid., 43–53, 100–02, 109, 125–26, 128–29. In fairness to Fr. Harrison, it should be here noted that, in a letter to me, dated February 8, 1995, he denies that his book asserts that *DH* asserts the natural right to be free to publicly manifest or propagate some non-Catholic religions in predominantly Catholic countries. If that, however, is not what he meant to say, it is nevertheless the meaning of what was written by him. The reader, of course, must judge for himself.
17 *RLC*, 126.
18 Ibid., 63–64. Notes omitted.

within due limits, he may neither be forced to act against his conscience, nor prevented from acting in accordance with it.

C3. The "due limits" mentioned in C2 are to be determined in accordance with the objective moral order, by the requirements of that fundamental component of the common good which in contemporary usage is termed the care of "public order." These requirements are: first, the protection of the rights of all citizens and the peaceful settlement of conflicts of rights; secondly, the protection of a just public peace; and finally, the protection of public morality.

C4. The freedom of the Church, which she claims before every public authority in her capacity as (utpote) the spiritual authority appointed by Christ for propagating the Gospel, is the fundamental principle governing relations between the Church, public authority, and the whole civil order.

10. The foregoing, I think, is a substantially accurate statement for our purposes. I shall not, however, concern myself herein with points C1 (because his discussion of this point in his book does not impact issues of religious liberty[19]) and C4 (insofar as the freedom of the Church is conceived as a matter of divine positive law). Here, we notice Fr. Harrison's observation: "It is immediately evident that our preconciliar proposition 5 above (forbidding coercion on anyone to embrace the faith) is not contradicted by any affirmation of *Dignitatis Humanae.*"[20] Indeed, that the freedom of the act of faith has a corresponding component of the natural right to religious liberty is expressly affirmed by *DH.*[21] Fr. Harrison, noting "the harsh mediaeval practice of the Church towards heretics,"[22] explains that *DH* developed the traditional doctrine of freedom of the act of faith by

19 See ibid., 64–82, where Fr. Harrison discusses C1 ("The 'traditional Catholic doctrine' concerning the 'moral duty of men and societies towards the true religion and the one Church of Christ' remains 'intact'") only in connection with issues pertaining to the duty to honor God and to recognize the Catholic religion as uniquely true. The book's discussion of the postconciliar coercive power does not refer at all to C1. See also ibid., 83–111.

20 Ibid., 64.

21 *DH* ##6.5, 9.1, 10, 12.1: *Decrees of the Ecumenical Councils,* eds. Norman P. Tanner & Giuseppe Albergigo (Washington: Georgetown Press, 1990) (hereafter "Tanner"), vol. II, 1003, 1005, 1006–1007, 1009.

22 *RLC,* 125. See also 32, where he refers to sixteenth-century Catholics "accustomed to a long tradition of ecclesiastically sanctioned heretic-burning."

having it also encompass whether or not to retain the faith. Thus, "it emerges as an implication of the traditional doctrine that people should not be coerced by governments simply for wanting to opt out of the Church by private acts of heresy, schism or apostasy."[23]

11. Before proceeding further, we should first examine the most relevant text in *DH*, that is, #7. It declares:[24]

> The exercise of the right to religious freedom takes place in human society and is therefore subject to certain modifying principles.
>
> The moral maxim of personal and social responsibility must be followed in the exercise of all liberties; in the use of their rights individuals and social groups are found by the moral law to have regard to the rights of others, to their own duties towards others and to the common good of all. All should be treated with justice and humanity.
>
> Further, as society has the right to protect itself against the abuses that can occur under the guise of religious liberty, it is chiefly for the state to provide the relevant safeguards. This should be done neither arbitrarily nor with inequitable discrimination, but by legal norms in accord with the objective moral order. Such rules are required for the effective protection and peaceful harmonizing of the rights of all citizens. They are required to make adequate provision for that general peace and good order in which people live together in true justice. They are required for the due protection of public morality. These factors together constitute a fundamental part of the common good, and are included in the idea of public order. Nevertheless, that principle of full freedom is to be preserved in society according to which people are given the maximum of liberty, and only restrained when and in so far as is necessary.

12. *DH* essentially defines religious liberty as immunity from coercion in religious matters, within due limits.[25] The declaration uses "due public

---

23 Ibid., 125.
24 Tanner II, 1005–06.
25 *DH* #2.1, Tanner II, 1002: "[Religious] freedom consists in this, that all should have such immunity from coercion by individuals, or by groups, or by any human power, that no one should be forced to act against his conscience in religious matters, nor prevented from acting according to his conscience, whether in private or

order"[26] as equivalent in meaning to "due limits." Hence, we may more succinctly define "within due limits" (or its equivalent expression) as: subject to those legal norms, determined in conformity with the objective moral order, necessary for the effective protection and peaceful harmonizing of the rights of all citizens, for the adequate provision for genuine public peace, and for a proper guardianship of public morality. It should be here noted that #7.3 is concerned with the legal limits of the immunity from coercion as to religious matters, whereas the second paragraph is concerned with the moral limits of the same. Fr. Harrison treats the two terms, "rights of others" as used in #7.2, and "rights of all citizens" as used in #7.3, as essentially synonymous – a matter, as we shall see, of great importance, since the former are moral (or quasi-moral) rights and the latter are legal (or juridical) rights.[27] Fr. Harrison correctly explains that

in public, whether alone or in association with others, within due limits." The legislative intent is clearly, to quote Fr. John Courtney Murray, "that the word 'conscience,' found in the Latin text, is used in the generic sense, sanctioned by usage, of 'beliefs,' 'convictions,' 'persuasions'" *(The Documents of Vatican II,* ed. W.M. Abbott [New York: America Press, 1966], 679, # 5). According to Cardinal Pietro Pavan: "It must first be stated that here the term 'conscience' means above all responsibility, so that the statement must be understood thus: In the religious sphere no one may be compelled to act in a way different from that in which he himself has decided to act, and no man may be prevented from acting according to this way." (Pietro Pavan, "Declaration on Religious Freedom," in 4 *Commentary on the Documents of Vatican II,* ed. Herbert Vorgrimler [New York: Herder and Herder, 1969], 66). See *Acta Synodalia Sacrosancti Concilii Oecumenici Vaticani II* (Rome: Typis Polyglottis Vaticanis, 1978) (hereafter *AS*), vol. IV/pt. VI, 734: "In textu conscientia connotat etiam responsabilitatem"; ibid., 769: "'Conscientiam' . . . indicans propriam persuasionem."

26   *DH* #2.2, Tanner II, 1003. The term "iusto ordine publico" is also translated as "the limits set by due public order" (#3.4, Tanner II, 1003).

27   See, e.g., *RLC,* 93, 97, 107, 110. Cf. *DH* #4.4, Tanner II, 1004, which condemns improper proselytizing ("any kind of action that savours of undue pressure or improper enticement, particularly in regard to the poor or uneducated") by religious communities as a "course of action [which] must be held an abuse of their own rights and an infringement of the *rights of others*" (emp. added). Since # 7.3 should not be understood as including within the meaning of legal "rights of all citizens" all the rights encompassed in # 7.2, not every violation of the right not to be subjected to improper proselytizing (#4.4) is a violation of the legal (or juridical) rights of all citizens, within the meaning of # 7, par. 3. Of course, some kinds of such action may violate such legal rights. The late Cardinal Jerome Hamer (a *peritus* at the Second Vatican Council) is reported by A.F. Carrillo de Albornoz as having said (as a member of the Secretariat for Christian Unity) at a "recent meeting in Geneva that the conciliar statement in question [*DH*, #4.4]

religious liberty is not to be understood as consisting of any moral right to hold or manifest any false belief with respect to religion, but rather as consisting of a natural right to be legally tolerated, as he puts it, by civil authority with respect to any such belief, within the limits of just public order. Thus, doctrinal or moral error cannot constitute the objective ground of religious liberty as a natural right.[28] As the Council itself teaches, this right "is firmly based on the dignity of the human person as this is known from the revealed word of God and from reason itself."[29] Indeed, "the right to religious freedom is based on human nature itself, not on any merely personal attitude of mind."[30]

C. Fr. Harrison's Book on the "Public Order" and "Objective Moral Order"

13. Fr. Harrison's reconciliation of preconciliar papal doctrine and that of *DH* is accomplished in the following manner. He first alleges that the public order, considered as the fundamental component of the common good, consists of three components which are identical with all those components of the common good that are concerned with the exercise of coercive power by civil authority. How is this possible? It is possible because "[t]he three grounds given by Vatican II [for civil restrictions on religious propaganda] cover generically all of the grounds recognized by the preconciliar doctrine. This is true by virtue of the Council's 'catch-all' category, 'the rights of all citizens.'"[31] According to Fr. Harrison, the term "rights of all citizens" as used in #7.3 includes the moral (or quasi-moral) rights of citizens not to have eternal life imperiled by, for example, temptations against faith occasioned by exposure to heretics.[32] As he further explains:[33]

> referred only to *moral rights* and that these moral rights neither could nor should be enforced by laws; thus this assertion [concerning improper proselytizing] rightfully belongs in the preceding paragraph of Section 7 where *moral* regulation of religious freedom is discussed" *(Religious Liberty* [New York: Sheed and Ward, 1967], 124–125). On the other hand, Fr. Harrison holds that the any improper proselytizing is potentially a violation of a just public order. *RLC*, 98, 110–111.

28 Ibid., 114–17, 129–30, 142. Unfortunately, Fr. Harrison insists on speaking of religious liberty in terms of the "right to be tolerated," which in my view tends more to confusion than clarification.

29 *DH* #2.1, Tanner II, 1002.

30 *DH* #2.2, Tanner II, 1003.

31 *RLC*, 93.

32 Ibid.

33 Ibid., 97.

The first consideration – protecting and reconciling "the rights of all citizens" is particularly broad. This may have been deliberate . . . [I]t is this very vagueness which saves *Dignitatis Humanae* from making any "blanket" condemnation of the Church's own traditional public law: as Bishop De Smedt's *relatio* about the "relative" and "evolving" nature of the "common good" implied, the Council did not wish to condemn the idea that, in certain social and cultural conditions which no longer obtain in the contemporary world, the public diffusion of non-Catholic ideas as such might have been justly restrained as an infringement of the rights of an overwhelmingly Catholic populace.

14. Fr. Harrison's reference to Bishop De Smedt requires further elaboration. He refers in the preceding passage to remarks made by Bishop De Smedt, the official *relator* of *DH*, in the course of his presentation to the Council on November 19, 1965. To quote Fr. Harrison's translation of Bishop De Smedt's remarks about # 7 of *DH*:[34]

Venerable Fathers, this elucidation regarding the common good clarifies many points in the text, and renders a number of other suggested changes unnecessary. Let me give an example. In no. 12 the issue was raised of reprehensible behaviour – behaviour contrary to the spirit of the Gospel – which has sometimes arisen during the history of the People of God. Now, some Fathers wanted us to add that in judging these shortcomings of the past, one should take into account the fact that human society itself has exhibited different modes of thinking and living in different ages. This is quite true, but it is equivalently expressed when we affirm that the norm for the care of religion is the common good. The common good, as everyone knows, is something relative: it is linked to the cultural evolution of peoples and has to be judged according to that development.

15. Bishop De Smedt's statement is made much of by Fr. Harrison as confirming his position that the "just public order" of *DH* is equivalent in scope only to the coercive components of the common good within the meaning of preconciliar doctrine. But this reliance is unwarranted. First, Bishop De Smedt was reading from a written *relatio,* which had been

---

34   Ibid., 89, quoting from, *Acta Synodalia Sacrosancti Concilii Oecumenici Vaticani* (Vatican City: Typis Polyglottis Vaticanis) (1978), vol. IV/pt. VI, p. 723 # 15.

made available to the Council Fathers on November 17, 1965.[35] The above-quoted remarks on the common good were not contained in the written *relatio* but rather were made in *oratione*. Hence, these appear to have been incidental, surely extemporaneous remarks – very likely without any considerable impact. Indeed, Fr. Harrison appears to have been the first person, writing in 1988, to have taken public notice of the bishop's statement. Second, the remarks in question are inconsistent with the statement in the written report: "The common good is taken in its full extent *(sumitur in sua amplitudine)* as a norm when it is a question of guarding or promoting the right to religious liberty. When it comes to imposing limits, however, the more basic component *(parte fundamentali)* of the common good is taken to be the norm."[36] If the common-good coercive power includes the power to guard religious liberty, it is clear that the scope of the common-good coercive power is greater than that of its public-order component. Third, although what a *relator* says is of value in determining the meaning of a conciliar text, this factor is subordinate to the most important consideration: the objective meaning of the text as is supplied by the text itself where sufficient to that purpose. The text of *DH* itself shows that the Council Fathers understood that the common-good coercive power (as historically understood with respect to the *cura religionis)* is much broader in scope than the public-order coercive power. Fourth, the probative value of the bishop's *in oratione* statement is swamped by other matters disclosing the legislative intent of Pope Paul VI and the Council Fathers.

16. There are many more ways in which Fr. Harrison is erroneous in his opinion that *DH* can be properly interpreted such that the coercive power based upon just public order is equivalent to the coercive power based upon the common good, as conceived in preconciliar doctrine and practice. Let us examine some of them. The reference in # 7, par. 3, quoted above, to freedom in religious matters as "not to be curtailed except when and insofar as necessary," discloses awareness on the part of the Council Fathers that the coercive power of civil authority in this domain should only extend to what is necessary to limit, rather than to also what is appropriate or useful (but not necessary) to limit. Thus *DH*, also with respect to religious liberty, had at the outset acknowledged that the "people of our time . . . also urge that bounds be set to government by law, so

---

35 Ibid., 703 (text at pp. 718–23); Pietro Pavan, "Declaration on Religious Freedom," 4 *Commentary on the Documents of Vatican II,* supra, 61–62.

36 Fr. Harrison's translation in RLC, 90.

that the limits of reasonable freedom should not be too tightly drawn for persons or for social groups."[37]

17. *DH* itself proclaims: "In addition, religious communities are entitled to teach and to give witness to their faith publicly in speech or writing without hindrance."[38] True, this component of the right of religious liberty must be exercised "within due limits." However, it is nonsense to say there is a corresponding legal right – within the meaning of the term "rights of all citizens" in #7.3 of *DH* – of a Catholic not to be exposed to such public teaching and witness by a non-Catholic religious community even if he freely wills to be, or assumes the risk of being, so exposed. Moreover, the same paragraph of *DH* proceeds to add a proviso about the duty to abstain from improper proselytizing – a qualification which is pointless unless some proselytizing for some non-Catholic religion is deemed within the scope of legitimate public teaching and witness. Clearly, the "rights of all citizens" in #7.3, cannot refer to such *rights* as those which entail limitations on liberty in religious matters and which also presuppose the truth of the Catholic religion as such.[39]

18. Similarly, *DH* teaches: "Truth, however, is to be sought in a manner befitting the dignity and social nature of the human person, namely by free enquiry assisted by teaching and instruction, and by exchange and discussion in which people explain to each other the truth as they have discovered it or as they see it, so as to assist each other in their search."[40] *DH* also declares "that it is wrong for a civil power to use force or fear or other means to impose the acceptance or rejection of any religion, or to prevent anyone from entering or leaving a religious body."[41] A civil power forecloses "free enquiry" and uses "force or fear or other means . . . to prevent anyone from leaving [the Church]" by protecting believers from temptations against faith presented by propaganda, even if those believers are freely willing to be, or assume the risk of being, exposed to such propaganda.

19. Thus, additionally, *DH* explains: "[T]his right to non-interference persists even in those who do not carry out their obligation of seeking the truth and standing by it; and the exercise of the right should not be

---

37 *DH* #1.1, Tanner II, 1002.
38 *DH* #4.4, Tanner II, 1004.
39 A law does not necessarily limit liberty in religious matters simply because the truth of the Catholic religion is presupposed by the legislature. For example, a law which forbids abortion or polygamy does not limit liberty in religious matters.
40 *DH* #3.2, Tanner II, 1003.
41 *DH* #6.5, Tanner II, 1005.

curtailed, as long as due public order is preserved."[42] For Catholics, the individuals described in this passage clearly include a believing Catholic who virtually neglects the study of apologetical writings but, nevertheless, avidly reads literature subversive of his faith.

20. Surely, it would not be difficult to multiply other reasons, based upon the textual analysis of *DH*, to show why Fr. Harrison egregiously errs in holding that the "rights of all citizens" as used in #7.3, includes a *right* not to be subjected to temptations against the faith presented by propaganda involving persons freely willing to be, or assuming the risk of being, exposed to the same. Moreover, the entire framework of the declaration on religious liberty, and its stated purposes and functions, is utterly inconsistent with Fr. Harrison's thesis as to the meaning of "rights of all citizens."[43]

21. What is most interesting is that Fr. Harrison himself seems cognizant of the untenable nature of his position – though as we shall see he has an implausible argument by which he seeks to avoid a charge of inconsistency. This fissure in Fr. Harrison's position is disclosed in his discussion of Bernadino Montejano's contention that, to quote Fr. Harrison, "since, according to the Council, religious activity may be limited by the need to 'protect the rights of all citizens,' a Catholic State may justly claim that its citizens have a right 'to preserve their religious unity and to protect the humble faithful from a socially dissolvent proselytism.'"[44] Fr. Harrison's final statement on Montejano's point is worth quoting in part:[45]

> Having argued Montejano's case for him as strongly as seems possible, one feels bound to say that such an interpretation still seems rather forced . . . [T]o conclude with Montejano that a Catholic State could still today ban all non-Catholic propaganda, without infringing the norms laid down by Vatican II, would seem a thesis very difficult to sustain. Even if it does not contradict the letter of the Declaration, it contradicts very definitely the primary intention of many Council Fathers and *periti,* especially those coming from mainly Protestant countries, for whom the chief purpose of a

42 *DH* #2.2, Tanner II, 1003.
43 See, e.g., *DH* #15, Tanner II, 1010–11.
44 *RLC*, 84. Note omitted. The citation from Montejano comes from an article by Christopher Wolfe, "The Church's Teaching on Religious Liberty," *Faith & Reason,* vol. IX, no. 3, Fall 1983, 192.
45 *RLC*, 86.

conciliar statement on religious liberty was to counteract, for example, the discrimination against Protestantism in countries like Spain, where the Vatican-endorsed laws were seen as a scandalous embarrassment to the Church at large, and an insuperable obstacle to any significant ecumenical progress.

22. Fr. Harrison reconciles his position that *DH* does not contradict preconciliar papal doctrine, given his interpretation of the term "rights of all citizens" in #7.3 of *DH*, by contending that *DH* impliedly rescinded previous ecclesiastical public law or policy. He states that:[46]

> [*DH*] understood especially in the light of the authentic interpretations given by the Holy See in its various post-conciliar concordat revisions – implies (though it does not explicitly state) a new practical policy judgment by the Church: namely, that even in overwhelmingly Catholic countries, non-Catholic propaganda as such is *no longer* to be seen as the kind of threat to the common good which may justly be repressed by civil law. In effect, then, *Dignitatis Humanae* has rescinded the previous public law of the Church on this point.

23. To provide an example of such a change in church law, Fr. Harrison writes: "Since Vatican II, understood especially in the light of how the Holy See has applied the conciliar Declaration in various concordat revisions, the new law is that even in the most predominantly Catholic countries, the right of at least the more moderate and upright non-Catholic groups to immunity from government interference takes precedence over the right of Catholics not to be 'led into temptation' towards sins against their faith, as a result of the diffusion of false religious ideas."[47]

24. In any event, it seems to me singularly unusual that the "authentic interpretation" of *DH* by the Holy See's postconciliar policy is understood by Fr. Harrison not to confirm the thesis that the change in Church policy was determined by virtue of a doctrinal basis supplied by *DH*. On the contrary, he urges that "*Dignitatis Humanae* contradicts no previously existing doctrine (it goes no further than rescinding a previous norm of ecclesiastical public law)."[48] Accordingly, he contends that the fact that the Church in *DH* "did not explicitly and formally condemn as intrinsically unjust her

46   Ibid., 87–88.
47   Ibid., 142; see also 87–88.
48   Ibid., 144.

own existing public law – the law which was then still in force in Spain – is not without significance."[49]

25. Now. *DH* itself rather weakly refers to the fact that "at times in the life of the people of God, as it has pursued its pilgrimage through the twists and turns of human history, [and] there have been ways of acting hardly in tune with the spirit of the gospel, indeed contrary to

---

49   Ibid., 87. Fr. Harrison uses "intrinsically [unjust, immoral, evil, or vicious]" to refer to something which is essentially or *per se* unjust, immoral, evil, or vicious, and therefore absolutely (i.e., without exception "always and everywhere") unjust, immoral, evil, or vicious. Ibid., 87, 134–136. But see RLC, 135, where he appears to hold that an act, not intrinsically evil, may nevertheless be immoral in specific contexts because it leads to evil consequences. He also appears to hold that a law or policy, not intrinsically unjust, can conceivably be objectively unjust (as distinguished from being imprudent) in some determinate circumstances because of its evil consequences (LT93. 5–6: F89, 40–41). Such injustice can, I think, be properly called extrinsically or instrumentally unjust. For an example of usage by a writer exemplifying the distinction between intrinsic and extrinsic (i.e., non-intrinsic) violations of the natural law, see James J. Fox, "Natural Law," *Catholic Encyclopedia* (New York: Robert Appleton, Co., 1910), vol. ix. 77, and ibid., "Slavery," *Catholic Encyclopedia* (1912), vol. xiv, 39–41. For John Paul II's teaching about *intrinsically evil acts,* see *Veritatis Splendor* (August 6, 1993) (Washington, D.C.: United States Catholic Conference, 1993), ##79, 80, 81, 83, 137, 95, 172, in which such acts are defined as being *"per se* and in themselves, independently of circumstances, [which] are always seriously wrong by reason of their object" (# 80). However, as Germain Grisez points out, "[m]ost specific moral norms are non-absolute because they are open to further specification by recourse to the same principles from which they are derived" *(The Way of the Lord Jesus: Vol. 1, Christian Moral Principles* [Chicago: Franciscan Herald Press, 1983] 256).

It is possible that a judgment that a particular act or practice is morally evil, whether or not intrinsically so, may well depend upon the discernment of empirical facts which have neither been divinely revealed nor are necessarily connected thereto. See *Donum Veritas: Instruction on Ecclesial Vocation of the Theologian* (May 24, 1990) (Boston: St. Paul Books & Media, n.d.), #24. For example, *DH*, # 9, declares that "the right of people to religious freedom have their basis in the dignity of the person, the demands of which have come to be more fully known to human reason from the experience of centuries" (Tanner II, 1006). Similarly, the Congregation for the Doctrine of the Faith has declared: "the legitimate demand for freedom in the absence of constraint is a necessary condition for the loyal inquiry into truth" *(Donum Veritas,* # 32).

Some writers, it should be noted, classify any violation of the natural law as intrinsically evil, and any violation of the positive law as extrinsically evil. See, for example, Anthony Koch (ed. Arthur Preuss), *A Handbook of Moral Theology* (St. Louis: B. Herder Book Co.. 1919). vol. 1, 266–267.

it."[50] However, Pope John Paul II in his apostolic letter, *Tertio Millennio Adveniente*[51], has emphatically condemned the injustice of civil intolerance committed on behalf of the Church. The Pontiff declared:

> Another painful chapter of history to which the sons and daughters of the Church must return with a spirit of repentance is that of the acquiescence given, especially in certain centuries, *to intolerance and even the use of violence in* the service of truth.
>
> It is true that an accurate historical judgment cannot prescind from careful study of the cultural conditioning of the times, as a result of which many people may have held in good faith that an authentic witness to the truth could include suppressing the opinions of others or at least paying no attention to them. Many factors frequently converged to create assumptions which justified intolerance and fostered an emotional climate from which only great spirits, truly free and filled with God, were in some way able to break free. Yet the consideration of mitigating factors does not exonerate the Church from the obligation to express profound regret for the weaknesses of so many of her sons and daughters who sullied her face, preventing her from fully mirroring the image of her crucified Lord, the supreme witness of patient love and of humble meekness. From these painful moments of the past a lesson can be drawn for the future leading all Christians to adhere fully to the sublime principle, stated by the Council: "The truth cannot impose itself except by virtue of its own truth, as it wins over the mind with both gentleness and power."[52]

50   *DH* #12.1, Tanner II, 1009.

51   (10 November 1994) (Boston: Pauline Books & Media, 1994), # 35 (note omitted).

52   Quoting from *DH* #1.3 (note omitted). In his message to the participants in the Congress on Secularism and Religious Freedom marking the thirtieth anniversary of *DH* (7 December 1995), the Pontiff stated (*L'Osservatore Romano*, Eng. Ed., no. 51/52, 10/27 Dec. 1995, 7) (http://www.vatican.va/holy_father/john_paul_ii/speeches/1995/december/index.htm): "On their part, *religious believers must be deeply committed to the method of dialogue and persuasion.* As we prepare to celebrate the 2,000th anniversary of the birth of Christ, the Church acknowledges, in a spirit of profound repentance, those times in history when 'acquiescence (was) given . . . to intolerance and even the use of violence to the service of truth' (John Paul II, *Tertio Millennio Adveniente*, #35). With the Fathers of the Second Vatican Council, the Church today holds firmly to that basic tenet of the Declaration on Religious Freedom: 'the truth cannot impose itself except by virtue of its own

26. *Pace* Fr. Harrison, the assertion of a natural right to religious liberty (i.e., immunity from coercion as to religious matters, within the limits of just public order) does indeed entail the objective injustice of such preconciliar public ecclesiastical policy or law as was rescinded, as it were, by the adoption of *DH*.[53] We must reject as without merit Fr. Harrison's contention that *DH* rescinded the preconciliar public ecclesiastical law or policy (by which any non-Catholic manifestation or propaganda in predominantly Catholic countries could legitimately be repressed) but did so without changing doctrine. *DH* expressly declared that the Council "in treating of this religious freedom [it] intend[ed] to develop the teaching of more recent popes [recentiorum summorum pontificum doctrinam] on the inviolable rights of the human person" (#1.3). Hence, *DH* declared a *doctrine* concerning religious liberty, i.e., that there is a natural right to be immune from coercion in religious matters within due limits (#2.1), and "due limits" (or its equivalent expression "iustus ordo publicus") is thereafter defined or described (#7.3). It is in virtue of this doctrine that the Church's policy was changed in that *DH* calls upon the recognition of religious liberty as a civil right in all political communities (#2.1; # 6.2; #15.4).

27. Thus, on 28 June, 1967, Spain eliminated that provision of Article 6 of the Charter of 13 July, 1945 (*Fuero de los Españoles*) by which "[n]o one shall be disturbed for his religious beliefs nor the private exercise of his religion. There is no authorization for external ceremonies or manifestations other than those of the Catholic religion." In its place was substituted: "The State guarantees the protection of religious liberty, which shall be

truth, which wins over the mind with both gentleness and power' *(Dignitatis Humanae,* 1). The Church neither seeks nor desires to seek any worldly power placed at the service of the truths she bears. She asks only to be allowed to address man in freedom: and she asks for all human beings the freedom to respond to the Gospel in the full measure of their humanity." See also the Pope's Homily and the Prayers of the Faithful during the Day of Pardon Mass (12 March 2000), 45 *The Pope Speaks* 242–248 (http://www.vatican.va/holy_father/john_paul_ii/homilies/2000/documents/hf_jp-ii_hom_20000312_pardon_en.html}; the Pope's Catechesis of 1 September 1999, 45 *The Pope Speaks* 49–50.

53 See note 49 *supra*. Whether or not such objective injustice was intrinsically so would require an extended discussion, to be deferred to another time since we are focusing on the meaning of the central doctrine set forth in *DH*. An analysis of each important component of the natural right of religious liberty would have to be undertaken in order to determine whether or not a corresponding violation should be properly deemed intrinsically or extrinsically unjust.

guaranteed by the effective juridical provision which will safeguard morals and public order." The preamble to the act, which was changed with Vatican approval, explained:[54]

> The fundamental law of 17 May 1958, in virtue of which Spanish legislation must take its inspiration from the doctrine of the Catholic Church, forms the basis of the present law.
>
> Now, as is known, the Second Vatican Council approved the Declaration on Religious Freedom on 7 December 1965, stating in Article 2: "The right to religious freedom has its foundation in the very dignity of the human person, as this dignity is known through the revealed word of God, and by reason itself. This right of the human person to religious freedom is to be recognized in the constitutional law whereby society is governed. Thus it is to become a civil right."
>
> After this declaration of the Council, the necessity arose of modifying article 6 of the Spaniards' Charter in virtue of the aforementioned principle of the Spanish State.

28. Returning to #7 of *DH*, we now consider the relevance of the term "objective moral order" as used in the proposition that relevant safeguards by civil authority against possible abuses which occur under the guise of religious liberty should be done "by legal rules in accord with objective moral order." Fr. Harrison contends that objective moral order refers not only to the natural moral law but to the divine positive law as well. He states:[55]

> [A]ccording to preconciliar doctrine, violations of revealed truth or divine positive law – not only of natural law – might also be penalized by public authority to the extent required by the common good. It is important to note that this teaching is not contradicted by Vatican II, which nowhere speaks of natural law as the *only* criterion by which civil authorities may decide what to permit or prohibit. The Council speaks of the "objective" moral order; and divine positive law, for Catholics, is certainly as "objective" as natural law, since both have God as their source.

---

54 Michael Davies, *The Second Vatican Council* (*supra* note 7), 275–76. For the postconciliar development of Spanish law respecting religious liberty, see Roland Minnerath, *L'Église et Les États Concordataires (1846–1981)* (Paris: Les Éditions du Cerf, 1983), 101–12.

55 *RLC*, 100.

29. Asserting that Vatican II does not deserve Pope Leo XIII's rebuke of those who reject supernaturally revealed truths or who assert that the State should not publicly advert to them. Fr. Harrison proceeds to say:[56]

> While [the Council] no longer wishes to allow civil powers to treat all public non-Catholic propaganda as a punishable offence in our own day, it leaves open the possibility that at least *some* activity which violates revealed truth, but not naturally knowable truth, might endanger the "public order," and hence be subject to civil restrictions.

30. Fr. Harrison explains that "the Church herself, according to Catholic belief, is the unique authentic interpreter of the 'objective moral order.'"[57] The significance of this must be understood in the light of his statement:[58]

> Vatican II does not say that the State may penalize violators of the Catholic religion *only* to the extent that such violators are opposed to reason or the natural law as well. "Reason" or "natural law" are not so much as mentioned in the Council's exposition of the limits to religious activity, only the "objective moral order." And in a Catholic document – particularly in the light of the Declaration's re-affirmation in article I of the civic community's duty to act in accordance with "the true religion and the one Church of Christ" – the "objective moral order" (without further restriction or quali-fication) can mean only one thing: the law of God (both natural and revealed).

31. As to all this, it should immediately be protested that *DH* nowhere requires or authorizes repression of any violations of the Catholic religion, as such. *DH* allows, as it were, civil authority to justly repress violators of

---

56 Ibid. Fr. Harrison expressly states that, by virtue of the public ecclesiastical law or policy brought about by Vatican II, applicable even in an overwhelmingly Catholic country, non-Catholic "ideas and practices" which would merit classification as a punishable threat to the common good "would now usually (but not invariably) have to be the kinds of anti-Catholic propaganda which also assault or threaten (by virtue either of their content or their methods) those norms of truth, justice, civic responsibility, sexual morality, and respect for persons which are accessible in principle to unaided human reasons, without any appeal to the supernatural authority of divine revelation" (ibid., 143).

57 Ibid., 99.

58 Ibid., 107.

the public peace, or of public morality, or of the rights of all citizens – an entirely different matter.

32. Fr. Harrison errs, I submit, when he claims that the term "objective moral order," as used in #7 of *DH*, encompasses divine positive moral law. In the first place, *DH* declares and vindicates religious liberty as a natural right, to be universally recognized in all political communities as a fundamental civil right. Second, Vatican II's declaration on the Church in the World, *Gaudium et Spes,* was promulgated on the same date as *DH*, December 7, 1965. *Gaudium et Spes* (#16) describes that "[d]eep within their conscience individuals discover a law which they do not make for themselves but which they are bound to obey, whose voice, ever summoning them to love and do what is good and to avoid what is evil, rings in their heart when necessary with the command: Do this, keep away from that." *Gaudium et Spes* is here referring to the natural law and to the human conscience. It proceeds to comment: "And the more a correct conscience prevails, so much the more do persons and groups abandon blind whims and work to conform to *the objective norms of morality.*"[59] Citing this passage in his encyclical, *Veritatis Splendor,* Pope John Paul II has explained:[60]

> The great concern of our contemporaries for historicity and for culture has led some to call into question *the immutability of the natural law* itself, and thus the existence of "objective norms of morality" valid for all people of the present and future, as for those of the past.

33. The reader should recall that *DH* declares that "the right to religious freedom is based on human nature itself" (*DH* #2.2), and refers to the duty of the Church not only to "announce and authentically teach the truth which is Christ, [but] at the same time to give authoritative statement and confirmation of the principles of the moral order which derive from human nature itself" (# 14.3).[61]

---

59   Tanner II. 1077–78. Emphasis added.
60   Encyclical *Veritatis Splendor* (August 6, 1993) #56.
61   Tanner II, 1010. Leo XIII, in *Libertas Praestantissimum* (1888), #25, refers to two kinds of truths, natural and supernatural. He writes: "Of natural truths, such as the principles of nature and whatever is derived from them immediately by our reason, there is a kind of common patrimony in the human race. On this, as on a firm basis, morality, justice, religion, and the very bonds of human society rest." *The Church Speaks to the Modern World: The Social Teachings of Leo XIII,* ed. Étienne Gilson (Garden City: Doubleday & Co., 1954), 73. Similarly, Pius IX in *Quanta Cura* (1864), #2, distinguished between "the [C]atholic Church and her salutary

34. The principle of religious liberty, a natural right to be universally protected by civil authority, applies to any political community, whatever its official position respecting religion. Accordingly, the objective moral order governs the process by which the just public order (which includes the "due protection of public morality" as a component factor) is to be determined.

35. The conclusion – that the natural moral law (and not the divine positive law) is to provide the foundation by which the requirements of just public order are to be determined by the civil authority of any political community – is not inconsistent with the doctrine that civil authority is bound by the moral law, both natural and positive, of God. However, *DH* necessarily presupposes that the law of God (whether positive or natural) does not require or authorize what would otherwise constitute violations of religious liberty.

36. Moreover, although it is only the natural moral law (and therefore not also the divine positive law) which provides the basis by which limitations on civil immunity from coercion in religious matters are to be determined, it does not necessarily follow that it is only the natural moral law that civil authority may properly consider in otherwise determining public policy issues not involving those pertaining to religious liberty.

37. *DH* codifies the principle of the narrowly construed term "just public order" as the basic component of the common good in order to limit radically the traditional scope of the coercive power of civil authority with respect to religious matters. Historically, the coercive power was chiefly exercised in the following ways in "predominantly Catholic countries" ostensibly to promote or protect the common good (in addition to doing what was necessary to protect public morality and to preserve public peace): (1) to promote indirectly or preserve national or political unity, or public tranquility, by preventing the divisiveness brought about by religious dissent or pluralism; (2) to protect believers from temptations against the faith presented by the propaganda or the scandalizing exercise of dissident religions; (3) to vindicate divine honor against blasphemy, actual or constructive (and of other cognate offenses), as acts which by their malice especially require or warrant punishment by civil authority; (4) indirectly to protect public morality (which includes good citizenship) against the subversion of its principal source, religious truth; and (5) to act as the

doctrine and venerable rights, but also to the eternal natural law engraven by God in all men's hearts, and to right reason."

26

secular arm of the Church in the execution of its judgments against offenders.[62] Indeed, Cardinal Alfredo Ottaviani presented a doctrinal schema for consideration at Vatican II, on behalf of the Theological Commission, which incorporated that particular view of the common good referred to above. The schema proposed, *inter alia,* that:

> Thus then, in the same way that the civil Authority judges that it has the right to protect public morality, likewise, in order to protect the citizens against the seductions of error, in order to keep the [Catholic] City in the unity of faith, which is the supreme good and the source of manifold, even temporal, benefits, the civil authority can, by itself, regulate and moderate the public manifestations of other cults and defend its citizens against the spreading of false doctrines which, in the judgment of the Church, put their eternal salvation at risk.[63]

38. The schema nevertheless confirms the freedom of the act of faith as also a civil right, and confirms that the common good, both on the national and international level, can warrant a just civil tolerance in the Catholic City.[64] However, the doctrine of *Dignitatis Humanae* concerning religious liberty is not just a disguised codification of Cardinal Ottaviani's schema. "Public order" as used in #7 of *DH* must narrowly be construed in order to conform to the clearly manifested legislative intent to exclude the above-described traditional components of the common-good coercive power.

39. Fr. Harrison's thesis, as presented in his book, as to how the preconciliar papal doctrine and that of Vatican II respecting religious liberty agree depends upon the legitimacy of his contention that *DH* radically changed public ecclesiastical law or policy but without contradicting

---

62 Civil authorities have also violated religious reasons for purposes unrelated to concern for the public good: for example, exploiting popular religious sentiments simply to remain in power for essentially corrupt or self-serving motives.

63 Davies, note 7 *supra*, 300. Davies incorporates the complete text of this schema at 295–302, less its numerous notes. Cardinal Ottaviani's schema, however, does not appear expressly to warrant reliance by the Church upon civil authority acting as its secular arm to enforce the judgments of its courts against offenders. The Latin Text of the schema (i.e., "Schema De Ecclesia, caput IX, De Relationibus Inter Ecclesium et Statum Necnon de Tolerantia Religiosa," appears in the *Acta et Documenta Concilio Oecumenico Vaticano II Apparando* [Typic Polyglottis Vaticanis, 1973]): s. II/vol. II/pt. IV/ 657–672.

64 Davies, note 7 *supra*, 300–01.

preconciliar doctrine. He indeed asserts that *DH* propounds the doctrine "that when the common good is not significantly endangered, the followers even of false religions have the natural right, not indeed to propagate their mistaken ideas or practices, but to be left free by human authority to do so."[65] His argument depends upon two major premises. The first is that the term "the rights of all citizens," as used in #7.3 of *DH*, somehow includes the *right* (in some sense) of a Catholic, even though freely willing to be (or assuming the risk of being) so exposed, to be protected against temptations against his faith presented by non-Catholic propaganda. The second is that the term "objective moral order," as also used in #7, encompasses the divine positive law. We have seen how both premises must be rejected as erroneous.

40. There are, I submit, several tensions evident in Fr. Harrison's book. *DH*, it is claimed, does not contradict preconciliar papal doctrine (i.e., the civil authority may legitimately repress public manifestation or propagation of doctrinal error as to faith or morals to the extent that the common good requires). Yet this preconciliar doctrine was not supposed to have condemned the proposition that there is a natural right to be free to propagate publicly or manifest some non-Catholic religions in predominantly Catholic countries. This proposition, according to what Fr. Harrison plainly says, is affirmed by *DH*. However, according to preconciliar public ecclesiastical law or policy, all public manifestations or propagation of non-Catholic religions in overwhelmingly Catholic countries could legitimately be repressed by civil authority. On the other hand, *DH* somehow impliedly rescinded this policy. However, Fr. Harrison does not explain the mechanism of such rescission in his book.

D. The Development of Fr. Harrison's Doctrine in His Subsequent Writings

41. We now turn to so see how Fr. Harrison has modified his theory significantly, as to the meaning of the doctrine of *DH* concerning religious liberty, in his later articles and reviews. In his July/August 1989 article in *Social Justice Review,*[66] he remains focused on preconciliar papal doctrine on religious liberty issues. This article contains two major points which are of special significance for us. The first is that Fr. Harrison, repeating that *DH* does not contradict preconciliar papal doctrine, provides an

---

65 *RLC*, 141–42.
66 Fully cited in note 2 *supra*.

explanation of why *DH* nevertheless changed ecclesiastical public law or policy warranting the repression, in some situations, of all public non-Catholic manifestations or propagation in predominantly Catholic countries. He writes:[67]

> [I]t seems probable that the precisions given in article 7 of *DH* in regard to the limiting criteria on religious activity are to be seen as new norms of ecclesiastical public law rather than immutable doctrine. The central *doctrinal* affirmation of the entire Declaration is found in article 2 . . . The Council simply affirms there that there are "due limits" to legitimate religious activity in civil society; and article 7 then gives concrete application to this general doctrinal principle by specifying how the Church in our own day wishes these limits to be determined by civil governments.

42. In short, the alleged doctrine of *DH* concerning religious liberty is essentially vacuous. It reminds one of those sham legal constitutional provisions in totalitarian states which (in substance) affirm the right of the people to be free, as to a particular matter, but only within the limits of law.

43. The second major point is that Fr. Harrison now turns to his proposition C1 to buttress his argument that *DH* did not change preconciliar papal doctrine. C1 states: "The 'traditional Catholic doctrine' concerning the 'moral duty of men and societies towards the true religion and the one Church of Christ' remains 'intact.'"[68] Fr. Harrison contends in his SJR article that this particular traditional Catholic doctrine referred to in # 1.3 of *DH* includes the first four of the five cardinal propositions of preconciliar papal doctrine set forth at pages 60–62 of his book. These include the three propositions (C2, C3, C4) which pertain to the coercive power of civil authority with respect to the expression or manifestation of non-Catholic religions.[69]

44. Fr. Harrison's reliance on his interpretation of proposition C1 is wholly unwarranted. To demonstrate this, we must quote from the relevant text in the preamble to *DH*. That text, following a description of how God has revealed Himself to humanity and that "this one and only true religion subsists in the catholic and apostolic church," reads:[70]

---

67   SJR89 (*supra* note 2), 110.
68   *RLC*, 63.
69   SJR89 (*supra* note 2), 106–11.
70   *DH* # 1, Tanner II, 1002.

[A]ll people are bound to seek the truth, especially about God and his Church, and when they have found it to embrace and keep it.

The synod further proclaims that these obligations touch and bind the human conscience, and that truth imposes itself solely by the force of its own truth, as it enters the mind at once gently and with power. Indeed, since people's demand for religious liberty in carrying out their duty to worship God concerns freedom from compulsion in civil society, it leaves intact the traditional [C]atholic teaching on the moral obligation of individuals and societies toward the true religion and one [C]hurch of Christ. Furthermore, in treating of this religious freedom the synod intends to develop the teaching of more recent popes on the inviolable rights of the human person and the regulating of society by law.

45. It is patently clear that "the moral obligation of the individuals and societies toward the true religion and one church of Christ" only encompasses the duty "to seek the truth . . . about God and his Church, and when they have found it to embrace and keep it" and "to worship God." Assuming, for the sake of argument, that this obligation impliedly confirms the traditional doctrine of the duty of the political community to recognize especially and support the Catholic religion and the Catholic Church, it has nothing to do with the question of the coercive power as to religious matters. The preamble itself negatives this by, among other things, referring to the "people's demand for religious liberty in carrying out their duty to worship God concerns freedom from compulsion in civil society." Indeed, the *Catechism of the Catholic Church* (#2105) itself conclusively shows that Fr. Harrison's view is erroneous. It declares (in part):[71]

> The duty of offering God genuine worship concerns man both individually and socially. This is "the traditional Catholic teaching on the moral duty of individuals and societies toward the true religion and the one Church of Christ."

71 (Liguori: Liguori Publications, 1994). 511. Nothing in #2105 pertains to coercion. Interestingly enough, Fr. Harrison also indicated in his article that "whether or not non-Catholics may practice their religion publicly" has nothing to do with his Thesis I (*"The civitas – the civic community as such – has a duty to pay public honour to God and to recognize as uniquely true the religion entrusted by Christ to the Catholic Church"* (SJR89) (supra note 2), 109). In the same article he also writes: "A state can give special favour and protection to the true religion in various important ways without repressing all public manifestations of other religions" (ibid., 108).

46. In his review of the late Archbishop Marcel Lefebvre's book,[72] Fr. Harrison again focuses on papal preconciliar doctrine with respect to the issue of continuity of doctrine with that of *DH*. He erroneously states that *Ecclesia Dei,* John Paul II's apostolic letter pertaining to Archbishop Lefebvre's illicit ordinations, "calls on the Church's scholars to study the Vatican II documents more deeply, with a view to bringing out more clearly their essential continuity with *traditional doctrine.*"[73] Nevertheless, he appears to limit the discussion of proposition C1, discussed in the immediately preceding paragraphs, to church-state issues other than those pertaining to religious liberty.[74] The greater part of his discussion pertains to the proper interpretation of preconciliar papal documents bearing upon religious liberty, which need not concern us here since we assume for the sake of argument the substantial accuracy of Fr. Harrison's summary of preconciliar papal doctrine concerning religious liberty. The review essentially restates the major theses of his book concerning pre- and postconciliar papal doctrine and public ecclesiastical law or policy concerning coercive power as to religious matters. However, Fr. Harrison states:[75]

> The *new doctrinal development* of Vatican II can be reduced quintessentially to the proposition – neither affirmed nor denied by the preconciliar magisterium, but seemingly implied in *Ci Riesce* of Pius XII – that under some circumstances (namely, when the common good of society is not seriously endangered) the public exercise of non-Catholic cults may not be justly repressed by human authority. In other words, the Declaration clarifies and affirms the teaching that there *can be* a right to immunity from human

---

72   Fully cited in note 2, *supra*.

73   (Note 2 *supra*) F89, 38. Emphasis added. *Ecclesia Dei* (July 2, 1988) #4 (http://www.vatican.va/holy_father/john_paul_ii/motu_proprio/documents/hf_jp-ii_motu-proprio_02071988_ecclesia-dei_en.html) refers to "Tradition," and not to "traditional doctrine" – a very different matter.

74   F89, 38–39. Indeed, his synthesis of the relevant statements in #1, #6, and #7 of *DH* is as follows (at 39): "In those particular circumstances where a people as a whole professes the Catholic faith, the society and its public authorities must fulfill their moral duty to give special recognition to the true religion and the one Church of Christ. This special recognition, however, should be such as to recognize and respect the right of religious liberty of all other citizens and religious communities, insofar as their activities do not violate public peace, public morality, or other rights of citizens."

75   F89, 44.

coercion for those who believe and practice a religion other than the Catholic religion.

Fr. Harrison makes an interesting point. That public authority may not justly enact or enforce a particular law limiting a liberty entails the existence of a corresponding right. However, it does not follow that we have a natural right – "natural right" being understood as one fundamentally based upon the natural dignity of human persons.

47. The review also asserts that the guarantee of infallibility does not apply to the Church's prudential judgments concerning an appropriate means to a good end. Moreover, Fr. Harrison notes *en passant* that "a consensus of theologians has traditionally held that the Holy Spirit could not allow the Church to impose a universal disciplinary norm which was intrinsically evil – as would be, for instance, a command to do what was intrinsically sinful, or a universal prohibition of some activity which is objectively required by divine law."[76] However, he does not pursue this matter further.

48. Next, we turn to Fr. Harrison's review of Michael Davies' book.[77] This review is quite remarkable, as we shall see, because in it Fr. Harrison closes up some loose ends. He affirms that *DH* "teaches the following thesis (not explicitly, but by undeniable implication): non-Catholics (like all human beings) have a natural right to immunity from government coercion in publicly expressing their beliefs, in circumstances where this does not violate public morality, public peace, or the rights of other citizens." He admits "that no Pope before Vatican II ever actually taught this thesis," but denies that preconciliar popes had actually condemned it.[78]

49. The vacuous nature of religious liberty as a natural right, as interpreted by Fr. Harrison, clearly appears since he affirms that the "rights of other citizens" (read, "rights of all citizens") includes the right of Catholics to be defended "against the spreading of false doctrines which, in the judgment of the Church, put their eternal salvation at risk."[79] He comments:[80]

---

76   Ibid.
77   Michael Davies argued in his book (*supra* note 7) that there is an apparent contradiction between preconciliar papal teaching on religious liberty and that of *DH*, and does not see how they can be reconciled.
78   LT93 (note 2 *supra*), 5.
79   Ibid. He asserts that "[t]he other two limits mentioned in [#] 7 are really rather redundant, since it is plain that those who violate 'public peace' and/or 'public morality'" are thereby also violating the "'rights of other citizens [read, "rights of all citizens"]'" (ibid., 10). Given Fr. Harrison's understanding that "rights of all

It is evident that a contradiction of the above thesis [i.e., concerning the natural right of non-Catholics to religious liberty] affirmed by Vatican II would affirm or imply the following: no violation of a natural right of non-Catholics is ever committed by a government which represses the public expression of their beliefs, not even in circumstances where such expression does not violate public morality, nor public peace, nor any rights of other citizens. This amounts to the doctrine that public religious error may always and everywhere be repressed without injustice, simply because it is erroneous; that is, without any regard for the social consequences of either repression or non-repression. (Such social considerations, according to this doctrine, could be relevant only to whether repression is prudent or imprudent, nor just or unjust.)

50. The second statement, I submit, is fallacious. It assumes that the injustice of a particular statute necessarily entails a corresponding natural right that would be violated by the application of the statute. This assumption, it seems to me, is unjustified. What the natural law would entail, in such circumstances, is what could be properly called a natural-law right. A natural right is a right entailed by the natural law where the basic ground of the right is the natural dignity of human persons. Given this analysis, it is clear that the set of natural-law rights includes all natural rights as its proper subset. However, not all natural-law rights are natural rights.

51. Fr. Harrison essentially repeats the same fallacies elsewhere in his review. Thus, he refers to the teaching of Pope Pius XII in *Ci Riesce* to the effect that in certain circumstances the common good may not only permit the toleration of evil by civil authority but may require it. Fr. Harrison writes:[81]

citizens," as used in # 7.3, encompasses all the moral rights encompassed in # 7.2, it is not surprising that he concludes that this term renders redundant the two other factors constituting the public order.

80   LT93 (note 2 *supra*), 5.
81   LT93 (note 2 *supra*), 6. Cardinal Ottaviani's schema declared that in a "non-Catholic City . . . [t]he civil Authority must, in matters of religion, conform at least to the precepts of the natural law. Under these conditions, the non-Catholic Authority should concede civil liberty to all forms of worship that are not opposed to natural religion" (Davies, *supra* note 7, 301). Based upon this schema, it is fairly arguable that civil liberty in a non-Catholic City need not be accorded to the public or notoriously conducted exercise of polytheistic or idolatrous worship.

If at times the state has no God-given right to repress certain errors, that seems to imply that those who propagate them have a God-given right, under those circumstances, to be immune from such repression. It would be interesting to know Davies' answer to the following question: in countries where Catholics are a minority, do the non-Catholic citizens have a natural right to immunity from coercion in publicly practicing their religion (at least insofar as they remain within the bounds of natural law)? After all, article 7 of the preparatory schema for Vatican II (praised by Davies as a good summary of preconciliar doctrine) asserts that the state "should concede" that sort of immunity under those circumstances; and there seems only a short distance between saying that those non-Catholics "should" be given this immunity and saying they have a right to be given it.

52. If there is no God-given right to repress X, then there is a corresponding God-given right not to be repressed as to X. However, it does not follow that this natural-law right is a natural right. Similarly, to say that A should have an immunity does not imply that the entailed right to the immunity is a natural right. Fr. Harrison, as we have seen, fallaciously assumes that all natural-law rights are necessarily natural rights.

53. He then proceeds to develop a thesis, not expounded by him in his previous writings. First, he asserts that non-Catholics in non-Catholic countries have a natural right to immunity from coercion within the bounds of natural law. He then says that "this core affirmation of *Dignitatis Humanae* does not say anything one way or another about the treatment of public non-Catholic manifestations in Catholic states."[82]

54. Now we come to the *pièce de résistance* in Fr. Harrison's review. He declares that it is true that "traditional doctrine excludes the possibility that, *in a predominantly Catholic society,* there can be any natural right of non-Catholics to be tolerated in the public profession of their religion." He also declares that it is false that *DH* "affirms (or at least implies) such a right."[83]

55. The reader will recall that Fr. Harrison had ostensibly stated in his book that preconciliar papal doctrine did not contradict the proposition, although affirmed by *DH*, that there is a natural right to be free to publicly manifest or propagate (peacefully) some non-Catholic religions in

82   LT93 (note 2 *supra*), 7.
83   Ibid., 8.

predominantly Catholic countries. We discerned here a striking incongruity because this proposition cannot justify, as it were, the preconciliar public ecclesiastical law or policy which required or permitted the repression of the public manifestation or propagation of all non-Catholic religions in predominantly Catholic countries. Fr. Harrison now proposes in his review of Davies' book that "a correct understanding of *Dignitatis Humanae* leads us to see the 'right' to immunity from coercion which non-Catholics now enjoy in predominantly Catholic states, not as a *natural right,* but as an acquired right granted by the Church."[84] According to Fr. Harrison, it was by virtue of the change in public ecclesiastical law that this was accomplished.[85]

56. Since, according to Fr. Harrison, non-Catholics do not have a natural right to be free to publicly manifest or propagate any non-Catholic religion in predominantly Catholic countries, he can no longer ostensibly rely upon the supposed fact that preconciliar papal doctrine had not condemned the proposition that there is a natural right to be free to publicly manifest or propagate (peacefully) some non-Catholic religions. He therefore provides another explanation:[86]

> [I]t must be acknowledged that Leo XIII and the other earlier Popes certainly did frequently urge (in concordats and other lesser documents) the repression of all public non-Catholic manifestations in Catholic states or societies. This policy was such a firm and unanimous norm of public ecclesiastical law – universally applied throughout centuries of Christendom – that I believe (as I am sure Davies does) that the Holy Spirit could not have permitted it if it were, *per se* and intrinsically, a violation of natural law. Indeed, all traditional theologians (and thus, the Popes and Bishops who approved their works) have taught it as theologically certain – a conclusion inseparable from revelation and therefore part of the infallible Ordinary Magisterium – that the Church's sanctity and indefectibility exclude the possibility that any general disciplinary norm of the universal Church (as distinct from a merely local norm) could be intrinsically (*per se*) contrary to divine law, whether natural or positive. It follows that if *Dignitatis Humanae* affirmed a natural right not to be prevented from

84   Ibid., 11.
85   Ibid.
86   Ibid., 9.

publicly propagating non-Catholic religions in Catholic societies, then indeed the Declaration would implicitly contradict the afore-said doctrine of the Ordinary Magisterium.

57. Given the foregoing, Fr. Harrison's laborious attempt to show that preconciliar papal documents did not condemn the proposition that there is a natural right to be free to publicly manifest or propagate (peacefully) some non-Catholic religions turns out to be rather pointless. He finally comes to realize that he can no longer rely solely upon his reading of the relevant preconciliar papal documents to serve as the total justification of preconciliar Church law or policy with respect to non-Catholic religions in Catholic countries. Moreover, unlike his book, which studiously avoids the doctrinal infallibility issue with respect to religious liberty issues, his review of Davies' book contends that (at least some) relevant preconciliar doctrine of the ordinary universal magisterium is infallible.[87] Finally, he expressly relies upon (what I term) practical infallibility with respect to universal disciplinary laws of the Church.

58. Alas, his argument is rather sketchy. It is, however, essential to take notice of his implicit assumptions. First, he assumes that a universal doctrine of "traditional theologians," that a particular proposition is a true theological conclusion, is necessarily a doctrine of the ordinary universal magisterium simply because popes and bishops have approved the works of these theologians. Second, he assumes that a given doctrine of the ordinary universal magisterium, albeit classified as theologically certain or as a theological conclusion, falls necessarily within the scope of the secondary object of the Church's infallibility (i.e., truths, not themselves divinely revealed, but which are necessarily connected to divinely revealed truths). Third, he assumes that a doctrine taught by the universal ordinary magisterium is necessarily taught as one to be held definitively by the faithful. Fourth, he assumes that theologians have assigned substantially the same meaning to the terms "theologically certain" and "theological conclusion." Fifth, he assumes that, if a policy or law rescinded by *DH* is held to have violated divine law, it must be held as having been "*per se* and intrinsically" contrary to natural law – rather than as having been instrumentally or extrinsically contrary to such law. Sixth, he assumes that the rescinded public ecclesiastical law or policy respecting repression of non-Catholic

---

87   In the same article, Fr. Harrison for the first time states his opinion that Pope Pius IX's encyclical *Quanta Cura* includes "teaching [which is] *ex cathedra* and irreformable" (LT93 [note 2 *supra*], 8).

religions falls within the ambit of what is meant by a general disciplinary norm of the universal Church to which a sound doctrine of practical infallibility properly applies. These assumptions, of course, require further discussion. However, for the present, I shall content myself with the maxim: *quod gratis affirmatur, gratis negatur* – what can be gratuitously affirmed can be gratuitously denied. In any event, Fr. Harrison deserves credit for expanding his inquiry as to preconciliar doctrine beyond the confines of papal documents of the last two centuries. Of course, Fr. Harrison may well disclose to what extent he agrees or disagrees with the "implicit assumptions" which I think underlie his argument.

59. Suffice to say that Fr. Harrison appears to have painted himself into a corner with regard to his views on *DH*. We should recall that it was also part of the public ecclesiastical law or policy, for many centuries, for the Church itself, or civil authorities acting at her behest, physically to coerce[88] Catholics for heresy, schism, and apostasy, and cognate offenses. Indeed, this law or policy was once universal in scope in Catholic Christendom.[89] Fr. Harrison, the reader will recall, stated that *DH* teaches

---

88 See note 9 *supra*.

89 See, e.g., canon 3 of the Fourth Lateran Council (1215) (constitution *Firmiter*) requiring secular rulers to "expel from the lands subject to their jurisdiction all heretics designated by the church in good faith" (Tanner I, 233–235). The adoption of the code of canon law in 1917, which took effect in 1918, abrogated the public ecclesiastical law sanctioning physically coercive penalties for these offenders, such law having already fallen into desuetude during the nineteenth century. Incidentally, Pope Pius XII, in his encyclical *Mystici Corporis* (1943), # 104, used language concerning freedom of the act of faith broad enough to mean that the freedom also pertains to remaining in the faith. See too his Allocution to the Sacred Roman Rota (6 October 1946) [38 AAS (1946) 392] *Catholic Mind*, vol.45 (March 1947), 129, 130–133). See also Pope John XXIII, *Pacem in Terris* (11 April 1963), AAS 55 (1963), 299–300 (Paulist Press, 1963), #158, 53–54.

In his Message for World Day of Peace of January 1, 1999, John Paul II observed [in # 5] that the "inviolability [of religious freedom] is such that individuals must be recognized as having the right even to change their religion, if their conscience so demands . . . [N]o one can be compelled to accept a particular religion, whatever the circumstances or motives." (http://www.vatican.va/holy_father/john_paul_ii/messages/peace/documents/hf_jp-ii_mes_14121998_xxxii-world-day-for-peace_en.html.) For similar remarks about religious freedom as including the right to be free to change one's religion, see also John Paul II, Message for World Day of Peace of January 1, 1991 at #IV/5, (http://www.vatican.va/holy_father/john_paul_ii/messages/peace/documents/hf_jp-ii_mes_08121990_xxiv-world-day-for-peace_en.html), and Benedict XVI, Message for World Day of Peace, January 1, 2011, at #5.2 (http://www.vatican.va/

that the freedom of the act of faith applies to keeping the faith as well as to embracing it initially – thereby entailing a corresponding natural right. The reader will also recall that Fr. Harrison, in his book, expressly approved of this "development of doctrine." Clearly, the teaching of *DH* on this point is incompatible with the now long defunct, but very much longer observed, law and practice of the Church concerning apostates, heretics, and schismatics. Given his views on practical infallibility – since Fr. Harrison reads *DH* such that there can be no natural right with respect to the public manifestation or propaganda of any non-Catholic religion in predominantly Catholic countries – he should *a fortiori* also read *DH* such that Catholics do not have any natural right to be immune from physical coercion by civil authority or the Church with respect to apostasy, heresy, or schism. However, this view would contradict his book's position that *DH* had developed the doctrine of the freedom of the act of faith so as to encompass the decision whether or not to retain the faith or remain in the Church.

60. Adverting to his opinion that *DH* rescinded that preconciliar ecclesiastical public policy or law by which the public manifestation or propaganda of all non-Catholic religions could legitimately be repressed in predominantly Catholic countries, Fr. Harrison repeats his view as to how one must distinguish between "norms" and "doctrine." He proceeds to elaborate:[90]

> Formally speaking, [article] 6 of *Dignitatis Humanae* contains no new doctrinal affirmations over and above what have been affirmed in [article] 2. It simply states that, if one religion is given state recognition, "the right to religious liberty of other citizens and religious communities" must be respected as well. But since this right has already been defined as an intrinsically limited one, [#]6, taken just as it stands and from a strictly logical viewpoint, leaves just as open as [#]2 does the question as to whether, in predominantly Catholic societies, the public manifestation of non-Catholic cults might, as such, be considered a transgression of the "due limits," and hence subject to legitimate repression.

holy_father/benedict_xvi/messages/peace/documents/hf_ben-xvi_m.). *DH* teaches "that it is wrong for a civil power to use force or fear or other means to impose the acceptance or rejection of any religion, or to prevent anyone from entering or leaving a religious body" (# 6, Tanner II, 1005).

90   LT93 (note 2 *supra*), 10.

61. From a strictly logical viewpoint, Fr. Harrison's position here presents difficulties. He holds that *DH* somehow affirms that non-Catholics have a natural right to be free, in non-Catholic countries, to publicly manifest and propagate non-Catholic religions within the bounds of natural law, and this right exists because the common good requires civil authority to tolerate such manifestation and propagation. On the other hand, he also holds that there cannot be a natural right to be free to publicly manifest and propagate any non-Catholic religion in predominantly Catholic societies. Thus the "acquired right" of non-Catholics in predominantly Catholic countries with respect to religious liberty is a matter of legislative grace. According to Fr. Harrison, as we have seen, A does not have any natural right to be free to do (or not do) X unless B has a corresponding duty to permit X. Hence, he should hold that it is impossible for the common good, national and international, of the political community and of the Church, to be considered as ever imposing upon civil authority in predominantly Catholic countries the duty of tolerating the public manifestation and propagation of any non-Catholic religion within the bounds of natural law. Therefore, it seems that Fr. Harrison's explanation of the "acquired" right of non-Catholics (allegedly granted by *DH*) as to some non-Catholic religions in predominantly Catholic countries is inconsistent with the doctrine of Pope Plus XII in *Ci Riesce* that, under certain circumstances, the toleration of public manifestations or propagation of religious error within Catholic states is a duty required by the common good.[91]

62. Finally, we have two points to consider: Fr. Harrison's understanding of "the common good" and "public order," and his remarks at the National Wanderer Forum held on 24–26 September 1993. Fr. Harrison refers in his *Living Tradition* article to how "the new *Catechism of the Catholic Church* . . . restores the traditional term *common good,* and indeed gives it priority over *public order,* the novel term preferred by *Dignitatis Humanae.* [Number] 1738 of the *Catechism* says that the civil power should protect the exercise of religious liberty 'within the limits of the common good and the public order.'"[92]

63. There are serious difficulties with Fr. Harrison's views. Number 1738 reads in full:[93]

91 See *RLC*, 18–20 and F89 (note 2 *supra*), 40, where Fr. Harrison appears to acknowledge that *Ci Riesce* teaches this doctrine.
92 LT93, 10 (note 2 *supra*).
93 *Catechism*, 431. Note omitted.

Freedom is exercised in relationships between human beings. Every human person, created in the image of God, has the natural right to be recognized as a free and responsible being. All owe to each other this duty of respect. *The right to the exercise of freedom,* especially in moral and religious matters, is an inalienable requirement of the dignity of the human person. This right must be recognized and protected by civil authority within the limits of the common good and public order.

64. The freedom mentioned in number 1738 is the "power, rooted in reason and will, to act or not to act, to do this or that, and so to perform deliberate actions on one's own responsibility." Number 1747, a summary "in brief," indicates the purpose of number 1738. Number 1747 reads:[94]

The right to the exercise of freedom, especially in religious and moral matters, is an inalienable requirement of the dignity of man. But the exercise of freedom does not entail the putative right to say or do anything.

65. It is therefore puzzling to see why number 1738 includes a reference to the civil authority at all. It should have, I think, referred to the limitations of the moral law. The confusing character of number 1738 also appears because it states that the right in question "must be recognized and protected by civil authority within the limits of the common good and public order." The inclusion of both the "common good" and "public order" is mystifying. On the one hand, it is redundant to mention them conjunctively since public order is a component of common good. (It would not, to give an example, be good usage to say: "All birds and pigeons have feathers.") If, on the other hand, the two terms ("common good" and "public order") are synonymous, it also does not make sense to use both in the conjunctive. (To give another example: "all male bachelors and unmarried men are unhappy.") If the third sentence in number 1738 refers to civil authority, it would make sense were it to read: "This right must be generally recognized and protected by civil authority within the limits of the common good as to moral matters but specifically within the limits of public order as to religious matters."

66. In this connection, we should here digress to consider number 2109 of the *Catechism* as well. Number 2109 reads:[95]

---

94 Ibid., 433.
95 Ibid., 512.

The right to religious liberty can of itself be neither unlimited or limited only by a "public order" conceived in a positivistic or naturalist manner.[96] The "due limits" which are inherent in it must be determined for each social situation by political prudence, according to the requirements of the common good, and ratified by the civil authority, in accordance with "legal principles which are in conformity with the objective moral order."[97]

67. Here, reference to the "requirements of the common good" as part of the process of determining the due limits (of public order: "debitos limites" or "iustus ordo publicus") is quite understandable – given that due limits encompass the three factors (i.e., the rights of all citizens, the public peace, and public morality) which together constitute the fundamental part of the common good.

68. Finally, we briefly discuss Fr. Harrison's remarks at the National Wanderer Forum held on 24–26 September 1993. In this talk, he

96   The English edition of the *Catechism*, in note 39 that accompanies the relevant text in #2109 (i.e., that the "right to religious liberty can of itself be neither unlimited nor limited only by a 'public order' conceived in a *positivistic* or *naturalist* manner"), cites only "Pius VI, *Quod aliquantum* (1791) 10; Pius IX, *Quanta cura* 3." (*Catechism of the Catholic Church* (2nd ed.) (Libreria Editrice Vaticana, 1994), 512.). However the official Latin text of #2109 reads: "Ius ad libertatem religiosam neque potest, natura sua, esse illimitatum[58] neque limitatum solummodo ordine publico qui modo « positivistico » vel « naturalistico » concipiatur."[59] [notes 58 and 59 in original text]. Note 58 (pertaining to religious liberty as unlimited) cites only Pius VI's *Quod Aliquantum*. Note 59 (pertaining to religious liberty as limited only by a 'public order' conceived in a positivistic or naturalist manner) reads: "Cf. Pius IX, Litt. enc. *Quanta cura*: DS 2890." (*Catechismus Catholicae Ecclesiae* (1997) (http://www.vatican.va/archive/catechism_lt/lettera-apost_lt.htm.) DS 2890 consists a quotation of the first two complete sentences of *QC* #4 (and not #3) [i.e., "And … interests?"]. The English translation is accessible at http://www.papalencyclicals.net/Pius09/p9quanta.htm. What the *Catechism* appears to do is to warn against any interpretation of "public order" that would preclude the promotion of religious life or subvert the freedom of the Church. See *DH*, # 3.5 and # 13, Tanner II, 1004, 1009. See # 5 in John Paul II's message of December 7, 1995, cited in note 52, supra; and ##6, 8 in Benedict XVI's Message for the World Day of Peace, January 1, 2011. (http://www.vatican.va/holy_father/benedict_xvi/messages/peace/documents/hf_ben-xvi_mes_20101208_xliv-world-day-peace_en.html) and his Address to the Members of the Diplomatic Corps, January 10, 2011. (http://www.vatican.va/holy_father/benedict_xvi/speeches/2011/january/documents/hf_ben-xvi_spe_20110110_diplomatic-corps_en.html).

97   Citing *DH* #7.3.

emphatically confirmed the view that the adoption of *DH* did nothing to contradict the "doctrine of the previous one and a half millennia";[98] that the common good was the criterion to which "Catholic governments, in conformity with Church teaching, had always appealed [to] in order to limit or even prohibit entirely the public manifestation of anti-Catholic doctrines or rites in predominantly Catholic societies."[99] According to this doctrine, such restriction by Catholic governments "is in itself morally legitimate, and may be imposed in the interest of the 'common good' of society, since heresy and apostasy are grave dangers to the eternal salvation of Catholic citizens, whose welfare – spiritual as well as temporal – is the legitimate concern of civil authority."[100]

69. This view is quite remarkable. Fr. Harrison urges that the preconciliar doctrine cannot be reversed "with as little damage to the Church's credibility as that which was occasioned by the Vatican's self-contradiction in regard to the Galileo case."[101] On the other hand, he candidly acknowledges:[102]

> [*DH*] . . . *sounds* more liberal than it really is. Conscious of the Church's public image at a time when dialogue with non-Christians and non-Catholics was being given high priority, Vatican II gave prominence to language which seems to allow for very few government restrictions on religious propaganda. But then, in the "fine print" and official commentary, which was not even published in Latin by the Vatican Press until thirteen years after the Council, it is revealed that this language is not to be understood in a way which would contradict the doctrine of the previous one and a half millennia, which in fact allowed for many more such government restrictions.

70. Thus we are to suppose that the credibility of the Church is not

98   "Roma . . . Est," (note 2 *supra*), 42.
99   Ibid., 41.
100 Ibid.
101 Ibid.
102 Ibid., 42. Fr. Harrison acknowledges that the term "public order" in #7 "seemed to imply that the state can never intervene unless religious (or anti-religious) activity involves actual rioting, fraud, public obscenity, instigations to violence or sedition, and so on: the kind of thing we normally think of as breaches of 'law and order' or 'disturbing the peace.'" He also argues that the *Catechism of the Catholic Church* confirms his position that the preconciliar doctrine was not contradicted by *DH*.

more seriously damaged if it is indeed the case that *DH* was adopted so that it *appears* to the unsuspecting to mean one thing, but was covertly intended *actually* to mean another. Apparently Fr. Harrison thinks so, although he disarmingly acknowledges that "if that strikes you as all rather confusing and less than straightforward, then I am inclined to agree with you."[103] But would it really be a good thing for the world to believe that the Council Fathers were guilty of such a subterfuge?

71. Fr. Harrison argues that such preconciliar doctrine as is apparently contrary to that of *DH* (but not, according to him, actually so) had been definitively taught by the Church.[104] But that raises another question, namely, whether preconciliar doctrine, apparently inconsistent with that of *DH*, had been *definitively* taught by the Church. My principal concern in this article has been to establish that the doctrine of *DH* is radically different from that presupposed by the concededly abrogated public ecclesiastical law or policy by which governments of predominantly Catholic countries had severely limited the public exercise or manifestations, or propaganda, of non-Catholic religions (and I should add, irreligions).

Conclusion

72. We end this article with an expression of dismay as to how the text of *DH*, read in the light of its legislative history, as further authentically interpreted by the diplomatic and ecumenical practice of the Holy See, apparently can be misconstrued so radically by Fr. Harrison. The credibility of

---

103 "Roma . . . Est," (note 2 *supra*), 42.

104 See ibid., 41–42, where Fr. Harrison argues that *DH*, if understood as being actually inconsistent with preconciliar doctrine, must be read as condemning the abrogated public ecclesiastical law or policy based upon such doctrine as intrinsically evil. Fr. Harrison overlooks the possibility that such law or policy may have been extrinsically evil because the right to religious freedom is (at least partly) only instrumentally necessary to secure basic human goods, and that the religious freedom as a natural right is grounded in large part upon the discernment of empirical facts not within the deposit of faith or necessarily connected thereto. See note 49 *supra*. Fr. Harrison erroneously claims that "Pius IX declared personally in the encyclical *Quanta Cura* that this 'evil opinion' [alleged by him to the effect "that government repression of anti-Catholic doctrine for the sake of the common good is intrinsically evil and unjust"] must be absolutely held as reprobated, denounced and condemned by all the children of the Catholic Church'" ("Roma . . . Est," 41). What Pius IX condemned was the quite different proposition: "the best condition of human society is that wherein no duty is recognized of the Government of correcting, by enacted penalties, the violators of the Catholic religion, except when the public peace requires it" (as quoted in *RLC*, 15).

the Church, ecumenical progress, as well as fruitful dialogue between Catholics and fellow-Christians, fellow-theists, and others, would be seriously jeopardized were Fr. Harrison's theory of religious liberty perceived to be widely held within the Church. Nevertheless, Fr. Harrison's sincere and honest concerns cannot be dismissed as unworthy of serious and respectful consideration by those who disagree with him as to the meaning of *DH*. He, and those who share or sympathize with his position, are very much bothered by the issue of the consistency between preconciliar doctrine and that of *DH*. Fr. Harrison, with very considerable polemical and analytical skill, has argued thoroughly, candidly and vigorously for his position. The fact remains, however, that there is something fundamentally wrong about his approach to the problem at hand – however intellectually stimulating it has proven to be. Surely, one can argue that there is something very wrong about an approach which ultimately leads Fr. Harrison to conclude that there is no natural right to be free to publicly manifest or propagate any non-Catholic religion in predominantly Catholic countries, and that the doctrine of *DH* is consistent with this position.

73. Fr. William Most has well pointed out: "The use of correct method is vital in all study."[105] Addressing the nature of the correct method is outside the scope of this article. It suffices to say that essential to the correct method for the study of *Dignitatis Humanae* is first to endeavor to determine its manifestly intended meaning, as disclosed by its text and legislative history, rather than to construct what appears to be a theory especially contrived in order to "save appearances."

---

105 Fr. William Most, "Religious Liberty: What the Texts Demand," *Faith & Reason,* vol. IX, no. 3, Fall 1983, 196.

Part II:

What Does *Dignitatis Humanae* Mean?*
A Reply to Arnold Guminski
Brian W. Harrison, O.S.

The foregoing essay by Mr. Arnold T. Guminski (which is a slightly edited version of the original that was published in the Christendom College journal *Faith & Reason*[1]) criticizes the ensemble of my own writings, published between 1988 and 1993, upholding the doctrinal continuity between the Vatican II Declaration on Religious Liberty, *Dignitatis Humanae* (*DH*), and traditional Catholic doctrine regarding Church, State, and religious toleration. In this response, I hope to defend substantially my position, while also correcting and clarifying it on some points in the light of my critic's observations.

A. Guminski vs. Harrison: the *Status Quaestionis*
1. It will be helpful to begin by trying to summarize as clearly as possible the central issue about which Mr. Guminski and I continue to disagree. First of all, among those points that I believe we *agree* upon, the following reading of the traditional magisterium (let us call it proposition **X**) has particular relevance for our discussion:

---

*   The title of this essay is abbreviated throughout this book as "WD."

1   Arnold T. Guminski, "*Contra Harrison in Re Libertatis Religiosae*: On the Meaning of *Dignitatis Humanae,*" *Faith & Reason*, Vol. XXVI, No. 1, Spring 2001, 39–83. The article is hereafter referred to in this book simply as "CH." The present response to Mr. Guminski's critique was also originally published in the same journal: "What Does *Dignitatis Humanae* Mean? A Reply to Arnold Guminski," *Faith & Reason*, Vol. XXX, Nos. 3 & 4, Autumn & Winter 2005, 243–295. This essay too has been slightly modified for this present publication in book form. These two journal articles by Mr. Guminski and myself are republished in this book with the kind permission of the editor of *Faith & Reason*.

X: According to preconciliar Catholic doctrine, there can be (or have been) circumstances wherein government prohibition of all public (and, under Old Testament and medieval circumstances, even private) religious manifestations other than those of the true religion does/did not involve the violation of any natural human right.

2. While Mr. Guminski would agree with that, he appears to think the traditional doctrine went a good deal further in its severity. For he opines that, "according to preconciliar papal doctrine, . . . there is no natural right *whatsoever* to freely (i.e., to be immune from coercion by civil authority) engage in the public manifestation or propagation of any non-Catholic religion."[2] His expression, "no natural right *whatsoever*," especially given his italicization of the last word, sounds as though it is equivalent, in his mind, to "*never under any circumstances* any natural right." If so, then I disagree. Certainly, pre-Vatican-II papal doctrine never positively taught that there *could* in fact be circumstances in which non-Catholics might have a natural right to the said immunity. But neither, as far as I can see, did the teaching of the magisterium (as distinct from that of certain theologians) *exclude* such a possibility, especially as regards societies with non-Catholic or non-Christian majorities.[3] My view has

2   CH, n. 13.

3   Cf. Brian W. Harrison, O.S., *Religious Liberty and Contraception* (Melbourne: John XXIII Fellowship Coop., 1988, hereafter referred to as *RLC*), 44. (To obtain this book, write to the publishers at P.O. Box 22, Ormond, Victoria 3204, AUSTRALIA, or use their online bookstore: www.fidelitybooks.com.au.) At this point in my book I expressed the above view by saying that this lacuna in earlier papal teaching "left the door open" for Vatican II to subsequently teach, without contradicting traditional Catholic doctrine, that "*Some* peaceful non-Catholic propaganda has a right to immunity from civil prohibition." This is presented on p. 44 as proposition (b). I assumed readers would understand (as most apparently have) that I meant the word "some" in the most extensive sense, i.e., as meaning some such propaganda *in at least some times and/or places*. However Mr. Guminski thought – and, in spite of my protestations in private correspondence, has continued to insist (cf. CH, 8, and n.16) – that the "objective meaning" of the above proposition (b) includes its implicit qualification by the words "in a predominantly Catholic country." I confess to being utterly mystified by this insistence, for neither on p. 44, nor anywhere else in that chapter (which spans pp. 31–51) is there any mention of "predominantly Catholic" societies or countries.

    I think the above explanation sufficiently answers Mr. Guminski's criticism that there is a "tension," and indeed, a "striking incongruity" (CH, ##40, 55), in my position by virtue of my acknowledgment that preconciliar Church-approved concordats forbade *all* public non-Catholic propaganda in many Catholic-majority states. Such tension or incongruity would exist only if, as Mr. Guminski has

consistently been[4] that this question was left obscure and undecided in the traditional magisterium, and that the essential development (i.e., non-contradictory change) in Catholic doctrine brought about by *DH* has been to clarify and answer it. The Declaration's new and authoritative answer is that there can indeed be circumstances wherein governmental prohibition of public non-Catholic religious activity – at least in its normal and more innocuous forms – would violate the natural right to religious freedom of the non-Catholics in question. It should be noted, however, that traditional doctrine (summarized in the maxim "error has no rights") certainly did exclude the idea that there can ever be any natural right even to believe – much less to propagate publicly – any false religious doctrine or practice. But Vatican II does not teach that there is, or ever can be, any such right. Traditionalist dissenters from *DH* frequently betray confusion over this point, because they fail to appreciate the important difference between affirming: **(a)** a natural right *to propagate* a given religion R, and **(b)** a natural right *to immunity from human coercion* in propagating R.[5] Not all objectively sinful acts can justly be criminalized.

3. I believe Mr. Guminski would also agree with me on the following proposition:

Y: According to *DH*, government prohibition of all public (and, *a fortiori*, private) religious manifestations other than those of the true religion would, under modern circumstances, have to be judged as involving a violation of the natural human right to religious liberty, in any country on earth.

However, Mr. Guminski's assent to **Y** would certainly only be a *placet iuxta modum*, as it were, because he definitely thinks that it is *not only* "under modern circumstances" that such prohibitions have violated the right in question. Herein lies our principal disagreement. I understand him to hold the following proposition to be true, while I hold it to be false:

Z: According to *DH*, government prohibition of all public (and, *a fortiori*, private) religious manifestations other than those of the true

---

    unjustifiably supposed, my proposition (b) referred only to "predominantly Catholic countries."

4   Cf. *RLC*, 129–130.

5   Cf. *RLC, ch. 8* and the adaptation of this chapter as "Religious Liberty: 'Rights' vs. 'Tolerance'?", *Living Tradition*, no. 16, March, 1988, accessible at www.rtforum.org/lt/lt16.html#II.

religion involves, *and always and everywhere has involved*, a violation of the natural human right to religious liberty.[6]

4. Now, it can readily be seen that the position ascribed to *DH* in **Y** does not imply the falsity of the traditional Catholic doctrine outlined in **X**. However, it is equally clear that if **Z** is true, *DH* has *contradicted* that doctrine, even though my critic seems reluctant to spell this out too starkly. Unfortunately, his penchant for euphemism rather than the "C-word" leads him to misrepresent my own position. He more than once chides me[7] for maintaining that *DH* did not "change" the preconciliar doctrine. He should have used the verb "contradict" here, for I have never sustained the implausible "no-doctrinal-change" thesis. Authentic doctrinal development is always change – but of a non-contradictory sort.

5. Indeed, the very fact that Mr. Guminski's interpretation of *DH* has it contradict traditional Catholic doctrine is fundamental to my disagreement with him. He claims that my interpretation, if perceived by non-Catholics as being widely held within the Church, would "seriously jeopardize" her "credibility,"[8] since, he says, it makes the document "essentially vacuous"[9] and reminiscent of the "sham legal constitutional provisions in totalitarian states.[10] However, I shall argue in due course that his own reading of *DH*, which sees in chapter I (articles 2–8) an outright reversal of preconciliar doctrine, turns the declaration as a whole into something even less credible: a self-contradictory and even *lying* document![11]

6. Moreover, lest Mr. Guminski's use of the conditional mood in his

---

6   I am now avoiding the language of "intrinsic" evil, or "intrinsic" violations of rights. For Mr. Guminski has remarked, perhaps rightly, that certain classes of action which might not be intrinsically evil (i.e., whose *object* is not evil *per se*), might nevertheless be evil (and I take him to mean here *always and everywhere* evil) in an "extrinsic" way, i.e., because of certain invariable circumstances or consequences accompanying those acts which can be learned by empirical observation and experience (cf. CH, nn. 49, 104). I shall prescind here from the question of whether this view is valid or not, since the expression "always and everywhere" seems to cover both possibilities adequately for present purposes.

7   Cf. CH, ##26, 43.

8   CH, #72, also cf. #70.

9   CH, #41.

10   CH, #41.

11   This is because the relevant official *relationes* and *DH*'s own preamble (art. 1) deny any such doctrinal reversal. Mr. Guminski thinks that, according to the preamble, the declaration leaves only *part* of the existing doctrine intact. However, I hope to show below that this exegesis of *DH* #1 is untenable.

conclusion[12] might suggest to some readers that my own position is in fact an idiosyncratic or isolated one, it seems appropriate to point out that I am far from alone in holding that proposition **Z** above is an incorrect reading of *DH*. Many examples could be given, but one will suffice here. The late Fr. John Courtney Murray, S.J., scarcely lies at the right of the Catholic spectrum in these matters. Indeed, I have argued in two other essays[13] that he leans too far to the left, particularly in his reading of *DH*'s teaching on the establishment of religion. It is significant, therefore, that Mr. Guminski's position situates him even farther to the left[14] than Fr. Murray, who explicitly denied that a Vatican-II-type understanding of the right to religious liberty condemns retrospectively, at least by implication, the kind of Church-sponsored repression mentioned in our propositions **X**, **Y** and **Z**. His view (which he took to be in substance that of the Council) was that any such retroactive verdict of injustice would be an "anachronism" wrongly based on "abstract deductive logic" and lacking in "historical con-sciousness."[15] For Murray, the right to full religious freedom "is a rational exigence of the *contemporary* personal and political consciousness."[16] I have expressed elsewhere[17] certain objections to this kind of psycho-his-torical hermeneusis. But for present purposes Murray's conclusion itself

12 "The credibility of the Church . . . *would be* seriously jeopardized *were* Fr. Harrison's theory . . . perceived to be widely held" (CH, #72, emphasis added).

13 Cf. Appendix I, "Church and State: John Courtney Murray," in *RLC*, 147–162; and "John Courtney Murray: a Reliable Interpreter of *Dignitatis Humanae?*," in D.J. D'Elia and S.M. Krason (eds.), *We Hold These Truths: Further Catholic Reflections on the American Proposition* (Steubenville, Ohio: Franciscan University Press, 1993), 134–165.

14 I am using the terms "left" and "right" in this paragraph not as journalistic catch-phrases, but in their strict and classical political sense. From the time of the French Revolution onwards, a political theory has come to be understood as "left-wing" (denoting a "radical, advanced or innovating" position, according to the Oxford Dictionary) in the degree to which it promotes radical innovations or departures from, and hostility toward, the European *ancien régime*, which was essentially the traditional order of Catholic Christendom.

15 "The Problem of Religious Freedom," in J. C. Murray (ed. J.L. Hooper), *Religious Liberty: Catholic Struggles With Pluralism* (Louisville, KY: Westminster/John Knox Press, 1993), 187. This essay was originally published in *Theological Studies*, vol. XXV, no. 4, December 1964, 503–575.

16 *Ibid.*, 186 (emphasis added, in accordance with many other passages in Murray's writings where he stresses the "contemporary growth in historical consciousness" as a *sine qua non* of the right to religious freedom as it is now understood).

17 Cf. my essay, "John Courtney Murray: a Reliable Interpreter . . .?" (referenced in note 13 above), 141–146.

(which I would reach by a rather different route) is what matters. My point is simply that, in holding *DH* to be wrongly interpreted by proposition **Z**, I have the support of the Catholic theologian generally acknowledged as the one whose thought, more than that of any other single scholar, lay behind the teaching of this conciliar Declaration.

B. Preliminary Criticisms of
Religious Liberty and Contraception

7. Having sought to clarify the central point at issue between myself and Mr. Guminski, I shall consider his criticisms, generally following the order in which he presents them. He begins by questioning my relative lack of interest in the *infallibility* or otherwise of the doctrines under discussion.[18] Indeed, that issue is, for me, quite secondary. For the mind of the Church, as I understand it, is that the Declaration is not to be understood in a way that would make it contradict *any* existing doctrine, whether infallible or "merely authentic." And my concern has always been to uphold that broad diachronic consistency of Catholic doctrine. (Why should the Church's apologist troops retreat to defend only the inner citadel when they hear her calling them not to abandon or surrender the city walls?)

8. Mr. Guminski also seems surprised that my book "limits" discussion of preconciliar doctrine to "papal declarations," thus neglecting (he thinks) what the "ordinary universal magisterium" may have had to say about religious liberty.[19] But the non-*ex-cathedra* statements[20] in a long series of papal interventions surely provide a pretty good indicator as to what *is in fact* the doctrine of the ordinary universal magisterium.

9. My critic also finds "remarkable" *RLC*'s failure to rely "upon any real or purported *practical* infallibility with respect to the Church's

---

18 Cf. CH, #3.

19 CH, #3.

20 That is, *all* statements in the relevant encyclicals and other papal documents (such as the 1864 *Syllabus*) with the exception of some found in Pius IX's *Quanta Cura*. I hold the errors set out in *QC* (those highlighted in the original text by the use of quotation marks) to be condemned in a form which manifestly meets Vatican I's requirements for *ex cathedra* papal definitions. In this I follow such theologians as Franzelin, Hervé, and Newman. Speaking of the well-known error in certain letters of Pope Honorius, Cardinal Newman declares it obvious that the said pontiff did not "intend to exert that infallible teaching voice which is heard so distinctly in the *Quanta cura* and the *Pastor Aeternus*" ("Letter to the Duke of Norfolk", in *Certain Difficulties Felt by Anglicans in Catholic Teaching Considered*, [London: Longmans, Green, 1920], 317).

legislation or policy, as distinguished from doctrine, bearing on religious liberty."[21] For the moment, it is sufficient to reply that, when writing *RLC*, I felt uncertain as to whether any Catholic *doctrine* must needs be deduced from the Church's traditional *practice* (policy or public law) of frequently urging governments to repress *all* public non-Catholic propaganda. Nevertheless, my book "covered that base": first, by pointing out that *DH* does not in any case state or imply that such practice, in earlier historical contexts, was always and everywhere unjust;[22] and secondly, by formulating the pertinent preconciliar doctrine in terms open-ended enough to allow for either answer to the said question. Note the parenthesized words in the following quotation: "Civil authority therefore has the duty to protect the true religion and the Catholic Church by restricting (to the extent that the common good requires) the free propagation of doctrinal error."[23]

10. I shall pass quickly over Mr. Guminski's section "B,"[24] which for the most part expounds, rather than criticizes, my position. However, he again misunderstands me here in stating:

> Fr. Harrison treats the two terms, "rights of others" as used in #7.2, and "rights of all citizens" as used in #7.3, as essentially synonymous – a matter, as we shall see, of great importance, since the former are moral (or quasi-moral) rights, and the latter are legal (or juridical rights).[25]

The truth is that in using the expression "rights of others," I am never quoting – and have never even had in mind – the merely moral rights referred to in #7.2. My repeated use of that expression as a quasi-synonym for "rights of all citizens" (used in #7.3) is purely stylistic – adopted for the sake of more precise expression in certain contexts. The term "all citizens" obviously includes the citizen who commits a (justly penalized) offence; but in committing such an offence he is not violating any right insofar as it is *his own*, only insofar as it is a "right *of others*." Indeed, the official *relator* himself used the term "rights of others" in exactly the same way I do.[26]

21 CH, #3.

22 Cf. *RLC*, 87–89. Thus, I have consistently denied what in the present essay appears as proposition **Z**.

23 *RLC*, 60, quoted in CH, #4.

24 CH, ##9–12.

25 CH, #12.

26 Cf. *Acta Synodalia Sacrosancti Concilii Oecumenici Vaticani* (Vatican City: Typis Polyglottis Vaticanis) (1970–1986): (hereafter *AS*) vol. IV/pt. VI. 722, quoted in *RLC*, 90.

C. RLC on "Public Order," "Public Law" and the "Objective Moral Order"

11. Mr. Guminski's section "C" contains his principal criticisms of my book, directed fundamentally at my interpretation of the aforesaid limits recognized by *DH*. They also reveal his concern to uphold proposition **Z**: that is, to argue that the Catholic Church in *DH* implicitly but clearly repudiates her own traditional repressive doctrine as having been false, and its application as having been always and everywhere unjust.

I. Past and present in relation to DH, chapter 1.

12. In this section my critic repeatedly assails another straw man instead of my true position. "According to Fr. Harrison," he writes, "the term 'rights of all citizens' as used in #7.3 *includes* the moral (or quasi-moral) rights of citizens not to have eternal life imperiled by, for example, temptations against faith occasioned by exposure to heretics."[27] He later claims that I "egregiously err" in holding that the said term "*includes*" that right.[28] These statements – and yet another where Mr. Guminski similarly uses a present-tense verb[29] – naturally create the impression that, according to me, Vatican II teaches that Catholics *today* have a right to be protected by law from such temptations against their faith. On the contrary, the pertinent passage of *RLC*[30] is plainly talking about earlier historical periods. Indeed, by that point, I have already recognized five pages earlier in my book that, in Vatican II's judgment, "non-Catholic propaganda as such is *no longer* to be seen as the kind of threat to the common good which may justly be repressed by civil law."[31]

13. Mr. Guminski might possibly reply that, in any case, the text of *DH* is such as to condemn *absolutely*, i.e., at any period of history or in any place, coercive measures against all public expressions of religion except the true religion. He seems to hold, for example,[32] that the more repressive preconciliar Catholic doctrine could under no conceivable historical circumstances be reconciled with *DH* #6's teaching that government may

---

27 CH, #13 (emphasis added).
28 CH, #13 (emphasis added), and again in CH, #39.
29 Cf. CH, #17, last sentence, saying that "it is nonsense to say there *is* a corresponding legal right . . . ." (emphasis added). But I never said there "is" such a right.
30 Cf. *RLC*, 93.
31 *RLC*, 88 (emphasis in original). This is also reiterated clearly in the book's conclusion (cf. 143).
32 Cf. CH, #18.

never use "force or fear or other means to impose on its citizens (*civibus imponere*) the acceptance or rejection of any religion, or to prevent anyone from entering or leaving a religious body." But what the Council intends to repudiate here is clearly the kind of government "imposition" which says, in effect, to citizens, "Believe X, and don't believe Y, *or else!*" In other words, *DH* teaches that government may not apply threats of "force or fear, [etc.]" *to those persons who wish (or might wish) to accept or reject* some given religion. But pre-Vatican II laws prohibiting the public diffusion of false religious propaganda among an already-Catholic populace did not apply any such threat to anyone. No Catholic in Franco's Spain, for instance, was legally subjected to force, fear or other "impositions" simply for lapsing into heresy, schism or apostasy. And the legal threats to those who would *publicly propagate* non-Catholic religions in such countries could not reasonably be construed as attempts to pressure those persons themselves into becoming Catholics. Nor do such laws "foreclose" free enquiry about religion, as my critic claims; they merely restrict it to some extent, while leaving room for such enquiry in private discussion, reading in libraries, etc.

14. Also, it should go without saying (since the limitations mentioned in *DH* #7 apply in "blanket" fashion to all the more specific freedoms spelt out in previous articles of the Declaration) that *DH* #6 cannot be read as denying that government may prevent people from "entering . . . a [given] religious body" which *itself* constitutes a threat to a just public order. In our own day Al Qaeda, for instance, can be considered a "religious body" – it most certainly considers itself to be one. Yet only like-minded Islamic *jihadists* would consider it unjust for governments to treat evidence of membership in this body as sufficient cause for arrest and detention. After all, even its "private" activities are in truth conspiracies aimed ultimately at overthrowing the present Western public order and replacing it with *sharia,* the Q'uran's religious legal code. Likewise, at least under some historical circumstances, even simple membership of the Freemasons and other heretical sects could have been justly considered a presumptive threat to the public order of Christendom.[33]

33 Our proposition **X** mentions the mediaeval/Old Testament repression of even "private" religious dissent. Space does not permit in this article any extensive argument for the essential doctrinal compatibility between *DH* and even this degree of severity; but the above comparison with twenty-first century *jihadism* sheds light on the issue. Fr. Basile Valuet, O.S.B., has emphasized, in his *magnum opus* upholding the continuity of *DH* with Catholic tradition, that in former centuries

15. More generally, if Mr. Guminski thinks that his citations of *DH* on pp. 47–49 prove that the Council gives us a "timeless," valid-for-all-ages doctrine against the kind of repression described in our propositions **X**, **Y** and **Z**, then he will need to provide further argumentation to that effect. In my view, we can know from circumstances independent of the text,[34] and also from what the text conspicuously *fails* to say, that the Council Fathers did not in fact intend their Declaration to *continue* allowing such repression in modern times. Nevertheless, I also maintain what the text itself actually *does* say in Chapter I (articles 2–7, the central section of the Declaration which my critic is appealing to) is intrinsically flexible and non-specific enough to be quite capable of accommodating the said repression under earlier historical circumstances.

16. Let me illustrate. Mr. Guminski thinks it is "nonsense" to attempt[35]

religious dissidents in Europe normally planned, in the event of their own rise to socio-political dominance, to be just as intolerant toward Catholics as Catholics had been toward them. Or (we might add) as the warriors of *sharia* now plan to be toward us. (Cf. *La liberté religieuse et la tradition catholique: un cas de développement doctrinal homogéne dans le magistére authentique*, 3 volumes in 6 *"fascicules"* [Le Barroux: Abbaye Sainte-Madeleine, 1998], vol. I, ch. 18.) In all these cases, those propagating false religious doctrine, even "privately," posed (or still pose) a very real threat to the Church's own freedom of action, and so could scarcely invoke *DH* in their demands for immunity from state coercion.

   As regards O.T. times, the divinely legislated eradication of religious dissent – and indeed, of the dissenters – was a basic pillar of ancient Israel's social order throughout the period of the Old Covenant. God, through Moses, commanded the Hebrews to treat the cult of pagans – "for as long as you live on [Israel's] soil" – as follows: "Tear down their altars, smash their sacred pillars, chop down their sacred poles, and destroy their idols by fire" (Deut. 12: 1, 3, cf. 6: 1–2; 7:5). "Prophets" or teachers of false religions were to be put to death for thereby promoting apostasy, while even private incitement of others to pagan worship was to be similarly punished (cf. Deut. 13: 6, 7–12). Catholic faith in the integral divine authorship of both Testaments rules out any simple condemnation of this pre-Christian harshness. Vatican II indeed recognizes in *Dei Verbum* #15 that some O.T. dispositions were "imperfect and temporary." But while divine justice might "temporarily" authorize what is "imperfect," it could never authorize something intrinsically (or always and everywhere) unjust.

34   Cf. *RLC*, 86, referring to the known aims and ecumenical consciousness of many Council Fathers and *periti,* the relatively liberal political attitudes of Paul VI, and the postconciliar revision of a number of concordats between the Vatican and Catholic-majority states.

35   To attempt it, that is, by postulating a right of Catholics to be protected from exposure to salvation-endangering propaganda, even when they are themselves willing to risk the possible consequences of such exposure. But if the mere willingness of

to reconcile such repression with *DH* #4's assertion that "religious communities are entitled to teach and give witness to their faith publicly in speech or writing without hindrance," especially since the same article mentions only coercive, dishonest or unworthy *methods* of such witnessing as violations of the rights of others.[36] But such attempts do not seem like "nonsense" at all, once we remember that *DH* #7's three limiting criteria apply as much to #4 as to any other preceding article. And it would clearly beg the vital question simply to *assume* that, according to Paul VI and the Council Fathers, the Church was always wrong in former times whenever she judged that non-Catholic religious manifestations as such endangered one or more of those three essential social values. Indeed, I submit that the following imaginary codicil sustaining that earlier position, would, if inserted into the Declaration immediately after *DH* #7, be logically quite consistent with all of the real conciliar text that precedes it:

> All that has been said so far in Chapter I expounds the right to religious liberty from the standpoint of reason and natural law alone. That is, it prescinds from divine revelation in order to consider the requirements of natural human dignity abstractly

individuals to expose themselves to a given risk were enough to render unjust any legislation forbidding that exposure, civil law could not oblige us to wear seatbelts in automobiles, forbid swimming in dangerous areas, etc. Indeed, it could do little or nothing to outlaw the sale of narcotic drugs, whose users, after all, begin by willingly exposing themselves to the risk of addiction and its catastrophic effects on their lives. But at least that catastrophe is only temporal, whereas the sins of heresy, apostasy and schism lead to something much worse – eternal perdition. Indeed, any coercive protection *at all* of "public morality" – explicitly mentioned as a right and duty of the state in *DH* #7 – seems problematical once we accept the premise that government can never, as it were, protect people from themselves. This same libertarian premise implies a "right" to free legal access to pornography, contraceptives, and practically all other forms of activity among "consenting adults," and is thus plainly seen as alien to Catholic doctrine.

36 CH, ##17–19. All one can reasonably conclude from *DH* #4's failure to mention the doctrinal tenets of "religious communities" (as distinct from unethical methods of spreading them) as a possible threat to public order is that in the Council's estimation, doctrinal tenets as such could not normally be seen, *under modern circumstances*, as constituting such a threat. Even so, there could still be exceptions. No one in the Vatican, as far as I know, complained when a radical Imam in London was silenced by the British authorities in 2003 for his inflammatory, proterrorist preaching, even though this was carried out only within a mosque (i.e., on private property), and only within the hearing of those who voluntarily came to hear him.

considered. Therefore, as regards observance of the right to religious liberty under contemporary circumstances, what has been said so far is sufficient to explain what should and should not be done in pluralistic societies where most of the populace are non-Catholics.

However, further precisions must be made in order to determine the just limits on religious activity where the great majority of the population already professes the true religion. For it is clear that not all of the aforementioned civil liberties will still be appropriate among those who have passed, by means of the virtue of faith infused at baptism, from the natural state of being *seekers* after religious truth to the supernatural state of *possessing* it. The need for a social environment providing ample freedom for public discussion and inquiry in religious matters (affirmed in #2 above), no longer exists in Catholic societies. Indeed, for baptized Catholic believers, *searching* for the true religion, far from being a moral obligation, would be a mortal sin. For this "search," to the extent that it was seriously and existentially undertaken, would constitute the grave sin of heresy (or even apostasy): that is, pertinaciously *doubting* the previously embraced truth of the Gospel, as proclaimed by the One, Holy Catholic and Apostolic Church. As the Sacred Synod has itself affirmed in #1 of this Declaration, man's moral obligation is to *hold fast* to the truth once he has found and embraced it. For this reason, the "due limits" to religious activity mentioned above in #2, paragraph 1, and specified in #7, paragraph 3, can be considered violated in predominantly Catholic societies by any and every non-Catholic religious manifestation in public. Such manifestations will inevitably tempt many Catholic souls toward perdition, and so can be considered a grave threat to public morality, and indeed, as a violation of the right of the faithful to be protected from such threats to their eternal welfare – a right comparable to their right to be protected from the tempting availability of perilous narcotic drugs which threaten their temporal welfare.

17. Once again, I am *not* saying that Paul VI and the Council Fathers intended the concrete requirements of "public order" in Catholic countries to be determined in this way *today*. I am simply saying that *the text itself* is not intrinsically contradicted by giving it this 'traditionalist' interpretation of "public order," and therefore does not exclude such an interpretation from having been a valid one for earlier times. This fact is in turn important, as we shall see, in establishing that the preamble (#1) neither lies nor errs in teaching that the Declaration "leaves entire and complete" (*integram*) the "traditional Catholic doctrine" on these matters.

II. "Common Good" vs. "Public Order"

18. At this point it seems appropriate to open a parenthesis in the main line of our argument, in order to elucidate the question of the precise difference between "common good" and "public order" as providing alternative limiting criteria on religious activity in society. It is a rather thorny question, bedeviled also by semantic confusion, because "public order" seems to be a relatively recent term in Catholic usage, and earlier writers often seem to have appealed to the "common good" as a limiting criterion on religious propaganda when what they really had in mind was "public order" in Vatican II's sense of the term. In writing *RLC* I concentrated on Bishop Emil De Smedt's final *relatio* on the religious liberty schema and failed to notice an earlier one where he had explained the difference more clearly to the Council Fathers.[37] I wrongly supposed *DH* to mean that "the positive social values which belong to the 'common good' are coextensive and identical with those linked to the 'public order,'" so that the latter term, in being described by *DH* #7 as the "fundamental part of the common good," meant "the coercive defence of those values, rather than the values themselves."[38] Mr. Guminski rightly points out that what De Smedt and the Council really mean is that the common good (in its entirety) includes *more* of those "positive social values" – or better, valued social conditions (hereafter VSCs) – than does the public order. The latter consists only of those most essential VSCs which society sees as *necessary for its very existence* or *survival* in an ordered form, and which, therefore, it has to protect by coercive measures. The common good (in its entirety), however, includes in addition other VSCs which, while not essential, are nonetheless valuable for the greater prospering and flourishing of society, that is, for its *perfection* rather than its very *survival*. And the Council certainly means to say that coercion may be used only against the kind of religious (or pseudo-religious) activity which threatens the former, "essential-for-survival," set of VSCs, not that which might threaten only the latter set of "nice-but-not-so-necessary" VSCs.

37   Cf. *AS* (1976), vol. IV/ pt. I, 194–195.
38   *RLC*, 94–95.

19. Nevertheless, the above error does not really weaken my case that proposition **Z** is an unwarranted reading of *DH*. To begin with, in earlier times the need to prevent the free propagation of heresy among a Catholic population most certainly *was* considered, by Church and State alike, to be the kind of VSC that was "essential for survival." For heresy radically undermined the foundations of Christendom as an integrated social order. Secondly, the precise content of "public order" is still left quite open-ended in *DH*. In the finally approved text of #7.3, it is made clearer that this general norm is being defined *in terms of* the three more specific norms mentioned in that paragraph. Hence, the first question to be answered is not, "What specific VSCs are in fact to be considered essential, rather than just desirable?," but rather, "What specific classes of activity are to be considered as violating public peace, public morality, or the rights of other/all citizens?" Then, *after* those classes of activity have been identified, they will have to be considered as being *ipso facto* a threat to public order and so subject to legal repression. Now, it is fairly easy to identify activities threatening public *peace*, because the absence of peace – violence and disorder – is something rather obvious to all concerned. But the Declaration still leaves it rather an open question, even as regards present-day circumstances, as to what sorts of specific activities *are in fact* to be considered such serious threats to "public morality" or "the rights of other/all citizens" as to warrant legal repression. Thirdly, since *DH* is to be understood, as we shall see shortly, as allowing for significant historical changes in the evolution of the common good, it must be read as being *still more* open-ended as to what kinds of limits on religious activity were objectively justifiable *in the past*. For when the requirements of the common good evolve, those of public order necessarily evolve along with them.[39]

---

39 The observations in this paragraph, together those regarding semantic confusion in the preceding one, imply that the "common good"/"public order" distinction is not really so important as is often claimed. They are therefore also relevant for evaluating Mr. Guminski's claim that the reason why *DH* presents public order as the "basic component" of the common good is "to limit radically the traditional scope of the coercive power of civil authority with respect to religious matters" (CH, #37). I think my critic is putting his own liberal "spin" on the Council's intentions here. Bishop De Smedt's pertinent *relationes* said nothing about an intention of "radically limiting" anything "traditional." To read Mr. Guminski without reading the *relator* himself, one would never guess that when De Smedt was explaining the *reasons for using* "public order" rather than "common good" (as distinct from explaining what these terms *meant*), his emphasis was much

III. Bishop De Smedt's final *relatio*

20. Let us now return to our main theme. What other arguments does Mr. Guminski adduce in order to sustain his thesis that *DH* retrospectively condemns the repressive doctrine and practice mentioned in our propositions **X**, **Y** and **Z**? This thesis requires him to deal with, among other things, the last official *relatio* on the religious liberty schema delivered by Bishop De Smedt. The Belgian prelate pointed out on the Council floor that the final revision of the schema provided reassurance for those Fathers who did *not* want the document to imply too harsh a verdict on earlier Church doctrine and practice. Following John Courtney Murray's critique of that "anachronistic" approach which denounces certain past legal dispositions in abstraction from their historical context,[40] De Smedt agreed with the said group of Council Fathers that:

> . . . one should take into account the fact that human society itself has exhibited different modes of thinking and living in different ages. This is quite true, but it is equivalently expressed when we affirm that the norm for the care of religion is the common good. The common good, as everyone knows, is something relative: it is linked to the cultural evolution of peoples and has to be judged according to that development.[41]

21. Now, Mr. Guminski recognizes this *relatio* as bearing at least the appearance of a formidable weapon in my own armory, and so strives to expose it as a mere dummy. His efforts, however, are unpersuasive. Unfortunately, he begins by misinterpreting me yet again, claiming that I see this *relatio* "as confirming [my] position that the 'just public order' of *DH* is equivalent in scope only to the coercive components of the common good within the meaning of preconciliar doctrine."[42] But I do not see it thus. My citation and appeal to the *relatio* come at the conclusion of a section of *RLC* (pp. 85–89) arguing for the more general and fundamental

more on the purely semantic issue: i.e., the value of using the same term (i.e., "public order") as is now commonly used in civil law codes in connection with coercive government action, so as to render the Council's document more readily intelligible in the modern world, and also to help clarify that term at a time when communist regimes were appealing to it as a pretext for violating the Church's own freedom. (Cf. *AS* (1978), vol. IV/ pt. VI, 722, cited and translated in *RLC*, 90.)

40 Cf. above, para. 7, discussion referenced by footnotes 15–17.
41 *AS* (1978), vol. IV/ pt. VI, 723, n.15 (my translation), cited in *RLC*, 89 and CH, #14.
42 CH, #15.

conclusion that (our present) proposition **Z** is a false reading of *DH*. This appeal precedes altogether my argument regarding the relationship between "common good" and "public order,"[43] and does not depend for its validity on that of the latter, and quite secondary, argument.

22. My adversary first tries to squeeze the maximum mileage from the fact that De Smedt's observations, cited above, were added orally to the printed text of his *relatio* which the Fathers had before them. Gratuitously, Mr. Guminski says that this addition "appear[s] to have been incidental, surely extemporaneous . . . – very likely without any considerable impact." "*Surely* extemporaneous"? Back in 1965 all documents destined for distribution had to be submitted a day or so earlier to the Vatican press. So, for all we know, De Smedt may have spent an hour or two, the night before he was due to deliver his *relatio*, meticulously preparing the Latin text of this additional paragraph. As regards the probable "impact" of these words, it is notorious that the Fathers were constantly swamped in such a volume of *printed* material that many or most never got round to reading it all. So it is precisely the orally presented commentary which is most likely to have made the greatest impact. In any case, *all* of this particular *relatio* – its printed and oral parts – forms part of the official and public *Acta* of the Council, and the final text of *DH* should therefore be understood in the light of its content.

23. Mr. Guminski next objects – *a priori* rather implausibly – that the *relator's* orally added remarks "are inconsistent with" what he himself says in his written report.[44] He evidently thinks that since De Smedt, in those remarks, was referring to government *limitations* on religious activity, consistency required him to speak of "public order" rather than "common good." But the *relator* did not need to make that distinction in these additional remarks. For here he was simply concerned to point out that the latest revision of the text, by reducing the prominence and importance of the relatively non-traditional *term*[45] "public order," and by *defining* it in terms of the "common good,"[46] made the schema more clearly compatible with a relatively benign judgment toward the Church's more repressive stance in

---

43   Cf. *RLC*, 89–95.

44   CH, #15.

45   The revision did not reduce the importance of the specific and substantive *content* which the Council wished to ascribe to that term. Nevertheless, that content itself – the three points mentioned in *DH* #7, par. 3 – is understood to be historically "relative" and "evolving," along with the conditions that constitute the "common good" in its totality.

46   Cf. *RLC*, 89–91, and note 7 (spanning pp. 91–92).

earlier times. De Smedt was taking it for granted that the Fathers he was addressing, since they realized the relationship of common good to public order is that of a whole to some of its parts, would understand that since the common good is ("as everyone knows") something "relative" and "evolving," so likewise is public order. His orally added words, using "common good" rather than "public order," were, in this context, no more inconsistent with his printed ones than the statement "I gave up smoking for the sake of my health" is inconsistent with the statement "I gave up smoking for the sake of my throat and lungs." This rebuttal of Mr. Guminski' second objection also covers his third, which depends for its validity on this supposed incompatibility.[47]

24. His fourth and final objection is that "the probative value of the bishop's *in oratione* statement is swamped by other matters" which supposedly show that the Pope and Council Fathers really meant *DH* to oppose that statement.[48] Now, what my critic needs to establish, of course, is that this abundance of "other matters" proves that the Council's judgment as to what *today* would constitute a violation of the right to religious liberty is necessarily retroactive for all of past history. I think that our prior discussion is sufficient, for present purposes, to show that he has failed to establish that.

IV. *Tertio Millennio Adveniente*

25. Mr. Guminski then seeks to show that John Paul II himself teaches, at least implicitly, that *DH* has brought about a doctrinal contradiction. He cites[49] the 1994 Apostolic Letter *Tertio Millennio Adveniente* (*TMA*), #35, where the Pontiff calls for "a spirit of repentance" for the historical acquiescence of "sons and daughters of the Church" in "intolerance and even the use of violence in the service of truth." Expressed in these terms, such a judgment is too rhetorical to be of much help in addressing our present questions.[50] However, the Pope is more specific in the next paragraph quoted by Mr. Guminski, where he expresses "profound regret" for the

---

47   Cf. CH, #15.
48   *Ibid.*
49   Cf. CH, #25.
50   The words "intolerance" and "violence" are morally charged terms *by definition*: what they really mean here is "*unjust/excessive* restriction" and "*unjust/excessive* physical force" respectively. For that reason, they do not answer the vital question that now interests us, namely, *what specific types or levels* of restriction and physical force, employed or endorsed by Catholics in the defense of religion, *were in fact* unjust and/or excessive.

views and practices of many earlier believers who thought "that a sincere witness to the truth simultaneously required eradicating, or at least isolating, the opinions of others (*sinceram veritatis testificationem simul iubere alienas opiniones extingui vel saltem secludi*[51])." Several comments on this statement seem relevant.

26. First, in contrast to *DH* and the Pope's own *Catechism*,[52] the above judgment omits completely all mention of public order and the legitimate limits on diffusion of harmful propaganda. Taken literally and in isolation, such an unqualified rebuke might seem to indicate papal endorsement of an absolute, unlimited liberty of propaganda in matters touching faith and morals. But since we know that this is *not* John Paul II's true position, we can infer that his broad generalization, situated in a pastoral exhortation, is not intended as a precise formulation of authentic doctrine requiring a submission of mind and will on the part of the faithful.

27. Secondly, this "non-doctrinal" reading of *TMA* #35 is supported by the Pope's cautiously worded identification of the *target* of his criticism, namely, "many sons and daughters of the Church" in former ages. The Holy Father thereby makes it clear that he is not here intending to censure and reverse any previous Catholic *doctrine*. For doctrine – even authentic but non-infallible doctrine – must always, by definition and in all honesty, be attributed to *the Church herself*, not just to individuals or groups among her children.

28. Thirdly, further corroboration of this interpretation is found in the Pope's use of the verb *iubere*, which should be translated here as "required" or "demanded." By denying that the "eradication" or "isolation" of anti-Catholic ideas was *required* in the interests of the true faith, John Paul is expressing only a historical judgment that such repression was *unnecessary*, not a formally ethical judgment that it was *unjust*. Admittedly, if this judgment is correct, it would follow from the teaching of *DH* that the repression in question was unjust as well as unnecessary.[53] But the relevant point here is that all judgments about the effectiveness or necessity of

---

51   *AAS* 87 (1995), 27 (my translation). Mr. Guminski uses a defective translation wherein these words are rendered: ". . . could include suppressing the opinions of others or at least paying no attention to them." What the Pope plainly means here by *secludi* (lit., to be secluded, enclosed, fenced in, isolated) is legislation restricting or prohibiting the diffusion of such opinions.

52   Cf. *Catechism of the Catholic Church*, #2109.

53   Cf. section III.b above (paragraphs 18–19).

certain practices as means to achieve a given end, are by their nature prudential judgments about questions of contingent fact, not doctrinal judgments about immutable moral norms.

29. Fourthly, in announcing, nearly three decades after *DH*, this prudential historical judgment that neither the "eradication" nor even the "isolation" of anti-Catholic opinion in Christendom was necessary (at least, for the most part) in the interests of religious truth, His Holiness cannot be assumed to be handing down an authentic interpretation of the conciliar document. For he expresses no intention of doing so. The Pope's only reference to the Vatican II declaration in the *TMA* passage invoked by Mr. Guminski is a brief citation of the preamble's affirmation that "the truth cannot impose itself except by virtue of its own truth, as it wins over the mind with both gentleness and power" (*DH* #1). And this teaching presents no problem for my own thesis, since traditional Catholic *doctrine* never taught that religious repression was for the purpose of "imposing" truth on unbelievers or dissidents themselves, but rather, for preventing them from doing spiritual, moral or material harm to others.[54]

30. In short, while John Paul II's independent postconciliar prudential judgment on religious repression within old Christendom seems more severe, at least implicitly, than the position I am attributing to the Council itself, that by no means constitutes evidence that my reading of the conciliar doctrine is wrong.

V. Postconciliar changes in Spanish law

31. My position in *RLC* is that the new *doctrinal* development in *DH*[55] has been appropriately accompanied by (though it does not, *per se*, require) a reversal of the earlier norm of ecclesiastical public law which was reflected in concordats and other legal documents prohibiting, in certain

---

54 Cf. discussion in paragraphs 13–14 above. I emphasize the word "*doctrine*" in the above sentence, because common medieval theological *opinion* did indeed hold that physical force could be used against heretics and apostates not only to protect Christian society from their dangerous influence (i.e., in the interests of public order), but also in order to compel such persons themselves to re-embrace the orthodox faith of their baptism. (Cf., for instance Aquinas, *ST*, IIa IIae, Q. 10, a.8c, and discussion in *RLC*, 125.) I know of no evidence, however, that the legitimacy of *this particular rationale* for the use of force – i.e., aiming more at "rehabilitating" the offender himself than at protecting the rest of society from him – was ever insisted upon by the Church's magisterium as a truth requiring the assent of all Catholics.

55 Cf. para. 2 above.

states, the public manifestation of all religions except Catholicism. I hold that such changes reflect a new practical pastoral/political judgment of the Church to the effect that such manifestations, as such, can no longer be seen as a threat to public order (i.e., as a sufficiently serious threat to the common good as to require legal repression).[56] That kind of change does not imply any contradiction of *doctrine*, i.e., of what the Church had previously presented as *divine* law. Mr. Guminski, however, thinks that such doctrinal contradiction is assumed to have taken place at Vatican II by the authors of postconciliar legal revisions in certain Catholic countries. He cites as evidence[57] the Spanish law of 28 June 1967 which eliminated the previous (1945) norm prohibiting public manifestations of all non-Catholic religions. Well, even if Mr. Guminski were right in thinking that the Spanish lawmakers in question agreed with him on this point, a sufficient short answer would be: "So what?" The said lawmakers scarcely constituted a kind of Iberian branch of the Holy Office, endowed with the faculty of authoritatively interpreting the teaching of Ecumenical Councils.

32. In any case, I by no means concede that the gentlemen in question did in fact agree with my critic's reading of *DH*. Their law simply states that "After this declaration of the Council" – that is, after the promulgation of the Declaration *Dignitatis Humanae* – it has become necessary, in view of Spain's 1958 "establishment" principle, for her to amend the earlier (restrictive) law of 1945. And, of course, the position I expound in *RLC* fully recognizes that necessity. But whether the Spanish legislators understood the Council to mean that this amendment was required by immutable divine law itself (as Mr. Guminski thinks), or only by a new ecclesiastical specification, suitable for our day, of a far more general and flexible divine law (as I think) – this, I submit, cannot possibly be determined solely on the basis of this brief legal text itself. Indeed, since those who draft and promulgate civil legislation are usually practical men, not theologians or natural-law philosophers, it seems quite probable that this theoretical distinction disputed by Mr. Guminski and myself passed completely undetected beneath their radar screen.[58]

56 Cf. *RLC*, 57–58, 87–88.
57 CH, #27.
58 These Spanish legislators (as cited by Mr. Guminski) do indeed begin the 1967 law by quoting the existing (1958) constitutional principle that all legislation in Spain "must take its inspiration from the *doctrine* of the Catholic Church" (emphasis added). But their decision to cite that principle is entirely explicable

VI. *DH* #1 and doctrinal "development"

33. Mr. Guminski has one more argument for "reject[ing] as without merit" my view that *DH* rescinded preconciliar public law without contradicting preconciliar doctrine. But this argument is the weakest of all, because it depends on a conciliar text which, correctly understood, conflicts with his own position and endorses mine. He reminds us that, in its preamble, "*DH* expressly declared that the Council, 'in treating of this religious freedom, . . . intend[ed] to develop the doctrine of more recent popes [. . .] on the inviolable rights of the human person.'"[59] Indeed. But simply by using the verb "develop," the Council Fathers *deny* the very thing my critic would have us believe they imply, namely, that the doctrine they now intend to propose is incompatible with preconciliar doctrine. Can it be that Mr. Guminski is unaware that ever since Blessed J. H. Newman's landmark essay propelled the concept of doctrinal "development" into mainstream Catholic theology, it has been taken for granted, as a *sine qua non* for ecclesial recognition of this concept, that any authentic "development" has to be in harmony, not in conflict, with the existing doctrine? That was fundamental to Newman's whole argument. Or does Mr. Guminski at least confusedly realize this, while supposing nevertheless that the Council's specification of "more recent" popes as being those whose doctrine it proposes to "develop" is a gentle, diplomatic, way of indicating that the doctrine of *earlier* popes may – alas! – have to be *corrected* (i.e., contradicted), rather than developed, in the course of carrying out this proposal?

34. If so, he is still wrong – on three counts. First, orthodox theology has always recognized, and insisted, that any development of doctrine, to be authentic and acceptable, must be compatible with *all* previous Catholic doctrine, not just with certain parts of it.

35. Secondly, upon identifying those "more recent" Popes whom the Council had in mind, we find that *their own* doctrine, and not only that of their predecessors, is such as would have been contradicted, not authentically developed, by the doctrine Mr. Guminski ascribes to the Council (cf. our proposition **Z**). Named in note 2 to the next paragraph (#2, par. 1), these popes are those whose writings are cited as the main magisterial sources for the Council's central doctrinal affirmation of religious liberty as a natural right: John XXIII, Pius XII, Pius XI, and Leo XIII, in that

simply by the appropriateness of indicating, in a legislative document, why it is that a magisterial document of the said religious denomination could, as such, be seen as requiring a change in Spanish civil law.

59   CH, #26, citing *DH* #1.3.

order. But every one of these popes accepted the justice, under some circumstances, of legally prohibiting all public manifestations of non-Catholic religions: such prohibitions, of course, were papally endorsed in Spain, Colombia and elsewhere right up until the Council. Hence, to argue that the more innovative statements of these popes which are invoked here in #2 somehow imply, and so can be "developed" into, the doctrine which proposition **Z** ascribes to *DH*, would imply the implausible claim that the position of all these Pontiffs on religious freedom was fundamentally incoherent – i.e., that each one of them embraced mutually contradictory doctrines in different statements or policies of his own pontificate.

36. Thirdly, the word *recentiorum* ("more recent") was added to the final draft by the express order of Paul VI – and certainly not with the intention of smoothing the way for a contradiction of *earlier* popes. On the contrary, this and several other vital last-minute amendments to *DH* #1 were introduced with the avowed intention of "reassuring" those Fathers who feared such a contradiction. The fact that these amendments – together with two full paragraphs of the final *relatio* explaining them – were dictated word for word by Paul VI was not made public till more than a quarter-century after the Declaration was promulgated. Their importance, therefore, could not be fully appreciated in commentaries on *DH* written before the early 1990s.[60]

37. How does "*recentiorum*" serve this avowedly conservative purpose? First, it must be taken in conjunction with the other simultaneous papal

60   I was unaware of this intervention when writing *RLC* and my earlier articles on *DH*. The archivist of Vatican Council II, Msgr. Vincenzo Carbone, finally published in 1991 the text of an important handwritten note from the Pope, dated November 15, 1965. It reads as follows (my translation): "Proposals for new amendments to the text *De lib. rel.* have been seen. To Msgr. Felici Pericle [secretary-general of the Council]. Please make known the following: some reassuring retouches will be added (*saranno apportati alcuni ritochi tranquillizzanti*); – but the schema must be printed immediately after that (this evening) so as to be distributed on Wednesday 17 and put to the vote on Friday 19. Already phoned to Most Rev. Dell'Acqua" (V. Carbone, "Il ruolo di Paolo VI nell'evoluzione e nella redazione della dichiarazione 'Dignitatis Humanae'", in *Paolo VI e il rapporto Chiesa-mondo al Concilio* [Brescia: Istituto Paolo VI, 1991], 169). What these "reassuring retouches" were can be seen by comparing the final text of *DH* #1 with the penultimate draft (*textus recognitus*). Article 3 was also modified by this papal intervention, so that the final text no longer excludes all trans-temporal concerns from the state's legitimate area of competence, and *does* exclude the "laicist" ideal of state "neutrality" as between religion and irreligion. It says the state "must recognize and favor the religious life of citizens."

additions to the same paragraph (#1.3) of the final draft (viz., the words "traditional" before "Catholic doctrine" and "and societies" after "men"). Then, the ensemble of these additions must be understood in the light of the relevant portion of Bishop De Smedt's final *relatio*,[61] which was also dictated to him in a communication from the Pope.[62] The idea of saying that the Council proposed to develop the doctrine of "more recent" Popes was to underline the insistence that what *earlier* Popes had taught (i.e., the "*traditional* Catholic doctrine") was to be left "*un*developed" i.e., "left intact" (*integram*, meaning "in its integrity," i.e., "entire and complete," "unchanged"). As the *relatio* says, these "recent" popes have "retained" the doctrine of "the papal documents up to Leo XIII . . . on the moral duty of public authorities toward the true religion" (a doctrine which certainly included the duty of those authorities, in some circumstances, to restrain the spread of *false* religions), but have also "complement[ed] it by highlighting another duty of the same authorities, namely, that of observing the exigencies of the dignity of the human person in religious matters as a necessary element of the common good." And (we are told) the Council now proposes to develop, in the sense of "clarify," this "more recent" papal teaching which complements the older, "undeveloped" (but still "intact") teaching.[63]

38. Readers will recall that in my view, this complementary *doctrinal* clarification consists essentially in the Council's implied teaching that "*Some* peaceful non-Catholic propaganda (in at least some times and/or places) has a right to immunity from civil prohibition."[64] Now,

---

61 Cf. *AS* (1978), vol. IV/ pt. VI, 719 (reproduced over n. 31 in *RLC*, 75, my translation).

62 The Council's archivist informs us that on the same day Pope Paul ordered the above insertions into the final draft to #1 and #3, he also intervened directly to dictate their official explanation: "At the bottom of a sheet of paper containing the section of the *relatio* from '*Aliqui patres*' down to '*adiunximus*' [the section referenced in n. 61 above], the Pope added the following hand-written annotation: '15–XI-1965. For Mons. C. Colombo. This text will be inserted into the final *relatio* on the Schema *De libertate religiosa*, **in order to respond to the objection alleging discontinuity in the magisterium**'" (Carbone, 169–170, bold type added). These papal interventions indeed seem to have had a significant "reassuring" effect for several hundred Fathers. The percentage of "*placets*" (positive votes) for articles 1–5 in this new version of the schema rose on November 19 to approach the necessary consensus: 88% (1954 out of 2216), compared to only 72% (1539 out of 2138) in the vote on the previous draft on October 26 (cf. Carbone, 170 and *RLC*, 67).

63 Cf. references in n. 61 above.

64 Cf. note 4 above and corresponding discussion in para. 2.

this newly developed proposition of divine and natural law is very general (non-specific) in character. Yet at the same time we know – mainly from the declaration's *silence* about any possible differences in the application of *DH* in Catholic, as distinct from non-Catholic, societies – that the Council's specific will and determination was to disapprove any continued restrictions on non-Catholic propaganda *as such*, even in officially Catholic nations like Spain. It follows that this disapproval must be understood as a prudential judgment – that is, a new norm of public ecclesiastical law – which gives concrete specification to the more general divine law by ruling that *under modern circumstances* the said propaganda can no longer, as such, be considered a threat to the just public order of any country on earth (cf. our proposition **Y**). For if, as my adversary is anxious to prove, the said disapproval were presented by *DH* as being itself a point of *divine* law (i.e., as *doctrine*, valid for all places and times, past, present and future), then it would plainly not "complement" the traditional Catholic doctrine, nor leave it "intact," but rather, radically contradict it. And it is the chief signatory to *DH*, Paul VI, who assures us via the *relator* that the declaration *cannot* be interpreted in any such radical sense.

VII. What is the "objective moral order"?

39. Mr. Guminski's final argument in the third section of his article has to do with whether or not the "objective moral order" (specified in #7, par. 3 in connection with the norms for legitimate governmental restriction on activity carried out in the name of religion), is to be understood – as Catholics would normally understand that expression – to include both the natural moral law and revealed (divine positive) law. In *RLC* I maintain that it should be understood to include both;[65] but my critic claims its meaning must be restricted in this context to the former. The short answer to Mr. Guminski, I suppose, is to ask him why on earth, if the Council Fathers had meant to teach that natural law provides the *only* legitimate criterion for setting legal limits to religious activity, they did not simply say so. However, his labored attempts to justify his narrow reading of the conciliar expression merit an answer.

40. My critic first protests that admitting divine positive law as a criterion would imply "authoriz[ing] repression of . . . violations of the Catholic religion, as such," and that *DH* does not allow for such repression.

---

65   Cf. CH, ##28–30, citing various passages of *RLC*.

But I deny the validity of this inference as regards the words "as such." Authorizing government to repress "violations of the Catholic religion *as such*" would be handing it a *carte blanche* for the repression of *any and every* religious manifestation which conflicts with Catholic orthodoxy. And, of course, I have consistently recognized that according to *DH*, that degree of repression would, at least under modern circumstances, violate the right to religious liberty. But it by no means follows from this that divine positive law, at least in our own day, has to be excluded *totally* from the criteria by which the government of a predominantly Christian or Catholic country determines the requirements of a just public order (and, therefore, the legal limits to religious activity). For an intermediate position is possible, by which *certain points* of divine positive law could still be included among such criteria, not *simply because* they are revealed by God, but because, *in addition*, they are judged to have a particular and direct social importance in maintaining a Christian or Catholic public order.[66]

41. We read next an appeal to the authority of *Gaudium et Spes* and *Veritatis Splendor*: passages are cited which indeed emphasize the natural law in connection with "objective norms of morality." But readers can readily see that neither quotation in any way excludes divine positive law from the role which my reading of *DH* #7 ascribes to it.[67]

42. Mr. Guminski further argues that since religious liberty is "a natural right to be universally respected by civil authority" in all political communities regardless of their official religion (if any), it follows that "the natural moral law (and not the divine positive law) is to provide the foundation by which the requirements of just public order are to be determined."[68] But this is a non sequitur, for the conclusion depends on another premise which *DH* neither states nor implies, namely, that the "due limits" which are inherent to the said natural right must be determined *uniformly*, at least as regards their "foundation," in all political communities – those which recognize the truth of Catholicism and those which do not. But *DH* nowhere denies that God, if He wishes, can authorize civil authorities to set the bar for communal conduct higher in a Catholic community than

---

66 Cf. *RLC*, 100–101, where several examples are suggested: divine positive law regarding polygamy, Sunday observance, and the *per se* duty of political communities themselves (along with all other "societies," according to *DH* #1, par. 3), to recognize Roman Catholicism as true.

67 Cf. CH, #32.

68 CH, #35.

would be fair in a non-Catholic community, i.e., forbidding in the former certain things that it would not be right to forbid in the latter.

43. Finally, it should be pointed out that Mr. Guminski's attempt to keep divine positive law separate from natural law runs up against this further obstacle: according to Catholic doctrine, every violation of the former indirectly violates the latter as well. For it is precisely the *natural* moral law, known by the light of reason, which requires individuals and societies (even though only the former can possess the supernatural virtue of faith) to recognize the truth of Roman Catholicism, along with what it proclaims as divine positive law.[69]

44. I submit that my observations so far constitute a sufficient reply to Mr. Guminski's claim that the position I expound in *RLC* regarding the meaning of *DH* and its reconciliation with traditional doctrine is "unjustified" and "fundamentally flawed."[70]

D. Articles Published After RLC

I. The meaning and status of *DH* #7

45. The final section (D) of Mr. Guminski's critique covers several of my articles on the religious liberty issue published after *RLC*: articles in which, as he quaintly puts it, my own "doctrine" has been "developed." He refers first to an article in *Social Justice Review*[71] in which, noting that "the central *doctrinal* affirmation of the entire Declaration is found in article 2," I also suggest that "it seems probable that the precisions given in article 7 of *DH* in regard to the limiting criteria on religious liberty are to be seen

---

69 Cf., for instance, Vatican Council I, DS 3033–3034, and Leo XIII, *Immortale Dei*, #6: "Since, then, no one is allowed to be remiss in the service due to God, and since the chief duty of all men is to cling to religion in both its teaching and practice – not such religion as we may have a preference for, but the religion which God enjoins, *and which certain and most clear marks show to be the only one true religion* – it is a public crime to act as if there were no God. So too it is a sin in the State . . . [to adopt] out of many forms of religion . . . that one which chimes in with fancy; for we are bound absolutely to worship God in that way which He has shown to be His will" (emphasis added, cited in *RLC*, 13). The *Catechism of the Catholic Church*, #2105, references this encyclical in its entirety in expounding the social duty of religion.

70 CH, #2.

71 "Vatican II and Religious Liberty: Contradiction or Continuity?," *Social Justice Review*, July/August 1989, 104–112. This article was republished in *Catholic Dossier*, vol. 6, no. 2, March-April, 2000, 21–30. I will follow Mr. Guminski in referring to this article as "SJR*89*."

as new norms of ecclesiastical public law rather than immutable doctrine."[72]

46. First, I should remark that if I were writing that sentence again today, I would use the word "possible" instead of "probable." For, as the foregoing argumentation in this present essay will have made clear to the reader, my considered opinion is that the limiting criteria of *DH #7* are sufficiently broad and indeterminate *in meaning* as to constitute an umbrella large enough to shelter a number of *concrete applications* of varying degrees of tolerance or intolerance, in accordance with the Church's changing prudential judgment in different historical situations. If this is true, it will follow that article #7 affirms something which the Council understands and teaches to be true *at all times and in all places.* Indeed, the very breadth or vagueness of its *meaning* will help to guarantee the universality of its *truth.* And teachings which the Church requires Catholics to accept as true for all times and all places are, by definition, *doctrines.*

47. However, I recognize that the meaning of article 7, especially its terms "public morality," the "rights of all citizens," and "the objective moral order," is less than crystal-clear, so that my own reading of the text is at least open to debate. And in fact, Mr. Guminski and I are busy debating it. Now, let us suppose for the sake of argument that I am wrong and he is right, i.e., that the Council Fathers did *not* intend the criteria to be as broad and indeterminate in meaning as I think they are. Let us suppose, concretely, that my adversary could prove his claim that the Fathers intended "the objective moral order" in *DH #7* to mean the natural moral law *alone.* On that basis, the revealed or supernatural considerations[73] which underpinned the Church's more intolerant preconciliar stance would have to be judged "inadmissible evidence" by State authorities – even in solidly Catholic countries – in determining legal limits on religious activity. In other words, it would then follow that the very *meaning* of the terms "rights of all citizens" and "public morality" in *DH #7* would be restricted to those rights and moral norms which can be directly and persuasively established on the basis of "secular" or philosophical ethics, i.e., unaided human reason.

48. Supposing all this to be true, would it then mean that Mr. Guminski is right in the main point at issue between us, namely, his claim that proposition **Z** expresses the true meaning of the conciliar declaration? Not

---

72   *SJR89,* 110, cited in CH, #41.
73   These would have been, principally, the unique truth of the Roman Catholic religion and the consequent threat to the eternal salvation of Catholic citizens arising from the spread of heresy in society

at all. The point I alluded to (but did not expound) in my 1989 article is that in that case *DH #7*, by deciding that divine revelation as such (together with any consequences flowing from it) is to be ruled "out of court" by even Catholic civil authorities as a basis for legal limitations on religious activity, would be establishing a norm that could in no way be seen as implied by, or as being a harmonious development of, any existing Catholic doctrine. Indeed, such a norm would not only be a complete novelty – and for that reason alone be excluded from doctrinal status by Catholic tradition[74] – but would actually fly in the face of traditional doctrine if it were itself proposed *as doctrine*. For these reasons, and in the light of *DH* 1's repeated assurances that the declaration remains in harmony with traditional doctrine, the criteria of *DH #7*, if they mean what Mr. Guminski thinks they mean, would have to be understood as constituting a "new norm of ecclesiastical public law" or policy, as I suggested in SJR89. The status of this norm would then be rather like that of the present Pontiff's recent prudential judgment that the death penalty can rarely if ever be justified *under modern circumstances*. Precisely because of its non-doctrinal status, the putative new norm of *DH #7* would not imply any retroactive condemnation of all previous Church-approved religious repression (prompted mainly by considerations of revealed truth). In short, whether I am right or wrong about the meaning of *DH #7*, proposition **Z** remains false either way.

48. Let us return to Mr. Guminski's critique of my position. After citing my *SJR89* observations, he retorts sardonically: "In short, the alleged doctrine of *DH* concerning religious liberty is essentially vacuous. It reminds one of those sham legal constitutional provisions in totalitarian states which (in substance) affirm the right of the people to be free, as to a particular matter, but only within the limits of law."[75]

49. I think the foregoing discussion sufficiently justifies my 1989

74 The First Vatican Council, for instance, insists that, in the light of the completeness of divine revelation, "the Holy Spirit was not promised to the successors of Peter in order for them to make known any new revealed doctrine, but rather, so that through His assistance, they might devoutly guard and faithfully expound revelation handed down by the Apostles, that is, the deposit of faith" (DS 3070 = Dz 1836).

75 CH, #42. In CH, n. 67, Mr. Guminski understandably expresses puzzlement at my use of the term "immutable doctrine" (SJR89, 110, cited in CH, #41) in reference to what we both agree is an exercise of the non-infallible magisterium. A distinction needs to be made between the immutability (or mutability) of a given ethical norm *itself* and the immutability (or mutability) of the Church's *expressed judgment* that this norm is true. Consider the following two propositions:

comment for present purposes. But I will add several further comments on Mr. Guminski's retort. First, on any possible reading of *DH*, not just mine, merely human, positive law in different times and places will have to decide the "limits" on acceptable religious activity in varying ways. Indeed, the authentic interpretation of *DH* furnished by the *Catechism* recognizes this: "The 'due limits' which are inherent in [the right] must be determined for each social situation by political prudence, according to the requirements of the common good, and '. . . in conformity with the objective moral order.'"[76] Secondly, the invidious comparison between *DH* and "the sham . . . provisions of totalitarian states" is unfair insofar as such regimes certainly do *not* follow this "objective moral order" in imposing their legal limits. Thirdly, we should not be surprised that some natural rights, precisely in order to be valid for all times and places, have to be so general as to be quite "vacuous" unless and until they are given concrete specification by a multiplicity of human positive laws which will vary greatly according to circumstances. It is obvious that such "vacuity" must also be admitted, for instance, in regard to the natural right of workers to receive a just wage[77] and the "inalienable right to education" of "[a]ll men, . . . in virtue of their dignity as human persons."[78] Ah, but *how much* pay constitutes a just wage? And *what sort* of education truly befits human dignity? Only human positive law and prudential policy judgments, varying greatly according to changing historical, cultural and economic circumstances, will be able to answer those vital questions satisfactorily.

II. The meaning of *DH* #1.

51. Still commenting on my *SJR89* article, Mr. Guminski brands as

> 1. *Dignitatis Humanae* teaches that X is an immutable right of the human person.
> 2. *Dignitatis Humanae* teaches immutably that X is an immutable right of the human person.
>
> When I used the word "immutable" I had in mind the first proposition, but did not express myself well. I meant that *DH* proposes (authentically but not infallibly) that the right to RL is "immutable" simply by virtue of being a *natural* right, in contrast to other kinds of rights which are derived from changeable circumstances or mere positive law (the will of a human legislator).

76   *CCC* #2109.
77   Cf. *CCC* #2434.
78   Vatican Council II, Declaration on Christian Education, *Gravissimum Educationis*, #1

"wholly unwarranted"[79] my contention therein that the preamble to *DH* upholds the preconciliar doctrine acknowledging the right of civil authority to use coercion in protecting the true religion. Now, if the Secretariat for Christian Unity had wanted to present a schema contradicting *any part* of the existing doctrine of the Church, then of course honesty would have required that this be acknowledged openly on the floor of the Council. The *relator* would have had to adduce evidence and argumentation in order to convince the Fathers that the (putatively) erroneous doctrinal thesis they were now being asked to repudiate had never been proposed with *infallible* force by either the ordinary or extraordinary magisterium. There is of course not a trace of any of this in the Council's *Acta*. On the contrary, the Fathers were assured, in the pertinent *relationes*, that *no* doctrinal contradiction was involved. Moreover, I insist that the preamble itself, implicitly and explicitly, repeats that same assurance – three times, in fact. (Hence my earlier remark that Mr. Guminski's interpretation of *DH*, chapter I, far from making the declaration more "credible," turns it into a scandalous piece of lying hypocrisy.)

1. We have already seen one instance of this in discussing the implications of the verb "develop" near the end of *DH* #1.[80]

2. Next, we have another of Paul VI's last-minute amendments: the first paragraph's all-encompassing affirmation that the Council, in evaluating modern man's ever-increasing demand for freedom, "examines the Church's sacred tradition *and doctrine*, from which it draws forth new things which are *always in harmony* with the old."[81] The "doctrine" in question is not said to be limited to the "infallible" (as distinct from merely "authentic") category; nor is it said to be limited to some particular *area* of doctrine. In short, *anything* "new" proposed by the Declaration is affirmed in advance to be in harmony with any and every aspect of the "old" doctrine.

3. My critic has apparently not considered any of the points presented in the preceding three paragraphs. (I myself have never raised them in previous publications.) So he discusses only the third relevant text of *DH* #1, to wit, that better-known passage affirming that religious freedom (as the Council understands it) "leaves intact the traditional Catholic doctrine on

---

79   CH, #44.

80   Cf. paras. 35–37 above.

81   ". . . *sacram Ecclesiae traditionem **doctrinamque** scrutatur, ex quibus nova **semper** cum veteribus **congruentia** profert*" (emphasis added).

the moral obligation of individuals and societies to the true religion and the one Church of Christ." Specifically, while Mr. Guminski does not contest my view that *DH* includes here the "moral obligation" of civil authorities to recognize Catholicism as uniquely true,[82] he rejects my contention that it also includes their right to use coercion against false religious propaganda "to the extent that the common good requires"[83] (that is, in the interests of a just public order).

52. Failing to appreciate the importance of the last clause in quotation marks, which I would maintain is essential in order to express the traditional (preconciliar) doctrine correctly, my critic asserts that the "moral obligation" reaffirmed by *DH* #1 "has nothing to do with the question of the coercive power as to religious matters," and that "[t]he preamble itself negatives this" by referring to the "people's demand for religious liberty . . . [which] concerns freedom from compulsion in civil society."[84] Now we know, of course, that repeated statements throughout the rest of the declaration make it clear that the religious liberty affirmed briefly in article 1 is not to be understood as an *unlimited* liberty. But this fact in turn implies that there is no incompatibility between the said affirmation of the preamble and my own reading of the paragraph in which it occurs. For it is obvious that "leaving intact" a "traditional doctrine" which allows the State to restrict the diffusion of religious and moral falsehood in the interests of a just public order is perfectly compatible with affirming a "religious liberty" which can be *limited* in the interests of a just public order.

53. Moreover, since Mr. Guminski finds it "patently clear" that the coercion-justifying aspect of preconciliar doctrine is *not* included within that "traditional Catholic doctrine" which *DH* #1 claims to leave "intact," he must, logically, sustain the thesis that the coercion in question was *not* traditionally understood by the Church's magisterium as finding its

---

82 As Mr. Guminski points out, I had already defended *this* thesis in detail in chapter 6 of *RLC*. He does not seem particularly concerned to dispute the propriety, or even the theoretically normative status, of such state "establishment" of Catholicism, provided this has no discernible restrictive consequences for non-Catholic minorities.

83 *RLC*, 60 (proposition 2); cf. CH, ##43–44. As we have seen in paragraph 18 above, coercion which the common good *requires* (i.e., which is truly *necessary*) – as distinct from coercion which (putatively) would be *beneficial*, but not *necessary*, for the common good – is precisely what *DH* means, according to the *relator*'s official explanation, by coercion in the interests of a "just public order."

84 CH, #45.

justification in the "moral obligation" of the "public power"[85] (that is, government) "toward the true religion and the one Church of Christ"; for the preamble clearly means to say that *everything* traditionally understood to be included in that "moral obligation" is being "left intact" by *DH*. I submit, however, that this thesis is historically indefensible, and indeed, preposterous. For while the *civil* authorities of Christendom who actually enforced the traditional restrictions on heretical and Jewish propaganda might often have been motivated largely by political or other non-religious considerations, it is manifest and undeniable from all the relevant preconciliar magisterial documents and theological treatises that, as far as "traditional Catholic *doctrine*" was concerned, such restrictions were very much part of the State's duty to protect the true religion and the souls of those constituting "the one Church of Christ."

54. A reading of Mr. Guminski's 15–line citation of the last part of the preamble[86] may well leave an initial impression that his bland (and, as it were, "toothless") interpretation of this *social* obligation toward the true religion reflects the true mind of the Council. But it should be remembered, first, that this final version of *DH* #1 is a product of some last-minute "doctoring" or "retouching" of the second-last draft. That previous draft had indeed implied nothing favorable to coercion, since it spoke only of upholding the moral duty of *individuals* to the true religion. And traces of this previous more liberal and individualistic perspective remain embedded in the general structure and phraseology of the final text.

55. Secondly, and perhaps more importantly, the translation used by Mr. Guminski – like every other published translation I have come across – fails to render adequately one of those final papally mandated "retouches": the replacement of *Itaque* by *Porro* to begin the second sentence of the preamble's last paragraph.[87] Dictionaries show that *porro* is a rather flexible connecting word, meaning "again, in turn, next, furthermore, moreover, on the other hand." In ecclesiastical Latin this last meaning, indicating a certain contrast with what has just been said, is common. For while *porro* here can still be more "neutral," and even (like *autem* or *vero*) a mere

---

85 The papally dictated section of the final *relatio* unquestionably implies that the word "societies" in *DH* #1 includes the "public power" (*potestas publica*), i.e., the State (cf. *AS*, vol. IV/ pt. VI, 719, reproduced over n. 31 in *RLC*, 75).

86 Cf. CH, #45.

87 Cf. *AS* (1978), vol. IV/ pt. V, 78, for the pertinent section of the second-last draft (*textus recognitus*), and *AS*, vol. IV/pt. VI, 704 for the corresponding section of the final text (*textus denuo recognitus*).

stylistic variant for "and," it often has the adversative force of "on the other hand," or "but."[88] In short, it is used to introduce a new thought that represents a *break or contrast* from the preceding statement. Now, *itaque* indicates just the opposite: continuity, reinforcement, or logical consequence from what has just been said. It means "and so, and thus, accordingly, therefore, consequently." Hence, the replacement of *Itaque* by *Porro* as the first word in the sentence reaffirming the "traditional Catholic doctrine" is highly significant. It means that this sentence *no longer* expresses something which is an implication or consequence of the preceding one, with its "coercion-unfriendly" insistence that truth "imposes itself solely by the force of its own truth, [etc.]." Given this textual change, and given also the fact that all these final amendments were, in the handwritten words of Paul VI, introduced precisely to "in order to respond to the [conservative] objection alleging discontinuity in the magisterium,"[89] the word following *Porro*, namely, *quum*, should also be re-translated in a more "conservative-friendly" way: that is, as "while" or "although," instead of "since." I submit, therefore, that the following rendering of the first two sentences of *DH* #1, final paragraph, expresses their true meaning more accurately than the commonly used translations. (The Pope's "retouches" are italicized so that the reader can see where the final text differs from the previous draft.)

> The Sacred Synod further proclaims that these obligations touch and bind the human conscience, and that truth imposes itself solely by the force of its own truth, as it enters the mind at once gently and with power. *On the other hand,* although religious liberty – which men demand in fulfilling their duty to worship God – concerns immunity from coercion in civil society, it leaves intact the *traditional* Catholic doctrine on the moral obligation of men *and societies* toward the true religion and the one Church of Christ.

56. The harmony between the text, thus translated, and the interpretation I am giving to it is now much more apparent. The train of thought is as

---

88 See for instance the Douay-Rheims rendering (a very close and literal one) of the Vulgate Bible, in such texts as Lk 10: 42 (Martha and Mary): "But one thing is necessary . . . ."; Lk. 11: 20: "But if I by the finger of God cast out devils, ..." and Mt. 8: 27: "But the men were astounded . . . ." Cf. also I Chron. 5: 2; 11: 5, I Kings (= I Samuel) 22:30; III Kings 11: 32. In all these texts (and many others) "but" in the Douay-Rheims version translates *porro* in the Vulgate.

89 Carbone, *op. cit.,* 169–170.

follows: Given that religious liberty "concerns immunity from coercion in civil society," *it might seem* that if the Council now recognizes a natural right to such liberty, this will inevitably involve a repudiation of the *traditional* Catholic doctrine on the moral duty *of societies* toward the true religion. For that doctrine, after all, certainly included society's right and duty to protect the true religion with coercive measures. However (we are reassured), there will be no such repudiation. For *although* religious liberty (as the Council understands it) does indeed concern immunity from coercion, it *nevertheless* "leaves intact" (or "whole and complete"[90]) that traditional doctrine. (The seeming tension between the "old" and the "new": doctrinal positions would then be resolved by drawing attention, as I have done above, to the *limited* character of both the previously authorized coercion and the newly acknowledged liberty.)

III. The *Catechism of the Catholic Church* on *DH* #1

57. Mr. Guminski next appeals to the *Catechism*'s authentic commentary on the preamble, which, he claims, "conclusively shows that Fr. Harrison's view is erroneous.."[91] My adversary asserts this claim without argument, apparently thinking it is self-evidently vindicated by the very words of the *Catechism*. He simply quotes #2105, according to which the "traditional Catholic doctrine" mentioned in *DH* #1 is "constituted by" (Lat. *constituit*) the following principle: "The duty of offering God authentic worship (*cultum authenticum*) concerns man both individually and socially" (my translation).

58. Now, this laconic affirmation of the *Catechism* needs to be "unpacked" in the light of its historical and literary context. First, given the papally mandated *relatio* we have considered above, there can be not the slightest doubt that among those bound to carry out "authentic" (i.e., Roman Catholic) worship "socially," the *Catechism* means to include civil authorities as such. Father (later Cardinal) Jérome Hamer, who had been a conciliar *peritus* for the Secretariat for Christian Unity, comments authoritatively as follows on the words "and societies" in *DH* #1: "The reference here is to all social groups, from the most modest and spontaneous to nations and States, and covering everything in between: trade unions, cultural associations, universities."[92] Article #2105 itself clearly implies that this "social" duty binds nations and states by referring in its sources to the

90 Latin *integram*.
91 CH, #45.
92 *La libertá religiosa nel Vaticano II* (Torino-Leumann, Elle Di Ci, 2nd Ed., 1967), 145. Hamer's comment is also cited in *RLC*, 77 (translation mine, emphasis added).

encyclicals *Immortale Dei* (1885) and *Quas Primas* (1925), both of which are principally concerned to uphold and emphasize that duty.[93]

59. So far, Mr. Guminski will probably not disagree; but he evidently thinks the *Catechism* excludes the view that governmental *coercive* measures against non-Catholic manifestations as such can ever (past, present or future) find any justification in the aforesaid social duty. Well, if that were the case, the *Catechism* itself would be open to the objections I have already leveled at Mr. Guminski's own position in section IVb above, especially that of its unhistorical character (cf. para. 52). It is a clearly documented fact that "traditional Catholic doctrine" *did* include coercive measures as part of the State's "moral duty to the true religion." And if not even God can change the past, much less can a church catechism do so.

60. However, I do not concede that the *Catechism* does in fact exclude all coercive measures in fulfillment of the said duty. Bearing in my mind that this social duty of "offering authentic worship" to God involves not only *recognizing* Catholic truth in this way but also *keeping, conserving* or *guarding* it[94] so that the next generation (and the next, and the next) will still offer that same worship, the need for some degree of coercion to restrict anti-Catholic propaganda follows as a *practical* corollary.[95] According to both Old and New Testaments, "worship," no matter how outwardly reverent and orthodox, will not in fact be "authentic" if it is not carried out in the context of a life-style (individual or national as the case may be) marked by justice and the observance of God's commandments.[96] Accordingly, this same article (#2105) of the *Catechism* reminds

---

93 Significantly, the final (1997) version of the *Catechism* omits the original (1992) references specifying articles 3 and 17 of *ID*, and articles 8 and 20 of *QP*. These encyclicals, two classic *pièces de résistance* for Catholic traditionalists, are therefore now referenced in their entirety, making it clear that the Church is not repudiating any part of their doctrine.

94 Latin *servare* (*DH* #1, last word, second paragraph).

95 It does not indeed follow with a strict *logical* necessity. As I have noted in my other writings, state establishment of religion is theoretically compatible with a very wide variety of legal dispositions vis-à-vis the treatment of other religions, philosophies and life-styles, ranging from the fiercest intolerance to almost unrestricted liberty.

96 Cf., for example, "The sacrifice of the wicked is an abomination" (Prov. 21: 27); "Away with your noisy songs! I will not listen to the melodies of your harps. But if you would offer me holocausts, then let justice surge like water, and goodness like an unfailing stream" (Amos 5: 23–24); also Is. 1: 11–17, Sir. 34: 19–20, Jer. 6: 20, Mk. 12: 38–40, etc.

Catholics that their duty to evangelize includes working to "infuse the Christian spirit into the mentality and mores, laws and structures of the communities in which [they] live." But experience amply demonstrates that in those states (for instance, postconciliar Spain, Italy, and the northern European monarchies) which have maintained merely nominal, ceremonial church 'establishments' while imposing few if any restrictions on anti-Christian propaganda, the aforesaid "Christian spirit" gradually withers and disappears from their "mentality and mores, laws and structures." (That, of course, was precisely what the nineteenth-century popes had predicted in their crusade against excessive religious and other civil liberties.) Legislation eventually permits such evils as divorce, pornography, abortion, the sale of contraceptives, euthanasia, and even homosexual "marriage."[97] This massive atrophy of the grass-roots substance of a Christian social order has already led inexorably to the calm (generally uncontroverted[98]) abolition of even the nominal Catholic "establishments" of Spain and Italy, where seventeen centuries of the Constantinian era officially ended with a mere whimper – certainly not a bang – in the 1980s.

61. Further light on what lies beneath the surface of the *Catechism's*

97   Indeed, a new intolerance toward *Christian* religious expression is now looming in some of these officially "Christian" states. Since 2002, the law in Lutheran Sweden prohibits speech showing "disrespect" for homosexuals (among other groups). The then-Prime Minister, Göran Persson, admitted publicly at the time that this would penalize the use of the word "unnatural" in reference to sodomy. A Pentecostal pastor, the Rev. Ake Green, was sentenced to a month's imprisonment under this law in June 2004 for preaching (to his own flock, inside his own church building) that homosexual acts are "perverse" and abominable in God's sight. On appeal, the Supreme Court decided in 2005 that Green had indeed violated *Swedish* law, but acquitted him on the grounds that the European Court of Human Rights would probably object to his imprisonment. Nevertheless, the intimidatory effect of the said law against free Christian speech in Sweden is obvious. (Cf. "The Ake Green Case," www.akegreen.org .) As is well known, strong legal pressures against any religious or moral criticism of homosexual activity, and even coercing believers into acting against their religious convictions (e.g., punishing professional photographers simply for declining to cover homosexual "commitment" ceremonies), are steadily mounting in other traditionally – even if not officially – Christian nations and states. Cf. for instance, A. Sears & C. Osten, *The Homosexual Agenda: Exposing the Principal Threat to Religious Freedom Today* (Nashville, TN: Broadman & Holman, 2003).

98   However, for a fine, patriotic polemic against the disestablishment of Catholicism as Italy's State religion, cf. Roberto de Mattei, *L'Italia Cattolica e il Nuovo Concordato* (Rome: Centro Culturale Lepanto, 1985).

insistence on a "social" (i.e., national or civic) duty to give "authentic worship" to God is shed by the celebrated preconciliar theological exchanges in the U.S. between John Courtney Murray and his conservative critics. For, as a leading scholarly commentator on those debates has pointed out, the existence or non-existence of such a duty lay at the very heart of this debate.[99] Pavlischek selects as the paradigmatic attack on Murray's position a 1952 essay in which Msgr. Joseph Clifford Fenton insisted that the entire edifice of orthodox Catholic doctrine regarding Church, State and religious repression/toleration is squarely based on the bedrock principle that "not only individual men, but also all societies or groups of men are bound" to acknowledge and honor God, and that:

> . . . the one acceptable and authorized social worship of God is to be found summed up in the Eucharistic sacrifice of the Catholic Church. It is God's will that men should pay the debt of acknowledgment and gratitude they owe to Him in the worship and according to the rite of His own Church.[100]

62. Both Murray and his critics such as Fenton realized that this principle was inseparable from all the practical (if not strictly logical) consequences that flowed from it, especially the legitimacy of some degree of government restriction on manifestations contrary to the Catholic religion (which of course includes both "faith" and "morals"). Precisely for that reason, Murray denied the said principle: in his view, the State's incompetence to recognize religious truth is the real basis for the human right to religious liberty. After the Council Murray tried to present *DH* as supporting his own position on this point; but in fact, thanks to the last-minute papal intervention, the declaration had quietly vindicated the traditional doctrine expounded by Fenton (along with other critics of Murray such as George W. Shea and Francis J. Connell). And #2105 of the *Catechism* vindicates it even more explicitly. In short, once that "stone" of "authentic worship" is cast into the "pool" of man's social and national duties, certain restrictions on anti-Catholic propaganda are among the ripples it inevitably produces.

99 Cf. Keith J. Pavlischek, *John Courtney Murray and the Dilemma of Religious Toleration* (Kirksville, Missouri: Thomas Jefferson University Press, 1994), 44–47.

100 J.C. Fenton, "Principles Underlying Traditional Church-State Doctrine," *American Ecclesiastical Review*, vol. 126, June 1952, 455–456 and 457, quoted in Pavlischek, *op. cit.*, 44 and 45–46.

IV. My review of Michael Davies' *The Second Vatican Council and Religious Liberty*

63. Mr. Guminski goes on to criticize my most recent substantial piece on *DH*, a 1993 review of the late Michael Davies' book of the above title.[101] Here, I think that some of his objections are better founded than those we have considered so far, and I shall modify my position accordingly. However, I shall pass quickly over his opening volley[102] because it depends entirely on a distinction which I find specious. Mr. Guminski wants to distinguish between a "natural right" and "what could be properly called a natural-law right." The former, but not the latter, would have as its "basic ground . . . the natural dignity of human persons," and the set of all natural rights would be "a proper subset" of "the set of natural-law rights."[103] The implication, namely, that certain rights whose "basic ground" is *not* "the natural dignity of human persons" can nevertheless pertain to the *natural* moral law, seems to me both incomprehensible and (as far as I know) unsupported by the Catholic natural law tradition. (My critic cites no other authors, Catholic or otherwise, in support of this distinction.)

64. More important, I think, are other issues arising from my critique of Davies. I have already acknowledged that my book *RLC*, in concentrating only on the major papal encyclicals (those from 1864 onwards), had left unanswered the question as to whether there had already been in place, since before the time of Pius IX, any authentic Catholic doctrine teaching that governmental bans on *all* public non-Catholic manifestations could be just in some circumstances. The book recognized, of course, the obvious historical fact that the Church's centuries-long *practice* (her policy and public law) approved such comprehensive bans in many Catholic countries. But whether or not that very fact (and/or, perhaps, other earlier magisterial documents) implied or amounted to a corresponding church *doctrine* was a question I did not address in *RLC*. Nevertheless, as has been noted,[104] *RLC*'s case for integral doctrinal continuity already "covered that base," both by understanding and formulating the traditional doctrine in

---

101 This review was originally published in *Living Tradition*, No. 44, January 1993, 4–12 (abbreviated by Mr. Guminski as *LT93*). However, I will refer here also to the more accessible and widely distributed version published in *Fidelity* (May 1993, 39–47), under the title (chosen unilaterally by the editor), "Did the Church Change Her Teaching on Religious Liberty?" (hereafter abbreviated as *F93*).

102 Cf. CH, ##48–62.

103 CH, #50.

104 Cf. paragraph 9 above.

sufficiently open-ended terms, and by arguing that *DH* does not in any case condemn the said earlier practice retroactively as having been always and everywhere unjust.

65. More recently, I have become convinced that the correct answer to that previously unresolved question is affirmative: i.e., that Church endorsement of such comprehensive government bans (those allowing *no* public non-Catholic manifestations) did indeed attain the status of at least authentic doctrine (as distinct from mere common theological or canonical opinion). I noticed, for instance, that in his 1832 encyclical *Mirari Vos*, Pope Gregory XVI, in condemning demands for an "immoderate liberty of opinions," appealed to St. Augustine's argument for repressing fifth-century Donatist propaganda: "What worse death of the soul is there than liberty for error?" (". . . *quae peior mors animae, quam libertas erroris?*")[105] The Pontiff's clearly implied doctrine here is that since religious error *as such* threatens the salvation of Catholic souls, *any and every* public manifestation of religious error could justly be repressed (at least in the circumstances he was presupposing and addressing, namely, predominantly Catholic societies in the early nineteenth century). The "risk" to the "eternal salvation" of Catholic citizens arising from "the spreading of false doctrines" was also presented as justifying government intervention in the relevant preparatory schema for Vatican II,[106] whose authors (notably Cardinal Alfredo Ottaviani, head of the Holy Office) were very well qualified to identify the content of existing (i.e., traditional) Catholic doctrine as taught by the ordinary magisterium. Even Pius XII's most "progressive" statement in *Ci riesce* – that in which he affirms that "*in determined circumstances*" God does not grant "the right to repress what is erroneous and false"[107] – clearly presupposes the teaching that in *other* circumstances God certainly does grant that right. That Pius presupposed this is confirmed by the fact that he himself, only a few months before giving this allocution, had endorsed the 1953 Vatican concordat with Franco's government which legislated the repression of "what is erroneous and false" in Spain. These considerations explain my expressed agreement with Mr. Guminski about proposition **X** at the beginning of this essay.

66. On the other hand, I now believe that my original formulation of, and proposed grounding for, this more long-standing doctrine of the

---

105 DS 2731, = Dz 1615.
106 Quoted in M. Davies, *The Second Vatican Council and Religious Liberty* (Long Prairie, Minnesota: Neumann Press, 1992), 300.
107 Cf. *AAS*, 45 (1953), 798–799. Cf. English translation in Davies, *op. cit.,* 311.

ordinary magisterium was (as set out in my review of Davies' book) inexact. I then wrote: "[T]raditional doctrine excludes the possibility that, *in a predominantly Catholic society*, there can be any natural right of non-Catholics to be tolerated in the public profession of their religion."[108] But that formulation would amount to a doctrine according to which this one social circumstance alone (viz., the presence of a "predominantly Catholic" population), regardless of any other contemporary cultural, social, religious or political conditions, is, *always and everywhere*, a sufficient condition for the moral legitimacy of repressing all public manifestations of other religions. Catholic "predominance" (whatever percentage of the population that might be defined as) would enjoy doctrinal status as a simple "litmus test," perpetually and universally valid, guaranteeing that such comprehensive repression would not, as such, violate any human right of the religious minorities affected by it.

67. I now think that this view I expressed in 1993 involved a rather too abstract and ahistorical reading of the earlier ordinary magisterium. Certainly, whenever the question came up in earlier centuries with regard to "predominantly Catholic societies" (or Christendom), the legitimacy of such comprehensive repression was always insisted on. But I would now argue that the earlier popes and bishops who originally arrived at that judgment were, at least implicitly, making it relative to the *whole ensemble* of contingent social circumstances which then existed. These would have included not only the percentage of Catholics in a given area, but also (among other things) the generally low level of culture and education amongst largely illiterate populations, and the generally accepted "paternalistic" view of the role of government in general, in the era before the rise of modern Western democracy gave birth to increasing popular demands for individual and group autonomy vis-à-vis state authority. Another relevant change in recent historical circumstances has been the revolution in technology, communications and "globalization," which has rendered Catholic "societies" (in the commonly understood sense of "countries" under a unified political regime) far less insulated from the non-Catholic world than they were in earlier centuries. The pre-nineteenth-century guardians of Catholic doctrine can scarcely be assumed to have foreseen an era when their own successors might arrive at a new prudential judgment to the effect that the *relevant region* requiring uniform religious policies (for the common good and public order) would no longer be a given "country" (sovereign state or colony

---

108 *LT93*, 8 (= *F93*, 41–42), quoted in CH, #54 (emphasis in original).

as the case may be), but rather, a much larger *community* of countries – even encompassing the entire planet – in which the population, taken as a whole, is definitely not "predominantly Catholic."[109]

68. For all these reasons I no longer think it correct to elevate the category of "predominantly Catholic societies" to *doctrinal* status, and so have omitted it from the wording of the doctrinal theses under discussion in this essay (cf. propositions **X**, **Y** and **Z** in section I).

69. So much for my 1993 *formulation* of the doctrine in question. I also believe now that I was mistaken in the *grounding* or *basis* which I then offered for it, namely, the "infallibility" supposedly implicated in the very *practice* (policy or public law) of the Church in urging for many centuries the civil repression of all public manifestations of non-Catholic religions. Mr. Guminski takes me to task at some length over this point;[110] but it is not necessary to consider his arguments in detail, because I am now retracting the premise which drew his fire. There is indeed a long-standing (though now largely forgotten) common teaching of approved theologians, dating back (in explicit form) to sixteenth- and seventeenth-century authors such as Melchior Cano, Bellarmine, and Suarez, that the Church's *universal disciplinary legislation* is "infallible" in the sense of being guaranteed not to command or urge any behavior which would be *per se* immoral or contrary to Catholic faith.[111] This is a teaching which I still accept as both authoritative and reasonable. However, further study has persuaded me that I was previously misunderstanding the term "universal," as used by these approved authors. They base their reasoning on Christ's promises that the Holy Spirit will constantly guide the Church *as a whole* in the path of eternal salvation, and so will never permit her supreme authority to "oblige all the faithful"[112] – i.e., the great bulk of the People

---

109 Pius XII had already raised this issue a decade before Vatican II in his allocution *Ci riesce* (6 December, 1953), published in *AAS* 45 (1953), 794–802. Cf. Davies, *op. cit.*, 310–312 for an English translation of the relevant section.

110 Cf. CH, ##57–59.

111 Cf. M. Davies, *I Am With You Always* (Long Prairie, Minnesota: 1997), 32. Cf. also such standard texts as J.M. Hervé, *Manuale Theologiae Dogmaticae*, vol. I (Westminster, Maryland: Newman Bookshop, 1946), 515–516; L. Lercher, S.J., *Institutiones Theologiae Dogmaticae*, 5th ed. (Barcelona: Herder, 1951), 304–305; E. Dublanchy, s.v. "Église" (section IV), in *Dictionnaire de Théologie Catholique*, vol. IV (Paris: Letouzey, 1911), cc. 2185–2186.

112 ". . . *omnes fideles obligare*" (Lercher, *loc. cit.*); ". . . *omnibus fidelibus praecipere*" (Hervé, *loc. cit*); ". . . *pour tout le peuple chrétien*" (Dublanchy, *loc. cit.*).

of God – to carry out objectively sinful actions. But they never claim that church laws obliging only a *small proportion* of Christians – even if decreed by the Church's "universal" authority (Pope or Council) and/or for a geographically "universal" area – *ipso facto* generate or presuppose a corresponding infallible *doctrine*. After all, Providence has permitted Satan to win limited and local battles against the Church, including her leaders, ever since he managed to intimidate Peter and corrupt Judas. The concrete examples given by these classical authors are nearly always in the area of liturgical and sacramental law – norms of public worship applying to faithful Catholics as a whole. But papal decrees, letters, etc., urging secular authorities to repress all non-Catholic manifestations within their jurisdiction never obliged – even indirectly – any more than a tiny fraction of the faithful: rulers, magistrates, and other enforcers of "law and order."

70. In short, I no longer hold, as I did in 1993, that according to traditional *doctrine*, there can *never* (i.e., from Pentecost until Judgment Day) be a natural right of any non-Catholics "in predominantly Catholic states" to be tolerated in the public profession of their religion. This modification enables me to withdraw in turn another claim – rather shaky, as I now see it – which I logically had to make in the same book review in order to sustain my central thesis that *DH* does not contradict traditional doctrine. I refer to the claim – severely criticized by Mr. Guminski – that the right to public freedom implicitly recognized by *DH* for non-Catholics living "in predominantly Catholic states" is not in fact, according to the Council, a *natural* right, but only "an *acquired* right granted by the Church."[113] My critic points out that this expression effectively reduces the public religious liberty of non-Catholics in such states to "a matter of legislative grace"[114] – a mere *privilege*, in effect. I am now inclined to agree with him that this reading of the Council "presents difficulties," and probably does not do justice to the mind of the Pope and Council Fathers. It would imply, for instance, that the right of non-Catholics in Spain to immunity from coercion in publicly manifesting their religion *began to exist* only on December 7, 1965, *precisely by virtue* of the Church's promulgation of *DH*. I now think it more likely that the true mind of the Church at that moment was that she was *discerning* an *already-and-independently-existing* reality, not *creating* a *new* reality by her own legislative fiat. In other words, I suspect that most Fathers of Vatican II understood themselves to be discerning and recognizing – though without passing judgment against Spanish-style

113 F93, 45.
114 Cf. CH, #61.

repressive legislation under earlier historical circumstances – that at least under mid-twentieth-century circumstances, that degree of repression in Spain *had already ceased* to be compatible with the natural human right to religious liberty (insofar as such repression could no longer reasonably be portrayed as *essential* for the common good of society, i.e., as required by a just public order). Nevertheless, I think it is worth emphasizing again that this concrete discernment did not flow simply and directly from *DH*'s strictly *doctrinal* content, which is too blunt an instrument, as it were, to attain such surgical precision; rather, it logically depended also on a distinct, complementary, *prudential* judgment, namely, that assessment of the contemporary, contingent facts expressed in parenthesis in the last part of the previous sentence. That is why, in summarizing *DH*'s implied position in my proposition **Y** (cf. section I), I have used the expression "would . . . have to be judged as involving," and not simply "would . . . involve."

71. I do not think Mr. Guminski's final two substantial points need a detailed response. In the first of these, involving the *Catechism of the Catholic Church,* my critic announces "serious difficulties" in my reading of #1738, but then directs his concern mainly at the *CCC*'s own bracketing together here of "common good" and "public order."[115] I will also pass over his objections to my 1993 address to the National Wanderer Forum, which are concerned with a quite secondary and rather "subjective" question, namely, how the Church's public image might (in his view) be affected by the kind of understanding of *DH* which I expressed in that address.[116]

Conclusion

72. Readers may perhaps welcome a thumb-nail summary of my overall thesis. My basic position is that the big difference between the Church's stance on religious liberty before and after Vatican II lies not in her old and new *doctrinal* teachings respectively; for these, though certainly not identical, are quite compatible, thanks largely to their very general (non-specific) content. Rather, it lies in the Church's very different pre- and postconciliar prudential judgments as to *how much* restriction on false and immoral propaganda is *in fact* required by a just public order, given the dramatic social and political changes of recent centuries.

115 Cf. CH, ##62–67. He finds the wording of #1738 "confusing," "puzzling" and "mystifying." Those readers who find my previous discussion of the "common good"/"public order" distinction persuasive (cf. sections IIIb and IIIc above), will probably not share much of my opponent's puzzlement.
116 Cf. CH, ##68–69.

73. I would like to end simply by thanking Mr. Guminski for his thoughtful critique. He concludes it by stressing – very rightly – the importance of following a "correct method" if we are to determine the true meaning of *Dignitatis Humanae*. I leave it to readers to judge for themselves whether his method or mine sheds more light on the Council's treatment of this important but complex issue.

Part III:

Further Reflections on Freedom in Religious Matters: A Response to Father Harrison[*]
Arnold T. Guminski

1. Father Brian W. Harrison, O.S., has replied to my article on religious freedom (RF)[1] in that hearty polemical yet analytically astute manner so characteristic of his writings.[2] So I continue our dialogue inspired by the

---

[*] The title of this essay is abbreviated throughout this book as "FR."

[1] For our purposes, I define *religious freedom* (RF) as civil and social freedom in religious matters (FRM) within due (just) limits, i.e., within the limits of a just public order as defined in *DH* #7.3. *The Catechism of the Catholic Church* #2108 similarly defines the right to RF as "neither a moral license to adhere to error, nor a supposed right to error, but rather a natural right of the human person to civil liberty, i.e., immunity, within just limits, from external constraint in religious matters by political authorities." Essentially, *DH* #2.1 defines RF as the immunity, within just limits, from being coerced into acting against one's conscience or from being impeded from acting in accord with one's conscience, in matters religious. For convenience sake, I shall ignore the first component of RF since our principal concern pertains to public propaganda and manifestations in matters religious. RF, within the meaning of *DH*, is not necessarily identical in all respects with the notion of *religious freedom* within the meaning of the First Amendment to the Constitution of the United States of America. But this article concerns itself only with the meaning of RF in the sense of *DH*. For my views on the First Amendment, and related constitutional issues, see my *The Constitutional Rights, Privileges, and Immunities of the American People: The Selective Incorporation of the Bill of Rights, the Refined Incorporation Model of Akhil Reed Amar, Dred Scott, National Citizenship and Its Implied Privileges and Immunities, the Second Amendment Right, and Much More* (Bloomington IN: iUniverse, 2009), 108–51.

[2] My article, "*Contra Harrison in Re Libertate Religiosa*: On the Meaning of *Dignitatis Humanae*" (hereafter CH), appears in *Faith & Reason* 26 (2001): 39–83. Fr. Harrison's response, "What Does *Dignitatis Humanae* Mean? A Reply to Arnold Guminski" (WD) appears in *Faith & Reason* 30 (2005) 243–95. CH and WD, as published in this volume, slightly differ in several details from the versions published in *Faith & Reason*.

words of St. Thomas Aquinas: "If any wish to write replies to my defence, I shall be delighted. For there is no better way of disclosing truth and refuting error than by opposing the opposition: 'Iron sharpens iron; friend shapes up friend.'"[3]

A. The Basic Procedural Approach Necessary for Our Inquiry

2. Fr. Harrison's position is that the Church's "*doctrinal* teachings [on RF before and after Vatican II] though certainly not identical, are quite compatible, thanks largely to their very general (non-specific) content." "Rather," he contends, "it lies in the Church's very different pre- and post-conciliar prudential judgments as to *how much* restriction on false and immoral propaganda is *in fact* required by a just public order, given the dramatic social and political changes of recent centuries." (WD, #72.)[4]

3. My position, on the contrary, is that the doctrine of *Dignitatis Humanae (DH)*[5] concerning RF (i.e., *civil and social freedom in religious matters* (FRM) *within just limits*) is indeed incompatible in very important respects with the preconciliar doctrine of the Church, as propounded by Gregory XVI, Pius IX, and Leo XIII.[6] However, I hold that any part of

3   The quotation is from John Finnis, *Aquinas* (New York: Oxford University Press, 1998), 12.
4   Unless otherwise indicated, bracketed matter within quotation marks are my editorial changes; emphasis and parenthesized matter within quotations were supplied by the source; omission of notes to quoted matter is not indicated. I shall use the term *definitively*, with respect to the Church's doctrine, to mean *in the exercise of the infallible magisterium. Nondefinitive doctrine* refers to only such authoritative doctrine that all the faithful are obliged to believe as true (if only defeasibly so).
5   Norman P. Tanner, ed., *Decrees of the Ecumenical Councils* (Washington DC: Georgetown Univ. Press, 1990) (hereafter, Tanner), II: 1001–11.)
6   By "preconciliar doctrine" I refer to the relevant doctrine of Gregory XVI, Pius IX, and Leo XIII. I shall follow this procedure (except as otherwise noted) since Fr. Harrison holds that preconciliar doctrine both before and after the pontificate of Pius X until the promulgation of *DH* are consistent. Fr. Harrison's charges that I have a "penchant for euphemism" such that I should have chided him for maintaining that *DH* contradicted preconciliar doctrine instead of changing it since "[a]uthentic doctrinal development is always change – but of a non-contradictory sort." (WD, #4.) But *au contraire* I made it abundantly clear in *CH* that: (1) Fr. Harrison's "efforts [had been] directed toward showing that there is no inconsistency, and that there is indeed, a legitimate continuity, between the doctrine of [*DH*] and that of the preconciliar Church" (CH, #1); and (2) that my intention was

preconciliar doctrine incompatible with that of *DH* was not definitively (i.e., infallibly and irreformably) taught doctrine of the Church.

4. Although Fr. Harrison appears at times to have believed that some relevant preconciliar doctrine is definitive (WD, n20),[7] he nevertheless protests that his interest in the infallibility of preconciliar doctrine is quite secondary. "For," he explains, "the mind of the Church ... is that [*DH*] is not to be understood in a way that would make it contradict *any* existing doctrine, whether infallible or 'merely authentic.'" (WD, #7.)

5. The basic procedural presupposition of my inquiry is (and has been) that the reader actually believes, or assumes for argument's sake, the truth of the Catholic religion as understood by (what I term) *standard-orthodox Catholics.*[8] A standard-orthodox Catholic (SOC) is a professed Catholic who, inter alia, believes: (1) The Catholic Church has the divinely instituted authority to definitively (i.e., in the exercise of its infallible magisterium) teach such propositions as are to be believed as being divinely revealed truths within the deposit of faith. (2) The magisterium includes the divinely instituted authority to definitively teach other doctrines, including those pertaining to morals, that are to be believed as being necessarily connected (in the requisite sense) to truths within the deposit of faith. (3) The Church has the divinely instituted authority to nondefinitively teach other doctrines concerning faith and morals even if not *necessarily* connected to the deposit of faith. (4) The Church's magisterium (both definitive and nondefinitive) extends to truths concerning specific moral precepts contained within the deposit of faith. (5) The Church's teaching authority extends also to precepts of the *natural moral law* (NML) – whether or not any such precept

to show "that Fr. Harrison's interpretation of the doctrine of *DH* on religious liberty is unjustified, and that his thesis as to how that doctrine can be reconciled with preconciliar doctrine is fundamentally flawed." (CH, #2.)

7   See also his "Roma Locuta Est; Causa Finita Est," in *For the Glory of God and the Salvation of the World* (*Proceedings of the 26th Annual National Wanderer Forum September 24th–26th, 1993*) (The Wanderer Forum Foundation), 41–42. This address is also accessible online at http://www.rtforum.org/lt/lt57.html.

8   I use the term *standard-orthodox Catholic* to preclude any need to discuss whether a professing Catholic is *orthodox* even though he denies, as Frank Mobbs does, or explicitly declines to affirm principles (2) and (5) as stated in the accompanying text. In his writings, Mobbs denies that the Church's infallible magisterium extends to the so-called secondary object (i.e., doctrines necessarily connected to but not within the deposit of faith) and that even its nondefinitive magisterium extends to propositions stating NML norms not within the deposit of faith. (See his *Beyond Its Authority: The Magisterium & Matters of Natural Law* [Morehouse Pub. Co., 1997.])

is also within the deposit of faith or necessarily connected thereto.[9] A well-informed SOC is someone who sincerely professes that a "[t]he willingness

9   Propositions (1)-(5) in the accompanying text are distilled from: Vatican Council
    I (1870), *Dei Filius,* ch. 3 & *Pastor Aeternis,* ch. 4; Vatican Council II (1964),
    Lumen Gentium #25; Congregation for the Doctrine of the faith (CDF), declara-
    tion *Mysterium Ecclesiae* (1973) #3 & instruction *Donum Veritatis* (1990)
    ##13–20, 23–24; John Paul II, apostolic letter motu proprio, *Ad Tuendam Fidem*
    (1998); *Catechism of the Catholic Church,* ##85–88, 888–92, 1960, 2032–36,
    2049–51. For a very useful exposition of the foregoing matters, see *Magisterium:
    Teacher and Guardian of the Faith* (Naples FL: Sapiente Press, 2007), 49–99, by
    Cardinal Avery Dulles. The Glossary to the *Catechism of the Catholic Church* use-
    fully defines the *deposit of faith* as "the heritage of faith contained in the Sacred
    Scripture and Tradition, handed on in the Church from the time of the Apostles,
    from which the Magisterium draws all that it proposes for belief as being divine-
    ly revealed." According to the apostolic letter (motu proprio), *Ad Tuendam Fidem,*
    ##3,4, truths necessarily connected to divine revelation, either for historical rea-
    sons or by a logical relationship, are "those things required for the holy keeping
    and faithful exposition of the deposit of faith" (*Code of Canon Law,* c. 750, §2;
    Code of Canon Law of the Eastern Churches, c. 598, §2). According to the doc-
    trinal commentary: "'everything definitively proposed by the Church regarding
    teaching on faith and morals' .... includes *all those teachings belonging to the
    dogmatic or moral area, which are necessary for faithfully keeping and expound-
    ing the deposit of faith, even if they have not been proposed by the Magisterium of
    the Church as formally revealed*" (emphasis in original). Cardinal Joseph
    Ratzinger & Archbishop Tarciso Bertone (then prefect and secretary, respectively
    of the CDF), "Doctrinal Commentary on the Concluding Formula of the
    'Professio fidei'" (hereafter, Doctrinal Note) (June 29, 1998) #6.1.
    (http://www.vatican.va/roman_curia/congregations/cfaith/documents/rc_con_cfai
    th_doc_1998_professio-fidei_en.html). The Church's authoritative doctrines are
    "all those teachings – on faith and morals – presented as true or at least as sure,
    even if they have not been defined with a solemn judgment or proposed as defin-
    itive by the ordinary and universal Magisterium." (Ibid., #10.) (Fr. Harrison and I
    think that it is very plausible that the Ratzinger-Bertone note misspoke itself when
    it used "sure" (or any of its equivalents in other approved versions) rather than the
    term "safe" in the just-quoted passage because #10.3 of the note refers to some
    censurable "teachings of the prudential order, as *rash or dangerous* and therefore
    'tuto doceri non potest' [cannot be taught safely].")
        The Doctrinal Note, although published in the *Acta Apostolicae Sedis* [90
    (1998) 544–51], is a very important but rather anomalous curial document since
    it was not approved by John Paul II either *in forma communi* or *specifica.*
    According to then Cardinal Ratzinger, prefect of the CDF: "[The] whole text was
    composed by the Congregation, its successive stages of development were pre-
    sented to the College of Cardinals, and its final version was approved by them. It
    also received the approval of the Holy Father. But all were agreed that the text
    itself was given no binding force; rather, it was only offered as a help to the under-

to submit loyally to the teaching of the Magisterium on matters *per se* not irreformable must be the rule."[10] The denial of any foregoing principle would render rather moot or uninteresting the issue of whether some preconciliar doctrine is actually inconsistent with the doctrine of *DH*, or that such preconciliar doctrine had been definitively taught.

6. An SOC believes that God has willed that his Church have a teaching authority that may either be exercised definitively or nondefinitively.[11] The Church's credibility seriously suffers when apologists and theologians operate upon the principle of a de facto inerrancy of the Church with respect to the exercise of its nondefinitive magisterium. It is equally implausible and inopportune to operate with the principle that there is a de facto impossibility of an actual inconsistency between an earlier doctrine, A, and a later doctrine B. Whenever nondefinitive doctrine B supersedes doctrine A and is inconsistent with it, the loyal SOC's ordinary and presumptive (but defeasible) duty of religious assent to doctrine B nevertheless obtains. Although the credibility of the Church suffers should it markedly change, or even totally rescind, nondefinitive doctrine as to a particular matter, its credibility would suffer even more should quite implausible arguments be offered to explain, or explain away, apparent inconsistencies. It seems reasonable that the burden of proof in showing that an actual inconsistency obtains between two ostensibly inconsistent doctrines considerably differs between a case in which both doctrines are

standing and was not to be published as an independent document of the Congregation itself. However, the particular form of its publication was purposely chosen to indicate that it was not a private work of the Prefect and the Secretary of the Congregation, but instead was an authorized aid to understanding the texts…. In any case … the examples [of doctrinal propositions] included in this text have no more weight than they had before…." Statement by Joseph Cardinal Ratzinger, *Stimmen der Zeit* 217 (1999) 169–72, trans. by Dr. Londa Maloney and published in Ladislas Orsy, S. J., *Receiving the Council: Theological and Canonical Insights and Debates* (Collegeville MN: Liturgical Press, 2009), 121–24, at 124. (See also Dulles, *Magisterium*, 86n7.) The Doctrinal Note, issued on June 30 by the CDF, is available on-line in Latin, English, and several other languages. (http://www.vatican.va/roman_curia/congregations/cfaith/doc_dottrinali_index.htm).

10 *Donum Veritatis,* #24.2.
11 Germain Grisez, that SOC par excellence, has carefully explained how and why Catholics only have a defeasible duty to give religious assent to nondefinitive doctrines. See his *Christian Moral Principles* (Chicago: Franciscan Herald Press, 1983), 853–54, and *Living a Christian Life* (Quincy IL: Franciscan Press, 1993), 46–55.

nondefinitive and another case in which only one apparently conflicting doctrine is nondefinitive. Surely, the burden of proof in the former case should be considerably lighter than in the latter.[12]

7. Fr. Harrison agrees (*RLC*, 102) that *DH* was promulgated in the nondefinitive exercise of the Church's magisterium, albeit as an act of an ecumenical council. For this reason, the very adoption of *DH* constitutes a very important datum for the SOC. The Pope and the Fathers of Vatican II manifested their collective judgment that the doctrine of *DH* concerning RF is consistent with all preconciliar definitive doctrine and with truths within the deposit of faith.

B. Why No Relevant Preconciliar Doctrine Is Definitive

8. From the outset, Fr. Harrison has candidly acknowledged that *DH* "bear[s] at least a prima facie appearance of contradicting previous papal statements." (*RLC*, 14.) But, as he observes, any error in preconciliar doctrine respecting FRM, if this was indeed a fact, would be one of the relatively few occasions when the Church has erred in the exercise of its nondefinitive magisterium – assuming momentarily for argument's sake the consistency of the doctrine of *DH* with all preconciliar definitive doctrine.[13] In any event, he assures us that his discussion prescinds from the issue whether any relevant preconciliar doctrine is definitive. (See, e.g., *RLC*, 138–39; WD, #7.) However, I shall address this issue because many readers may think that for our purposes there is no procedural difference between the issue of the consistency between two nondefinitive doctrines and that of the consistency between one definitive doctrine and another that is not definitive. Moreover, other readers may not be persuaded (even after diligent inquiry) that preconciliar doctrine is consistent with that of *DH*, and they would rightly in that case be very concerned whether the former is indeed definitive.

9. Fr. Harrison's position is that Pius IX's encyclical *Quanta Cura*

---

12   It is not altogether clear whether Fr. Harrison holds that the burden of proof would be the same with respect to the two scenarios. See his *Religious Liberty and Contraception* (hereafter *RLC*) (Melbourne: John XXIII Fellowship Coop., 1988), 102–03, where he indicates that the burden of proof would be "very heavy" were the preconciliar doctrine definitive.

13   Thus Fr. Harrison has written that this is "one of the very few areas in which it has been plausibly – though I believe incorrectly – argued that Vatican II really did contradict the previous teaching of the Church, namely in regard to Church-State relationships and religious liberty." ("Roma Locuta Est" [note 7 *supra*], 40.)

(*QC*) (1864) is the only papal document that contains definitively taught doctrine respecting FRM that is apparently inconsistent with the doctrine of *DH*.[14] The relevant text from *QC* reads:[15]

> [#2.] But now, as is well known to you, Venerable Brethren, already, scarcely had we been elevated to this Chair of Peter (by the hidden counsel of Divine Providence, certainly by no merit of our own), when, seeing with the greatest grief of Our soul a truly awful storm excited by so many evil opinions, and (seeing also) the most grievous calamities never sufficiently to be deplored which overspread the Christian people from so many errors, according to the duty of Our Apostolic Ministry, and following the illustrious example of Our Predecessors, We raised Our voice, and in many published Encyclical Letters and Allocutions delivered in Consistory, and other Apostolic Letters, we condemned the chief errors of this most unhappy age, and we excited your admirable episcopal vigilance, and we again and again admonished and exhorted all sons of the Catholic Church, to us most dear, that they should altogether abhor and flee from the contagion of so dire a pestilence. And especially in our first Encyclical Letter written to you on Nov. 9, 1846, and in two Allocutions delivered by us in

14 See, e.g., WD, #8 where Fr. Harrison refers to "non-*ex cathedra* statements [about religious liberty] in a long series of papal interventions," (ibid., n20) which are constituted by "*all* statements in the relevant encyclicals and other papal documents (such as the 1864 *Syllabus*) with the exception of some found in Pius IX's [*QC*]." He then explains that "the errors set out in *QC* (those highlighted in [QC] by the use of quotation marks) to be condemned in a form which manifestly meets Vatican I's requirements for *ex cathedra* papal definitions." He cites in support "such theologians as Franzelin, Hervé, and Newman." (Ibid.) However, it seems that Fr. Harrison did not believe that any definitive doctrine is actually inconsistent with *DH*. Thus, in his "The 'Secondary Object' of Papal Infallibility: A Reply to Frank Mobbs," *Irish Theological Quarterly*, 65 (2000): 319, 333, Fr. Harrison, referring to that preconciliar doctrine claimed by Mobbs to be "the error admitted by [*DH* #12] regarding religious coercion," states that this "real or imagined error has … [not] been proposed as definitive moral doctrine; that is, the Church has never 'bound her children to accept [it] as certainly and *irrevocably* true.'" (Note omitted.)

15 This translation (emphasis added; notes omitted and bracketed matter added) appears in the *Dublin Review* 4 (N.S. 1865): 503–505; and (with very few minor editorial changes) is available online at www.papalencyclicals.net/Pius09/p9quanta.htm. The brackets enclosing "QC1" through "QC5" signify the individual propositions condemned in the passage.

Consistory, the one on Dec. 9, 1854, and the other on June 9, 1862, we condemned the monstrous portents of opinion which prevail especially in this age, bringing with them the greatest loss of souls and detriment of civil society itself; which are grievously opposed also, not only to the Catholic Church and her salutary doctrine and venerable rights, but also to the eternal natural law engraven by God in all men's hearts, and to right reason; and from which almost all other errors have their origin.

[#3.] But, although we have not omitted often to proscribe and reprobate the chief errors of this kind, yet the cause of the Catholic Church, and the salvation of souls entrusted to us by God, and the welfare of human society itself, altogether demand that we again stir up your pastoral solicitude to exterminate other evil opinions, which spring forth from the said errors as from a fountain. Which false and perverse opinions are on that ground the more to be detested, because they chiefly tend to this, that that salutary influence be impeded and (even) removed, which the Catholic Church, according to the institution and command of her Divine Author, should freely exercise even to the end of the world – not only over private individuals, but over nations, peoples, and their sovereign princes; and (tend also) to take away that mutual fellowship and concord of counsels between Church and State which has ever proved itself propitious and salutary, both for religious and civil interests. **For You well know, Venerable Brethren, that at this time men are found not a few who, applying to civil society the impious and absurd principle of *naturalism*, as they call it, dare to teach that [QC1] "the best constitution of public society and [also] civil progress altogether require that human society be conducted and governed without regard being had to religion any more than if it did not exist; or, [QC2] at least, without any distinction being made between the true religion and false ones." And, against [(or) contrary to] [*contra*] the doctrine of Scripture, of the Church, and of the holy Fathers, they do not hesitate to assert that [QC3] "that is the best condition of society, in which no duty [(or) function] [*officium*] is recognized, as attached to the civil power, of restraining by enacted penalties, offenders against the Catholic religion [(or) violators of the Catholic religion] [*violatores catholicae religionis*], except so far as** public peace may require." From which totally false idea of social government they do not fear to foster that erroneous opinion, most fatal in its effects on the Catholic Church and the salvation of souls, called by Our Predecessor, Gregory XVI, an *insanity*, viz., [QC4] that "liberty of conscience and worships is each man's personal right, which ought to be legally proclaimed and asserted in every rightly-constituted society; [QC5] and that a right resides in the citizens to an absolute liberty, which should be restrained by no authority whether ecclesiastical or civil, whereby they may be able openly and publicly to manifest and declare any of their ideas whatever, either by word of mouth, by the press, or in any other way." But, while they rashly affirm this, they do not think and consider that they are preaching the *liberty of perdition*; and that, "if human arguments are always allowed free room for discussion, there will never be wanting men who will dare to resist truth, and to trust in the flowing speech of human wisdom; where we know, from the very teaching of our Lord Jesus Christ, how carefully Christian faith and wisdom should avoid this most injurious babbling."

10. I believe that the contradictory of proposition QC3 *rightly understood* is ostensibly inconsistent with the doctrine of *DH*. I also hold, but with somewhat less certainty, that the contradictory of QC4 (also rightly understood) is ostensibly inconsistent with the doctrine of *DH*. But, for all purposes, I maintain that the contradictory of either QC5 or QC4–5 (the latter considered as one integral, compound proposition) is actually consistent with *DH* because: (1) either condemned proposition denies the authority of the Church to regulate the public expression of opinion on religious matters by Catholics even in cases where the ecclesiastical sanctions do not involve external coercion of the kind characteristic of civil authority only; or (2) it extends a *virtually unlimited* freedom of expression of opinion in religious matters to "any other way" besides that of the spoken, written, or printed word, as a right required in "every rightly-constituted society."

11. After a statement of several other errors in *QC*, the pontiff makes a declaration relied upon by Fr. Harrison in WD (and by others) as providing the allegedly firm basis for concluding that Pius IX ex cathedra condemned the numerous (approximately twenty, depending on how they are counted) errors described in *QC*. This (what I call the) *operative declaration* (OD) reads (*QC* #6):

> Amidst, therefore, such great perversity of depraved opinions, We, well remembering Our Apostolic Office, and very greatly solicitous for our most holy Religion, for sound doctrine and the salvation of souls which is entrusted to Us by God, and [solicitous also] for the welfare of human society itself, have thought it right again to raise up Our Apostolic voice. Therefore, by Our Apostolic Authority we reprobate, proscribe, and condemn all and singular the evil opinions and doctrines severally mentioned in this letter, and will and command that they be thoroughly [*omnino*] held by all children of the [C]atholic Church as reprobated, proscribed and condemned.[16]

Fr. Harrison refers in *RLC,* 30, to the OD as constituting "a strong censure." He also declares as to QC3: "[T]he censure is very strong. The Pope says it is not only 'totally false,' but that it is also 'contrary to the teachings of the Holy Scriptures, of the Church, and of the Holy Fathers.'" (Ibid., 33.)

12. Any inquiry concerning whether a papal act constitutes an ex cathedra definition should proceed in compliance with the precept contained in canon 749(3) of the *Code of Canon Law*: "No doctrine is understood to be infallibly defined unless it is clearly established as such." Significantly, other than as specifically describing each of the propositions QC1 through QC5 as an opinion that is "evil," "depraved," "erroneous," or "false and perverse," or as being an "impious and absurd principle," or as a "totally false idea of social government," Pius IX does not otherwise characterize these condemned propositions with any customary theological censure. The OD only obliges Catholics to hold that each condemned proposition "as reprobated, denounced, and condemned." Thus Catholics are not obliged by the OD to believe that the contradictory of each condemned proposition is a divinely revealed truth or a truth, not divinely

---

16 *Dublin Review,* 506–509 (bracketed matter in original). *The Companion to the Catechism of the Catholic Church* (San Francisco: Ignatius Press, 1994), 761 and Claudia Carlin, IHM, *The Papal Encyclicals 1740–1878* (Ann Arbor: Perian Press, 1990), 384, both provide the same translations of the OD as that in the *Dublin Review*. Fr. Basile (Valuet), O.S.B., in both his treatises *La Liberté Religieuse et la Tradition Catholique* (2nd ed.) (Le Barroux FR.: Abbaye Sainte-Madeleine, 1998), IIA, 1060, and *Le droit à la liberté religieuse dans la tradition de L'Église* (Le Barroux: Éditions Sainte-Madeleine, 2005), 234, adopts "entièrement" (i.e., "entirely') as the French translation of *omnino*.

revealed, but one necessarily connected to one that is. Moreover, the word *omnino* in the last clause of the OD is best to be translated as *thoroughly* or *entirely*, in the quantitative sense of *without exception*, rather than as *absolutely*, in the epistemic sense of what is to be *unconditionally* or *irrevocably* believed; since the pontiff wanted to make clear that every proposition condemned in *QC* was intended by him to be regarded by the faithful as reprobated, proscribed and condemned.

13. But it might be objected that a stronger case for the ex cathedra status of QC3 can be made. For in QC3, the condemned proposition is described as being "against the doctrine of Scripture, of the Church, and of the holy Fathers." However, it is axiomatic that a solemn definition does not as such include arguments or incidental statements. "Only the doctrine itself, to which those arguments lead and which these *obiter dicta* illustrate, is to be considered as infallibly defined."[17] These same considerations apply a fortiori to the condemnation of QC3, whether or not definitive. Thus the terse description of the condemned proposition as being contrary to doctrine of Scripture and the Holy Fathers (besides that of the Church) is but a preliminary point constituting a ground for the condemnation. True, *QC* manifestly indicates that the contradictory of QC3, for example, was Catholic doctrine before the publication of the encyclical, but it cannot be justly concluded that this doctrine is definitive.

14. On the other hand, the fact that the propositions condemned in *QC* are characterized as *errors* does not provide an additional reason for or against concluding that all of their contradictories are definitive doctrines. The rationale for this caution is that the collective characterization in *QC* does not technically constitute, in the strict sense, a formal authoritative (or judicial) censure of the condemned propositions by the magisterium because it appears in prefatory passages rather than in the OD. Moreover, the term *errors* is used in *QC* in such a broad sense that it can very reasonably be understood to encompass contradictories of definitive doctrines, whether concerning revealed truths or truths necessarily connected to revealed truths, as well as contradictories of authoritative, but nondefinitive, doctrines.[18] Accordingly, the interesting

---

17 (J. H. Harty) "Definition" *Catholic Encyclopedia* (New York: Robert Appleton, Co., 1908) 4: 676.

18 Pius IX in #3 of *QC* refers to how "in many published Encyclical Letters and Allocutions, delivered in Consistory, and other Apostolic Letters, we condemned the chief errors of this our most unhappy age." He explained how in certain deliverances he had "condemned the monstrous portents of opinion which prevail espe-

question as to what specific formal censures apply to contradictories of definitive doctrines pertaining to truths necessarily connected to

cially in this age ... and from which/ almost all other opinions have their origin." In #4 of *QC*, although he declared he "[had] not omitted often to proscribe and reprobate the chief errors of this kind," that it was necessary "to exterminate other evil opinions, which spring forth from the said errors as from a fountain." *QC* #3 refers to the propositions specifically condemned in the encyclical as *false and perverse opinions*, but these propositions must also be *errors* in the same broad sense as those already denounced as *chief errors* and from which the propositions condemned in *QC* "spring forth ... as from a fountain." The use of the term *errors* in ##2–3 of *QC* embraces not only the propositions condemned in *QC* but also the eighty propositions condemned in the accompanying *Syllabus*. (The complete title of the *Syllabus* reads: "Syllabus, Embracing the Principal Errors of Our Time Which are Censured in Consistorial Allocutions, Encyclicals, and other Apostolic Letters of Our Most Holy Father, Pope Pius IX.") The collective characterization of the condemned propositions in *QC* as *errors* appears in prefatory passages but not in the doctrinal judgment embodied in OD. The OD itself only uses the term *evil opinions and doctrines* to collectively refer to the condemned propositions in *QC*.

There are unquestionably some propositions condemned in the *Syllabus* and in *QC* that SOCs would agree are formally censurable as *heretical* because they contradict divinely revealed truths. There are other propositions condemned in the *Syllabus* and in *QC* that SOCs would agree are censurable because they are contradictories of truths necessarily connected to divinely revealed truths. But it can be very plausibly, if not persuasively, argued that there are some condemned propositions in the *Syllabus* that well-informed SOCs would not hold are contradictories of either any truths that are either divinely revealed or are necessarily connected to divinely revealed truths – including but not limited to propositions 12 ("The decrees of the Apostolic See and of Roman Congregations interfere with the free progress of science"), 23 (insofar as it asserts that "Roman Pontiffs and ecumenical Councils have exceeded the limits of their power [and] usurped the rights of Princes"), 58 ("The Roman pontiffs have, by their too arbitrary conduct, contributed to the division of the Church into Eastern and Western"), and 72 (Boniface VIII was the first who declared that the vow of chastity taken at ordination renders marriage void). See the comments concerning these particular propositions by Cardinal Joseph Hergenröther, in his *Catholic Church and Christian State : A Series of Essays on the Relation of the Church to the Civil Power* (London: Burnes & Oates, 1876), I: 210–12.

Thus the collective characterizations in *QC* ##2–3, the encyclical's prefatory passages, of the propositions condemned in both *QC* and the *Syllabus* as *errors* must be taken in a broader sense, and therefore not in a strict technical sense as used in a formal authoritative censure by the Church. Furthermore, assuming arguendo that the collective characterization of the condemned propositions in *QC* and the *Syllabus* as *errors* constitute a formal authoritative censure, *errors* would nevertheless still have to be considered as having such a broad sense in *QC* and

revealed truths and to nondefinitive doctrines is practically irrelevant for our purposes.[19]

> the *Syllabus* that it encompasses not only propositions contradicting definitive doctrines of *fide credenda* (i.e., those concerning divinely revealed truths) and *fide tenenda* (i.e., those concerning truths necessarily connected to divinely revealed truths), but also propositions contradicting nondefinitive doctrines.
>
> Nevertheless Fr. Harrison maintains, but I do not, that quite independently of the status of the collective characterization in *QC* ##2–3 of the condemned propositions as *errors*, the terms of the OD as such are sufficient to warrant the conclusion that the contradictories of all the propositions specifically condemned in *QC* are definitive doctrines of the magisterium. More precisely, Fr. Harrison affirms, and I deny, that the OD by its terms manifestly obliges "all children of the [C]atholic Church" to a full and irrevocable assent to the contradictories of all the propositions condemned in *QC*.

19 The English version of the Doctrinal Note to the apostolic letter *Ad Tuendam Fidem* (1998) reads: "A proposition contrary to these doctrines [i.e., those that "have not been defined with a solemn judgment or proposed as definitive by the ordinary and universal Magisterium"] can be qualified as *erroneous* or, in the case of teachings of the prudential order, as *rash or dangerous* and therefore '*tuto doceri non potest* [cannot be taught safely].'" (Doctrinal Note, #10.3; see note 9 *supra*.) However, the word *falsum* instead of *erroneum* appears both in the *AAS* (note 9 supra, 549) and in the Vatican website's Latin version.

Unfortunately, the Doctrinal Commentary fails to identify the formal authoritative censure applicable to contradictories of definitive doctrines about truths necessarily connected to revealed truths. Because the characterization in *QC* of *errors* is not a formal authoritative censure, the question of what are or should be the technically correct censures applicable to definitive and nondefinitive doctrines need not be further pursued in this essay. However, interested readers may consult the following authorities (to name but a few) about these matters: Sixtus **Cartechini**, S. J., *De valore notarum theologicarum et de criteriis ad eas dignoscendas ad usum auditorum,* (Rome: Pontificia Universitas Gregoriana, 1951) (see summary chart at 134–35). Joseph Clifford **Fenton,** *The Concept of Sacred Theology* (Milwaukee: Bruce Publishing Co., 1941), 121–125, and his articles "The Religious Assent Due to the Teachings of Papal Encyclicals," 123 *American Ecclesiastical Review* (1950) 59–67 and "The Question of Ecclesiastical Faith," 128 *American Ecclesiastical Review* (1953) 287–301. Edwin G. **Kaiser**, *Sacred Doctrine: An Introduction to Theology* (Westminster MD: Newman Press, 1958), 311–19. Bernard **Lucien**, *Révelation et Tradition: Les lieux médiateurs de la Révelation divine publique, du depot de la foi au Magistère vivant de l'Église* (Brannay FR: Editions Nuntiavit, 2009). 287–301 (summary chart at http://www.salve-regina.com/Theologie/VALEUR_ET_CEN-SURES.htm). Ludwig **Ott**, *Fundamentals of Catholic Dogma* (4th Eng. Ed.) (Rockford, IL: TAN Books, 1974) 8–10. G. **Van Noort**, *Dogmatic Theology Vol. III – The Sources of Revelation: Divine Faith* (Westminster MD: Newman Press, 1960), 282–91 (summary chart at 290).

15. Nevertheless it is not at all evident that Pius IX in *QC* manifested an intent to give an *absolutely* final (and therefore *irrevocable*) judgment such that he can truly be said to have directed the faithful to give an assent with *absolute* certainty (i.e., without apprehension of possible error) such that the assent is *irrevocable* with respect to the contradictories of the propositions condemned in the OD.[20] An SOC would not violate the OD were he to believe that QC3, for example, contradicts neither a divinely revealed truth nor a truth necessarily connected thereto, but rather a proposition the denial of which is prejudicial, injurious, or dangerous to faith or morals, or opposed to the natural moral law, or to the legitimate interests of the Church and civil society.[21]

20 *Catechism* #88 reads: "The Church's Magisterium exercises the authority it holds from Christ to the fullest extent when it defines dogmas, that is, when it proposes, in a form obliging the Christian people to an irrevocable adherence of faith, truths contained in divine Revelation or also when it proposes, in a definitive way, truths having a necessary connection to these." When the Church definitively teaches a doctrine as necessarily connected to divinely revealed truth, then "there is no difference with respect to the full and irrevocable character of the assent which is owed" to "truths set forth by the church as divinely revealed" and to those other truths "to be held definitively." "Doctrinal Commentary" (*supra* note 9), #8. See also *Catechism* #2035: "The supreme degree of participation in the authority of Christ is ensured by the charism of *infallibility*. This infallibility extends to all those elements of doctrine, including morals, without which the saving truth of the faith cannot be preserved, explained, or observed."

21 Well before Vatican II, some eminent SOC scholars denied or questioned that the condemnations of the propositions described in *QC* had been shown to be infallible definitions. These include: **Franz Xavier Wernz**, S.J., *Jus Decretalium* (Rome, 1905), I: 385n58 ("plane improbabilis" [i.e., manifestly improbable]); **E. Vacandard**, "La Nature Du Pouvoir Coercitif De L'Église," *Études De Critique Et D'Histoire Religieuse (Deuxième Série)* (Paris: Librarie Victor Lecoffre, 1914), 241; **Joseph-Eugène Mangenot**, "Encycliques," *Dictionnaire de Théologie Catholique* (Paris: Librairie Letouzey et Ané, 1924), 5: c15 ("Les encycliques des papes ne constituent pas jusqu'à present des definitions *ex cathedra* d'autorité infaillible" [the papal encyclicals do not constitute up to the present ex cathedra definitions of infallible authority]); **Nicolas Iung**, *Le Droit Public de L'Église* (Paris: Procure Générale Du Clergé, 1948), 90–91("dans l'encyclique [QC] … où sans promulguer, semble-t-il au moins, une definition *ex cathedra*, it faut une declaration solennelle sur un point de doctrine qu'il serait désormais téméraire de nier …." [in the encyclical [*DH*] … where without promulgating, so it seems at least, an ex cathedra definition, it seems a solemn declaration on a point of doctrine which will from then on be temerarious to deny …], the writer specifically referring to a proposition other than QC3 but that was similarly condemned in the OD of *QC*); **Joseph Clifford Fenton**, "The Theology of the Church and the State,"

16. Discussing his "contention [in his 1989 article] that the preamble to *DH* upholds the preconciliar doctrine acknowledging the right of civil authority to use coercion in protecting the true religion" (WD, #51), Fr. Harrison comments (ibid.):

> Now, if the Secretariat for Christian Unity had wanted to present a schema contradicting *any part* of the existing doctrine of the Church, then of course honesty would have required that this be acknowledged openly on the floor of the Council. The *relator* would have had to adduce evidence and argumentation in order to convince the Fathers that the (putatively) erroneous doctrinal thesis they were now being asked to repudiate had never been proposed with *infallible* force by either the ordinary or extraordinary magisterium. There is of course not a trace of any of this in the Council's *Acta*. On the contrary, the Fathers were assured, in the pertinent *relationes*, that *no* doctrinal contradiction was involved.[22]

17. This strikes me as a strange argument. For since "the Fathers were assured, in the pertinent *relationes*, that *no* doctrinal contradiction was involved," there would then be no need by "[t]he *relator* ... to adduce evidence and argumentation in order to convince the Fathers that the [putatively] erroneous doctrinal thesis they were now being asked to repudiate had never been proposed with *infallible* force by either the ordinary or extraordinary magisterium."[23] But Fr. Harrison never once reports in his

Proceedings of the Catholic Theological Society of America, 2 (1947): 15, 31 ("The teaching of the [*QC*] cannot, of course, be classified as a solemn definition of the Sovereign Pontiff, in the technical sense in which the Bull *Ineffabilis Deus* had contained a definition. Nevertheless the [*QC*] was and remains very obviously a tremendously important document of the ordinary *magisterium* of the Church"). See also Cardinal Joseph Hergenröther, *Catholic Church and Christian State: A Series of Essays on the Relation of the Church to the Civil Power* (London: Burnes & Oates, 1876), I: 204–12, and especially 208–10 for his comments about the condemnation in globo of the propositions in the Syllabus, which can be applied equally mutatis mutandis to *QC*.

22 The quoted matter continues with the additional contention "that the preamble itself, implicitly and explicitly, repeats that same assurance – three times in fact. (Hence my earlier remark that Mr. Guminski's interpretation of *DH*, chapter I, far from making the declaration more "credible," turns it into a scandalous piece of lying hypocrisy.)" Strong words these!

23 Bishop Emile Joseph De Smedt indeed expounded at length in his first *relatio* (November 19, 1963) how the proposed doctrine of *DH* would not contradict

reply that in his opinion Paul VI and the Council Fathers were sold the proverbial bill of goods with respect to the meaning of the nineteenth-century papal documents. He had elsewhere most emphatically argued that the Council Fathers were presented with an unhistorical and inaccurate exegesis of the relevant texts.[24] Moreover, according to Fr. Harrison, there was a "manipulation of the more conservative, but rather complacent and unsuspecting, majority by the powerful and 'progressive' Northern European bishops and their *periti*."[25] So it turns out that his argument from silence fails and becomes a self-inflicted wound.[26]

18. How convenient it is indeed that Fr. Harrison holds that neither

> preconciliar doctrine in the nineteenth-century papal documents, although he admitted some difficulties. (*AS* (1978), vol. II/pt. V, 491–92. Trans. in Michael Davies, *The Second Vatican Council* [Long Prairie: Neumann Press, 1992], 288–94.) However, in his *relatio* concerning the final draft, De Smedt stated: "Some Fathers affirm that the Declaration does not sufficiently show how our doctrine is not opposed to the ecclesiastical documents up till the time of the Supreme Pontiff Leo XIII. As we said in our last *relatio*, this is a matter for future theological and historical studies to bring to light more fully." *AS* (1978), vol. IV/pt. VI, 719; trans. in *RLC*, 75.)

24 *RLC*, 40–41; "Vatican II and Religious Liberty: Contradiction or Continuity?" *Social Justice Review* (July/August 1989), 105–06.

25 See Fr. Harrison's "Skeletons in the Conciliar Closet," *The Remnant* (2004) (available at http://www.remnantnewspaper.com/Archives/archive-skeletons.htm) for remarks disclosing his rather uncomplimentary opinion of Bishop De Smedt, as well as of "the more conservative, but rather complacent and unsuspecting, majority" of the Council.

26 See also Fr. Harrison's comments in *RLC*, 107, about the term *public order* in *DH*: "[T]he Council has followed the example of Lewis Carroll's Humpty Dumpty: *in this document* [i.e., *DH*], '[P]ublic order' must be taken to mean whatever the Church chooses it to mean, not what it may mean for the rest of the world – especially for the nations whose constitutions are based on a separation of Church and State." In his address "Roma Locuta Est" (note 7 *supra*), 42, he thus explains why *DH*'s use of some terms (such as *public order*) is "all rather confusing and less than straightforward": "[*DH*] . . . *sounds* more liberal than it really is. Conscious of the Church's public image at a time when dialogue with non-Christians and non-Catholics was being given high priority, Vatican II gave prominence to language which seems to allow for very few government restrictions on religious propaganda. But then, in the 'fine print' and official commentary, which was not even published in Latin by the Vatican Press until thirteen years after the Council, it is revealed that this language is *not* to be understood in a way which could contradict the doctrine of the previous one and a half-millennia, which in fact allowed for many more such government restrictions." So much for the integrity of the authors of *DH*!

Gregory XVI's encyclical *Mirari Vos* (1832),[27] nor the *Syllabus of Errors* (1864), nor Leo XIII's *Immortale Dei* (1885) (*ID*), nor his *Libertas Praestantissimum* (1888) (*LP*), nor Pius XII's *Ci Riesce* (1953), contains any ex cathedra definition apparently inconsistent with the doctrine of *DH*. Furthermore, despite several claims by others to that effect, there has yet to be a serious effort to plausibly show that the preconciliar doctrine as to FRM had been taught *definitively* (and not simply just authoritatively) by the universal ordinary magisterium rather than as a solemn definition. This effort would necessarily involve showing that the Catholic faithful were required to believe that the preconciliar doctrine is (at least implicitly) within the deposit of faith as divinely revealed truth, or hold that it is necessarily connected to divinely revealed truth. Fr. Harrison, as I understand him, does not presently make any such claim. Therefore, given my conclusion that *QC* does not contain ex cathedra definitions, I proceed henceforth with the assumption that no relevant preconciliar doctrine (i.e., such rightly understood preconciliar doctrine as is ostensibly inconsistent with the doctrine of *DH*) was definitive. And recall that both Fr. Harrison and I maintain with good reason that the doctrine of *DH* is nondefinitive.

---

27 Nothing in this encyclical itself indicates that its teaching is in the exercise of the infallible magisterium. The claim that *Mirari Vos* contains an ex cathedra definition is based on the declaration by Gregory XVI in his encyclical *Singulari Nos* (1834), in which he explained how, in *Mirari Vos*, he had defined [*definivimus*] Catholic doctrine [*catholicam doctrinam*] concerning the unlimited license of opinions and of speech, as well as absolute liberty of conscience. However, it is highly unlikely that the mere use of "definire" in one encyclical can be properly taken as persuasive evidence of an intent to make an ex cathedra definition in an earlier papal document especially since *Mirari Vos* was issued well before the definition of papal infallibility by Vatican I in 1870. Some writers have noted that *define* and its derivatives have frequently been used in papal and other ecclesiastical documents in a rather broad sense with respect to any authoritative doctrine of the Church. (See, e.g., Edmond D. Bernard, "The Doctrinal Value of the Ordinary Teaching of the Holy Father in View of *Humani Generis*," *Proceedings of the Sixth Annual Convention* (1951) (Catholic Theological Society of America), 78, 83–84: Lucien Choupin, *Valeur des Décisions Doctrinales et Disciplinaires du Saint-Siège* (Paris: Gabriel Beauchesne, 3d ed. 1928), 26; see also Hergenröther, *Catholic Church and Christian State*, *supra* note 21, 2: 206–210 for similar remarks about the terms "dogmatic judgment" or "dogmatic decision." Finally, the term "Catholic doctrine" is ambiguous. It could mean a doctrine authoritatively taught by the magisterium but as neither within the deposit of faith nor *necessarily* connected thereto; however, the term is applied sometimes to teachings of a higher (but never a lower) order. Cartechini, *De valore* (note 18 supra), 68–70.

C. Why the Issue of the Consistency of Relevant Preconciliar Doctrine with that of *DH* Is Legitimately Open for An SOC

19. So what we are now to make of Fr. Harrison's point that "the mind of the Church ... is that [*DH*] is not to be understood in a way that would make it contradict *any* existing doctrine, whether infallible or 'merely authentic'"? (WD, #7.) Fr. Harrison has not cited any ecclesiastical document that declares that Catholics are *obliged* (albeit if only in a defeasibly presumptive manner) to believe that preconciliar doctrine is consistent with that of *DH*. Benedict XVI's remarks in his 2005 Christmas address to the Roman Curia are determinative as to what is the current mind of the Church. In this address, he sharply criticized "a hermeneutic of discontinuity and rupture [which] asserts that the texts of the [Vatican II] as such do not yet express the true spirit of the Council." The pontiff, however, distinguished "a hermeneutic of reform" from that of discontinuity and rupture as follows:[28]

> It is precisely in this combination of continuity and discontinuity at different levels that the very nature of true reform consists. In this process of innovation in continuity we must learn to understand more practically than before that the Church's decisions on contingent matters – for example, certain practical forms of liberalism or a free interpretation of the Bible – should necessarily be contingent themselves, precisely because they refer to a specific reality that is changeable in itself. It was necessary to learn to recognize that in these decisions it is only the principles that express the permanent aspect, since they remain as an undercurrent, motivating decisions from within. On the other hand, not so permanent are the practical forms that depend on the historical situation and are therefore subject to change.... *The Second Vatican Council, with its new definition of the relationship between the faith of the Church and certain essential elements of modern thought, has reviewed or even corrected certain historical decisions, but in this apparent discontinuity it has actually preserved and deepened her inmost nature and true identity.*[29]

28 Address to the Roman Curia (December 22, 2005) (www.vatican.va/holy_father/benedict_xvi/speeches/2005/december).

29 The correction of "certain historical decisions" with respect to RF appears to have been due to the contemporary recognition that RF had been formerly "considered an expression of the human inability to discover the truth and thus [became] a

D. Why the Authentic Doctrine of *DH* Does Not Contradict Sacred Tradition and the Doctrine of the Church

20. Fr. Harrison claims that *DH*'s preamble itself assures us three times that there is no doctrinal contradiction between its doctrine on RF and relevant preconciliar doctrine (which, for argument's sake, he assumes to be nondefinitive). (WD, #8.)[30] First, we address the significance of the statement in *DH* #1.1 that the Council "examine[d] the sacred tradition and teaching of the church from which it continually draws new insights in harmony with the old." The term *sacred tradition* pertains to the deposit of faith, and its living transmission through the magisterium. The term *sacred tradition and teaching of the church* is equivalent in meaning to *sacred tradition and sacred teaching of the church.* The term *sacred doctrine* refers to those doctrines which teach about divinely revealed truths within the deposit of faith – including doctrines necessarily connected to divinely revealed truths, and doctrines proposed in order "to aid a better understanding of Revelation and make explicit its contents, or to recall how some teaching is in conformity with the truths of faith, or finally to guard against ideas that are incompatible with these truths." *Donum Veritatis,* #23.3.[31]

canonization of relativism." But for "those who believe that the human person is capable of knowing the truth about God and, on the basis of the inner dignity of the truth, is bound to this knowledge," RF will be "perceive[d] … as a need that derives from human coexistence, or indeed, as an intrinsic consequence of the truth that cannot be externally imposed but that the person must adopt only through the process of conviction." Ibid. The pope propounded essentially the same view about continuity in his 2005 address that he did as Prefect of CDF when, in the course of his remarks on June 25, 1990, he stated: "The text [*Donum Veritatis*] also offers different forms of binding which arise from different levels of magisterial teaching. It states – perhaps for the first time with such clarity – that there are magisterial decisions which cannot be and are not intended to be the last word on the matter as such, but are a substantial anchorage on the problem and are first and foremost an expression of pastoral prudence, a sort of provisional disposition. Their core remains valid, but the individual details influenced by the circumstances at the time may need further rectification. In this regard one can refer to the statements of the Popes during the last century on religious freedom as well as the anti-modernistic decisions at the beginning of this century, especially the decisions of the Biblical Commission of that time." (*L'Osservatore Romano* (Eng. Ed.) N. 27 – 2 July 1990, 9.)

30   His discussion of the issues based upon the text of *DH* and its legislative history appears in WD, ##33–37, 51–56.

31   Thomas Aquinas: "It was necessary for man's salvation that there should be a knowledge revealed by God besides philosophical science built up by human reason. Firstly, indeed, because man is directed to God, as to an end that surpasses the

21. But the Church's magisterium is not limited to only what constitutes sacred doctrine. As *DH* (#14.3) declares, the charge of the Catholic Church as the teacher of truth "is to announce and authentically teach the truth which is Christ, and at the same time to give authoritative statement and confirmation of the moral order which derives from human nature itself." The *Catechism* #2036 teaches that "[t]he authority of the Magisterium extends also to specific precepts of the *natural law*" – although precepts could also be within the deposit of faith and can also be the object of the magisterium.[32] Fortunately, Fr. Harrison himself agrees

> grasp of his reason.... It was therefore necessary that besides philosophical science built up by reason there should be a sacred science learned through revelation." (*Summa Theologiae,* Ia q 1 ad 1) [(tr. Fathers of the English Dominican Province, 2nd & Rev'd ed., 1920) available on-line at http://www.sacred-texts.com/chr/aquinas/summa/sum003.htm.)

32 *Donum Veritatis* #16: "[T]he competence of the Magisterium also extends to that which concerns the natural law. Revelation also contains moral teachings which *per se* could be known by natural reason.... It is a doctrine of faith that these moral norms can be infallibly taught by the Magisterium." The doctoral dissertation of now Cardinal William J. Levada, Prefect of the Congregation of the Faith, argued that the Church's infallible magisterium does not extend to doctrines formulating NML norms, unless they are also within the deposit of faith or necessarily connected thereto, because such doctrines are essentially grounded upon the data of human experience not found within the deposit of faith. (*Lex Naturae et Magisterium Ecclesiae,* Pontifical Gregorian University Doctoral Thesis No. 4276/1968, July 18, 1968, Vol. II, p. 617. This dissertation was partially published in English: *Infallible Church Magisterium and the Natural Moral Law: Excerta ex dissertatione ad lauream in Facultate Theologiae Pontificiae Universitatis Gregorianae* [Roma: Pontificia Universitas Gregoriana, 1971].)

  Also noteworthy is a response by representatives of the Congregation of the Doctrine of the Faith at the February 1999 meeting at the Vallombrosa Center in Menlo Park, California with members of the doctrinal commissions and/or conference presidents or their representatives from North America and Oceania. The CDF response stated that "the Magisterium has the competence to teach infallibly and make obligatory the definitive assent of the members of the faithful with regard to the knowledge and application in life of [all negative moral norms that concern intrinsically evil acts]." However, "[w]ith regard to the particular applications of the norms of the natural moral law that do not have a necessary connection with Revelation – for example, numerous positive moral norms that are valid *ut in pluribus* [in most cases] – it has not been defined nor is it binding that the Magisterium can teach infallibly in such specific matters." CDF Representative, "Some Brief Responses to Questions Regarding the *Professio fidei, Proclaiming the Truth of Jesus Christ: Papers from the Vallombrosa Meeting* (Washington DC: United States Catholic Conference, 2000), 61–66, at 66 (quoted in Dulles, *supra*

with me that the doctrinal issues pertaining to FRM "are fundamentally concerned with points of natural law," and hence I claim they do not pertain as such to sacred doctrine.[33]

22. Fr. Harrison also wrote in *RLC* that the Leo XIII's encyclical *ID* discloses "beyond any shadow of a doubt, that [Leo XIII's] intention is to declare either revealed truth, or else truths required for the safeguarding the deposit of faith." (*RLC*, 29.) What Fr. Harrison refers to is Leo XIII's declaration that his teaching on the Christian constitution of states "is the necessary growth of the teachings of the Gospel," and that it is "of the highest moment, and a strict duty of [his] apostolic office, to contrast with the lessons taught by Christ the novel theories now advanced touching the State."[34]

23. But the issue is how much doctrine in *ID* constitutes sacred doctrine in the requisite sense. For the reader is invited to carefully read its text to see just how much falls within the rubric of political-social doctrine based partly upon the NML and just how much of it is sacred doctrine.[35]

note 9, at 80). The Church's preconciliar doctrine concerning FRM pertained to positive moral norms.

33   *RLC*, 9–10: "We have chosen this 'case-study' approach partly because ... the case in question [i.e., RF] is of particular theoretical and practical importance in the life of today's church. The two doctrines [contraception and RF] we have chosen to compare bear certain 'family resemblances' which render such a comparison a feasible project: both are ethical issues; both came to a head within the same general historical and ecclesial context – the era of Vatican II with all its insistence on the rights of persons over and against institutions; both are fundamentally concerned with points of natural law, one set within the matrix of the family and the other within that of civil society."

Fr. Harrison wisely does not appear to draw upon the doctrine of the kingship of Christ as taught in the encyclical *Quas Primas* (1925) to support the thesis that civil authority has the coercive power to restrict freedom in religious matters in ways incompatible with a liberal (but nevertheless theologically correct) theory of the doctrine of *DH*. (See *RLC*, 14, 77; "Roma Locuta Est" (note 7 supra), 44; WD, #58 and n93.) *Quas Primas* (#32) (http://www.vatican.va/holy_father/pius _ix/encyclicals/documents/hf_p-xi_enc_11121925_quas-primas_en.html) reminds "rulers and princes. . . . that the State should take account of the commandments of God and of Christian principles, both in making laws and in administering justice, and also in providing for the young a sound moral education." They are also admonished to "exercise their authority piously and wisely, and . . . make laws and administer them, having in view the common good and also the human dignity of their subjects." (Ibid., #19.)

34   *Immortale Dei* (November 1, 1885) #2.

35   See, e.g., how in *ID*, Leo XIII expressly relies (# 6) upon the teaching of "[n]ature and reason" upon which he bases the moral duty of civil society to recognize and favor Catholicism as uniquely true, and (#32) on "the laws and dictates of nature"

But how could the doctrine of *DH* possibly conflict with preconciliar sacred doctrine? – since the Vatican II Fathers declared that the Church "sees the principle of religious freedom as in accord with human dignity and the revelation of God."[36]

24. Insofar as we consider the scope and limits of the natural right as to FRM with respect to the public manifestation and propagation of false doctrines in religious matters, we are concerned with secondary or instrumental human goods rather than those that are primary.[37] We are also

> upon which to condemn "the State . . . whenever it permits the license of opinion and of action to lead minds astray from truth and souls away from the practice of virtue." Fr. Harrison comments: "In regard to the State's duty to profess religion publicly, we have seen Pope Leo assert that this is a 'command' of 'nature and reason'" (*RLC,* 29); and notices "that the Pope is insisting that natural law requires the State universally and absolutely to prevent false opinions from 'leading minds astray from truth and souls from the practice of virtue'" (ibid., 53). But he cautions: "[t]he sentence from Leo XIII just referred to should not be plucked out of context. As we have seen, Leo acknowledges elsewhere that civil authorities not only *may* sometimes tolerate such errors, but under some circumstances even 'should' do so." (Ibid.)

36 *DH* #12.1. I am not begging the question in view of what immediately follows the just quoted matter: "Throughout the centuries [the Church] has guarded and handed on the teaching received from the master and from the apostles" – surely this is what is meant by *sacred tradition and doctrine.* [Cf. Vatican Council II, *Dei Verbum* (Dogmatic Constitution on Divine Revelation), #24: "Sacred theology takes its stand on the written word of God, together with tradition, as its permanent foundation. By this word it is made firm and strong, and constantly renews its youth, as it investigates, by the light of faith, all the truth that is stored up in the mystery of Christ." (Tanner II, 980).] *DH* #12.1 continues: "Although at times in the life of the people of God, as it has pursued its pilgrimage through the twists and turns of human history, there have been ways of acting hardly in tune with the spirit of the gospel, indeed contrary to it, nevertheless the Church's teaching that no one's faith should be coerced has held firm. Thus the leaven of the gospel has long been at work in the minds of people and has played a great part in the course of time in the growing recognition of the dignity of the human person, and in the maturing of the conviction that in religious matters this dignity must be preserved intact in society from any kind of human coercion."

37 In the case of RF, the supposed factual basis for the nineteenth-century (and earlier) public ecclesiastical law and policy calling for total repression of public manifestation and propagation of non-Catholic religions in predominantly Catholic countries included the denial that the "legitimate demand for freedom in the sense of absence of constraint as a necessary condition for the loyal inquiry into truth" (*Donum Veritatis* #32), and that a sufficient zone of freedom of inquiry and expression in matters religious is virtually necessary in order to ensure that the freedom of the act of faith (in either initially embracing, or continuing to adhere

concerned with the *remote precepts* of the NML, as to which honest and indeed more or less reasonable errors as to factual matters frequently occur.[38] So it may well be the case that doctrinal error with respect to the NML is possible; but that such doctrinal error does not entail what is *intrinsically* unjust but rather what is, for other reasons, *objectively* unjust.[39]

E. Why the Authentic Doctrine of *DH* Does Not Contradict the Traditional Catholic Doctrine on the Moral Duty of Individuals and Societies toward the Catholic Religion

25. We now turn to Fr. Harrison's major thesis that "[i]t is a clearly documented fact that 'traditional Catholic doctrine' *did* include coercive measures as part of the State's moral duty to the true religion.'" (WD, #58.) In which statement, I wholly concur – provided the term *traditional Catholic doctrine* is

to, the faith) involves the offer of a *rational* homage to God (ibid., #36). *DH* #9.1 explains: "The statements made by this Vatican synod on the right of the people to [RF] have their basis in the dignity of the person, the demands of which have come to be more fully known to human reason from the experience of centuries." (Tanner, II: 1006.) The natural right to RF does not come to obtain when a sufficiently puissant and effective consciousness arises that human dignity requires such freedom. Rather, the natural right to RF already obtains but does not become a juridically established right until the requisite consciousness arises. John Paul II rightly noted: "moral principles are not dependent upon the historical moment in which they are discovered." (*Veritatis Splendor* (1993) #112.)

38 The article on natural law in the *Catholic Encyclopedia*, 9: 78, points out that the *remote precepts* of the natural morality involve "conclusions … which are reached only by a more or less complex course of reasoning. These may remain unknown to, or be misinterpreted even by persons whose intellectual development is considerable. To reach these more remote precepts, many facts and minor conclusions must be correctly appreciated, and, in estimating their value, a person may easily err, and consequently, without moral fault, come to a false conclusion."

39 Speaking of "the acquiescence given, especially in certain centuries, to *intolerance and even the use of violence* in the service of truth," John Paul II declared in his apostolic letter *Tertio Millenio Adveniente* (1994) #35: "It is true that an accurate historical judgment cannot prescind from careful study of the cultural conditioning of the times, as a result of which many people may have held in good faith that [a sincere] witness to the truth [simultaneously required eradicating, or at least isolating, the opinions of others]. Many factors frequently converged to create assumptions which justified intolerance and fostered an emotional climate from which only great spirits, truly free and filled with God, were in some way able to break free." (Bracketed matter includes improved translation by Fr. Harrison in WD, #25 and n52.)

understood to also refer to those doctrines of the Church that pertain to NML norms not within the deposit of faith or necessarily connected thereto. But I call upon the reader to carefully consider the pertinent text in *DH* #1.3 in which the Council announces that "it leaves intact the traditional catholic [doctrine] on the moral obligation of individuals and societies towards the true religion and the one church of Christ." The passage in question is most emphatically not simply using the term *traditional Catholic doctrine* (hereafter TCD) without additional qualification. Moreover, the Council is not expressly using the term TCD to refer to *the State's moral duty or right with respect to coercive measures limiting FRM in the interest of the true religion* (or words to that effect). Since the passage refers to the moral obligation of individuals *and* societies towards the true religion and the one church of Christ, the passage patently pertains only to a moral obligation common to both individuals and to societies (including among them, civil societies) mentioned in the preceding sentence "to worship God."[40] For that moral obligation common to individuals and societies would not include an obligation (to whatever extent it exists) that is specific to, or proper of, only political authority since it is that authority alone that is generally conceded to legitimately possess the power to use externally coercive means to protect civil society.[41]

26. The preamble does not appear to precisely define or describe the

---

40 The legislative history of this part of the preamble to *DH* amply confirms that the moral duty of societies and that of individuals towards the true religion and the one church of Christ are essentially identical. Thus, as Fr. Harrison narrates: "In the third-last draft (the *textus reemendatus*), article one [provided in part]: 'Moreover, this treatment of religious liberty leaves intact the Catholic doctrine concerning the one true religion and the one Church of Christ.'" (*RLC*, 71.) Thereafter, the revised draft text (the *textus recognitus*) (after substituting a comma for 'and' after 'religion') simply added the words "and the moral duty of men towards that Church." (Ibid., 72.) The final draft text (the *textus denuo recognitus*) inserts "traditional" before "Catholic doctrine," and adds "and of societies" after "the moral duty of men." (Ibid., 75.)

41 I assume that Fr. Harrison still agrees that the Church itself lacks divinely instituted authority to use (or to require Catholic rulers to use) coercive means typical of civil authority only (*RLC*, 125, and see CH, ##10, 59); and that, therefore, the Church's authority *jure divino* to impose nonconsensual temporal penalties not typical of civil authority only are solely those incident to her inherent *household rights*. That the Church in fact exercised the power to impose externally coercive sanctions is explained as being due to: (a) acting upon the erroneous premise (but never proposed as authoritative doctrine) that its authority *jure divino* was broad enough to include the power in question; and/or (b) the power in question was warranted by the *jus publicum* of medieval Catholic Christendom. For informative

nature of the moral obligation in question. The second paragraph declares: "But all people are bound to seek for the truth, especially about God and his Church, and when they have found it to embrace and keep it." This obligation *could* be part of the moral duty in question, but appears to refer to only individuals.[42] The third paragraph then goes on to say: "The synod further proclaims that these obligations touch and bind the human conscience," adding "that truth imposes itself solely by the force of its own truth, as it enters the mind at once gently and with power." Then follows a very important passage (Tanner II: 1002): "Indeed, since people's demand for religious liberty in carrying out their duty to worship God concerns freedom from compulsion in civil society, it leaves intact the traditional catholic teaching on the moral obligation of individuals and societies."

27. From this passage, it appears that the term *duty to worship God* refers to *the moral obligation of individuals and societies towards the true religion and the one church of Christ.*[43] (Here I note my agreement with Fr.

accounts as to how this *jus publicum* came about, see Joseph Fessler, *The True and the False Infallibility of the Popes: A Controversial Reply to Dr. Shulte* (New York: Catholic Publication Soc., 1875), 119–26; Jean-Edmé-Auguste Gosselin, *The Power of the Popes during the Middle Ages* (London: C. Dolman. 1853), I: 1–176; and Joseph Cardinal Hergenröther, *Catholic Church* (note 21 *supra*), I: 293–332; II: 301–84. (See also ##9, 10 in John Paul II's address to the European Parliament of Strasbourg, October 11, 1988, concerning the *jus publicum* of medieval Christendom.[http://www.vatican.va/holy_father/john_paul_ii/speeches/1988/oct ober/documents/hf_jp-ii_spe_19881011_european-parliament_fr.html].) The *jus publicum* of medieval Catholic Christendom, in its final form, was the end-product of ever-increasing coercive repression throughout the preceding centuries by Church and State of non-Catholic activities, both public and private, as well as of apostates and heretics. That every country in this commonwealth became overwhelmingly Catholic was to a great extent the fruit of the poisoned tree of extensive and sustained intolerance by coercive means typical of only civil authority. For succinct accounts of this process with respect to the Roman Empire see Joseph Lecler, S.J., *Toleration and the Reformation* (trans. T.L. Westow) (London: Longmans, 1960), 32–64, and Thomas Owen Martin, "Theodosius' Laws on Heretics," *The American Ecclesiastical Review* 123 (Aug. 1950) 117–130.

42 It was not long after the publication of my CH that I perhaps too quickly concluded that the so-called "'moral obligation of individuals and societies towards the true religion and one church of Christ'" also includes the duty "to seek the truth ... about God and his Church, and when ... found to embrace and keep it." (CH, #45.)

43 But it is not even enough to speak of the "duty to worship God"; what is necessary is to speak of the duty to worship (i.e., to owe reverence to) God in ways authorized by him. Leo XIII declared in *ID* #6: "we are bound absolutely to worship God in that way which He has shown to be His will."

Harrison that that the term "societies" in the above quoted passage includes civil societies.[44]) This supports the position that whatever is that moral obligation common to individuals and societies, referred to in the preamble to *DH*, it does not include whatever is encompassed by the specific moral duty or right of civil authority with respect to externally coercive measures limiting FRM.

28. The foregoing analysis is confirmed by the #2105 of the *Catechism*, which declares in part: "The duty of offering God genuine worship concerns man both individually and socially. This is 'the traditional Catholic teaching on the moral duty of individuals and societies toward the true religion and the one Church of Christ'" (citing *DH* #1.3). The term *genuine worship* is to be understood as equivalent to *authentic* (i.e., authoritative) *worship*, since this is the meaning manifestly intended by the term *cultum authenticum* in the official Latin text.[45] Hence *genuine worship*, as used in #1205, is to be understood as referring to such worship as is authorized by God. The divinely authorized worship of God (in the sense intended in *DH* #1.3 and #2105 of the *Catechism*) includes the recognition (in some way or another, whether explicit or implicit) by individuals and societies that the Catholic religion is uniquely true and that the Catholic Church is the one true church of Christ. Because my argument is with Fr. Harrison, I shall not burden this essay with an argument as to why I maintain that *DH* and postconciliar exercises of the magisterium have not superseded preconciliar doctrine pertaining to the prima facie duty of civil

44 Fr. Harrison rightly notes that I "do not contest [his] view that *DH* [# 1.3] includes the 'moral obligation' of civil authorities to recognize Catholicism as uniquely true." (WD, #51.) In the accompanying endnote (ibid., n. 82), he remarks that "[Guminski] does not seem particularly concerned to dispute the propriety, or even the theoretically normative status, of such state 'establishment' of Catholicism, provided this has no discernible restrictive consequences for non-Catholic minorities." But churchmen should have paid much stricter heed to the biblical injunction: "Put not your trust in Princes" (Prov. 146: 3). In this article, I prescind entirely from the wisdom, prudence, and expediency of the particular ways in which civil society has discharged (explicitly or implicitly, directly or indirectly) its prima facie obligation to recognize Catholicism as uniquely true. I also prescind from what extent political authority is relieved for now and the reasonably foreseeable future from satisfying the obligation in question simply because of the lessons of history and experience, especially in view of the revolutionary changes in communication, technology, mobility, demographics, economics, popular education, and political structures that have characterized the last century.

45 Fr. Harrison refers in WD, #57, to "authentic worship (*cultum authenticum*)" as part of his translation of #2105 of the *Catechism*.

authority to recognize the Catholic religion as uniquely true except to the extent that this might be inconsistent with the doctrine of *DH* concerning RF. Of course, there are SOCs who would strongly disagree with this assessment – but then they would necessarily reject the proposition that RF may be abridged upon grounds that presuppose the truth of the Catholic religion. Bear in mind, however, that the proposition that civil authority, when certain conditions obtain, has the prima facie right to abridge RF in the interest of the spiritual welfare of citizens because the truth of the Catholic religion entails the proposition that civil authority has the prima facie right to recognize the Catholic religion as uniquely true – although the latter proposition does not entail the former.

29. But Fr. Harrison takes pains to assure us that he does "not concede that [#2105 of] the *Catechism* does in fact exclude all coercive measures in fulfillment of the said duty." He explains that (WD, #59):

> Bearing in mind that this social duty of "offering authentic worship" to God involves not only *recognizing* Catholic truth in this way but also *keeping, conserving* or *guarding* it so that the next generation (and the next, and the next) will still offer the same worship, the need for some degree of coercion to restrict anti-Catholic propaganda follows as a *practical* corollary.

30. As to the first point, Fr. Harrison refers us in the endnote immediately following the word *"guarding"*: "Latin *servare* (*DH* #1, last word, second paragraph)." (WD, n94.) But the passage in question plainly pertains to the duty of individuals "to seek for the truth, especially about God and his church, and when they have found it to embrace and keep it [*quaerere eamque cognitam ampecti ac servare*]." Thus *servare* refers to only an individual's cognitive duty with respect to the truth. Indeed, as Fr. Harrison has pointed out elsewhere: "a Catholic community cannot, as such, make an act of faith in the true sense." (*RLC*, 77.)

31. As Fr. Harrison has sometimes reminded us, the moral duty of offering authentic worship towards God by political authority does not preclude complete RF for *adherents* of non-Catholic religions.[46] However, Fr.

---

46 See, e.g., *RLC*, 31: "[T]he *civitas* as such – that is, the civic community and its official leaders – has a duty to recognize Catholicism as the true religion. State 'recognition' of a certain religion does not *by itself*, however, tell us very much about the treatment of other religions under such a regime. This can range all the way from the severest persecution at one end of the spectrum to total (or near-total) liberty at the other." In *RLC*, 76, he speaks simply of "the duty of the *civi-*

Harrison says in his reply article, "the need for some degree of coercion to restrict anti-Catholic propaganda follows as a *practical* corollary." Nevertheless he concedes that this "does not follow with a strict *logical* necessity." (WD, n95.) But the term *practical corollary* is an oxymoron in this context since Fr. Harrison candidly acknowledges: "As I have noted in my other writings, state establishment of religion is theoretically compatible with a very wide variety of legal dispositions vis-à-vis the treatment of other religions, philosophies and life-styles, ranging from the fiercest intolerance to almost unrestricted liberty." (Ibid.)[47] If so, then clearly the moral right or duty (under some circumstances) of the civil community to

tas as such to recognize and respect the true religion." But this is equally the duty of individuals and all other societies besides the *civitas*. Ibid., 77: "The core of the preconciliar doctrine is simply that when human beings act communally to order their temporal affairs, they have no objective right to consider themselves exempt from the duty of recognizing and respecting the will of God (both naturally knowable and revealed) simply by virtue of the fact that their action is communal rather than individual." Fr. Harrison also explains (ibid., 59): "Along with the institution of intolerance for other religions, [John Courtney] Murray's main foe is the principle that civil governments are bound by a *duty* to recognize and favour the true religion over other religions." In this passage, Fr. Harrison quite clearly distinguishes two different kinds of duty or right of civil government towards the true religion. See also his "John Courtney Murray; A Reliable Interpreter of *Dignitatis Humanae*," eds. Donald J. D'Elia & Stephen M. Krason, *We Hold These Truths and More: Further Catholic Reflections on the American Proposition* (Steubenville OH: Franciscan University Press, 1993), 135: "There were basically two issues, closely related but distinct, in the controversy between Murray and his conservative critics before and during the Council: first, the question of special state recognition or 'establishment' of Catholicism; and secondly, the question of state repression of public religious manifestations on the part of non-Catholics. The first of these legal dispositions does not necessarily imply the second, but the second clearly presupposes the first."

47 But see WD, #56 where Fr. Harrison inconsistently contends that "the [TCD] on the moral duty *of societies* toward the true religion.... certainly included society's right and duty to protect the true religion with coercive measures." Fr. Harrison erroneously states that Msgr. Joseph Clifford Fenton (an arch-adversary of Murray) "insisted" in his article "Principles Underlying Traditional Church-State Doctrine," *American Ecclesiastical Review*, 126 (1952), 455–56 and 457, "that the entire edifice of orthodox Catholic doctrine regarding Church, State *and religious repression/toleration* is squarely based on the bedrock principle [that all individuals and societies are bound to acknowledge and honor God in the worship and according to the rite of His own Church]." (WD, #61; emphasis added.) Fenton most definitely did not connect *religious repression/toleration* with the moral duty of civil societies to worship God.

recognize the Catholic religion as uniquely true is essentially distinct from and does not logically or analytically entail whatever is the right or duty (under some circumstances) of the civil authority to exercise its coercive powers to limit liberty in religious or nonreligious matters in ways that, indirectly at least, disclose reliance upon supernaturally revealed truths. I invite Fr. Harrison to consider that, as he writes, "the civic community's recognition of Catholic truth is primarily a duty which it owes *to God*" ("John Courtney Murray: A Reliable Interpreter of [*DH*]?"); whereas whatever power the civic community has to exercise externally coercive powers to repress the public manifestation and propagation of religious and moral error would primarily be a duty it owes *to man* "to the extent that common good requires" (*RLC*, 141).

32. The relevant text of the preamble to *DH* poses a grave analytical problem for Fr. Harrison. The logical structure of the relevant text is: *since* (or *because*) **p** is true, [*therefore*] **q** is true. But Fr. Harrison insists, on the contrary, that the relevant text when properly translated has the logical structure: *while* (or *although*) **p** is true, **q** is *nevertheless* true. Thus, according to Fr. Harrison, the relevant text should be understood as saying: "For *although* religious liberty (as the Council understands it) does indeed concern immunity from coercion, it *nevertheless* 'leaves intact' (or 'whole and complete') that traditional doctrine" (WD, #56) – *traditional doctrine* being understood to "certainly [include civil] society's right and duty to protect the true religion with coercive measures" (WD, #56). But nowhere has he shown that, distinguished from the claims made by some theologians, the Church herself had in her traditional doctrine taught that the moral duty of individuals and societies to recognize and favor Catholicism as uniquely true includes the duty of civil authority to use its coercive powers with respect to FRM.

33. Fr. Harrison refers to how the fact that, in November 1965, some "vital last-minute amendments to [*DH* #1] [together with two full paragraphs of the final *relatio* explaining them] were dictated word for word by Paul VI was not made public till more than a quarter-century after the Declaration was promulgated."[48] (WD, #36.) Fr. Harrison relies upon the papal intervention to justify his rendering of the relevant text in the preamble to *DH* in a candidly partisan ("conservative-friendly") way. (WD, #55.) But Fr. Harrison reports that he "was unaware of this intervention when writing RLC and [his] earlier articles on *DH*." (WD, n60.) The pontiff

48   Fr. Harrison's account of and comments about the papal interventions appears at
      WD, ##36–37, 55, and accompanying notes.

required that "some reassuring retouches will be added" to the preamble to *DH*, and that the final *relatio* be revised "in order to respond to the objection alleging discontinuity in the magisterium." (WD, nn60–61.) But, pace Fr. Harrison, the alleged discontinuity in the magisterium, referred to by Paul VI, appears to pertain to the issue of the moral duty of civil society to recognize and favor Catholicism as uniquely true (considered as merely a component of that moral duty common to individuals and societies towards the true religion and the one church of Christ), and not to that special moral duty of civil authority to coercively repress false religions – a matter sounding in NML rather than in sacred doctrine. Finally, although the papal intervention has great historical interest, it lacks substantial hermeneutical value because it was privately made and its contents not publicly disclosed for many years. In sum, therefore, the doctrine of *DH* does not contradict any doctrine of the Church embodying truths within the deposit of faith or necessarily connected thereto.

F. The Statement in DH that It Developed the Doctrine of the More Recent Popes on Human Rights Does Not Preclude the Fact that Some Preconciliar Doctrine Is Inconsistent with the Doctrine of *DH*

34. Fr. Harrison's *third assurance* is based upon the preamble's statement that "in treating [RF] the synod intends to develop the teaching of more recent popes on the inviolable rights of the human person and on the regulating of society by law." (Tanner II: 1002.) Fr. Harrison's point is essentially that "simply by using the verb 'develop,' the Council Fathers *deny* the very thing my critic would have us believe they imply, namely, that the doctrine they now intend to propose is incompatible with preconciliar doctrine." (WD, #33.) He rhetorically asks whether I am "unaware that ever since John Henry Newman's landmark essay propelled the concept of doctrinal 'development' into the mainstream Catholic theology, it has been taken for granted, as a *sine qua non* for ecclesial recognition of this concept, that any authentic 'development' has to be in harmony, not in conflict, with the existing doctrine." (Ibid.) Alas! I am unaware of what Fr. Harrison so confidently claims to be the case simply because it is only partially true. I readily agree that *genuine* doctrinal development of dogma or other definitive doctrine, and of the doctrines in the deposit of faith itself, cannot for the SOC admit of any contradiction with respect to any *candidate* doctrine proposed for noncontradictory development. But I believe that the term *doctrinal development* has a broader sense when we speak of the development of nondefinitive doctrine in some domain. (Of course, there will be a background, as it were, of relevant definitive doctrine, the deposit of faith, and well-established nondefinitive doctrines.) Thus, I submit there can be a *genuine doctrinal development*, in the broader sense of the term, of nondefinitive doctrine even though a contradiction in some respect obtains between A, the extant doctrine, and A', the proposed superseding doctrine. Thus I believe I conform to the declaration of Benedict XVI in his 2005 Christmas message to the Roman curia about continuity and discontinuity at different levels of doctrine. Necessarily, an SOC must believe that no proposed nondefinitive doctrine is acceptable unless it is consistent with definitive doctrine and the deposit of faith. But where both doctrines A and A' are consistent with definitive doctrine and the deposit of faith, one must make a further inquiry as to which doctrine, if any, is true or most probable – provided one has first ascertained their respective authentic meanings.

G. The Promulgation of *DH* concerning Religious Freedom Leaves in Place Important Authoritative Doctrines on Church-State Relations

35. The promulgation of *DH* does not annul or override several very important Church doctrines. What are they? It behooves us to briefly review them in turn. Essentially, they are embodied, entailed or presupposed, by the contradictories of the first two propositions (i.e., QB1 and QB2) condemned by Pius IX in *QC*.

36. First, *DH* does not abrogate the TCD that civil society as such has a right (and duty, in some circumstances) to recognize and favor (at least indirectly and implicitly) Catholicism in some fashion as uniquely true.[49] Rejection of so-called political naturalism as stated in QC1 and QC2 and the acceptance of RF (as defined by *DH*) can be perfectly compatible.[50] Fr.

---

49   Bishop De Smedt, in his *relatio* of November 19, 1964 (*AS*, vol. III/pt. VIII, 452), stated that the proposed declaration did not directly treat of the juridical aspect of the relations between Church and State.

50   See Leo XIII, encyclical *Longinqua Oceani* #6 (1895); "But, moreover (a fact which it gives pleasure to acknowledge), thanks are due to the equity of the laws which obtain in America and to the customs of the well-ordered Republic. For the Church amongst you, unopposed by the Constitution and government of your nation, fettered by no hostile legislation, protected against violence by the common laws and the impartiality of the tribunals, is free to live and act without hin-

Harrison would agree that the discharge of this right does not require, although it is consistent with, a formal establishment of the Catholic religion or Church, historically understood as including an official endorsement of the Catholic religion as true, the financial endowment or support of Catholic Church and its clergy, and provision for special privileges and immunities for the Church and clergy in excess of those entailed by that freedom of the Church as required by divine positive law, or by constitutional entitlement to RF.[51] (See, *RLC*, 79–82, 159–60.)

37. Second, "[i]t is part of the Church's mission 'to pass moral judgments even in matters related to politics, whenever the fundamental rights of man or the salvation of souls requires it'" (*Catechism* #2245). According to the Church, political "[a]uthority is exercised legitimately only when it seeks the common good of [civil society] and it employs morally licit means to attain it" (*Catechism* #1903). Moreover, "[t]he exercise of authority is measured in terms of its divine origin, its reasonable nature and its specific object. No one can command or establish what is contrary to the dignity of persons and the natural law" (*Catechism* #2235). "Political authorities are obliged to respect the fundamental rights of the human person." (*Catechism* #2237.) Finally, "the State should take account of the commandments of God and of Christian principles, both in making laws and in administering justice, and also in providing for the young a sound moral education." (Pius XI, *Qua Primas* #32.) Nevertheless, although the doctrine of *DH* precludes political authority from abridging RF, it neither precludes political authority from using its coercive powers to abridge FRM *outside* the limits of a just public order nor from abridging freedom in nonreligious matters – provided, of course, that such abridgments are warranted by the common good, consistent with the

drance." However, the pontiff insisted that the Church "would bring forth more abundant fruits if, in addition to liberty, she enjoyed the favor of the laws and the patronage of the public authority." The cardinal point, for our purposes here, is that governmental endorsement and support of the Catholic religion and Church may obtain without the loss of any of that liberty to which non-Catholic religious communities were also constitutionally entitled prior to the establishment of the Catholicism as uniquely true.

51   The present policy of the Church, however, is that "[i]t does not put its hope in privilege tendered by civil authority, and it will even renounce its exercise of some rights it has lawfully acquired where it has decided that their exercise casts doubt on the sincerity of its witness or that new conditions of life call for a different arrangement." (Vatican Council II, pastoral constitution *Gaudium et Spes* 26.5 (Tanner II: 1124).)

exigencies of human dignity including respect for other fundamental natural rights, and otherwise compatible with the NML and the divine positive law.[52]

38. Third, *DH* expressly confirms the TCD that the Church should be juridically entitled to all such rights, privileges, and immunities as are constitutive of, or implied by, that freedom of the Church instituted by divine positive law. (*DH* #13.) *DH* also teaches that the Church and the faithful, independently of the foregoing, are juridically entitled to that RF to which all religious communities should be entitled (subject, of course, to the requirements of a just public order). The freedom of the Church as a divinely instituted right can exist de facto in harmony with civil societies which do not recognize (whether explicitly or implicitly) Catholicism as uniquely true, and indeed recognize some other positive religion as uniquely true, or even reject all positive religions as false. *DH* uses some language that appears to indicate that the scope and limits of the freedom of the Church are congruent with that freedom it should enjoy by virtue of RF. But it seems more likely that the proposition is not exceptionlessly true. Accordingly, in a well-ordered civil society that (at least implicitly) recognizes Catholicism as uniquely true, every particular component of the freedom of the Church must be juridically safeguarded by law even if it is not also a component of RF. In a civil society that does not (even at least implicitly) recognize the truth of any positive religion, juridical recognition of freedom of the Church in excess of what is required by RF should be urged in appropriate cases as being warranted by the theologically neutral common good considerations whenever this can be reasonably argued. The freedom of the Church, insofar as it is based upon divine positive law, entails a fundamental personal right to the free exercise of the Catholic religion grounded upon its truth-value.

52 Thus a general statute which prohibits sexually explicit public conduct does not limit FRM whether or not such conduct is religiously motivated. The reader will notice how frequently Fr. Harrison erroneously confounds freedom in matters religious with freedom in nonreligious matters. See, e.g., his remarks in *RLC*, 110, where he manages to cite legislation regarding pornography, monogamy, divorce, decency in dress, homosexuality, contraception "and so on" as falling within the *public morality* component of a just public order as a limitation on FRM – even though these examples plainly pertain to nonreligious matters. See also WD, n66, which discloses his continued failure to see that FRM does not encompass legislative policy pertaining "polygamy, Sunday observance, and the *per se* duty of political communities themselves … to recognize Roman Catholicism as true" – albeit "*certain points* of divine positive law" are considered as justifying such policy.

39. Fourth, in every well-ordered society, political authority is obliged "to give effective protection to the religious liberty of all citizens by just laws and other suitable means, and to ensure favourable conditions for fostering religious life." (*DH* # 6.2.) The latter obligation includes "ensur[ing] favourable conditions for fostering religious life" consistent with the doctrine of Catholicism taken as being uniquely true.[53]

40. Last, but not least, in every well-constituted society, political authority has the grave duty not to "establish laws or social structures leading to the decline of morals and the corruption of religious practice, or to 'social conditions that, intentionally or not, make Christian conduct and obedience to the Commandments difficult and practically impossible.'"[54]

H. On the True Meaning of that Preconciliar Doctrine Most Likely to Be Inconsistent with the Doctrine of DH concerning Freedom in Religious Matters

41. I shall not burden this article with an explanation of how and why the authentic meaning of the declarations of Pius IX on FRM as set forth in his *QC* and the accompanying *Syllabus* are such that they indeed set forth the authoritative (but not definitive) doctrine of the Church circa 1864 (and thereafter perhaps until and up to the pontificate of John XXIII) to the effect that there is no natural right (i.e., a right grounded on human dignity by virtue of the NML) *whatsoever* to even (what I call) a *special public RF.* The term *special public RF* means a freedom in religious matters that essentially includes: (i) a civil freedom of public manifestation[55] and

53 For example, *Catechism* #2188 declares: "In respecting religious liberty and the common good of all, Christians should seek recognition of Sundays and the Church's holy days as legal holidays." This section appears to recognize that official recognition of Sundays and other Church holy days of obligation as legal holidays is not required by RF.

54 *Catechism* #2285. Section 2354 declares that "[c]ivil authorities should ban the production and distribution of pornographic materials" – which seems to be implicitly defined as sexually explicit pictorial or similar graphic matter calculated to arouse sexual passion. Surely, it is to that extent an ill-constituted society in which constitutional freedoms of speech and of the press as such are understood to encompass rights to freely produce and distribute pornographic materials. Similar remarks apply mutatis mutandis to exploitive pictorial or other nonverbal depictions of scenes of violence and brutality especially likely to be morally and mentally injurious to the young and intellectually, morally, and emotionally immature adults.

55 By *public manifestation* and similar expressions (e.g., *exercise*) the term *public* as used in relevant Church documents appears ordinarily intended to include (but not

propaganda in religious matters (ii) in some but not all appropriate forms and channels of public expression[56] (iii) within the limits of a just public order; (iv) and as to which the truth of the Catholic religion, or of any other positive religion or of natural religion, is deemed (explicitly or implicitly) not juridically relevant to the determination of what constitutes a *just public order.*[57] For the purposes of this article, it has turned out to be unnecessary to include my argument as to the foregoing matter.[58] This is because, **fortunately,**

limited to) what occurs inside buildings and similar enclosed structures open to the public – even if the *public* is limited to members in good standing of the religious community in question. (See CH, n10.) See, e.g., c. 1214 of the *Code of Canon Law*: "The term church signifies a sacred building destined for public worship to which the faithful have a right of access for divine worship, especially its public exercise." Interestingly, in 1864 a Spanish statute "definitively established that a meeting is to be regarded as public and therefore subject to regulation by law if it consists of more than twenty persons." John David Hughey, Jr., *Religious Freedom in Spain: Its Ebb and Flow* (Nashville, Tenn: Broadman Press, 1955), 25 (citing Law of June 22, 1864, *Gaceta de Madrid,* June 23, 1864, p. 1). I assume, subject to correction, that Fr. Harrison agrees with my usage of *public* in this context

56   I use *forms and channels of public expression* to include, for example, what is published in the press and other mass media, as well as what is said in places open to the public, such as churches, temples, synagogues, lecture halls, auditoria etc. For example, unsolicited mass mailing and solicited mass mailing of propaganda would constitute two forms or channels of public expression. *Public propaganda*, which necessarily pertains to forms and channels of public expression, includes the publication of printed matter offered to the public within privately owned buildings, such as bookstores and libraries, or through the mails. What is said in the home, or in private conversation or personal correspondence, belongs to *forms and channels of private expression*.

57   The truth of the Catholic religion could be juridically relevant for civil authority for some purposes other than determining the limits of FRM (e.g., legislation limiting freedom in nonreligious matters). In my view, the doctrine of *DH* entails that there is a natural right to *general public RF* – a civil freedom of public propaganda and manifestation in religious matters in, and common to, all appropriate forms and channels of public expression within the limits of a just public order; and as to which the truth of the Catholic religion, or of any other positive religion or natural religion (and/or the desirability of it being believed) is necessarily deemed not juridically relevant to the determination of what constitutes a *just public order.*

58   The omitted argument referred to in the accompanying text is contained in my as yet unpublished article, "With How Great Care: The Authentic Meaning of the Doctrine of Pius IX's *Quanta Cura* and the *Syllabus of Errors* Concerning Freedom in Religious Matters." But let the following brief summary suffice. As Fr. Harrison explains in his book (RLC, 51–2, n46): "According to Lewis and

Fr. Harrison and I currently agree that, as disclosed in [nineteenth] century papal documents, preconciliar Catholic doctrine included the proposition that there is no natural right to

Short *(A Latin Dictionary,* p. 1994), an offense does not have to be very extreme in order to be a *violatio*. 'With abstract objects,' says the dictionary – and under that heading, certainly, comes 'the Catholic religion' – *violare* means 'violate, outrage, break, injure, etc.' [Fr. William G.] Most asks, 'What if a Protestant, orally or in print, defends his own doctrine. This is hardly *violare*. Not strong enough. So Pius IX would not ask for repression.' [Citation omitted.] On the contrary, not only Pius IX, but every subsequent Pope before Vatican II, did indeed 'ask for repression,' in some countries, where it was a question of Protestants publicly defending their own doctrine 'orally or in print.' .... It therefore seems unreasonable to call in question whether Pius IX would have seen each and every public defence of heretical or infidel doctrine as at least a 'breach' or 'injury' – and hence a *violatio* – of the Catholic religion." Political authority does not presume the truth of Catholicism as a supernatural religion when it duly discharges the office of repressing violators of the Catholic religion *only* to the extent the public peace requires. But it necessarily (at least implicitly) makes that presumption when it represses violators of the Catholic religion in excess of what the public peace duly requires. Political authority is not discharging the office of repressing violators of the Catholic religion in excess of what is required by the public peace just because: (1) it itself does not engage in violating the Catholic religion such as by hostile legislation abridging the freedom of the Church; (2) it appropriately discharges the office of repressing violators of the rights of all persons (prescinding from revealed or supernatural considerations) to security of person, privacy, and property; (3) it represses violators of the natural moral law alone or of natural religion. The contradictories of QC3 and QC4 (rightly understood) do not in themselves entail a denial that there is a natural right in all predominantly Catholic countries (including, of course, nineteenth-century countries) to a special public RF. But each does entail an affirmation that there is no natural right in any country to a *general public RF.* (See note 57 *supra* for the meaning of this term.) On the other hand, the duty of civil authority to repress violators of the Catholic religion in excess of what the public peace requires does not oblige them to do so in cases in which it would be contrary to the NML (assuming that the NML does not preclude the abridgment of some components of RF). Proposition 77 in the *Syllabus* (condemned as one of the "[e]rrors which have reference to the Liberalism of the day") asserted: "In this our age it is no longer expedient that the catholic religion should be treated as the only religion of the State, all other worships whatsoever being excluded." The authentic meaning of the term, "[Catholicism being] the only religion of the State, all other worships being excluded," read in the light of its legislative history, relates to a situation in which not only Catholicism is the solely established religion of the State but one in which it alone of all religions may lawfully be publicly manifested or propagated in the particular civil society in question. Spain and Ecuador circa 1864 provided examples par excellence of civil societies in which Catholicism "was the only religion of the State, all other worships

be civilly free to publicly manifest (or exercise) or propagate any non-Catholic religion during a particular period in a particular country if there then exists certain contingent social-political circumstances; and we further agree that the prudential judgment of the Church was that this antecedent condition actually obtained in several predominantly Catholic countries during the [nineteenth] century. The *certain contingent social-political circumstances*, as disclosed in the papal documents, chiefly include: that a specific country had been overwhelmingly Catholic (at least nominally so) for at least a few generations; that the population was largely poorly educated, if not illiterate or semi-literate; and that the form of government was fundamentally paternalistic.[59]

being excluded." [See article 1 of the Concordat between the Holy See and the Republic of Ecuador (September 26, 1862); article 1 of the Concordat with the Kingdom of Spain; Pius IX (allocution) *Quibus Luctuosissimus* (September 15, 1851 (*Acta Pii IX* 01, 294–302); Pius IX (allocution) *Nemo Vestrum* (July 26, 1855) (*Acta Pii IX* 02, 441–446); Hughey, *Religious Freedom in Spain* (note 55 supra), 22–25 (for a summary of relevant Spanish legislation 1848–1864).] See note 59 infra.

59   The foregoing was proposed to Fr. Harrison in my e-mail of April 19, 2007. He wrote in his reply dated the following day: "This proposal is OK by me." According to him, the above-stated formulation more accurately expresses his true position than some statements in his reply article appearing at WD, #64 ("More recently, I have come to the opinion … that Church endorsement of such comprehensive bans (those allowing *no* public non-Catholic manifestations) [in many Catholic countries in the nineteenth century] did indeed attain the status of at *least authentic doctrine*"); and ibid., n105: ("[Gregory XVI's] clearly implied doctrine [in *Mirari* Vos] that since religious error *as such* threatens the salvation of Catholic souls, *any and every* public manifestation of religious error could justly be repressed (at least in the circumstances he was presupposing and addressing, namely, predominantly Catholic societies in the early nineteenth century. The 'risk' to the 'eternal salvation' of Catholic citizens' was also presented as justifying the government intervention in the relevant preparatory schema for Vatican II, whose authors (notably Alfredo Ottaviani, head of the Holy Office) were very well qualified to identify the content of existing (i.e., traditional Catholic) doctrine."

The *certain contingent social-political circumstances* pertaining to the IPD undoubtedly obtained in Spain during the pontificate of Pius IX. Hughey, *Religious Freedom, supra,* 22–23; citing Joaquín Francisco Pacheco, *El código penal concordado y comentado* (1848), I, 336 f.; II f., 17 f., 35) summarized certain provisions of the Spanish Penal Code of 1848 as follows: "[B]y the terms of the Code the State [would not] permit public manifestations of other religions.... Anyone who might celebrate public acts of worship of a non-Catholic religion was

125

Fr. Harrison and I sharply disagree as to whether the foregoing (what I call this) *Included Preconciliar Doctrine* (IPD) is consistent with the doctrine of *DH* concerning RF.

42. Fr. Harrison and I radically differ upon the precise grounds for coming to our essentially identical conclusions about this IPD. But oddly enough, we agree (for quite different reasons however) that the apparent inconsistency of the IPD with *DH* does not necessarily depend upon the meaning of certain propositions condemned in *QC* or the *Syllabus*. The papal condemnations of QC5 and QC4–5 cannot in any event be actually inconsistent with whatever may plausibly be the true doctrine of *DH*. Nor can the sufficient basis for the IPD be grounded in QC3 or QC4 because either condemnation is consistent with the proposition that there is a natural right to a special public RF, i.e., a civil freedom to act in religious matters with respect to the public manifestations and propagation of *some* non-Catholic religions in *some* forms and channels of public expression in all civil societies.[60] Fr. Harrison (if I rightly understand him) holds that the IPD is to be found elsewhere than in *QC* or the *Syllabus*. I believe that the authentic meaning of the condemnation of proposition 77 of the *Syllabus*[61]

liable to exile ... Anyone guilty of ... persisting in publishing doctrines condemned by the ecclesiastical authorities was subject to imprisonment ... Recurrence in such offences was punishable by exile ... Any Spaniard who might apostatize publicly from the Roman Catholic religion would be punished with perpetual exile." (Ibid., 22–23 Article 3 of the 1851 concordat provides in part: "the government will give its powerful patronage and support to the bishops whenever it is requested, principally when they oppose malicious attempts to pervert and corrupt the souls of the faithful or when they wish to prevent the publication, introduction or circulation of harmful books." (Available on-line at http://www.concordatwatch.eu/showtopic.php?org_id=845&kb_header_id=3454 1.) Pius IX, in his allocution *Quibus Luctuosissimis* (September 15, 1851), approvingly noted how the Spanish concordat provided (as was previously done) for the Catholic religion to be exclusively dominant in the kingdom, of such sort that every other cult would be banished and forbidden. (Fr. Basile, *La Liberté Religieuse* (supra note 16), 1048.)

60   Fr. Harrison appears to agree that the contradictory of QC3 is consistent with, but does not entail, the IPD since he has explicitly stated that it is consistent with the public ecclesiastical law in force circa 1864 "which urged the penalization of all ***public*** non-Catholic propaganda *per se* in overwhelmingly Catholic countries." (*RLC*, 108.)

61   "Aetate haec nostra non amplius expedit religionem catholicam haberi tanquam unicam status religionem, ceteris quibuscumque cultibus exclusis." [In this age it is no longer expedient that the catholic religion should be treated as the only religion of the State, all other worships being excluded." See also proposition 78 of

entails that there is no natural right whatsoever to publicly manifest or propagate any non-Catholic religion. But Fr. Harrison's most recently expressed opinion of which I am aware is to the effect that proposition 77 "has nothing to do with whether or not non-Catholics may practice their religion publicly." (SJR, 109.) But he is quite right in thinking that the *else-where* includes what can be found in Gregory XVI's *Mirari Vos* (#14), the Leonine encyclicals *ID* (##32, 36) and *LP* (##23, 34), and Pius XII's *Ci riesce* (pt. V).[62] (See *RLC*, 15–20, 53–55; WD, #65.)

> the *Syllabus*: "Hinc laudabiliter in quibusdam catholici nominis regionibus lege cautum est, ut hominibus illue immigrantibus liceat publicum proprii cujusque cultus exercitium habere." ["Hence it has been laudably provided by law in some Catholic countries, that men thither immigrating should be permitted the public exercise of their own several worships."] (Trans. in *Dublin Review* 4 (N.S. 1865): 526–27.)] That the contradictory of each proposition condemned in the *Syllabus* is to be taken as having stated Catholic doctrine, see for example Pius IX's allocu-tion to bishops from the entire Church assembled in Rome to celebrate the eigh-teenth centenary of St. Peter's martyrdom (June 17, 1867): "'In the Encyclical of 1864,' he said, 'and in that which is called the Syllabus, I declared to the world the dangers which threatened Society, and I condemned the falsehoods which assail its life. That Act I now confirm again in your presence, and set it before you as *the Rule of your teaching*.'" [*Acta Sanctae Sedis*, 4: 635] William George Ward, *Essays on the Church's Doctrinal Authority* (London: Burns & Oates, 1880), 493 (emphasis added by Ward). See also Leo XIII, *Immortale Dei* #34, text accompa-nying note 22: "To the like effect, also, as occasion presented itself [referring to *Quanta Cura* and the *Syllabus* in note 22], did Pius IX brand publicly many false opinions which were gaining ground, and afterwards ordered them to be con-densed in summary form in order that in this sea of error Catholics might have a light which they might safely follow."

62   **Gregory XVI**, *Mirari Vos* (#14): "This shameful font of indifferentism gives rise to that absurd and erroneous proposition which claims that liberty of conscience must be maintained for everyone. It spreads ruin in sacred and civil affairs, though some repeat over and over again with the greatest impudence that some advantage accrues to religion from it. 'But the death of the soul is worse than freedom of error,' as Augustine was wont to say. When all restraints are removed by which men are kept on the narrow path of truth, their nature, which is already inclined to evil, propels them to ruin." **Leo XIII**, *ID* #32: "Whatever, therefore, is opposed to virtue and truth may not rightly be brought temptingly before the eye of man, much less sanctioned by the favor and protection of the law. A well-spent life is the only way to heaven, whither all are bound, and on this account the State is act-ing against the laws and dictates of nature whenever it permits the license of opin-ion and of action to lead minds astray from truth and souls away from the practice of virtue." *ID* #36: "The Church, indeed, deems it unlawful to place the various forms of divine worship on the same footing as the true religion, but does not, on that account, condemn those rulers who, for the sake of securing some great good

43. When all is said and done, both Fr. Harrison and I agree that "the *civil* authorities of Christendom who actually enforced the traditional restrictions on heretical and Jewish propaganda might also have been motivated largely by political or other non-religious considerations; it is manifest and undeniable that, from all the relevant preconciliar magisterial documents and theological treatises, as far as 'traditional Catholic *doctrine*'

or of hindering some great evil, allow patiently custom or usage to be a kind of sanction for each kind of religion having its place in the State." *LP #23:* "Men have a right freely and prudently to propagate throughout the State what things soever are true and honorable, so that as many as possible may possess them; but lying opinions, than which no mental plague is greater, and vices which corrupt the heart and moral life should be diligently repressed by public authority, lest they insidiously work the ruin of the State. The excesses of an unbridled intellect, which unfailingly end in the oppression of the untutored multitude, are no less rightly controlled by the authority of the law than are the injuries inflicted by violence upon the weak. And this all the more surely, because by far the greater part of the community is either absolutely unable, or able only with great difficulty, to escape from illusions and deceitful subtleties, especially such as flatter the passions." *LP #34:* "But, to judge aright, we must acknowledge that, the more a State is driven to tolerate evil, the further is it from perfection; and that the tolerance of evil which is dictated by political prudence should be strictly confined to the limits which its justifying cause, the public welfare, requires. Wherefore, if such tolerance would be injurious to the public welfare, and entail greater evils on the State, it would not be lawful; for in such case the motive of good is wanting. And although in the extraordinary condition of these times the Church usually acquiesces in certain modern liberties, not because she prefers them in themselves, but because she judges it expedient to permit them, she would in happier times exercise her own liberty; and, by persuasion, exhortation, and entreaty would endeavor, as she is bound, to fulfill the duty assigned to her by God of providing for the eternal salvation of mankind. One thing, however, remains always true — that the liberty which is claimed for all to do all things is not, as We have often said, of itself desirable, inasmuch as it is contrary to reason that error and truth should have equal rights." **Pius XII**, *Ci riesce #V:* "Could it be that that in [determinate] circumstances [determinate circostanze] He would not give men any mandate, would not impose any duty, and would not even communicate the right to impede or to repress what is erroneous and false? A look at things as they are gives an affirmative answer. Reality shows that error and sin are in the world in great measure. God reprobates them, but He permits them to exist. Hence the affirmation: religious and moral error must always be impeded, when it is possible, because toleration of them is in itself immoral, is not valid absolutely and unconditionally.... The duty of repressing moral and religious error cannot therefore be an ultimate norm of action. It must be subordinate to *higher and more general* norms, which *in some circumstances* permit, and even perhaps seem to indicate as the better policy, toleration of error in order to promote a *greater good*."

was concerned, such restrictions were very much part of the State's duty to protect the true religion and the souls of those constituting 'the one Church of Christ.'" (WD, #53.) And, a very important point, Fr. Harrison affirms (*RLC*, 60) that according to the preconciliar doctrine:

> Civil authority ... has the duty ... to *protect* the true religion and the Catholic Church by restricting (to the extent that the common good requires) the free propagation of doctrinal error – both that which opposes reason or the natural law and that which opposes revealed truth. (It then pertains to ecclesiastical and civil law, mutable according to circumstances, to propose norms governing *how much* restriction the common good does in fact require in particular cases.[63]

I. On the True Meaning of the Doctrine of *DH* on Freedom in Religious Matters within the Limits of a Just Public Order

44. My object in this article is not to propound a thesis as to what *should* have been the doctrine of *DH* concerning FRM. Rather, it is to defend a thesis as to what *is* (the actual or most probable) authentic meaning of the doctrine of *DH* on RF. Accordingly, my thesis is that the doctrine of *DH* is essentially that there is a natural right in every well-constituted civil society to a *total* civil FRM within the limits of a just public order – as to which the truth of Catholicism, or of any other positive religion or of natural religion, is deemed not juridically relevant in determining what constitutes a just public order. It follows, therefore, that the *concrete* rights of non-Catholics (of various kinds) with respect to FRM to which they are entitled as being components of a universal natural right are identical whether or not Catholics constitute a dominant majority in any given country, or just a politically insignificant minority. These concrete rights are the same whether or not the country in which non-Catholics reside is one in which civil society recognizes (explicitly or implicitly) the Catholic religion as uniquely true. Strangely, Fr. Harrison is able to assert both that: (1) "we know – mainly from the declaration's *silence* about any possible differences in the application of *DH* in Catholic, as distinct from non-Catholic, societies – that the Council's specific will and determination was to

---

63 See WD, #17, 39–43, 46–48, and accompanying notes, for the most current evidences of the same position.

disapprove any continued restrictions on non-Catholic propaganda *as such*, even in officially Catholic countries like Spain" (WD, #38);[64] and that (2) "*DH* neither states nor implies . . . that the 'due limits' which are inherent to the said natural right must be determined *uniformly*, at least as regards their 'foundation,' in all political communities – those which recognize the truth of Catholicism and those which do not" (WD, #41.)

45. Without seeing the incongruity of asserting both propositions (1) and (2), Fr. Harrison claims: "But *DH* nowhere denies that God, if He wishes, can authorize civil authorities to set the bar for communal conduct higher in a Catholic community than would be fair in a non-Catholic community, i.e., forbidding in the former certain things that it would not be right to forbid in the latter." (WD, #42.) But has God done so under the New Law (i.e., the Law of the Gospel) with respect to limitations on FRM? I submit that the well-informed SOC should emphatically say: "No!" As the *Catechism* #1972 teaches: "The New Law ... sets us free from the ritual and juridical observances of the Old Law [i.e. the Law of Moses]."[65] *DH* makes clear that the New Law, unlike the Law of Moses, does not contain any divine positive law that limits or authorizes political authority to limit FRM more than is independently authorized by the natural moral law. (*DH* ##9–12.) So granted that a particular statute required or even authorized by the now-abrogated juridical component of the Law of Moses for the ancient Israelite nation was not *intrinsically* evil,[66] it could be such as to violate NML absent the overriding or superseding divine positive law.[67] Thus most (if not virtually all) components of the FRM (insofar as it is a natural right)

64 But there is no *silence* about the matter. *DH* #6.3 reads in part: "If in view of particular demographic conditions special recognition is given in the constitution to one religious community, the right of all citizens and religious communities to religious freedom must at the same time be recognized and upheld." Tanner, II: 1005.

65 See St. Thomas Aquinas, *Summa Theologiae*, 1a IIae q. 104 and q. 105, about the judicial component of the Old Law.

66 See WD, n33: "[W]hile divine justice might 'temporarily' authorize what is 'imperfect,' it could never authorize something intrinsically (or always and everywhere) unjust."

67 Thus, for example, some moral theologians and philosophers have held that although polygamy is contrary to the NML (prescinding from divine positive law), it was nevertheless permitted under the Old Law. See, e.g., Antony Koch, *A Handbook of Moral Theology* (Arthur Preuss, ed.) (St. Louis MO: B. Herder Book Co., 1924), V: 488–89; Henry Davis, *Moral and Pastoral Theology* (London: Sheed and Ward, 1945), I: 128–29, and St. Thomas Aquinas, *Summa Theologiae*, Suppl. IIIae q. 65 a. 2

pertaining to public manifestation or propagation are such that some theo-logically possible divine positive law might, in some different scenario, dis-pense governments from the obligation to observe them. Such components as are theoretically dispensable by divine positive law pertain to secondary or instrumental human goods. For example, the seeking, embracing, and the keeping of the truth in religious matters that God wills all humans to have is a primary human good; the complementary secondary or instrumental good is the "psychological freedom and freedom from external coercion" that people should have in order to be "able to meet this obligation in ways that accord with their own nature."[68] (*DH* #2.2.)

46. Fr. Harrison has also apparently failed to notice the following explication in the *relatio* (November 19, 1964) of Bishop De Smedt:[69]

68   Fr. Harrison, for someone who thrives and profits from controversy, has a rather crabbed view of the value of free public discussion and inquiry in religious mat-ters because he affirms the putative right (or should we say potential right) of Catholics to be protected by externally coercive means from a willing exposure to non-Catholic "salvation-endangering" propaganda for the sake of their eternal sal-vation. (WD, n.35; see also #16; the last two sentences in his *imaginary codicil*.) He equates willing exposure of Catholics to such propaganda with willing expo-sure to narcotic drugs, riding automobiles without seat belts, etc. Human dignity does not entail a natural right to a civil freedom as to narcotic drug trafficking and acquisition. But the exigencies of human dignity do call for an ample civil and social freedom of publication and propaganda in religious matters, in sufficiently many forms and channels of public expression, so that free and mature persons are more efficaciously enabled to *rationally* and *responsibly* exercise their right (and discharge their duty) to seek for and discover, and to embrace and also retain, the truth in religious matters in intellectually worthy ways. Perhaps Fr. Harrison will recall his own remark in his RLC, 134: "[A] faith which can survive the challenge of hostile arguments may well emerge deeper, more mature, and more fervent than if it had been perpetually shielded from such challenges by paternalistic legisla-tion." Nevertheless, this essay prescinds from issues pertaining to the Church's *inherent* coercive power, whether by the natural or positive law, to regulate the reading or hearing by Catholics of anti-Catholic matter. Note, however, that the Holy See announced on June 14, 1966 the discontinuance of the *Index Librorum Prohibitorum, AAS* 58 (1966) 455) and decreed on November 15, 1966 that canons 1399 and 2318 of the 1917 Code of Canon Law (prohibitions and penalties per-taining to books) no longer retained the force of ecclesiastical law (*AAS* 58 [1966] 1186), adding nevertheless the continued force of the natural moral law concern-ing the reading of writings endangering faith and morals. The present Code of Canon Law (1983) does not include any provision similar to the abrogated canons 1399 and 2318.)

69   *AS* (1976), vol. III/pt. VIII, 454; translation by Dr. Michael Woodward, formerly Professor of Latin and History, and also Chief Librarian, Archbishop Vehr

Religious liberty is not impeded in any country with a Catholic majority where the Catholic Church benefits from certain privileges, or even an official recognition. This privileged condition, if it is sometimes granted by divine providence and the good will of men, does not of itself exclude other religious communities from the benefit of a true religious liberty. This is not contrary to true religious liberty, provided that non-Catholics are guaranteed that they will not be the object of coercion. On the other hand, the reciprocity is true: when the Church is in the minority, she is not judged to be injured in her rights if she does not share in all the privileges recognized to a more numerous religious community, provided that she is able to lead a free existence.

47. Fr. Harrison, that worthy son of an attorney, astutely identifies the fundamental issue that divides us. It pertains to the meaning of the term *objective moral order* found in *DH* #7.3, which in part reads that the provision by the state for relevant safeguards "against the abuses that can occur under the guise of religious liberty ... should be done neither arbitrarily, nor with inequitable discrimination, but by legal rules in accord with the objective moral order." Fr. Harrison contends that the term *objective moral order* "is to be understood ... to include both the natural moral law and revealed (divine positive) law." (WD, #39.) My position is that the NML alone (thus prescinding from supernatural revelation) constitutes the objective moral order, within the meaning of *DH*. But I must first address some difficulties posed by Fr. Harrison in order to satisfactorily resolve this fundamental issue upon which we strongly disagree.

48. First, he contends that my protest "that admitting divine positive law as a criterion would imply 'authoriz[ing] repression of ... violations of the Catholic religion, as such,' and that *DH* does not allow for such repression" is without validity. He argues that "[a]uthorizing government to repress 'violations of the Catholic religion *as such*' would be handing it a *carte blanche* for the repression of *any and every* religious manifestation that conflicts with Catholic orthodoxy." (WD, #40.) But he misunderstands the meaning of my position. Governmental authority to repress violations of the Catholic religion as such just means that the Catholic religion is to be protected by the law because it is *Catholic*; it being understood that all legislation must be warranted by the common temporal and spiritual good,

Theological Seminary, Denver CO. I am grateful to Dr. Woodward for his helpful comments concerning an earlier draft of this article.

broadly understood as encompassing revealed or supernatural considerations, and/or to give only the Catholic religion special protection as to some matter. For example, a law that prohibits the *unsolicited* mailing of published propaganda attacking certain described definitive doctrines of the Church (e.g., the divinity of Christ, the immaculate conception of the Virgin Mary, papal infallibility) would authorize the repression of violations of the Catholic religion as such, without any implied carte blanche to warrant prohibition of the *solicited* mailing of such published propaganda.[70] On the one hand, a law that prohibits willful disturbances of religious services of *any* lawful religious society would not protect the Catholic religion *as such* even though it would, together with other (civilly) lawful religions, benefit from this law. Were a statute, on the other hand, to make willful disturbances of Catholic religious services a greater offense than willful disturbances of other lawful religions, the statute in that respect would be targeted against violations of the Catholic religion as such.

49. Second, another difficulty posed by Fr. Harrison pertains to how he had first believed, quoting from an earlier writing:[71] "'[T]raditional doctrine excludes the possibility that, *in a predominantly Catholic society*, there can be any natural right of non-Catholics to be tolerated in the public profession of their religion.'" (WD, #66.) But he presently rejects this formulation because it "would amount to a doctrine according to which this one social circumstance (alone, viz., the presence of a 'predominantly Catholic' population), regardless of any other contemporary cultural, social, religious or political conditions, is *always and everywhere*, a sufficient condition for the moral legitimacy of repressing all public manifestations of other religions." (WD, #66.) Here again Fr. Harrison's reasoning is radically defective. For example, let us assume for argument's sake that according to TCD there is no natural right *whatsoever* to be civilly free in a predominantly Catholic country to publish non-Catholic religious propaganda. This does not entail that it would be morally legitimate for a government to totally prohibit the publication of such propaganda regardless of circumstances. The TCD allowed for governments to tolerate the publication of propaganda to the extent that such toleration was required for the

---

70 I use *solicited* as including (not limited to) a multiple mailing with the actual consent of a free person (an adult not in actual or constructive custody), or where an implied consent or a voluntary assumption of risk of such a person may be reasonably presumed.

71 The quotation is from his "Book Review: *The Second Vatican Council and Religious Liberty* by Michael Davies," *Living Tradition*, 44 (1993): 8.

sake of securing some great good, or for hindering some great evil (Leo XIII, *ID #36, LP #34*); and indeed that some circumstances would require toleration in order to promote a greater good (Pius XII, *Ci Riesce*). Thus a law that unjustly or improvidently limits FRM would not necessarily abridge RF insofar as it is a natural right – assuming there is no natural right *whatsoever* to be civilly free in a predominantly Catholic country to publish non-Catholic religious propaganda.[72]

50. Third, another proposition contained in Fr. Harrison's syllabus of my errors is my contention that we must distinguish between *natural rights* (i.e., those rights that human persons have by virtue of the natural law because such rights are *proximately*[73] grounded upon the exigencies of human dignity), and the class of (what I call) *natural-law rights* (i.e., rights that obtain by virtue of the NML whether or not *proximately* grounded upon the exigencies of human dignity). Thus, among *natural-law rights* are rights (even if not themselves natural rights) that are grounded upon the exigencies of the common good. (CH, ##50–52.) Thus A has a common-good right to be civilly free to do (or not do x) where the common good requires that civil society tolerate the doing (or not doing) of x because it would otherwise be unjust (as opposed to being just inexpedient) not to do so. Let these rights be called *common-good rights*. Fr. Harrison "passes over quickly over [my] opening volley because it depends entirely on a [specious] distinction." (WD, #63.) This is a rather strange way of disposing of my ground for the distinction – something based upon what Fr. Harrison himself appears to have unintentionally suggested. In his review of Michael Davies' book, Fr. Harrison refers to how "more recent Popes, especially Pius XII in *Ci riesce* [implied or insinuated that]: if at times the state has no God-given right to repress certain errors, that seems to imply that those who propagate them do have a God-given right, under those circumstances, to be immune from such

---

72 Because of our differences of opinion on this, and related matters, I hesitate to concede that propositions X, Y, and Z in WD. ##1–3 accurately "summarize[s] as clearly as possible the central issue about which [we] continue to disagree." (Ibid., #1.) Moreover, the term *modern circumstances* in proposition Y appears to be used by Fr. Harrison to only to *contemporary circumstances* starting sometime during the twentieth century.

73 See CH, #51 where I used the term *basic ground* instead of *proximate ground*. The term *proximate* (in the sense of *closely*) perhaps better expresses my meaning since it is plausible to maintain that all legislation legitimately promoting or protecting the common good is *remotely* grounded upon the exigencies of human dignity.

repression."[74] But you will look in vain for anything in Pius XII's *Ci Riesce* (Davies, supra note 23, 303–15) for anything that grounds a duty of political authority in some predominantly Catholic countries to guarantee the free public exercise or propagation of some non-Catholic religions upon the exigencies of human dignity. Rather the circumstances permit, or even at times require, the civil toleration of public moral or religious error in order to promote a greater good or avoid a greater evil pertaining to civil society in general or to the Church. Fr. Harrison also notes that "article 7 of the preparatory schema for Vatican II [which] asserts that the [non-Catholic] state 'should concede' that sort of immunity [i.e., the right of non-Catholics to immunity from coercion in publicly practicing their religion within the bounds of natural religion in predominantly non-Catholic countries]; and there seems only a short distance between saying that these non-Catholics 'should' be given this immunity and saying they have a right to be given it."[75] But here again the reader will look in vain in the preparatory schema for anything remotely suggesting that a FRM within the bounds of the natural religion in non-Catholic countries is proximately grounded upon the exigencies of human dignity, but rather in terms of spiritual and secular aspects of the common good of the political community and of the Church.

51. The foregoing discussion is directed towards showing how Fr. Harrison implausibly urges that although "pre-Vatican II papal doctrine never positively taught that there *could* in fact be circumstances in which non-Catholics might have a natural right to the said immunity [i.e., immunity from coercion by civil authority as to the public manifestation or

---

74   "Book Review: The Second Vatican Council and Religious Liberty *by Michael Davies*," 44 *LT* (1993): 6. Indeed before his *Ci riesce* (1953), Pius XII expressly had declared in his Allocution to the Sacred Roman Rota, October 6, 1946: "The ever increasing frequency of contacts and the promiscuity of the various religious confessions within the same country have led the civil tribunals to follow the principle of 'tolerance" and 'freedom of conscience.' And indeed there is a tolerance, political, civil, social, toward the adherents of other faiths which is, under these circumstances, a moral obligation also for Catholics." (IAAS 38/12 [1946]: T. Lincoln Bouscaren, *Catholic Law Digest: Officially Published Documents Affecting the Code of Canon Law* 1942–1953 (Milwaukee: Bruce Pub. Co.) 3: 652.)

75   "Book Review."44 LT (1993): 6. The English and Latin texts of the preparatory schema can be found respectively in Davies, *The Second Vatican Council* (note 23 supra), 295–302 and in *Acta et Documenta Concilio Oecumenico Vaticano II Apparando* (Typic Polyglottis Vaticanis, 1968): s.II/vol.II/pt.IV/ 657–672.

propagation of some non-Catholic religions] ... neither ... did the teaching of the magisterium ... *exclude* such a possibility, especially as regards societies with non-Catholic and non-Christian majorities." (WD, #2.) The implausibility is even more striking if the reader recalls that Fr. Harrison acknowledges that according to the TCD governments in many predominantly Catholic countries during the nineteenth century were warranted in repressing all public manifestations and propaganda of non-Catholic religions. (WD, ##53, 65–67.) But now he contends "that according to traditional *doctrine*, there can [*sometimes*] (i.e., from Pentecost until Judgment Day) be a natural right of [some] non-Catholics 'in predominantly Catholic states' to be tolerated in the public profession of their religion."[76] This seems, to paraphrase Fr. Harrison (WD, #54), a very "bland (and, as it were, 'toothless') interpretation" of TCD.

52. How odd Fr. Harrison's novel thesis appears to be, especially so since he has previously held that there is no natural right whatsoever to freedom of non-Catholic manifestation and propaganda in predominantly Catholic countries, even after the promulgation of *DH*. That these constructions are rather bizarre is all the more evident in the light of Fr. Harrison's statements in his book frankly acknowledging that: (1) "[*DH*] was intended to be addressed to the modern world in general, and to the separated Christian communities in particular" (*RLC*, 49); and (2) "[W]e have had an Ecumenical Council promulgating a Declaration which *sounds* more liberal than it really is. Conscious of the Church's public image at a time when dialogue with non-Christians and non-Catholics was being given high priority, Vatican II gave prominence to language which seems to allow for very few government restrictions on religious

76 WD, #70. I have substituted "*sometimes*" for "never"; and "some" for "any." However, my paraphrased quotation is in accord with Fr. Harrison's intention in the relevant paragraph. See also WD, #2: "The Declaration's new and authoritative answer is that there can indeed be circumstances wherein governmental prohibition of public non-Catholic religious activity – at least in its normal and more innocuous forms – would violate the natural right to religious freedom of the non-Catholics in question." Fr. Harrison forcefully protests that I have misunderstood his point about what he thinks is Vatican II's "implied teaching that '*[s]ome* peaceful non-Catholic propaganda (in at least some times and/or places) has a right to immunity from civil prohibition.'" He insists that he manifestly "meant the word 'some' in the most extensive sense, i.e., as meaning some propaganda *in at least some times and/or places*." (WD, n2; see also ibid., #38.). I persist in my view that the objective meaning of what he wrote, quite apart from what he actually intended to mean, is that his proposition pertains also (but chiefly) to predominantly Catholic countries. See CH, ##7–8 and accompanying notes.

propaganda" ("Roma Locuta Est," 42); (3) "[T]he use of the [term *public order* in *DH*] seemed to imply that the state can never intervene unless religious (or anti-religious) activity involves actual rioting, fraud, public obscenity, instigations to violence or sedition, and so on: the kind of thing we normally think of as breaches of 'law and order' or 'disturbing the peace.'" ("Roma Locuta Est," 42.) Fr. Harrison seems driven to construe the text of *DH* in (what I can only bluntly characterize as) a far-fetched manner because he wants, at all costs, to sustain the implausible thesis that relevant preconciliar doctrine and that of *DH* are actually consistent.[77]

53. Nevertheless, Fr. Harrison is quite right: the central issue pertains to the meaning of *objective moral order* as well as that of *just public order*. His position is that the *objective moral order* (as used in *DH*) "is to be understood . . . to include both the natural moral law and revealed (divine positive) law." (WD, #39.) He explains the issue so well (WD, #47):

> Let us suppose, concretely, that my adversary could prove his claim that the [Council] Fathers intended "the objective moral order" in *DH* #7 to mean the natural moral law *alone*. On that basis, the revealed or supernatural considerations [n73] which underpinned the Church's more intolerant preconciliar stance would have to be judged 'inadmissible evidence' by State authorities – even in solidly Catholic countries – in determining legal limits on religious activity. In other words, it would then follow that the very *meaning* of the terms "rights of all citizens" and "public morality" in *DH* #7 would be restricted to those rights and moral norms which can be directly and persuasively established on the basis of "secular" or philosophical ethics, i.e., unaided human reason.[78]

54. It is quite evident how this appraisal conforms to the first two

---

77 Fr. Harrison dismisses the probative value of postconciliar changes in Spanish law as evidence that there was doctrinal change involving inconsistency because the Spanish legislators were "usually practical men, not theologians or natural-law philosophers." (WD, #32.) But the changes in Spanish law were done only after governmental negotiations with and approval by the Holy See – as required by the Concordat of 1953. Cf. Teodoro Jiménez-Urresti, "Religious Freedom in a Catholic Country: The Case of Spain," in *Religious Freedom* (*Concilium* volume 18) (New York: Paulist Press, 1966), 104–107.

78 The accompanying note after "revealed or supernatural considerations" reads: "These would have been, principally, the unique truth of the Roman Catholic religion and the consequent threat to the eternal salvation of Catholic citizens arising

sentences in Fr. Harrison's *imaginary codicil* "inserted immediately after *DH #7*, ([and] "logically quite consistent with all of the real conciliar text that precedes it"): "All that has been said so far in Chapter I expounds the right to religious liberty from the standpoint of reason and natural law alone. That is, it prescinds from divine revelation in order to consider the requirements of natural human dignity abstractly considered." (WD, #16.) The balance of the imaginary codicil, however, presupposes we are to take revealed or supernatural considerations into account when interpreting the terms *objective moral order*, *public morality*, and *rights of all citizens* in *DH #7.3*. My adversary urges that my construction of the foregoing terms such that they involve NML alone "would not only be a complete novelty – and for that reason alone be excluded from doctrinal status by Catholic tradition [n74] – but would actually fly in the face of traditional doctrine if it were itself proposed as doctrine." (WD, #47.) But, in the first place, my construction does not "fly in the face" of that traditional doctrine referred to in *DH # 1.3* because said doctrine pertains to a moral duty common to both individuals and societies, and not to only civil societies with its exclusive power of external coercion for the common good. In the second place, note 74 in WD cites only to a statement of doctrine by Vatican I concerning divine revelation – and the doctrine of *DH* is fully grounded in the NML insofar as it concerns rights pertaining to the public anti-Catholic manifestations and propaganda.

55. I shall not repeat the arguments in my article that the term *objective moral order* means the NML alone. (CH, ##28–32.) But I do need to respond to the more important of Fr. Harrison's counter-arguments in his reply article which I have not already addressed. He demands, as his short

from the spread of heresy in society." (WD, n73.) Moreover, if the truth of Catholicism as a supernatural religion is not judicially cognizable in determining the limits of FRM, then political authority cannot in the course of that enterprise enact laws repressing spiritual offenses, or otherwise predicate culpability or assess the degree of malice as to offenses such as heresy, apostasy and other sins of infidelity based upon the deliverances of supernatural revelation. Fr. Harrison has so well explained: "The fact that infidelity (considered in its formal, not material, aspect) is one of the least obvious of sins is no reason at all to presume its rarity; for its hiddenness can be explained very well as a result of the completely *supernatural* quality of divine faith, against which it offends. As Bernard Häring observes, 'The dreadful malice of this sin is shown in its true light only through revelation.'" "Heresy – An Uncommittable Sin?" *Faith & Reason* 13 (1987), 26. The bottom line is that *DH* calls for both Catholics and non-Catholics to be equally free from external coercion with respect to matters religious.

answer, "why on earth, if the Council Fathers had meant to teach that natural law provides the *only* legitimate criterion for setting legal limits to religious activity, they did not simply say so." (WD, #39.) But why should they have done so? – since the plain meaning of chapter I of *DH* (i.e., ##2–8) was to describe and define a right to FRM in terms of the NML in a document addressed to all humanity, including non-Catholic Christians. He briefly refers to my "appeal to the authority of *Gaudium et Spes* and *Veritatis Splendor*," but dismisses the same as unpersuasive without argument. (WD, #41.) Alas! I should have pointed out in my article that *DH* #3 (Tanner II: 1003) proclaims that:

> [T]he supreme rule of life is the divine law itself, the eternal, objective and universal law by which God out of his wisdom and love arranges, directs and governs the whole world and the paths of human community. God has enabled people to share in this divine law, and hence they are able under the gentle guidance of God's providence increasingly to recognize the unchanging truth [n3].[79]

56. Professor William E. May has well argued that this passage (considered in the light of its accompanying note's reference to St. Thomas Aquinas) together with the relevant texts in *Gaudium et Spes* and *Veritatis Splendor* (as noted in my article) discloses that the *objective moral order* is indeed the NML alone.[80] Fr. Harrison in a desperate ploy urges: "[My] attempt to keep divine positive law separate from natural law runs up against this further obstacle: according to Catholic doctrine, every violation of the former indirectly violates the latter as well." (WD, #43.) But surely this does not entail that the NML incorporates by reference the

---

79 Note 3 to the just quoted text reads: "Cf. Thomas, Summa Theologica, I-II, 91, a.1; q. 93, a. 2–3." Professor William E. May has remarked in his *An Introduction to Moral Theology* (Huntington, IN: Our Sunday Visitor Publishing Division, 2nd ed. 2003), 132n74: "[F]or some reason neither the Abbott nor the Flannery translations of the documents of Vatican Council II include this important note [i.e., note 3 to *DH* #3]. Yet it is found in the official Latin text of [*DH*]."

80 May, *Introduction*, 87–91. ("Clearly, the demands of God's divine and eternal law are one and the same as the requirements of natural law" [ibid., 87].) See text accompanying notes 1–9 in May's article "The Church's Moral Teaching, Holiness, and Personal Vocation" (May 2003), accessible online at www.christendom-awake.org/pages/may/holiness.htm; and John M. Finnis, "The Natural Law, Objective Morality, and Vatican Council II," in William E. May, ed., *Principles of Catholic Moral Life* (Chicago: Franciscan Herald Press, 1981), 113–50.

divine positive law, anymore that the NML incorporates by reference such Church or State law which we are obliged by the NML to obey. Almost needless to say, Fr. Harrison himself quite frequently refers to the NML alone, thus prescinding from supernatural revelation. (See, e.g., WD, ##16, 39, 4.) And it should not be overlooked that the *Catechism* teaches: "The natural law....expresses the dignity of the person and determines the basis for his fundamental rights" (#1956), which include the "natural right of the human person [to RF]" (#2105); and that "it provides the *indispensable* moral foundation for building the human community" (#1958; emphasis added).

57. Finally, as to the meaning of *objective moral order,* I refer the reader to the relatio in which it was stated:[81]

> It pertains to the right of the public power to restrain the public exercise of religion on occasion, if it gravely injures the public order. Thus, in effect, the public power acts in the civil order, and not in the religious order as such. But on the other hand, it is not permitted for the public power to impede by the law or by administrative action the public exercise of any religion whatever it may be, supporting itself on a motive that this or that religion is judged false, or that its exercise proceeds from an erroneous conscience, or that it injures the good of the Church. For in such a case the coercive action of the public power would be operating in the order of religion as such, which is not permitted.

58. From all the foregoing elucidation of *objective moral order,* it follows that the putative right of Catholics not to be subjected to temptations against their faith presented by public non-Catholic propaganda and manifestations cannot be among the *rights of all citizens* because the so-called right in question presupposes that Catholicism, by virtue of revealed or supernatural considerations, has (explicitly or implicitly) been juridically deemed true.[82] Similarly what constitutes a breach of public morality is also determined by a consideration of the natural moral law

81 *Relatio de textu emendato, AS* (1976), vol. III/pt. VIII, 462–63 (dated November 11, 1964); distributed on November 19, 1964 to the Council Fathers. Trans. by Dr. Michael Woodward. Cf. #49 and n69 *supra.*

82 Instances of improper proselytizing in the sense of *DH* # 4 (i.e., "any kind of action that savours of undue pressure or improper enticement, particularly of the poor or uneducated") that are also violations of the *rights of all citizens* should likewise be determined without presupposing the truth of Catholicism as a supernatural religion.

alone,[83] because here too it is inadmissible to juridically presuppose the truth of Catholicism as a supernatural religion. Although it is clear enough that Fr. Harrison's thesis that the *objective moral order* encompasses both the NML and divine positive law is erroneous, it is still useful to briefly address some important remaining points made in his reply article.[84]

59. First, he claims that the *rights of all citizens* is justly used *quasi-synonymously* for *rights of others* because "the citizen who commits a (justly penalized) offense … is not violating any right insofar as it is *his own*, only insofar as it is a 'right *of others*.'" (WD, #10.) This is a rather captious objection because necessarily the *rights of all citizens* constitute a class of rights predicable of even a violator of a component right.

60. Second, he protests that I "naturally create the [erroneous] impression that, according to [him], Vatican II teaches that Catholics *today* have a right to be protected by law from such temptations against their faith." (WD, #12.) True, he does not hold that it would be to the common good *today* for civil authority to enact and enforce laws to protect Catholics from such temptations. But Fr. Harrison has only himself to blame for this naturally created impression because in his book he speaks of a "right of at

83 Some writers use some notion of *public morality* as a device by which all the traditional uses of the police power in the Catholic State to outlaw or severely limit the public propagation or manifestation of non-Catholic religions can be maintained upon the ground that it is against public morality to engage in such activities. But other writers in discussing the civil toleration of public rites of unbelievers in traditional Catholic countries, distinguish between those rites contrary to natural morality, and other rites (which although superstitious) contrary to the Christian religion but not intrinsically evil or contrary to natural morality alone. See, e.g., Francisco Suarez, *De Triplici Virtute Theologica, Fide, Spe, et Charitate* (1621), in Gwaldys L. Williams, ed., *Selections from Three Works of Francisco Suarez, S.J.*, (Oxford: Clarendon Press, 1944), 2: 244–45. Cardinal Ottaviani himself saw fit to distinguish in his proposed schema (#5) the right of civil authority to protect public morality from its right to protect people against the seductions of religious error in order to preserve civil unity in religious matters and to defend them against the spreading of false doctrines which put their eternal salvation at risk. Davies, *The Second Vatican Council* (*supra* note 23, 300) (*Acta et Documenta, supra* note 75, 666).

84 All points made in WD not specifically addressed in this response have been either (at least implicitly) answered in this article, or I have concluded that they are relatively unimportant. (E.g., Fr. Harrison's implausible claim in WD, # 6 that I am "further to the left than Fr. Murray.") Accordingly, my silence as to any point not specifically mentioned herein should not be deemed a concession.

least the more moderate and upright non-Catholic groups to immunity from government interference tak[ing] precedence over the right of Catholics not to be 'led into temptation' towards sins against the faith, as a result of the diffusion of false religious ideas." (*RLC*, 142.) Evidently he uses *right* at times to refer to a logically possible juridically recognizable interest, or to *moral* rights of others (in the sense of *DH* #7.2). In such a situation, the clear meaning of the passage in question is that one putative right trumps another.

61. Third, he sometimes uses *public order* to refer to the constitutional order of a civil society or an integrated social order, as if such usage conforms to the meaning of the term in *DH*.[85] To be sure, to engage in seditious activities aimed at overthrowing a constitutional order by force or violence, or similar overt acts, would constitute a breach of a just public peace. However, *public order* as used in *DH* refers only to that which is essential or indispensable for the existence of *any* morally legitimate constitutional order, not therefore to the particular constitutional order of a given civil society.

62. Fourth, he charges that "it would clearly beg the vital question simply to *assume* that, according to Paul VI and the Council Fathers, the Church was always wrong in former times whenever she judged that non-Catholic religious manifestations as such endangered one or more of those essential social values [constituting a *just public order*]."[86] (WD, #16.) But

---

85   See, e.g., WD, ##14, 19. Fr. Harrison also writes "at least under some historical circumstances, even simple membership in the Freemasons and other heretical sects could have been justly considered a presumptive threat to the public order of Christendom" (WD, #14); and this because "heresy radically undermined the foundations of Christendom as an integrated social order" (WD, #19). But, on the contrary, the establishment of Christendom as an integrated social order required a comprehensive repression of virtually all public (and much private) propagation and manifestation of non-Catholic religions. He also makes reference to "activities [by Islamic *jihadists*] ... aimed ultimately at overthrowing Western public order and replacing it with *sharia*, the Q'uran's religious legal code." (Ibid.) In my view, only private or public activities involving terrorism, insurrection, usurpation of public authority, or other unlawful force or violence (including other methods not restricted to peaceful propaganda urging constitutional change) calculated to subvert or overthrow the so-called western *public order* constitute juridically cognizable threats to the *just public order* within the meaning of *DH*. But, in any event, engaging in these activities does not even constitute exercising a freedom in *religious* matters.

86   Fr. Harrison himself has justly observed (*RLC*, 47): "If we take a global view of human society and history (and Vatican II certainly tried to do that), it is obvious

---

I make no claim that "the Church was always wrong [etc.]" – either as an assumption before or as a conclusion after due inquiry. Indeed, it is Fr. Harrison who begs the question in part since he presupposes the truth of his thesis as to the meaning of *objective moral order.*

63. Fifth, my learned critic confidently asserts "earlier writers often seem to have appealed to the 'common good' as a limiting criterion on religious propaganda when they really had in mind the 'public order' in Vatican II's sense of the term." (WD. #18.) But this is not the case. The term *public order* is used in *DH* because *common good* was deemed to be far too encompassing as a "limiting criterion" for the external coercive power of political authority. Thus, for example, consider the following passage from De Smedt's *relatio* of November 19, 1964 (*AS* [1976], vol. III/pt. VIII, 454; trans. by Dr. Michael Woodward):

> In the draft of the declaration that we proposed last year, we affirmed that the exercise of religious liberty was limited by the common good. But very numerous Fathers have remarked with just reason that this rule is too broad and opens the way to multiple abuses.

Thus the decision to use the term *public order* was only for the purpose of more aptly naming that three-fold fundamental part of the *common good* described in *DH* #7.3, rather than giving just another name for the traditional notion the *common good*. (*AS* [1978], vol. IV/pt. VI, 722; trans. in *RLC*, 90–91.)

64. Fr. Harrison persists in making a "big deal" out of some remarks made *in oratione* (i.e., orally but not in writing)[87] by Bishop De Smedt in his final *relatio* to the effect that the norm for the care of religion is the culturally relative common good.[88] But I persist in believing that the hermeneutic value of these remarks is grossly exaggerated by my critic given the fact that the term *common good* had historically provided the warrant for the comprehensive repression of non-Catholic public

that many false ideas and immoral practices, propagated or carried out in the name of some religion or other – even the Catholic religion, at times – *have been by their very nature* injurious to a *just* public order, even if we take into account the elements of relativity in differing historically and culturally conditioned legal and moral codes."

87 I concede that I should not have described in my article the bishop's remarks as having been made "surely extemporaneous[ly]." (CH, #15.)

88 WD, ##20–24. The bishop's remarks appear in *AS*, vol. IV/pt. VI, 723; trans. by Fr. Harrison at *RLC*, 89 and WD, #20.

propaganda and manifestation in Catholic states.[89] I look upon the bishop's remarks as at worst misleading and at best ambiguous since the bishop himself noted that the common good includes a care for RF. (*AS*, vol. IV/pt. VI, 722; trans. in *RLC*, 90.)

Conclusion

65. The doctrine of *DH*, rightly understood, is incompatible with preconciliar doctrine because in determining what are the legitimate limits to FRM it is necessary for this purpose (and not necessarily for others) to prescind from presupposing the truth of the Catholic religion and from other supernatural considerations.[90] But since the doctrine of *DH* is

---

89   See "Roma Locuta Est" (note 7 *supra*), 41: "[D]uring the final days of the conciliar debates on religious liberty, the conservative consortium known as the International Group of Fathers ... requested that the term 'common good' be substituted for 'public order' as the criterion which governments might appeal to in order to limit activities carried out in the name of religion. If this change were made, they informed the drafting committee, the several hundred members of this group would be prepared to give an affirmative vote to the document ... [H]owever, that 'the desired changes ... were not made.' The reason these conservative Fathers would have been satisfied with 'common good' is quite simple: that is precisely the criterion which Catholic governments, in conformity with Church teaching, had always appealed to in order to limit, or even prohibit entirely, the public manifestation of anti-Catholic doctrines or rites in predominantly Catholic societies. It is simply historical fact that practically ever since the emancipation of Christianity in the fourth century, the ordinary Magisterium of the Roman Pontiffs and the world's Catholic Bishops had insisted with the utmost constancy and firmness that such restriction is in itself morally legitimate, and may be imposed in the interests of the 'common good' of society, since heresy and apostasy are dangers to the eternal salvation of Catholic citizens, whose welfare – spiritual as well as temporal – is the legitimate concern of civil authority." Thus it appears that my adversary puts his own intransigent "spin" on the Council's intentions when he submits that Bishop De Smedt viewed *common good* and *public order* as essentially synonymous terms. (See "Roma Locuta Est," 42; WD, n39.)

90   In my opinion this is consistent with the current position of the papal magisterium. See, e.g., John Paul II, *Redemptor hominis* (1979) # 17 [http://www.vatican.va/edocs/eng0218/_pi.htm]: "This is the document called *Dignitatis Humanae*, in which is expressed not only the theological concept of the question [i.e., the right to religious freedom together with the right to freedom of conscience] but also the concept reached from the point of view of natural law, that is to say from the 'purely human' position, on the basis of the premises given by man's own experience, his reason and his sense of human dignity. Certainly the curtailment of the religious freedom of individuals and communities is not only a painful experience but it is above all an attack on man's very dignity, independent-

nondefinitive, Catholic theologians, philosophers, and others interested in the matter may legitimately engage in a free and responsible inquiry, in accordance with the appropriate norms governing such inquiry, as to whether the doctrine of *DH* should be modified in some respects. Careful inquiry, for example, might result in the conclusion that the Council Fathers went too far in judging that every component of RF is a component of a natural right, rather than perhaps a component of just a common-good (but nevertheless a natural-law) right.[91] Perhaps, some components might arguably find their justification upon only prudential or expediential grounds sounding in common-good considerations specific only to a particular nation or group of nations.

66. In my opinion, however, a morally sound philosophy of RF must incorporate the notion that there are hard-core components of RF that are the components of a natural right in religious matters applicable to all civil societies and to the benefit of which Catholics and non-Catholics (including former Catholics) are equally entitled; and that the just limits of public order pertaining to RF insofar as it is a natural right do not presuppose the truth of natural or of any positive religion (including Catholicism), or other supernatural considerations. Among hard-core components of RF are *natural rights* that preclude laws: penalizing spiritual/or ecclesiastical offenses such as apostasy, heresy, or schism; or that which prohibit the public exercise or manifestation of a purportedly false religion (but in accord with the just public order) within appropriate buildings or enclosed structures; or that which prohibit the free expression and propagation of purportedly doctrinal error (in accord with the just public order) in those

---

ly of the religion professed or of the concept of the world which these individuals and communities have. The curtailment and violation of religious freedom are in contrast with man's dignity and his objective rights." (Note omitted.)

91 Fr. Harrison should not be too surprised in reading the preceding two sentences as I had already related these possibilities to him in a letter dated 16 February 1995, at pages 11–12. Although, according to *DH*, the right to RF is a natural right, it is *also* a global common-good right. This appears, for example, in *DH* # 15.4 [Tanner II: 1010] where the Council declares: "For quite clearly all nations are daily becoming more united, people of different culture and religious belief are bound together by closer ties, and there is a growing awareness of the responsibilities of each. To the end, therefore, that relations of peace and harmony may be established and deepened in the human race, it is essential that religious freedom be given adequate legal protection throughout the world, and that the supreme duties and rights of people in regard to the freedom of their religious life in society should be upheld."

forms and channels of public communication substantially less likely to be prejudicial to judicially cognizable social interests (e.g., solicited deliveries of writings, or their sale or exposure within such structures as bookstores, libraries, public meeting halls, and reading rooms).

67. Among soft-core components of FR are *common-good* (but not *natural*) *rights* pertaining to forms and channels of public communication substantially more likely to be prejudicial to judicially cognizable social interests (e.g., unsolicited deliveries, house-to-house canvassing, public open-air assemblies, live or motion picture plays, mass media pictorial publications in places of public accommodation, convenience, or necessity). I believe that, even if some soft-core components of RF are not components of a natural right, *DH* should be understood as teaching, based upon the lessons of experience and history, that every abridgment of RF violates the NML because every such abridgment is contrary to the common good of civil society throughout the world. Furthermore, religious freedom, as to both its hard- and soft-core components, is to the overall good and interest of the Church and the Catholic religion, especially in recent modern times – which, for our purposes, can be deemed to begin with the end of World War II.

68. Moreover, granted that "the principle of religious freedom ... is in accord with human dignity and the revelation of God" (*DH* # 12.1), further inquiry may also be called for in order to assess to what extent the right to RF, beyond what is necessary to secure the freedom of the act of faith, can be independently justified upon grounds that include supernaturally revealed truths, and Catholic doctrine, and the deliverances of the lessons of history and common experience. *DH* does not claim that the universal right to RF is fully grounded in revelation except to whatever extent it obtains by virtue of the freedom of the act of faith. (See ##9.1, 11.2.) Therefore any plausible argument justifying components of RF (in excess of that pertaining to the freedom of the act of faith) partially grounded upon revelation and Catholic doctrine does not entail that it is even implicitly within the deposit of faith or necessarily connected thereto because its probability also depends upon the deliverances of reason concerning empirical matters of fact based upon the lessons of history and experience.

69. In closing, I again express my gratitude to Fr. Harrison for having encouraged me to write my first article and to submit it to *Faith & Reason*, despite his awareness that I am a former Catholic and not even a theist. That Fr. Harrison has engaged in a dialogue pertaining to Catholic doctrine on FRM with an unbeliever is itself evidence of his intellectual hospitality, and of his paramount desire that the subject of our controversy be thoroughly explored because of its theoretical and practical importance for believers and unbelievers alike. He has vigorously, courteously, and ably advocated what he sincerely believes to be true (leaving no stone unturned in the process), nevertheless engaging in our candid and thoroughgoing exchange with the same hope that it will issue into something good. Since by mutual agreement he will have the last word in our exchange, it is likely that he may state things in his response to which I would have liked to reply had we a different arrangement. But in controversy, just as in litigation, there must be an end for the sake of the weary reader if not for the participants.

Part IV:

Dignitatis Humanae:
A Final Reply to Arnold Guminski[*]
Brian W. Harrison, O.S.

A. Some Preliminary Questions

I. Is anyone claiming "a de facto inerrancy" of the non-definitive magisterium?

1. While I thank Mr. Guminski for his courteous words in concluding his final contribution to this debate, I am afraid I cannot be so appreciative of the way he begins it. For he there alleges that I am "operat[ing] upon the principle of a de facto inerrancy of the Church with respect to the exercise of its nondefinitive magisterium . . . [and upon] the principle that there is a de facto impossibility of an actual inconsistency between an earlier doctrine, A, and a later doctrine, B."[1] These "principles," according to my critic, will make "[t]he Church's credibility seriously suffer," because they oblige apologists who adopt them to resort to "quite implausible arguments."[2]

2. Now, this is all quite gratuitous. Not only am I not *"operating"* on any such *a priori* "principles"; I believe I have never written anything that would suggest to an impartial reader that I am doing so. I have always acknowledged the fact of an inconsistency between earlier and later doctrinal teachings whenever I find the documentary evidence convincing. I recognize, for instance, that since the early 19th century[3] the Church's

---

[*]   The title of this essay is abbreviated throughout this book as "DHFR."

[1]   FR, #6.

[2]   Ibid. As we shall see, the main "quite implausible" argument that Mr. Guminski ascribes to me is actually a caricature of my position.

[3]   In 1758 Pope Benedict XIV removed most works promoting the Copernican cosmology from the *Index of Forbidden* Books, but the issue came up again for Vatican authorities in the 1820s and 1830s when *imprimaturs* were sought for

magisterium has permitted Catholics to hold the Copernican cosmology that it forbade them to hold in the 17th century; that since the 1950s it has permitted them to hold and publish certain scriptural theses that were earlier censured by the Pontifical Biblical Commission with Pope St. Pius X's endorsement; and that since 1992 it permits Catholics to "hope" for the salvation of infants dying without baptism,[4] even though Pope St. Innocent I in 417 had branded such a hope as "utterly foolish,"[5] and Sixtus V, in a papal Constitution of 1588, had declared it "certain" that the victims of abortion, since they die unbaptized, are "excluded" from "the blessed vision of God."[6] So my claim of doctrinal non-contradiction in regard to religious freedom is made on *a posteriori* grounds – *after* having studied the relevant documentation. However, the Church's credibility (for which my non-believing adversary graciously expresses concern) will indeed take a serious blow – more serious, in fact, than those inflicted by the aforesaid doctrinal flip-flops – precisely if his own position in this debate is correct. For Mr. Guminski is claiming that *Dignitatis Humanae* not only permits, but *requires*, Catholics to give their assent to a thesis[7] she had previously forbidden them to hold. I do not know of any precedent for a magisterial U-turn as sharp as that.

II. Do mainstream Catholics admit doctrinal discontinuity in *DH*?

3. Given that Mr. Guminski has begun his final rejoinder by depicting my case for doctrinal continuity as not just wrong, but *obviously* wrong, it seems appropriate to expand a little on my previous reminder[8] that the "pro-continuity" party in this debate is by no means some sort of fringe group. Within the Church, the compatibility of *DH* with earlier doctrine

---

heliocentric works destined for publication in Rome itself. Cf. the detailed account of this at times tortuous relaxation process in Robert A. Sungenis, Ph.D., *Galileo Was Wrong: the Church Was Right*, 4th ed. (Stateline, Pennsylvania: Catholic Apologetics International Publishing, Inc., 2008), vol. 2, 232–262.

4   Cf. *CCC*, #1261.

5   *"Perfatuum"* (cf. DS 219).

6   Cf. the relevant text in P. Gasparri (ed.), *Codex Iuris Canonici Fontes*, vol. I, 308. It is also cited and translated by the present writer in Aidan Nichols (ed.), *Abortion and Martyrdom* (Leominster, UK: Gracewing, 2002), 116–118.

7   To refresh the reader's memory, we can express the thesis in question thus: *Catholic civil authorities have always and everywhere violated the natural human right to religious freedom whenever they have forbidden and penalized all public manifestations of non-Catholic beliefs and practices.*

8   Cf. WD, #6.

is usually denied only by those at the liberal and traditionalist ends of the theological spectrum, while it is affirmed by mainstream theologians and leaders of the Catholic hierarchy. So, given Mr. Guminski's concern (as a benevolent outsider) that the spread of views like mine among Catholics will harm the Church, he should, logically, be still more concerned if he takes note of just how widespread they already are among churchmen far more important and influential than Harrison. Leading Catholic authorities have been no more inclined than I am to concede what Mr. Guminski thinks must be conceded in order for the Church to maintain her "credibility," i.e., that *DH* is in effect an historic *mea culpa* – an abjuration and correction of a doctrine she had taught for many centuries.[9]

4. For instance, *DH*'s own "iconic" theologian, Fr. John Courtney Murray, S.J., always denied that the change for which he battled so strenuously implied or required that sort of ecclesial breast-beating. Commenting on the 1862 concordat between Ecuador and the Holy See, which established that "no other dissident cult and no society condemned by the Church" was to be permitted in that country,[10] Murray said it would be an "anachronism" to "denounce the Church or the Republic of Ecuador for a violation of religious freedom in 1862." How so?

> The historical institutions of establishment and intolerance are to be judged *in situ*. They might well be judged valid *in situ*. The function of law, said the Jurist, is to be useful to the people. These institutions might well have been useful to the people, in the condition of the personal and political consciousness of the people at the time. This was Leo XIII's judgment. It would be anachronistic to question it.[11]

This liberality in evaluating the Church's illiberal past aroused considerable disappointment – even indignation – among certain non-Catholic observers who evidently thought along the same lines as Mr. Guminski. The Protestant ethicist Philip Wogaman, for instance, found Murray's position much too close for comfort to preconciliar Catholic "thesis-hypothesis"

9   The doctrine, that is, expressed in Proposition X at the beginning of my previous essay.
10   Cited by Murray in "The Problem of Religious Freedom" (originally published in 1964), in J. Leon Hooper (ed.), *Religious Liberty: Catholic Struggles With Pluralism* (Louisville, KY: Westminster/John Knox Press, 1993), 184.
11   Ibid., 189.

theology: he complained that the American Jesuit "has left the door open for the denial of religious liberty in other contexts."[12]

5. Other prominent churchmen who do not see *DH* as the renunciation and correction of an erroneous traditional doctrine include the distinguished scholars Msgr. Fernando Ocáriz,[13] the late Cardinal Avery Dulles, S.J. (who expressly endorsed my own argument for continuity[14]), Fr.

---

12   *Protestant Faith and Religious Liberty* (Nashville: Abingdon Press, 1967), 59, cited in K.J. Pavlischek, *John Courtney Murray and the Dilemma of Religious Toleration* [Kirksville, MO: Thomas Jefferson University Press, 1994], 168. More severe was A.F. Carillo de Albornoz, an official of the World Council of Churches, who, on the eve of the last session of Vatican II, penned a scathing review of Murray's essay entitled "Religious Freedom: Intrinsic or Fortuitous?" (*Christian Century* 82, September 15, 1965, 1122–1126). Bristling at Murray's claim that the right to (full) religious freedom is something relative to varying levels of popular "consciousness" in different cultural and historical situations, he retorted – though, as Pavlischek points out, "overstating his case" – that this approach "would in fact permit all situations of intolerance in the past, in the present and (why not?) in the future to be considered 'valid'." Carillo de Albornoz concluded brusquely that "if the Roman Catholic Church were to adopt . . . [Murray's] positivist, historical and pragmatic attitude," then "the ecumenical dialogue would be as impossible as before" (ibid., 1124, cited in Pavlischek, op. cit., 168–170). I of course am maintaining, against Mr. Guminski, that Vatican II, by declining to condemn the Church's traditional doctrine as false and unjust, did indeed endorse a "historical" understanding of human rights similar to Murray's. In any case, "the ecumenical dialogue" has been flourishing since the Council, partly, no doubt, because not all other non-Catholics are as intransigent as Carillo de Albornoz – an ex-Catholic evidently very resentful of the Church's repressive historical record. But another reason, frankly, may be the Declaration's own lack of perspicuity. Since the said "historical" approach is only implicit in *DH*, and needs to be teased out of the text and *relationes* by the kind of argumentation I am presenting in this debate, there has been plenty of scope for both Catholic and non-Catholic ecumenists – persons usually optimistic and eager in their search for common ground – to read the Council's guarantees of civil freedom for non-Catholics as being more absolute and trans-historical than they really are. (Mr. Guminski thinks that my comments of this sort impugn "the integrity of the authors of *DH*" [FR, n26]. Not at all. I am not suggesting that thousands of like-minded bishops cunningly conspired to weave critical ambiguities into their declaration. On the contrary, the final text of *DH* emits mixed signals precisely because its multiple authors were *not* like-minded! This is a document whose internal tensions and obscurities reflect the sincere but conflicting views of churchmen who spent three sessions of the Council trying to push and pull it in different directions.)

13   Fernando Ocariz, "Sulla libertà religiosa: continuità del Vaticano II con il magistero precedente," *Annales Theologici*, III, June 1989, 71–97. See also n19 infra.

14   Cf. "*Dignitatis Humanae* and the Development of Catholic Doctrine," in K.L.

Bertrand de Margerie, S.J.,[15] the Gregorian University's Dean of Philosophy, Fr. Kevin Flannery, S.J.,[16] and Fr. Basile (Valuet), O.S.B., whose massive (6–volume) dissertation[17] won him both a *summa cum laude* doctorate from Rome's Pontifical Athenaeum of the Holy Cross, and warm public praise from the Vatican Cardinals Joseph Ratzinger, Alfons Stickler, Johannes Willebrands, Jerôme Hamer, Augustin Mayer, and Jorge Medina Estévez.[18] The subsequent Prefect of the Congregation for the Doctrine of the Faith (CDF), Cardinal William Levada, showed no more readiness than did his predecessor (now Pope Benedict XVI) to admit any magisterial self-contradiction over religious liberty. He personally passed on and recommended to me the already cited defense of

Grasso and R.P. Hunt (eds.), *Catholicism and Religious Freedom: Contemporary Reflections on Vatican II's Declaration on Religious Liberty* (Lanham, MD: Rowman & Littlefield, 2006), 43–67. After discussing three competing views about the relationship between *DH* and earlier doctrine, the late Cardinal Dulles (the only American ever awarded the "red hat" for his theological work) concludes as follows: "The most satisfactory position, I believe, is the third: that there has been true progress without reversal, even on the plane of propositional declarations. The teaching has developed in important ways but has not undergone contradictory change. In describing the development we may suitably follow Harrison, who takes note of three features" (ibid., 61). Dulles then goes on to summarize these features as I have treated them in my own writings.

15   *Liberté religieuse et règne du Christ* (Paris: Ed. du Cerf, 1988).

16   "*Dignitatis Humanae* and the Development of Doctrine," *Catholic Dossier,* vol. 6, no. 2, March-April 2000, 31–35.

17   *La liberté religieuse et la tradition catholique*, (Le Barroux: Abbaye Sainte-Madeleine, 1998).

18   On the back covers of successive volumes of Fr. Basile's *magnum opus* (referenced in n17 *supra*) can be found warm endorsements from the first five Roman prelates listed above, as well as a commendatory letter from the Vatican Secretariat of State passing on Pope John Paul II's blessing to the author. Cardinal Medina wrote the preface to the one-volume synthesis of the foregoing work (*Le droit à la liberté religieuse dans la tradition de l'Église*, [Le Barroux: Éditions Sainte-Madeleine, 2004] 11–15). Among the many other scholars who argue for doctrinal continuity between *DH* and Catholic tradition are F. Russell Hittinger ("The Declaration on Religious Freedom, *Dignitatis Humanae,*" in M.L. Lamb and M. Levering [eds.], *Vatican II: Renewal Within Tradition*, Oxford University Press, 2008, 359–382) and V. Rodríguez, O.P. ("Estudio histórico-doctrinal de la declaración sobre libertad religiosa del Concilio Vaticano II," *La Ciencia Tomista*, 93 [1966], 193–339). Fr. Basile, in the abridged (one-volume) version of the work already mentioned, references over thirty other authors holding for continuity: cf. *Le droit à la liberté religieuse dans la tradition de L'Église* (Le Barroux: Éditions Sainte-Madeleine, 2005, 55, nn168–175).

continuity by Msgr. Ocáriz, mentioning that this scholar is a consultor for the CDF. [19]

III. Are the condemnations in *Quanta Cura* irreformable?

6. Another preliminary question concerns the degree of authority attaching to Blessed Pope Pius IX's condemnations of certain liberal errors in his 1864 encyclical *Quanta Cura* (*QC*). Conspicuous by its absence from both the Ocáriz article and the Congregation's private 50–page response of 1987 to Lefebvre's *dubia*[20] is any concession of what Mr. Guminski insists must be conceded, namely, that the said continuity can be defended only with regard to preconciliar doctrine that was proposed *definitively* (i.e., for Catholic believers, infallibly). The distinction between definitive and non-definitive preconciliar doctrine plays no role in the argument of either author, because neither of them concedes, any more than I do, that any point of the latter has now been repudiated by *DH*.

7. Nevertheless, since that distinction has considerable importance from Mr. Guminski's own standpoint,[21] it will be appropriate to devote some attention to it. In my previous essay I mentioned[22] that I regard the

19 Some years ago there came into my hands a photocopy of the Congregation's confidential, unsigned 50–page 1987 response to the thirty-nine formal *dubia* (doctrinal questions) about *DH* that had been submitted in 1985 by Archbishop Lefebvre. It had been written by a theologian who, as then-Cardinal Ratzinger informed the archbishop in his covering letter, was considered "particularly qualified and trusted" (Bernard Tissier de Mallerais, *Marcel Lefebvre: the Biography*, tr. B. Sudlow [Kansas City, MO: Angelus Press, 2004], 545, cf. n68). Since this CDF response makes some of the same points I have been making against Mr. Guminski (especially that *DH* should not be read as an implicit admission that the more repressive, Church-approved legislation in earlier historical periods was unjust), I wrote to Cardinal Levada asking permission to cite this private response in the present essay. In a reply of March 7, 2009, His Eminence declined my request; but at the same time he made it clear that the Congregation by no means concedes any doctrinal discontinuity between *DH* and Catholic tradition by kindly enclosing a published article by the above-mentioned consultor to the Congregation, who argues against any such discontinuity (see n13 *supra* for reference). Also, I feel free to cite a few key words of the confidential 1987 document, since they have already been published by the Society of St. Pius X (SSPX): while acknowledging the "novelty" embodied in *DH*, the unnamed CDF theologian also concludes that the Declaration represents "doctrinal development in continuity" (cited in Tissier de Mallerais, *op. cit.,* 546).

20 Cf. n19.
21 Cf. his reasoning in FR, #8.
22 Cf. WD, n20.

doctrinal theses enclosed in quotation marks in *QC*, together with their collective censure by Pius IX, as manifestly constituting an exercise of papal infallibility as defined shortly afterwards at Vatican I.[23] Now, according to Mr. Guminski, the condemnation of at least one of these theses (the one he calls "QC3") has been contradicted by Vatican II, which he thinks proposes that same thesis as true. It is therefore important for his overall objective in this debate to show, if he can, that I am wrong in thinking its condemnation back in 1864 to have been definitive. For if I am right on that point, Mr. Guminski will no longer be able to maintain that "standard-orthodox" Catholics are now in duty bound by their own religious principles to abjure (at least "presumptively") the teaching of *QC* and embrace, in docility to *DH*, the very doctrine that *QC* had condemned. For of course, those principles teach that a definitively proposed doctrine can never be "superseded" by another that contradicts it. All that is definitive is by its very nature irreformable.

8. Now, while Mr. Guminski realizes that, I think he is also assuming that *only* what has been proposed definitively (infallibly) is, for Catholics, irreformable. But this seems very questionable. To begin with, it is clear that not all *non*-definitive Catholic doctrines carry an equal probability of being true. Some are certainly "more equal than others."[24] Even supposing for the sake of argument that my critic is right in thinking the papal condemnation of the proposition QC3 to be non-definitive, the cumulative authority of its high magisterial status and forceful wording is so weighty that I do not believe any precedent could be found in two millennia of Church history for a magisterial *relaxation*, much less *rejection*, of a

---

23   I am not claiming, however, that it is a solemn *dogmatic* definition, like those of the Blessed Virgin's Assumption or Immaculate Conception, in which a doctrine is proclaimed precisely as *part of* the revealed deposit. The CDF commentary on *Ad Tuendam Fidem* makes it clear (as did the *relator* at Vatican I) that popes can also define and confirm definitively and infallibly truths that are necessarily connected to the revealed deposit without forming an integral part of it. Cf. *Nota Doctrinalis, AAS* 90 (1998), #9, 547–548. For further discussion of this question, see the present writer's article, "The Ex Cathedra Status of the Encyclical *Humanae Vitae*," *Faith & Reason*, Vol. XIX, No. 1, Spring 1993, 25–78. This article, originally published in *Living Tradition*, no. 43, September-November 1992, is also accessible online at www.rtforum.org/lt/lt43.html. I responded to criticism of this article in "The 'Secondary Object' of Papal Infallibility: A Reply to Frank Mobbs," *Irish Theological Quarterly*, vol. 65, no. 4, Winter 2000, 319–334.

24   Cf. *Nota Doctrinalis*, op. cit.,#10, 548–549, and #11, 551, where the CDF states that teachings in the non-definitive category require "various degrees of adherence" (*varium adhaesionis gradum*), to be determined on a case-by-case basis.

doctrinal proclamation such as this. For we are looking at the kind of teaching which *ex hypothesi* falls short of infallible status, but does so by only a hair's breadth (e.g., with everything standing or falling according to the precise understanding of a single Latin word such as *omnino*). In a recent article, John R.T. Lamont has persuasively argued that some doctrinal theses, though not infallibly proposed, can nevertheless be proposed "with such a degree of authority that it is unreasonable to suppose that there could ever be any good evidence against their being true."[25] In which case such a thesis will remain forever irreformable as Catholic doctrine; for it has been proposed as being so close to *absolutely* certain that the Church could never reach a degree of certainty that it is false equal to, or greater than, the degree of certainty with which previous popes have declared it to be true.

9. Now, the Congregation for the Doctrine of the Faith seems to be tacitly acknowledging that Pius IX's *Quanta Cura* condemnations are irreformable in *at least* the way Lamont speaks of here. The scenario Mr. Guminski would evidently like to see is one in which Rome concedes to SSPX-type traditionalists that they are correct in seeing *QC* and *DH* as irreconcilable, but insists at the same time that the latter document has "superseded" the former, so that all loyal Catholics must now withdraw their assent from *QC* and transfer it to *DH*. But the Vatican shows no signs at all of adopting that position. Throughout forty years of still unresolved tension with the SSPX, the CDF has never conceded that *QC* and *DH* are irreconcilable, and so has never required traditionalists to renounce their adherence to the former. Rome seems to sense that such a radical flip-flop – the official repudiation of one or more doctrines taught forcefully in a papal encyclical – would set a dangerous precedent, undermining the authority of other weighty papal documents such as those rejecting contraception, abortion, homosexual activity, women's ordination, and so on. So it is entirely understandable that the CDF should take the approach that requiring Catholics to give their assent to *DH* is credible and justifiable *only* if their assent can still, logically, be given also to *QC*.[26]

---

25   "Determination of the Content and Degree of Authority of Church Teachings," *The Thomist*, vol. 72, July 2008, 402–403.

26   This approach can be discerned in the CDF's admonition to Archbishop Lefebvre of January 28, 1978. Speaking of the right to religious freedom as taught in *DH*, the Congregation says that this point of doctrine "is clearly part of the teaching of the Magisterium, and though it is not the object of a definition, it demands docility and assent (cf. Const. Dogm. *Lumen Gentium*, 25). Faithful Catholics are

10. Indeed, another flaw in Mr. Guminski's "supersessionist" position comes to light here. Against it stands the undeniable fact that the 1965 Declaration cannot hold a candle to the 1864 Encyclical when it comes to imposing obligations. While Pio Nono hurls down a veritable thunderbolt, peremptorily commanding all the faithful to assent "absolutely" to his condemnation of various liberal errors, the language of *DH* is quite mild, in keeping with the Council's avowedly "pastoral" rather than "dogmatic" character. Only implicitly does this document impose any kind of obligation on the faithful; for while it "declares" certain doctrinal propositions to be true, it abstains altogether from reinforcing them with commands or prohibitions. Therefore (supposing the two documents were admitted to be incompatible) *DH* would be quite impotent, in itself, to overturn an existing obligation to accept a teaching as forcefully imposed as that of *QC*. Indeed, the same paragraph of the CDF Instruction that Mr. Guminski quotes as requiring (as a rule) the "loyal submission" of Catholics to even non-irreformable teachings continues with the following guidelines for theologians who might see problems in such a teaching: "[They] will need, first of all, to assess accurately the authoritativeness of the interventions, which becomes clear from the nature of the documents, the insistence with which a teaching is repeated, and the very way in which it is expressed."[27] On the basis of those criteria, *QC* will certainly trump *DH* (especially since a "Declaration" is known to be the least doctrinally authoritative type of conciliar document, coming in third after Constitutions and Decrees).[28] It is also noteworthy that the CDF does not say that the *chronological order* of pertinent magisterial documents is relevant to their relative authority. Certainly, the mere fact that *DH* is the more recent document would be insufficient to overturn the obligation imposed by *QC*, even assuming *QC* to be reformable in principle. Indeed, in the only case I know of wherein two papal pronouncements on a particular ethical question have been

therefore not permitted to reject it as erroneous, but must accept it in the exact sense and bearing given it by the Council, *keeping in mind 'the traditional Catholic teaching* on the moral duty of individuals and societies towards the true religion and the one Church of Christ' (cf. *DH*, 1)" (cited in M. Davies, *Apologia Pro Marcel Lefebvre*, [Dickinson, TX: Angelus Press, 1983] vol. II, 106, emphasis added).

27   *Donum Veritatis*, #24, §2; cf. FR, #5 and n10.
28   Cf. *AAS* 1966, 1202. As can be seen on this page of the index, where the documents promulgated in the last session of Vatican II are referenced, the Council's three Declarations are ranked together after the Dogmatic Constitution (*Dei Verbum*), the Pastoral Constitution (*Gaudium et Spes*), and the six Decrees.

plainly inconsistent, it was the earlier teaching that was correct.[29] Catholic doctrinal development cannot be simplistically linked to the Enlightenment's myth of Progress ("Later is always better").

11. In the light of the foregoing considerations, the question as to whether or not *QC* contains definitive (infallible) teaching appears more clearly than ever as one of secondary importance. For it is in any case still "on the books" as doctrine requiring the assent of Catholics, and will very probably remain there forever. Nevertheless, for the record, I will respond in an Appendix to Mr. Guminski's claim that the *QC* condemnations are not definitive in character.

B. The Central Issue: Has Guminski Shown that Proposition Z Is True?

1. Did the Council *intend* to reverse any existing doctrine in DH?

12. In view of Rome's evident unwillingness to concede that Bl. Pius IX taught any doctrinal error in his emphatic *Quanta Cura* condemnations, Mr. Guminski faces quite an uphill battle in trying to prove his central claim, to wit, that *DH* embodies a doctrinal *volte-face*. For "QC3" is really his *pièce de résistance* – the preconciliar doctrinal statement he thinks is most clearly irreconcilable with *DH*. As to whether there really is any such reversal of existing doctrine, the Council's own intentions in that regard will be of fundamental importance. Was it the *will* of Paul VI and the other Fathers to allow for any such contradiction of existing doctrine? Mr. Guminski claims I have "not cited any ecclesiastical document which declares that Catholics are *obliged* . . . to believe that preconciliar doctrine is consistent with that of *DH*."[30] The short answer is, first, that it is not

---

29 In 1252 Pope Innocent IV instructed imperial authorities to use "force" (i.e., torture) to extract confessions of guilt from those accused of heresy (cf. Bull *Ad Extirpanda, Lex 25* [§26], in *Bullarium Romanum* [Turin: Franco, Fory & Dalmazzo, 1858], Vol. III, 556). This precept, of course, presupposes that such a procedure is itself morally licit. However, nearly four centuries earlier, the use of torture for extracting confessions from suspected criminals had already been condemned by Innocent's predecessor St. Nicholas I as something that "neither divine nor human law in any way permits (. . . *nec divina lex nec humana prorsus admittit*)" – DS 648). The *Catechism of the Catholic Church* (cf. ##2297–2298) has recently confirmed the earlier pontiff's judgment on this matter.

30 FR, #19 (emphasis in original). Mr. Guminski goes on to appeal, here and in his n29, to Benedict XVI's 2005 Christmas address to the College of Cardinals. The Pope explained on that occasion that by rejecting a "hermeneutic of discontinuity"

incumbent on me to produce any such ecclesiastical document; and secondly, that in any case *DH* itself *is* in effect such a document by virtue of its preamble, Mr. Guminski's arguments to the contrary notwithstanding. True, the preamble does not actually "declare" such an obligation; but simply by asserting that the new and old teachings are in harmony, it implicitly obliges the faithful to accept that they are indeed in harmony. But all this needs further elaboration, and two general hermeneutical points will be helpful to begin with.

13. First, we need to remember that one of the reasons why this present debate between Mr. Guminski and myself – and many similar scholarly debates ever since the Council – is even possible is that the meaning of *DH* is by no means obvious on certain key points. Secondly, because of the very nature of the Church's teaching office, which claims to be handing down faithfully the doctrine she has already received, there will always be a very strong *presumption* of doctrinal continuity between important magisterial pronouncements on a given topic, even when neither (or none) of them is proposed as definitive or irreformable.

in the interpretation of Vatican II's documents he did not mean to exclude the kind of "hermeneutic of reform" which would acknowledge the Council's "correction" of certain "historical decisions" of the Church that were bound up with "contingent matters" – that is, "individual details influenced by the circumstances of the time" (as he had put it earlier, when speaking as Prefect of the CDF). But the Pope said nothing to suggest that any preconciliar *doctrine* might have been "corrected" by the Council. I have no problem with Benedict's contention that such secondary and historically contingent injunctions in previous papal documents might sometimes cease to be valid under future changed circumstances. Indeed, I had already said as much myself, even before then-Cardinal Ratzinger made the point (cf. *RLC*, 23–28). I would see as an example of the kind of "contingent matter" he had in mind the repeated insistence in nineteenth-century papal documents that laws recognizing religious freedom for non-Catholic groups involved the "absurdity" of "placing truth and error on the same level." This charge, which would strike most of us today as puzzling, seems to have been undergirded by a paternalistic political theory that is no longer current – at least, not in Western nations. The theory involved an assumption that if a state (Catholic or non-Catholic) establishes the free public exercise of different religions as a right in the juridical order, it is to be understood as thereby giving its positive *authorization and approval* to all these cults. And that would indeed be "absurd," since of course they all teach mutually contradictory doctrines. According to today's common view that sees political leaders as the delegated servants, not the "fathers," of their people, that kind of legislation is to be understood as merely reflecting the State's limited jurisdiction in such matters, not as its bestowal of endorsement or moral approval upon all the different religious activities and doctrines concerned.

14. Now, how might that presumption be overturned in particular cases? One way would be if doctrinal discontinuity is "intrinsic" to the relevant texts – that is, if it is manifest and indisputable from the very words of a given magisterial decision that it runs contrary to earlier doctrine. But when (as in the case of *DH, ##2–7*) there is no such clear and evident contradiction in the text itself, then something *extrinsic* will be needed to overturn the said presumption. And that "something" could only be a clear statement on the part of competent Church authority that the *intention* of the new document is in fact to discard and correct some earlier and erroneous doctrinal teaching. In that case, of course, the ambiguity will have to be resolved in favor of discontinuity. But in the absence of any such authoritative intervention, the "default" presumption of continuity will remain in place, so that any ambiguity or obscurity will need to be resolved in favor of harmony with the traditional doctrine.

15. Applying this norm to *DH*, we must infer that even if the Declaration began with the existing article 2 – that is, without any preamble at all and without making any explicit claims of doctrinal continuity – it would still have to be interpreted in harmony with all points of traditional doctrine. For, as I believe I have shown in section **IIIa** (##12–17) of my previous essay, there is no clear and evident contradiction of earlier doctrine, intrinsic to the text of Chapter 1 (*DH, ##2–7*),[31] which could overturn the strong *a priori* presumption of doctrinal continuity. Nor was there ever any official extrinsic intervention telling the Council Fathers that the document was *intended* to embody a correction of some previous doctrinal error. I made the point in my initial rejoinder to Mr. Guminski that if the drafting Commission had intended the Declaration to include such a correction, "then of course honesty would have required that this be acknowledged openly on the floor of the Council," with evidence being adduced to reassure the Fathers that the earlier doctrine "they were now being asked to repudiate" had never been proposed irrevocably.[32] In the light of what is said in the previous paragraph,

31 Few if any scholars, it seems, have claimed that the concluding Chapter 2 (articles 8–15), which deals with religious liberty in the light of Revelation, includes contradictions of traditional doctrine.

32 Cf. FR, #16, quoting WD, #51. At this point Mr. Guminski raises an *ad hominem* objection. *Harrison*, he claims, is in no position to use this "argument from silence." Significantly, my critic offers no rebuttal of the argument in itself. Indeed, rejecting it would appear to involve the curious claim that the Fathers of an ecumenical council could validly bring about a contradiction of existing Catholic doctrine without intending to do so – and even *contrary* to their own intentions! All Mr. Guminski claims is that, *coming from the pen of Harrison*, the

I would now add that such an open acknowledgement would have been necessary not only for the sake of honesty and transparency, but also for validly bringing into effect the putative doctrinal correction itself. For without it there would be no warrant for any Catholic to interpret the unclear statements and omissions of *DH* in a sense contrary to traditional doctrine.

16. I am not alone in holding that such open and frank explanations to the Fathers would be necessary in the case of any proposal to correct some putative error in existing Catholic doctrine. Few could speak more authoritatively about conciliar procedures than the late Cardinal Augustin Bea, S.J., who had chaired the Commission that prepared the Council's Dogmatic Constitution on Divine Revelation, *Dei Verbum*. Soon after the Council, indignant at some Scripture scholars' claims that article 11 of *DV* had replaced traditional Catholic belief in unrestricted biblical inerrancy by a novel doctrine of restricted inerrancy, Bea argued that in order for such a reading of DV, #11 to be justifiable, the final text itself (and therefore, inevitably, the *relator* who had previously presented it to the Fathers) would have had to admit openly that the Church's previous teaching was being altered. He wrote (my translation): "If the Council had wanted to introduce here a new concept, at variance with that expounded in the aforesaid recent documents of the Supreme Magisterium, . . . it would have had to explain that clearly and explicitly."[33]

argument "fails and becomes a self-inflicted wound" (FR, #17). Why? Because Harrison himself, in earlier publications, has expressed the view that "Paul VI and the Council Fathers were sold the proverbial bill of goods with respect to the meaning of the nineteenth-century papal documents" (ibid.). Now, the words in quotation marks here are Mr. Guminski's, not mine. And they by no means represent my position fairly. What I had attributed to Bishop De Smedt, in his first *relatio* to the Fathers, was "an unhistorical and inaccurate exegesis" of the said papal documents. The logic of Mr. Guminski's objection seems to be as follows: Harrison's argument from the *relator*'s silence (silence, that is, about any intention to correct some existing doctrine) depends on the premise of his honesty; but Harrison himself has elsewhere *denied* De Smedt's honesty ("selling a bill of goods" to someone means deliberately deceiving him); therefore, coming from Harrison, this argument is self-defeating. I reply that I never called in question De Smedt's *honesty* when he adopted Fr. Murray's interpretations of nineteenth-century papal documents in order to reassure the Council Fathers that the new RL schema was compatible with them. I merely argued that he was mistaken. It is therefore my opponent's *ad hominem* objection, not my argument from silence, that fails.

33 *"Se dunque il Concilio avesse voluto introdurre qui un nuovo concetto, diverso da quello esposto nei detti recenti documenti del Supremo Magistero, avrebbe dovu-*

17. It follows from the above discussion that it is not strictly speaking incumbent on me to give any rebuttal of Mr. Guminski's persistent and ingenious (but still, as we shall see, unsuccessful) attempts to show that the preamble does not guarantee in advance the Declaration's complete harmony with previous doctrine. For the mere absence of such a guarantee will in any case be quite insufficient to legitimize the admission of some possible doctrinal discontinuity. This becomes still more evident when we recall that what the Council's *Acta* reveal is not simply *silence* on the part of the *relator*, but rather, his positive assurances to the Fathers that the RL schema embodies *no* intention to revoke some existing point of Catholic doctrine. Mr. Guminski himself acknowledges this.[34]

18. Moreover, it is not only what was said and left unsaid by the Secretariat for Christian Unity and its spokesman that is relevant here. What was said and left unsaid by the other two thousand Fathers is even more decisive. That is, since all of them were clearly and repeatedly told that no contradiction of existing doctrine was either intended or present in the RL schema, and since not one of them (as far as I can discover) ever expressed any intention or desire to contradict any part of that doctrine, their collective silence on this point becomes quite deafening. It means that the Council as a whole did not intend any doctrinal *volte-face* of the sort Mr. Guminski thinks he finds in *DH*. And, clearly, any doctrinal change that the Council did not *intend* to bring about, it *cannot* have brought about. Hence, no contradiction of existing doctrine can legitimately be read into those statements of articles 2–7 that lack clarity – especially as to whether they are being proposed as having been true *always and everywhere*,[35] or only as being true in today's religiously pluralistic "global village."

---

to spiegarlo esplicitamente e chiaramente" (A. Bea, *La Parola de Dio e l'Umanità: la dottrina del Concilio sulla rivelazione* [Assisi: Citadella Editrice, 1967], 190).

34 Cf. FR, n23. However, in the same footnote Mr. Guminski follows this acknowledgment (i.e., that De Smedt's *relatio* for the first draft of *DH* offered an assurance of non-contradiction) with a short and selective citation from his *relatio* for the final draft, which, isolated thus from its context, might suggest that the *relator* ended up by casting doubt upon that previous assurance. Readers can see from my own exposition of this paragraph of the *final* relatio (cf. third paragraph of **B.II.2** below) that this is certainly not the case.

35 Cf. Propositions Y and Z in section I of WD.

II. The preamble (*DH* 1) revisited

19. We can now return to the text of the preamble itself, and to Mr. Guminski's claim that it does not exclude a possible reversal of some part of the traditional doctrine.

1. "Sacred doctrine"?

20. The first obstacle Mr. Guminski has to surmount is the preamble's affirmation that in this document on RL the Council "brings forth" from "the Church's sacred tradition and doctrine . . . new insights that are always in harmony with the old (*nova semper cum veteribus congruentia*)."[36] The key word here for present purposes is "doctrine"; and the fact that it is qualified by neither of the restricting adjectives "definitive" or "infallible" appears to support my case and does not bode well for that of my opponent. On the face of it, the Council is saying here that whatever "new insights" it brings forth about religious freedom in *DH* will "always" be in harmony with the "older" doctrine of the Church, whether definitively or merely authentically proposed.

21. Mr. Guminski's first step is to assert (without argument) that the adjective *sacram* qualifies *doctrinam* as well as *traditionem*, so that the complete expression "is equivalent in meaning to *sacred tradition and sacred teaching [= doctrine] of the church.*"[37] Now, this is already very debatable. The Latin expression *sacram Ecclesiae traditionem doctrinamque* is really just as ambiguous on this point as its literal English translation: "the Church's sacred tradition and doctrine." From a purely grammatical standpoint "sacred" here *might* apply also to "doctrine" – or it might not. However, when we come to look more closely at the true meaning of "sacred doctrine," it will become apparent that the Council Fathers probably did not intend that term to be read into *DH,* #1, and that even if they did, its meaning would still corroborate my own position, not Mr. Guminski's. His second step is to claim that "[t]he term *sacred doctrine* refers to those doctrines which teach about divinely revealed truths within the deposit of

---

36 My critic cites an inaccurate translation which says that from these sources the Church "continually draws new insights in harmony with the old." But *semper* manifestly qualifies the adjective *congruentia,* not the verb "draws" (*profert*), and so must mean "always," not "continually." (In any case the normal word for "continually" would be *iugiter.*) Of course, one might "continually" draw forth new insights in harmony with the old, while occasionally producing one or two that *lack* such harmony. The word *semper* rules out such a reading of the preamble.

37 FR, #20.

faith or necessarily connected truths."[38] The only justification given for this assertion is a quotation from St. Thomas (*Summa Theologiae* Ia, Q. 1, art. 2) to the effect that since revealed knowledge as well as philosophical truth is necessary for man's salvation, it was necessary in God's plan "that besides philosophical science built up by reason there should be a sacred science learned through revelation."[39] My critic's third step is to note that the term "sacred doctrine," understood as he has defined it, does not cover all areas of Catholic magisterial teaching: it excludes those areas (like RL) that pertain fundamentally to the natural moral law rather than to revealed truth.[40] On the basis of these three steps he concludes, quite logically, that this passage of *DH*'s preamble does not, after all, guarantee in advance that everything "new" that follows in the Declaration will necessarily be "in harmony with the old[er]" teachings of the magisterium.

22. Mr. Guminski has undoubtedly constructed an ingenious argument here. But I am afraid it is also a house of cards that collapses under the lightest touch. In the first place it makes nonsense of the whole thrust of the Declaration's first paragraph, which, after proclaiming the Council's intention to "attend diligently" in this document to modern man's increasing demand *for freedom in religious matters,* culminates in the affirmation that the Declaration's new insights are always in harmony with the old. That affirmation manifestly refers to the aforesaid topic, religious freedom – the specific topic of the entire Declaration. Indeed, the said affirmation was one of the "reassuring retouches" that Paul VI ordered to be inserted at the last minute, precisely in order to allay the fears of those Fathers concerned about the schema's compatibility with earlier magisterial teachings on RL. But how could these fears be in any way allayed by an assurance that the Council would "always" maintain continuity with older teachings *in another category that does not include RL?* A newly elected President might just as well seek to dispel voters' fears that he will soon break his promise not to raise taxes by loudly insisting that he will never, *never* break his promise to tighten up border control!

23. Mr. Guminski also fails to realize that "sacred doctrine" (or "sacred science"), in ecclesiastical parlance, has acquired a rather different connotation during the seven centuries since Aquinas wrote. It does not, as

38   Ibid.
39   FR, n31.
40   Cf. FR, #21. Since the relevance and value of Mr. Guminski's paragraphs 22–24 depend entirely on the validity of his definition of "sacred doctrine," which I show above to be incorrect, they need no separate rebuttal.

he supposes, mean only *one part* of magisterial teaching (namely, "about divinely revealed truths within the deposit of faith"). As can readily be verified by a search for "sacred doctrine" (or *sacra doctrina*) on the Vatican website, this is a term now used mainly in the context of catechesis and religious education (whether at an advanced or elementary level), and it designates the entire corpus of Catholic doctrine on faith and morals. For example, Blessed John XXIII, in his first encyclical, speaks thus of the need for a well educated clergy: "Men in Sacred Orders should gain an adequate knowledge of human affairs and a thorough knowledge of sacred doctrine that is in keeping with their abilities."[41] Of course the Pope would have wanted every priest's "thorough knowledge" to extend to the whole range of magisterial teaching, so he would scarcely have used "sacred doctrine" here if, like Mr. Guminski, he had understood that term to exclude a significant part of the Church's ethical teaching.

24. Likewise, in his 1992 Apostolic Exhortation *Pastores Dabo Vobis* on the formation of seminarians, John Paul II defines *sacra doctrina* as follows: "The intellectual formation of the future priest has its natural and principal foundation in sacred doctrine, that is, in theology."[42] And of course, "theology" curricula in all Catholic seminaries include courses on the Church's social doctrine, which includes RL, and on other Church teachings arising more clearly and directly from natural law than from revelation – for instance, on contraception, euthanasia, abortion, in vitro fertilization and other bioethical issues.[43] All topics expounded in the *Catechism of the Catholic Church* would also come under "sacred doctrine." Neither in John Paul's statement nor in any other of the instances of "sacred doctrine" found on the Vatican website is there any evidence supporting Mr. Guminski's claim that the term, in its modern usage, excludes those magisterial teachings that are based mainly on natural law.[44]

41   *Sacerdotii Nostri Primordia* (1 August 1959), #78.

42   "*Formatio autem intellectualis eius qui sacerdos futurus est, fundamentum naturale ac praecipuum habet in sacra doctrina, id est in theologia*" (*AAS* 84 [1992], 751, #53).

43   In any case, *DH* by no means presents the natural right to RL as something unconnected to revelation. While it makes no claim that this right is either *part of* the revealed deposit or deducible from it by strict logic, the Fathers devote the whole of Chapter II to RL "in the light of Revelation," after having already "declared" in Chapter I that the right to RL is founded on the very dignity of the human person, "as this is known by the revealed Word of God" as well as by reason (*DH*, #2.1).

44   The present writer's search in November 2010 for the English words "sacred doctrine" at www.vatican.va yielded only 19 occurrences of this term. Two of these

25. In short, whether or not *sacram* is meant to apply to *doctrinam* as well as *traditionem* – and it probably isn't, since *DH* is not concerned with religious education curricula – the *doctrina* in question most certainly includes that on RL, so that this first paragraph of the Declaration already rules out any supposed warrant for Catholics to interpret any of its subsequent teachings in a sense contrary to any traditional doctrine.

2. The "moral duty of men and societies"

26. Now, the conclusion arrived at in **B.II.1** has consequences. By toppling the first domino in Mr. Guminski's case, it will also topple the next . . . and the next. My critic goes on to address the passage in the preamble's second paragraph which says that the right to RL, as affirmed in this document, "leaves intact the traditional Catholic doctrine on the moral obligation of men and societies toward the true religion and the one Church of Christ." Offering no argument except to emphasize with italics the word "and" following "men," he assures us that "the passage patently pertains only to a moral obligation common to both individuals and societies . . . mentioned in the preceding sentence 'to worship God.'"[45] That, is, while Mr. Guminski "wholly concur[s]" with me that "traditional Catholic doctrine" did itself include the State's moral duty or right to use coercive measures

are from Vatican II, but neither accurately reflects the Latin original. First, following the Flannery edition of the documents, "sacred doctrine" is used to translate the single word *doctrina* in the Decree on Missionary Activity, because the context is again that of religious education: "Moreover, the churches should gratefully acknowledge the noble work being done by auxiliary catechists, whose help they will need. These preside over the prayers in their communities and teach sacred doctrine. Something suitable should be done for their doctrinal and spiritual training" (*Ad Gentes,* #17). This translation further illustrates the point that "sacred doctrine" is now simply taken to mean the whole range of Catholic doctrine (or theology). The other occurrence of "sacred doctrine" linked to Vatican II is in the English translation of Pope John's opening address to the Council on October 11, 1962. However his actual words were not *sacra doctrina* but *veneranda doctrina*, "venerable doctrine" (cf. *AAS*, 54 [1962], 792). If we also exclude two more occurrences of "sacred doctrine" that are in direct quotations from St. Thomas Aquinas, and so probably carry the older and more restrictive sense of the term that Mr. Guminski appeals to, that leaves just 15 relevant (i.e., modern) instances on the website, dating from 1893 to 1993. Of these, eleven (including the two cited in the main text above) occur in passages – or entire documents – dedicated to religious education, and the other four occur in a more general context.

45 FR, #25.

"in the interest of the true religion,"[46] he claims the Declaration has carefully *refrained* from saying that it will "leave intact" *this particular part* of the traditional doctrine on the duty of "societies." How so? Because coercive religious duties are not *common* to both individuals and societies. If they exist at all, they pertain only to the latter.

27. Again, this is all quite ingenious and subtle. Indeed, if such was the Council's intended meaning, then far from being "patent," it is so very subtly expressed that as far as I know, Mr. Guminski is the only commentator who has rediscovered it in over forty years of learned commentaries. The general assumption has been that the Council is here professing to leave "complete and untouched" (*integram*) the full corpus of traditional doctrine regarding: (a) the moral duty of individuals, and (b) that of societies, toward the true Church and its religion. As in the text considered in **B.II.1** above, the wording of this expression is not pellucid in meaning. Grammatically and in itself, it *might* mean what Mr. Guminski says it means – or, again, it might not. Other commentators appear to have thought not.[47] In Fr. Basile's detailed discussion of this "moral duty . . . of societies," neither he nor any of the other scholars he quotes – and they are scholars of differing theological persuasions – even hints at my critic's view that the Council has

---

46   Ibid.
47   For instance, the distinguished Thomist scholar Fr. Victorino Rodríguez, O.P., reads this statement as "ratifying the traditional Catholic doctrine [i.e., not just part of it] on the duty of societies toward the Catholic Church as the true religion" ("Estudio histórico-doctrinal de la declaración sobre libertad religiosa del Concilio Vaticano II," *La Ciencia Tomista* vo. 93 [1966], 308–309). The CDF consultor Ocáriz begins his case for *complete* doctrinal continuity by saying, "Before all else (*Innanzitutto*), one must adopt as an interpretative criterion the explicit assertion of *DH* that its doctrine on religious liberty 'leaves intact the traditional Catholic doctrine on the moral duty of individuals and of societies (*dei singoli e delle società*) to the true religion and the one Church of Christ'" (op. cit. [cf. n13 *supra*], 73). It is clear that Ocáriz takes it for granted that this "leaving intact" applies to *all* the pertinent doctrine; for if he had thought, or even suspected, that this text in art. 1 was *restricting* the scope of this doctrinal reaffirmation, then of course he would have needed to address this, as an objection to his case. As it is, he defends the compatibility of *DH* with *QC*, including "QC3" (cf. ibid., 79–80), which Mr. Guminski considers the clearest example of incompatibility. Consistently with this, Ocáriz goes on to affirm *DH* to be quite compatible with the traditional teaching that "the Catholic Church can and should be assisted *and protected in a special way* by the State (*aiutata e protetta in modo speciale dallo Stato*), arriving at the confessional State wherever possible" (ibid., 93, emphasis added). Such legal "protection" by its very nature will involve coercive penalties for behavior that might harm the "specially" protected party.

limited its reaffirmation of the "traditional doctrine" to those aspects of the said social duty which also oblige individual believers.[48]

28. There are other reasons why Mr. Guminski's novel interpretation of this expression is inadmissible: **(1)** Such a limitation would contradict the previous paragraph of the preamble, which, as we have seen, clearly means that *DH*'s teaching is "always" – i.e., on any subject whatever – to be understood in harmony with the "old" doctrine. **(2)** The phrase *"and of societies"* was what Paul VI called a "reassuring retouch," inserted precisely "in order to respond to the objection alleging discontinuity in the magisterium."[49] This plainly rules out the idea that the added words actually *allow* for an element of magisterial discontinuity. Far from "responding" to the objection and "reassuring" the objectors, the papal intervention would then clearly have produced exactly the opposite effect, adding fuel to the fire. **(3)** In a passage of his final *relatio* that was also mandated *verbatim* by the Pope, Bishop De Smedt acknowledged that those Fathers concerned about doctrinal discontinuity had in mind "ecclesiastical documents up till the time of the Supreme Pontiff Leo XIII," especially the "insistence" of these documents on "the moral duty of public authority (*potestas publica*) toward the true religion." He then assured the Fathers that the revised text, by virtue of the final amendments to articles 1 and 3, "recalls [these duties] more clearly," from which "it is manifest that this part of the doctrine has not been overlooked."[50] This could only have been understood by the Fathers as an assurance that these amendments "manifestly" constituted a reaffirmation of the *whole* "traditional doctrine" regarding the moral duty of "societies" and their public authorities toward the true religion. Nothing in the *relator*'s words even hinted that the revised text intended to reaffirm *only* that part of traditional doctrine which concerned duties common to both individuals and public authorities.

29. Mr. Guminski claims that the only allegation of doctrinal discontinuity that Paul VI wanted to reject as unfounded "appears to pertain to the

---

48   Cf. op. cit., vol. IB, 528–547. (See n17 *supra* for reference.) Mr. Guminski adds in a footnote that the "legislative history of this part of the preamble to *DH* amply confirms" this interpretation of "men and societies" (FR, n40). But his argument for this claim consists of nothing more than a summary of my own account (in *RLC*) of the textual evolution of this clause, which culminated in the final insertion of "and societies" after "men." I fail to see how this constitutes any sort of "confirmation" of my critic's position.

49   Cf. WD, nn61, 63.

50   ". . . *ex quo patet hanc doctrinae partem non praetermitti*" (*Acta Synodalia*, vol. IV, pt. VI, 719).

issue of the moral duty of civil society to recognize and favor Catholicism as uniquely true . . . and not to that special moral duty of civil authority to coercively repress false religions."[51] But, again, there is no hint of this distinction in either Paul VI's handwritten memo or the related passage of the final *relatio* that he dictated at the same time. The Fathers seeking reassurance were of course concerned about the possible discontinuity of *DH* with *any part whatsoever* of traditional Catholic doctrine; and I think readers will agree that the citations in the previous paragraph make it perfectly clear that the final *relatio* could only have been understood as an assurance that no contradiction of *any* nineteenth-century papal doctrine was left lurking in the text the Fathers were being asked to approve. The only reason Mr. Guminski gives for reading the above distinction into the mind of Paul VI is that precepts enjoining coercion against false religions would, he says, belong in natural moral law teaching "rather than in sacred doctrine."[52] But we have already seen in **B.II.1** that "sacred doctrine" itself encompasses magisterial teaching about the natural moral law.

30. It should be evident by now that I need not respond any further to Mr. Guminski's objections: (i) that I have not shown that *DH* considers "guarding" or "preserving" the true religion to be a duty incumbent on societies as well as individuals;[53] and (ii) that I have not shown that any coercive rights or duties toward false religions are themselves *entailed by*, or *included in*, the duty (which he recognizes as implicitly reaffirmed by *DH*) of societies "to recognize and favor Catholicism as uniquely true."[54]

51 FR, #33.
52 Ibid. Mr. Guminski also asserts at the end of FR, #33 that since Paul VI's personal intervention was "private" and was not publicly revealed until many years later, "it lacks substantial hermeneutical value." I think most theologians will agree with me that this is far too dismissive. Mr. Guminski is a lawyer, and it may well be that in interpreting civil legislation that has been in effect for many years, any such details finally coming to light would have to be judged irrelevant for practical purposes. But since documents of ecumenical councils depend radically for their validity on the consent given to them by this one man, Peter's Successor, any new light shed upon what he understood a given conciliar document to mean and teach will always be relevant to its interpretation.
53 Cf. FR, ##26, 30.
54 Cf. FR, ##31–32. According to Mr. Guminski (cf. FR, n47, referring to WD, ##61–62 and nn100–101), I have erred in saying Msgr. Fenton "insisted" that the "entire edifice" of Catholic Church/State doctrine, including such coercive duties, is "squarely based on the bedrock principle" that all societies, as well as individuals, are bound to worship God according to the rites of the Catholic Church. It is true that nowhere in the 1952 essay I cited does Fenton *explicitly* connect the said

For both objections depend on the mistaken premise that the preamble professes to "leave intact" *only part* of the traditional doctrine on the duty of
societies toward the true religion. Since my opponent already "wholly concur[s]" with me that this traditional doctrine did include the legitimacy of
coercive measures in the interests of the true religion,[55] it is sufficient, in
order to rebut the above two objections, for me to show that the preamble
professes to leave *all* of the said traditional doctrine intact. And I believe I
have shown precisely that in this section.

3. *DH*'s intention to "develop" the doctrine of recent popes

31. The third domino in Mr. Guminski's case for detecting a loophole for
doctrinal contradiction in the preamble is his claim that I am only "partially" correct in saying any authentic doctrinal development must always be
in harmony with existing doctrine. According to my critic, "genuine" doctrinal development (which *DH* says it proposes to bring about) can in fact
involve "a contradiction in some respect" between "A, the extant doctrine,
and A¹, the proposed superseding doctrine." Such contradiction, he says,
can take place provided A is not an instance of "dogma or other definitive
doctrine."[56]

32. Now, this domino is toppled rapidly. Even if what Mr. Guminski
says were sometimes true, it could not be true here, because reading the
verb "develop" in *DH* 1 as a euphemism for "partially contradict and correct" would make the preamble internally incoherent; for as I have shown
in sections **B.II.1** and **B.II.2** above, its two previous assurances of continuity promise that the rest of the Declaration will be in harmony with *all* the
traditional doctrine. But in any case, is what my critic says *ever* true? His
claim that this supposed "broader sense" of doctrinal development is
acceptable to "standard orthodox" Catholic theology is virtually gratuitous. He says he "believe[s]" this claim to be true, and "submit[s]" that it
is true; but he quotes no pope, bishop, or Catholic theologian who agrees

duties to that principle. But what is predicated of a whole is of course implicitly
predicated of each of its parts. And that the said coercive duties toward false religions were indeed, in Fenton's view, a part of that "entire edifice" whose foundation he was explaining in this essay is obvious from the whole years-long war
against Murray's views waged by Fathers Fenton, Shea and Connell in the
American Ecclesiastical Review. Indeed, upon what *other* possible "bedrock principle" could Fenton possibly have thought those coercive duties were based, if not
on the one he was expounding in this essay?

55   FR, #25.
56   FR, #34.

with him that it is true. The best he can do is claim that this idea "conform[s] to the declaration of Benedict XVI in his 2005 Christmas message . . . about continuity and discontinuity at different levels of doctrine."[57] But I have already pointed out that there is no suggestion in that papal address that Vatican II contradicted and corrected any existing *doctrine*, whether definitive or merely authentic, but only certain "historical decisions" of the Church that were bound up with "contingent matters."[58]

33. We can now leave the preamble. However, in order not to "lose sight of the wood for the trees," it is worth recalling once more that the whole of this section **B.II** has been written "over and above the call of duty." My case for complete doctrinal continuity does not *require* a rebuttal of Mr. Guminski's elaborately argued claim that article 1 leaves wiggle-room for the subsequent articles to contradict part of the traditional doctrine. For even if that claim were true, it would still be unreasonable, for the reasons given in **B.I** above, to interpret any of the less-than-clear statements in *DH*, ##2–7 in a sense contrary to traditional doctrine.

III. The *Catechism of the Catholic Church*

34. Does the teaching of the *CCC*, however, insinuate that *DH* has not left *all* points of earlier doctrine intact? Or does it at least leave room for that possibility? Mr. Guminski thinks so, and cites #2105 to that effect.[59] He acknowledges that the *Catechism* follows *DH* in confirming the traditional doctrine that societies as such are, by divine law, bound to recognize "in some way or another . . . that the Catholic religion is uniquely true and that the Catholic Church is the one true Church of Christ."[60] But he denies that *Catechism* says anything that could imply the legitimacy under some circumstances of coercive measures against non-Catholic manifestations as such. So we shall need to take a closer look at this text of the *Catechism*. (For brevity in the following paragraphs, the word "Catholicism" will be used to mean what *DH* 1, cited here by the *Catechism,* calls "the true religion and the one Church of Christ"; and "pro-Catholic coercive measures" will be used as shorthand for "coercive measures enacted to protect Catholicism (including faith and morals) from its violators, not excluding, in some historical circumstances, the legal repression of *all* religious manifestations incompatible with Catholicism.")

57 Ibid.
58 Cf. n30 *supra.*
59 Cf. FR, ##28–32.
60 FR, #28.

35. Here are the first two sentences of *CCC, #2105*: "The duty of offering God authentic honor and worship (*cultum authenticum*)[61] concerns man both individually and socially. This constitutes[62] 'the traditional Catholic doctrine regarding the moral duty of men and societies toward the true religion and the one Church of Christ' (*DH 1*)." I have translated *cultum* here as "honor and worship," rather than just "worship," as is found in the standard English edition. This is because we English speakers usually take "worship" quite narrowly, as designating only acts of prayer and liturgical rites. The Latin *cultus* is broader in meaning than this, and includes pretty much everything one does or establishes out of reverence and honor for the deity or deities one believes in, including laws and social customs. The very next sentence of *CCC, #2105* makes this clear, for it explains the social aspect of the required *cultus authenticus* by quoting Vatican II's Decree on the Apostolate of the Laity, which says Catholics should strive to "infuse the Christian spirit into the mentality and mores, laws and structures of the communities in which [they] live." So it is clear that the social duty of "authentic honor and worship" taught by the *Catechism* in this paragraph involves a theoretical and practical recognition of Catholicism's unique truth that goes a lot further than, say, the kind of recognition accorded by Britain and some Scandinavian countries to the Anglican and Lutheran Churches respectively: that is, a mere constitutional lip-service to the nation's adherence to these religions, adorned now and then by state-sponsored liturgical ceremonies carried out according to their rites.[63]

36. Now, going by Mr. Guminski's interpretation of the words quoted from *DH*, #1 in the second sentence of #2105, that sentence would mean that the previously affirmed duty "to offer God authentic honor and worship" constitutes the traditional Catholic doctrine *regarding the moral*

---

61   The word *authenticum* is rendered "genuine" in the standard English version; but the latter word, as applied in modern everyday English to human activity and attitudes, often connotes nothing more than subjective sincerity. ("Dear Jack is a very *genuine* fellow, you know.") But the "traditional Catholic doctrine" which the *Catechism* is expressly reaffirming here was of course very clear that the *cultus* offered to God by both societies and individuals should only be that of the one objectively true religion.

62   The normative text reads, "*Hoc constituit 'traditionalem doctrinam catholicam . . . .'*" The standard English edition says, "This is 'the traditional doctrine . . . ,'" as if the Latin said "*Hoc est . . . .*"

63   Cf. also the observations already made on this subject in my previous essay (WD, #60).

*duty toward Catholicism that is **common** to both individuals and societies*. In that case, of course, the *Catechism* would indeed be implicitly denying that civil societies could ever have a duty to enact and enforce pro-Catholic coercive measures, for such a duty is never incumbent upon individuals. However, on the strength of my critique of this interpretation in **B.II.2** above, I conclude that the *Catechism*, in citing these words from *DH* 1, does not mean them in that sense any more than the Council itself does.

37. Rather, the second sentence of #2105 should be taken to mean (in accord with the commonly accepted interpretation of its *DH*, #1 citation) that the previously affirmed principle regarding "authentic honor and worship" constitutes the traditional Catholic doctrine *regarding the moral duty of individuals, **as well as** that of societies,* toward Catholicism. In other words, the *Catechism* is saying that the *entire body* of traditional doctrine on the duty of civil societies toward Catholicism is encapsulated in, or implied by, the affirmation that man is bound to offer God authentic honor and worship "socially." And since that body of traditional social doctrine certainly included our Proposition X – i.e., the legitimacy in principle of pro-Catholic coercive measures – the *Catechism* is implicitly reaffirming that proposition. In view of this, there is no need for me to rebut my opponent's contention that I have nowhere shown that the Church herself (as distinct from certain theologians) traditionally taught that the right and duty of employing pro-Catholic coercive measures is itself *included* in civil society's duty to recognize Catholicism as uniquely true.[64] Perhaps the former duty was thought by some authorities to be relatively *independent* of the latter – a duty implied rather by the practical, not theoretical, exigencies of that overall "honor" (*cultus*) that society owes to God and the true religion. What matters is that, either way, the Church traditionally taught that this coercive duty of society *certainly exists* – as my opponent "wholly" agrees. So it is implicitly included in the doctrine that the *Catechism*, along with the Council, has reaffirmed. Indeed, if I am correct in my basic claim that the perennial *doctrine* of the Church, conciliar and preconciliar, is sufficiently broad and non specific to accommodate varying degrees of coercion over the centuries according to her changing *prudential judgments* in differing socio-historical circumstances,[65] then this reaffirmation in a universal Catholic catechism is exactly what we would expect.

---

64   Cf. FR, ##30–32.
65   Cf. for instance, WD, ##46–48 and #72.

IV. The "true meaning" of relevant preconciliar doctrine

1. Is *Quanta Cura* irreconcilable with *Dignitatis Humanae?*

38. In section **A.III** (and in Appendix B) we have considered the relative degree of magisterial authority attaching to *QC* and *DH* respectively. But what concerns us even more than their authority is their *meaning*, and whether or not they are doctrinally compatible. We saw that the Congregation for the Doctrine of the Faith has so far not admitted any contradiction between them, but is this present Vatican reticence tenable? Let us look again at the proposition QC3, condemned by Bl. Pius IX: **"The best condition of society is that in which there is not recognized as incumbent upon civil authority any duty to restrain violators of the Catholic religion by enacted penalties, except so far as the public peace may require."** What, precisely, is the Pope proposing as the truth *opposed* to this error?

39. As far as I can judge from his long footnote 58, Mr. Guminski's view of the respective meanings of QC3 and *DH*, and their mutual relationship, seems to be as follows: He thinks Pius IX is teaching, as the truth opposed to QC3, this thesis: **(a) "In the best condition of society, a duty is recognized as incumbent upon civil authority of penalizing violations of (= offences against) the Catholic religion *as such.*"** He also thinks that *DH* teaches thesis **(b): "Violations of (= offences against) the Catholic religion may not, *as such,* be penalized by civil authority in any well-constituted society."** Hence, he concludes, **(a)** and **(b)** are incompatible doctrinal theses.

40. Now, while I would agree that *DH* might be taken to mean **(b)**, depending on what precisely is meant by "violations," "as such" and "any," I do not think we can infer that Pius IX, by condemning QC3, is *ipso facto* proposing **(a)** as true. Neither do the respected theologians Fr. Basile and Msgr. Ocáriz draw that conclusion.[66] The thesis minimally incompatible

---

66 Cf. Basile (2005), 223–228. In this section, wherein he discusses QC3 in detail, the author does not use the words *"per se"* or "as such" (*comme tel*) in connection with "the Catholic religion." He favors a strong sense of "violator" which would mean not any and every public dissenter from Catholic doctrine, but only those seeking to cause harm or injustice to the Church and/or her members – possibly in ways that would violate the rights they enjoy not specifically *qua* Catholic, but *qua* members of a religious community and human individuals respectively. These "violators" might cause such harm or injustice, he says, even while perhaps staying within the limits of a positivist "public peace" legally defined by a secularist

with QC3 could be formulated thus as thesis **(c)**: "**In the best condition of society, the requirements of public peace are not the <u>only</u> consideration that can impose upon civil authority a duty of penalizing activity having to do with religion.**"[67] Indeed, expressions such as "in itself," "as such," "violators," or even "the Catholic religion," seem to me unwarranted in formulating the simplest proposition which is contradictory to QC3. For even if one holds a view as relatively liberal as **(c)**, one contradicts QC3, and so does not hold what Pius IX condemned. And since **(c)** is plainly in harmony with *DH*,[68] there is no contradiction between *DH* and *QC* on this point.

41. From my own standpoint, therefore, the central issue in the present debate with Mr. Guminski is not *QC*. Rather, it is what I now understand to be the at least authentic (although perhaps not definitive) teaching of the Church's ordinary magisterium over many centuries, to the effect that **civil authority can indeed have the right and duty, in certain circumstances, to penalize "violators of the Catholic religion"** *as such*. In other words, that **penal legislation of that sort cannot be described as intrinsically (or always-and-everywhere) unjust.** (My fuller enunciation of this traditional thesis is to be found as Proposition X at the beginning of my previous essay.) Even though, as I have argued here against Mr. Guminski, Pius IX did not teach this *by the very fact of condemning QC3*, I have in recent years come to believe there can be no serious doubt that he and countless other popes and bishops prior to Vatican II not only took for granted the truth of this thesis, which of course is similar to **(a)** above,[69] and proposed it elsewhere in their ordinary magisterium, for instance, in their frequent insistence to Catholic rulers that the latter had a duty to restrain the spread

---

or anti-Catholic regime (cf. 224–226). Fr. Basile also agrees with me that provided one admits the two other grounds for restrictive legislation that are specified in *DH*, #7 over and above a (just) "public peace," one does not hold what Pius XII condemned in QC3 (cf. 226–227). Ocáriz takes the same approach (cf. op. cit., 79–80).

67 Cf. my detailed argument in *RLC* 102–109 that this is all that Pius IX teaches *as true* by the very act of condemning QC3.

68 Cf. the other limiting criteria mentioned in *DH*, #7, as well as "public peace."

69 It differs from **(a)** by not stating that the said right and duty obtains "In the best condition of society." I have omitted that phrase, because while it would be part of the traditional ordinary magisterium if taken in one sense, it is ambiguous, and so possibly misleading, in a way analogous to the ambiguities I point out below (cf. section **B.V**) in discussing the Church's pre-nineteenth-century teaching against usury and circumcision.

of heresy in their realms.[70] And my main task in this debate is to show that even this more repressive doctrine – more repressive, that is, than **(c)** above – is not contradicted by *DH*.

2. Do we agree about the content of traditional doctrine?

42. This brings us to Mr. Guminski's section H. Taking note of the aforesaid recent change in my own position,[71] he says that we "currently agree" that "preconciliar Catholic doctrine, as disclosed in nineteenth-century papal documents, included" the "proposition" that "there is no natural right to be civilly free to publicly manifest . . . or propagate any non-Catholic religion *during a particular period in a particular country if there then and there exists certain contingent social political circumstances.*"[72] That "proposition," in itself, does indeed seem to me fairly similar to the thesis contained within (not asserted by[73]) my own Proposition X, which I expected Mr. Guminski would more or less agree on as a formulation of the relevant traditional doctrine.[74] However, some qualifications are in order. First, I never said that the nineteenth-century papal documents "included" or "disclosed" this doctrine in the form of a "proposition" which included the passage italicized above (or other words to the same effect). For that would have in effect been a claim on my part that the said doctrine, including the qualification regarding particular circumstances, is *explicitly formulated* in those documents; and I do not know of any of them which formulates it thus. Still less did I claim that we can find "in the [aforesaid] papal documents" a "prudential judgment" that: **(i)** *specifies* the circumstances I had mentioned (a Catholic but poorly educated populace, paternalistic government, etc.[75]); **(ii)** claims that such circumstances "actually obtained in several predominantly Catholic countries"; and **(iii)** concludes that under these existing circumstances pro-Catholic coercive

---

70   Evidence of that doctrine is preserved even in the Church's post-Vatican II liturgy. An excerpt from the thirteenth-century "spiritual testament" of Saint Louis of France to his son includes the following exhortation: "Endeavour to banish all sin, especially blasphemy and heresy, from your kingdom" (Office of Readings for August 25, second reading).

71   Cf. WD, ##65–70.

72   FR, #41 (emphasis added).

73   Note that what "Proposition X" asserts is not the *doctrinal thesis* enunciated within X, but rather, my own claim that this thesis *was* in effect the (relevant) "preconciliar Catholic doctrine."

74   Cf. WD, ##1–2. The reason for the qualification "more or less" is explained in #2.

75   Cf. WD, #67.

measures are justified.[76] Again, the "disclosure" of such a detailed "prudential judgment" would have required explicit papal formulations which I do not believe exist. What I claimed, rather, was that the earlier popes who, in their ordinary magisterium and acts of governance, denied the right to civil freedom for *any* non-Catholic religious manifestations[77] were, "*at least implicitly*, making [that teaching] relative to the whole ensemble of contingent social circumstances which then existed."[78] That is, I am not claiming they *consciously reflected* on the historical contingency of these circumstances and stated accordingly that their severity toward religious dissent was being conditioned by them. Rather, these pre-twentieth-century popes[79] (and his predecessors) most probably took for granted unreflectively the conditions they lived in and were addressing, just as a fish takes for granted its own watery world.

43. This *implicitly* relative character of the earlier papal teaching can be inferred partly by historical reflection on those contingent circumstances themselves – a gradually disintegrating Christendom which by the time of Vatican II had given way in the West to a secularized, and pluralistic sociopolitical culture. It can also be inferred by noting not just what the popes actually said in the relevant documents, but also what they significantly

76 Cf. FR, #41.
77 As I explained in WD, #65, it was above all further reflection (years after I published *RLC*) on Gregory XVI's *Mirari Vos*, not the encyclicals of his two successors, that led me to this conclusion. In his note 58, Mr. Guminski argues that no. 77 of the 1864 *Syllabus,* in asserting the continuing "expediency" of having Catholicism as State religion "to the exclusion of all others," teaches the legitimacy of "a situation in which not only [is] Catholicism the solely established religion of the State, but . . . in which it alone of all religions may lawfully be publicly manifested or propagated." In my book I already recognized this as one of two possible reasonable interpretations of no. 77, but I argued (both there and in more summary form in *SJR*, 109) that even if it is the correct one, that would not in itself imply that Pius IX was intending to propose the legitimacy of this comprehensively repressive legislation as a truth of *divine* law, i.e., as Catholic *doctrine* (cf. *RLC*, 58–60). In the light of my new overall position, whether I was right about no. 77 is now a moot point for present purposes.
78 WD, #67. The emphasis is added here to "at least implicitly," and deleted from "whole ensemble."
79 This greater readiness of the Church to repress religious dissent had its *origin* many centuries ago in these very different and less politically sophisticated historical circumstances; but, of course, this approach lingered on into the twentieth century (cf. WD, ##65–66), under gradually increasing challenges from within and without the Church, until the great majority of the Fathers at Vatican II concluded that in the modern world it had now become quite inappropriate.

failed to say. If some pre-Vatican-II pontiff had formulated the denial of a natural right to civil freedom for *any* public non-Catholic manifestations in predominantly Catholic countries using "absolutizing" language ("always and everywhere," "intrinsically," "under no possible circumstances," etc.), then of course we would have to recognize their strictly doctrinal teaching as being trans-historical universal, and exceptionless in scope (universal and exceptionless, that is, for all those countries on earth that ever have had, or ever will have, a predominantly Catholic population). And such a doctrine would certainly have been irreconcilable with the clear implication of *DH* that in the modern world, at least, the natural right to RL of non-Catholic minorities in "Catholic" countries normally extends to public manifestations of their own beliefs. But in fact, the (non-infallible) pronouncements in question stopped short of using that sort of "absolutizing" language. That is why, in my initial reply to Mr. Guminski, I corrected my earlier (1993) view that authentic preconciliar doctrine saw the presence of a predominantly Catholic population in any given country as being *always and everywhere* a sufficient condition – a simple "litmus test" guarantee – for concluding that nobody in that country had any natural right to civil freedom in publicly manifesting any non-Catholic doctrine.[80] (*A fortiori*, of course – as I had already recognized in my 1993 essay[81] – traditional doctrine stopped short of teaching that there can never under any circumstances be such a right in predominantly *non*-Catholic countries.)

44. My line of reasoning here is essentially that which Catholic scholars have long used in order to counter the charge of a self-contradiction in the Church's doctrine regarding usury. Earlier magisterial condemnations (up until the first half of the eighteenth century) of charging interest on a loan in the absence of specific "extrinsic titles" did not *spell out* that this doctrine was partly dependent on the whole existing economic situation of that time. But when, beginning in the second half of that century, the revolution in Western technology, communications and industry eventually produced a very different economic system that had been quite unforeseen in earlier times, it could finally be recognized by theologians, and by the Church herself, that the earlier and more rigorous teaching against the taking of interest was *implicitly* based on conditions which in fact had been, but were not at the time *recognized to be*, historically contingent. Therefore no true Catholic *doctrine*, whether infallible or merely authentic, was contradicted by the nineteenth-century Holy Office decisions introducing the

80   Cf. WD, #66.
81   Cf. WD, n102 for reference.

Church's present more relaxed position regarding the taking of interest on a loan. For a Catholic moral doctrine, by definition, is a norm proposed as being true everywhere and at all times (or at least since the New Covenant came into effect).[82]

45. The same relativizing hermeneutic must be applied to the Council of Florence's assertion that, ever since the New Covenant came into effect, "circumcision, . . . whether or not one places hope in it, . . . cannot be observed at all [by those who glory in the name of Christian] without loss of eternal salvation."[83] This is certainly a doctrinal affirmation, for it is prefaced by the Council's assertion that "the most holy Roman Church . . . firmly believes, professes and teaches" it. Has the Church in recent times, then, *contradicted* this doctrine by allowing Catholics to practice circumcision for purely secular (usually hygienic) reasons? No, because such reasons never even crossed the "radar screen" of the Florentine Fathers, centuries before anything was known about bacteria, the causes of urinary tract infections, etc. Even though they specified that practicing circumcision was always mortally sinful "whether or not one places hope in it" (i.e., whether or not one considered it a means of justification, as Aquinas and many others have thought it was under the Old Covenant), the Fathers still took it for granted that the only reason anyone would ever want to observe circumcision would be a belief or fear that God still required it. And it was precisely this attitude that they intended to condemn, in line with St. Paul's warning to the Galatian Christians that any of them who had themselves circumcised would be "separated from Christ, . . . fallen from grace."[84] So this implicit qualification – that only such *religiously motivated* circumcision is being formally condemned here – must be understood as integral to the Florentine doctrine itself. Am I saying, then, that Florence implicitly *approved* circumcision for non-religious reasons? No, only that Florence implicitly left that question open and undecided.

---

82 Cf. the entries by Arthur Vermeersch on "Interest" and "Usury" in the *Catholic Encyclopedia* (accessible online). The notion of something being true "always and everywhere" does not of course rule out the inclusion within that "something" of conditions that will *not* obtain always and everywhere. The Church's teaching on the conditions for a just war, for instance, would certainly qualify as doctrinal in character (cf. *Catechism of the Catholic Church*, no. 2309). What the doctrine means is that *always* (in any century) and *everywhere* (in any country or region on earth) the set of contingent conditions specified in the doctrine must obtain if a decision to go to war is to be considered just.

83 DS 1348 (= Dz 712).

84 Cf. Gal. 5: 2–4.

46. I have explained more fully here than in my previous rejoinder the idea that there can be merely "implicit" qualifications underlying some magisterial formulations, because it is critical for my defense of *DH*'s continuity with traditional doctrine; and I think Mr. Guminski has failed to appreciate this point sufficiently. Indeed, that failure seems to me to underlie his severely negative verdict ("striking[ly] . . . implausible"[85]) against my present understanding of the traditional doctrine, in which I emphasize what is *missing* from the relevant magisterial formulations, rather than what they state.

47. However, this brings us to what I fully agree is the "striking implausibility" of a claim which my adversary ascribes to me regarding the content of the traditional doctrine on religious freedom. But I never made such a claim. This straw man assailed by Mr. Guminski is one he sets up with an egregiously illogical inference that I find quite remarkable, coming as it does from so learned a jurist and philosopher. The opinion I said I *no longer* hold is this: **"[A]ccording to traditional *doctrine*, there can *never* (i.e., from Pentecost until Judgment Day) be a natural right of any non-Catholics 'in predominantly Catholic states' to be tolerated in the public profession of their religion."**[86] So my new position is simply that traditional doctrine did *not* include the above proposition ("[T]here can *never* . . . their religion"). But how does my critic "paraphrase" my new position? Well, as if to reinforce what will already be clear to attentive readers, he spells out for them in a footnote the fact that in his main text he has modified my own words in citing them: "I have substituted '*sometimes*' for *never*; and 'some' for 'any.'"[87] Indeed he has. Thus, in his main text, Mr. Guminski claims that my new position (i.e., that implied by my renunciation of the opinion in bold type above) is as follows: **"[A]ccording to traditional *doctrine*, there can [*sometimes*] (i.e., from Pentecost until Judgment Day) be a natural right of [some] non-Catholics 'in predominantly Catholic states' to be tolerated in the public profession of their religion."**[88] And this "paraphrased quotation," he assures readers in the footnote just cited, "is in accord with Fr. Harrison's intention."

48. It certainly is not. No more than my critic do I know of any traditional doctrinal statement to the effect that the said natural right could "sometimes" be enjoyed by "some" non-Catholics in such states (or in any

85   FR, #51.
86   WD, #70 (emphasis in original).
87   FR, n76.
88   FR, #51.

other states, for that matter); and it has never crossed my mind to claim that such a thesis was part of traditional doctrine. Indeed, I expressly affirmed at the beginning of my initial rejoinder that it "certainly" was not![89] Mr. Guminski's faulty logic here amounts to the following inference: Proposition A – **"The Church did not traditionally teach that X can never be the case"** – implies Proposition B: **"The Church traditionally taught that X can sometimes be the case."** But of course A does not imply B, because it is equally compatible with C: **"Traditional Church teaching *neither affirmed nor denied* that X can sometimes be the case."** And in this debate, my central claim is that since A and C are true, Vatican II does not contradict traditional doctrine when it clearly implies that X can sometimes – i.e., in the contemporary world that *DH* is addressing – be the case.

V. The "true meaning" of *DH*: the "always-and-everywhere" factor.

49. We now come to the heart of the dispute between Mr. Guminski and myself. I invite readers to recall that what he needs to show, in order to establish his basic claim that there is a doctrinal contradiction between *DH* and the traditional magisterium, is that our Proposition Z, although now with one amendment, is true. Here it is again, with italics as in the original and with the amendment added and underscored:

> **Z: According to *DH*, government prohibition of all public (and, *a fortiori*, private) religious manifestations other than those of the true religion involves, and <u>since the promulgation of the New Law</u> has *always and everywhere involved*, a violation of the natural human right to religious liberty.**[90]

---

89 "Certainly, pre-Vatican-II papal doctrine never positively taught that there *could* in fact be circumstances in which non-Catholics might have a natural right to . . . immunity [from coercion in publicly propagating their religion]" (WD, #2).

90 Cf. WD, #3. In FR, n72, Mr. Guminski says he "hesitate[s] to concede" that in my propositions X, Y, and Z I have achieved my stated aim of expressing the central issue we are disputing "as clearly as possible." However, as I hope to make clear below in commenting on FR, #49, the main thing prompting his hesitation seems to be my inappropriate choice of the words "moral legitimacy" (WD, #65). My failure to express clearly what I had in mind at that point has apparently led him to ascribe to me the view that in *all* cases where government restrictions on religious activity are unethical, the *reason* they are unethical is that they violate the natural right to RL. But in any case proposition Z itself (with or without the above amendment) does not imply that view. My X, Y and Z all simply take for granted

50. Without the above amendment, Z would not – or at least, would no longer – express exactly my opponent's understanding of *DH*. For in his final essay he makes the important admission that the Declaration need not be read as implying that the repression of religious dissent as such is *intrinsically* evil. That is because he recognizes that the Old Testament – which Catholics believe to be divinely inspired – mandated that repression in ancient Israel by an act of divine positive law which, he says, overrode a "secondary or instrumental human good" linked to the natural moral law.[91]

51. Now, it is in his section #I that Mr. Guminski turns his attention once again to where we disagree regarding the meaning of *DH*. And this disagreement involves especially our respective interpretations of the criteria laid down in the Declaration for deciding what limits or restraints civil authority may place on religious (or irreligious) activity in the interests of a "just public order." What my opponent emphasizes most in his final essay is the following thesis, which I will call **T**: **According to *DH*, the natural right to RL requires that, in deciding what limits are permissible, "the truth of Catholicism [be] deemed not juridically relevant in determining what constitutes a just public order."**[92] This norm, he says, is what the Declaration presents as being necessary for "every well-constituted society"; and its result, when implemented, will be that

the truth of Mr. Guminski's view, expressed in FR #49, that according to perennial Catholic teaching (both pre- and postconciliar), government repression of religion-related activity can be reprehensible for reasons *other than* that of violating the natural right to RL. Nor does Z imply that (according to *DH*) all restrictions that *do* violate the said natural right are wrong for that reason *only*. On the other hand, neither does Z depict *DH* as teaching that *each and every instance* of repression that occurs in implementing the policy in question will itself be unethical. (For in some cases, of course, the repressed activity would be one which *indisputably* transgresses the "due limits" contemplated by *DH*.) In fact, in formulating X, Y and Z, I chose the verb "involve" precisely so that proposition Z (which I have presented as Mr. Guminski's view) would not say or insinuate that, according to *DH*, each and every instance of repression, under such a regime, will necessarily violate the natural right to RL. I knew my opponent does not think that; but he surely does think that, according to *DH*, the consistent and nation-wide implementation of a policy that represses *all* manifestations of false religions will always (at least, ever since the Christian era began) violate *somebody*'s natural right to RL, i.e., it will *involve* a violation of that right. Hopefully, Mr. Guminski will now agree that Proposition Z, thus understood, adequately expresses his understanding of what *DH* teaches.

91   Cf. WD, n34 and FR, #45.
92   FR, #44.

the "*concrete* rights" of non-Catholics will be identical, regardless of the percentage of Catholics in a given country's population, and whether or not its constitution recognizes Catholicism as uniquely true.[93]

52. Whether the Council really insists on this surprisingly naturalistic concept of public order is a question we shall return to in section **C** below. However, let us concede for the sake of argument that it does so. Will Mr. Guminski then have shown that our (amended) Proposition Z is true, thereby defeating my own major and fundamental claim in this dispute? Not at all. For his thesis T itself does not even mention, and his arguments in its defense do not even seriously address, that very aspect of Z which I have made a point of repeatedly emphasizing, namely, the "*always-and-everywhere*" factor. That is, even if all his new arguments are valid, the most they will then prove is that, according to *DH*, the "due limits" inherent in the natural right to RL should, *in the religiously pluralistic and increasingly interdependent community of modern nations presupposed by the Declaration*, be determined uniformly according to a strictly natural-law, "revelation-free," concept of public order. But that will by no means contradict the traditional Catholic doctrine formulated in Proposition X and further explained in section **B.IV** of the present essay. For, far from demonstrating that *DH* proposes this putatively secular concept of public order *retroactively* – i.e., as having been always (except in ancient Israel) required in principle by human dignity – Mr. Guminski has really not even offered any new *argument* that it does so. In my previous essay I already addressed several observations wherein he seemed to be at least implying that the Council was proposing as valid *for all ages* certain norms which would (in that case) be inconsistent with traditional doctrine;[94] and I noted that he would "need to provide further argumentation"[95] in order to make his case. I then elaborated on this point in #47. But my adversary has failed to provide such further argumentation.[96] He does indeed attempt to rebut the reasons I adduce in #47 for denying that such a secular concept of public order (supposing it were implied in *DH*, #7) is proposed as retroactively valid for

---

93 Cf. ibid.

94 Cf. WD, section IIIa.

95 WD, #15.

96 In FR, #45, Mr. Guminski does indeed *assert* that, according to *DH* ##9–12, "the New Law" of Christ – a law which by its very nature has been valid "always and everywhere" ever since its promulgation at Pentecost – does not allow for any restrictions on religious freedom except those "independently authorized by the natural moral law." However, he offers no argument to support this curious interpretation of articles 9–12, which I will address in section **C.2** *infra*.

all countries all the way back to Pentecost.[97] However, even if this rebuttal were cogent in itself, it would not be sufficient to prove this alleged retroactive meaning and intention on the part of the Council; for one does not demonstrate the truth of a proposition simply by showing that some arguments for its falsity are invalid. This point of logic is especially relevant here, given the fact that the Declaration's core *doctrinal* passage, *DH, #2.1,* speaks vaguely only of "due limits," and does not mention the specific terms "public order" and "objective moral order" on which my opponent's case for *doctrinal* discontinuity depends crucially. Is Mr. Guminski perhaps assuming that since a natural human right is by definition one that obtains at all times and in all places, it follows that if the natural right to RL requires (at least under the New Law) a strictly secular notion of public order at even one time and in one place, it must necessarily do so at all times and in all places? If this is his assumption, I have also shown the invalidity of that sort of inference in my previous essay.[98]

53. I also rebutted there Mr. Guminski's attempt to dismiss as seemingly inconsistent – and even as inadmissible evidence (for being delivered "only" orally, not in print) – the *relator*'s explicit assurance to conservative Fathers that *DH* should not be taken as an implied condemnation of the severer stance endorsed by the Church in earlier times.[99] My opponent's only reply now is to repeat his unconvincing charge that Bishop De Smedt was inconsistent in this section of his final *relatio*, and to complain that I am making a "big deal" of it.[100] I think the problem is rather that Mr.

---

97 Cf. FR, #54.

98 Cf. WD, #50.

99 Cf. WD, section IIIc (##20–24).

100 Cf. FR, 64. Mr. Guminski again insists here that I have "grossly exaggerated" the hermeneutical value of these comments of the *relator*, given that they are (in his view) "at worst misleading and at best ambiguous." My critic now explains this complaint more fully by pointing out that the term "common good," used by the *relator* in these comments, "had historically provided the warrant for the comprehensive repression of non-Catholic public propaganda and manifestations in Catholic states." But Bishop De Smedt's *terminology* is in any case of only minor relevance to the point that he was making – and that I am emphasizing – namely, that the justice or injustice of government restrictions placed on a given type of religion-related activity is not necessarily something absolute and fixed for all times and places. Rather (as his mentor John Courtney Murray constantly insisted), some restrictions of that sort need to be judged according to historically evolving cultural standards. Just as a given legal restriction might objectively violate the natural right of an adult, but not that of a adolescent living at the same time and in the same culture, so, analogously, a given legal restriction that might be

184

Guminski is making a "small deal" of it – i.e., unduly minimizing its importance. All I have done, after all, is cite De Smedt's words and defend their manifest relevance to our dispute over the truth or falsity of Proposition Z.

* * * * * * *

54. Let me now summarize the main points made in the present section (**B**). I argued, first, that there is always a strong *a priori* presumption of doctrinal continuity in successive and weighty pronouncements of even the non-definitive Catholic magisterium, noting, however, that this presumption can be defeated either by unambiguously contradictory wording in the relevant documents themselves, or else by an extrinsic official statement that the later document is intended – and so should be interpreted – as a correction of some earlier magisterial error. We then saw that neither of these conditions is verified in the case of *DH*, and indeed, that the Declaration's preamble and final *relatio* explicitly *deny* (*pace* Mr. Guminski's insistence to the contrary) any intention on the part of the Council to "correct" some supposed error in the traditional doctrine.

55. I then defended and explained more fully my understanding of the *content* of that traditional doctrine, stressing what was only implicit and unformulated in it, and also pointing out that my critic has seriously misrepresented my position in this matter. Finally, I have shown that, far from refuting my arguments against the crucial "always-and-everywhere" clause in Proposition Z (our principal bone of contention in this dispute), Mr. Guminski has not even made a serious attempt to do so in his second rejoinder. It seems that, despite his ingenious analysis and precision in matters of detail, he has ended up losing the plot; and I submit that he has thereby lost this debate. My central claim in this exchange has been that since the Vatican II Declaration *may* reasonably be interpreted in the sense of Proposition Y rather than Proposition Z, it *must* be interpreted in that sense, so as to avoid making it contradict the traditional doctrine expressed in Proposition X – a contradiction which, in view of the preamble, would also render the Declaration self-contradictory, and therefore non-binding upon Catholic consciences. As regards *that* claim, I rest my case.

objectively unjust under certain historical and cultural circumstances could well be objectively justifiable under other circumstances wherein significantly different community standards and expectations hold sway. (See below, fourth paragraph of Conclusion.)

C. A Secondary Question: What Sort of "Public Order" Does *DH* See as "Just" for *Today's* World?

56. It remains to consider whether my critic, in his final reply, has succeeded in demonstrating that, *at least as far as the contemporary world is concerned*, his thesis T above is warranted, to wit, his claim that, according to *DH*, the natural right to RL requires that, in setting legal limitations to religion-related activity, "the truth of Catholicism [be] deemed not juridically relevant in determining what constitutes a just public order."

I. What does it mean to restrict non-Catholic propaganda "as such"?

57. First, Mr. Guminski sees an "incongruity" in my affirming *both* the following propositions: **(i)** *DH* implies that under modern circumstances there should be no "continued restrictions on non-Catholic propaganda as such, even in officially Catholic countries"; and also **(ii)** *DH* neither implies nor states that [under modern circumstances] the "due limits" inherent in the natural right to RL "must be determined *uniformly* [i.e., on the foundation of natural law alone, to the exclusion of divine positive law] in all political communities – those which recognize the truth of Catholicism and those which do not."[101] The question has relevance because I maintain that *DH*'s concept of public order would be consistent, even under modern circumstances, with at least a few legal restrictions which depend on certain points of the revealed Law of Christ rather than natural law – points which have a particularly direct and vital importance for a civil society based on Gospel principles. Notable among these would be Sunday observance,[102] the repudiation and disallowance of polygamy and divorce, and civil society's obligation to recognize, wherever politically feasible, the kingship of Christ and the Catholic Church's role as the unique authoritative interpreter of the whole divine law, both

---

101 Cf. FR, ##44–45, quoting WD, #38 and #42.

102 According to Mr. Guminski, *CCC*, #2188 "appears to recognize that official recognition of Sundays and other Church holy days of obligation as legal holidays is not required by [religious freedom]" (FR, n53). Whether or not the *Catechism* really "recognizes" that, my own point is in any case a different one, to wit, that *DH* does not imply that a state's prohibition of certain activities on such days, binding all citizens, Catholic and non-Catholic alike, will *ipso facto* violate the religious freedom of some citizens, even though such prohibition depends on divine positive law.

natural and positive.[103] The restrictions I have in mind in regard to this last point (the 'establishment' of Catholicism) would apply to "propaganda attacking it: propaganda, that is, in favor of total separation of Church and State."[104]

58. Now, is there in fact an "incongruity" or inconsistency between **(i)** and **(ii)** above? It depends on what exactly we mean by the disapproval of "restrictions on non-Catholic propaganda *as such.*" If **(i)** means that *DH* disapproves any civil legislation today which considers the opposition of public activity A to Catholic doctrine to be *even one reason among others* (though not in itself a sufficient reason) for restricting A, then the two are indeed inconsistent. For in that case **(i)** would mean that, according to *DH*, A's anti-Catholic character may no longer even be *taken into account* by any civil authority in deciding whether A may be restricted as a danger to public order. Rather, any restrictions on A would have to be based exclusively on secular, natural, considerations. And the aforesaid legal

103 Cf. WD, n. 67 and *RLC*, 100–101. Mr. Guminski chides me for "frequently . . . confound[ing] freedom in matters religious with freedom in nonreligious matters." This is because I include the above morally-related points of revealed truth, along with pornography, homosexual behavior, decency in dress and other points of the natural law (cf. *RLC*, 110), as matters relevant to the legal limits envisaged in *DH*, #7. According to my critic, "these examples plainly pertain to nonreligious matters" (FR, n52). Well, perhaps they are classified as nonreligious in civil law codes; but *DH* is an ecclesiastical document, and I insist that for our purposes they are very much "religious matters". For offences in these areas are certainly "violations of the Catholic religion" (cf. *QC*), as that religion – consisting of both "faith and morals" – is set out officially in magisterial documents and the *CCC*. (Mr. Guminski's objection is perhaps linked to his mistaken exclusion of natural law teachings from "sacred doctrine": cf. **B.II.1** above.) Moreover, the sorts of legal restrictions *DH*, #7.3 has in mind are by no means confined to restrictions on activity which is, or at least claims to be, religious in character or motivation. The Declaration aims, more broadly, at "abuses that can be carried out *under the pretext of* religious liberty (*abusus qui haberi possint **sub pretextu** libertatis religiosae*)" (emphasis added). Of course, people who do not even claim to be religiously motivated in wanting to overturn legislation against pornography, divorce, sodomy, "gay marriage," euthanasia, etc., use that pretext as one of their chief arguments, and are therefore among those targeted by *DH*, #7.3. Such activists invariably claim that the existing laws violate their own "religious freedom" in the sense that they constitute the "imposition" upon them of other folks' religious "dogmas" and "prejudices." Cf. discussion in **C.I** above, regarding the approach exemplified by the pro-abortion feminist slogan, *"Keep your rosaries off my ovaries!"*

104 *RLC*, 101.

restrictions that I claim would still today be consistent with *DH* could clearly not be justified on that basis *exclusively*.

59. However, the above is not what I mean by **(i)**. Rather, I mean – and have consistently maintained[105] – that *DH* disapproves (given modern circumstances) any civil legislation that would consider the simple fact of A's opposition to Catholic doctrine to be *in itself sufficient grounds* for restricting A. And this is compatible with **(ii)**, because I am not suggesting that (for instance) the mere incompatibility of public anti-establishment propaganda with Catholic doctrine could still (consistently with *DH*) be legally treated today in some countries as a *sufficient* reason for proscribing it as a danger to public order. Rather, my whole point is that, *over and above* the mere fact of its incompatibility with Catholic doctrine, such propaganda, in a predominantly Catholic society, embodies the gravely aggravating factor of constituting an attack against that central "moral duty" *of societies* to recognize the true religion and the Kingship of Christ. It also attacks the rightful authority of Christ's Church to exert a unique influence over human social and political life. Propaganda contrary to other revealed truths – the divinity of Christ, the sacraments, Marian dogmas, etc. – of course *indirectly* weaken a nation's Catholic identity; but the Church at Vatican II has clearly made a prudential judgment that this consideration, today, is insufficient to justify recourse to government power for the purpose of "quarantining" or silencing those minority citizens who may feel obliged in conscience before God[106] to publicly oppose these Catholic dogmas by respectful and honest means.[107] A

---

105 Cf. *RLC,* 143; WD, 40; and SJR89, where I say, "With Vatican II, the Church has decided that civil authorities should no longer – not even in 'Catholic' societies – regard *mere* incompatibility with Catholicism (i.e., without any aggravating factors) as representing a social evil serious enough to outweigh the claim to immunity from coercion which arises from the dignity of the human person and his or her good conscience" (cited from the republication of this article in *Catholic Dossier*, vol. 6, no. 2, March-April, 2000, 29, emphasis in original).

106 I add "before God," because *DH* does not imply any natural right to immunity from coercion, even under modern circumstances, for those who would publicly spread atheism or anti-religious propaganda. Rather, the natural right to RL recognized by Vatican II is carefully formulated so as to cover "the private and public acts *of religion* by which men direct themselves *to God* according to their convictions" (*DH*, #3, emphasis added). Cf. *RLC*, 109–110, including n28.

107 I add "by respectful and honest means," in view of *DH's* provision that "coercive," "dishonest" and other "unworthy" forms of spreading religious belief are not protected by the right to RL. On the contrary, they are said to constitute a "violation of the rights of others" (and, therefore, as a punishable offence against public order). Cf. *DH*, 4, 7. Cf. section **D. 1** infra.

new and more tolerant Christendom could live with this greater diversity under a "bigger tent" than was allowed by its more repressive medieval fore-runner. (A case could be made on historical grounds that the latter turned out in any case to be counter-productive in the long run.)

60. But anti-establishment propaganda seeks to tear down the tent itself. It lays the axe to the very root of all Catholic social teaching, as found in the First Commandment of the Decalogue.[108] It represents a direct, full-frontal assault on the very essence, the very possibility, of Christendom as such – i.e., of a socio-political order based on the Gospel of Christ. And such an order must forever remain the Church's pole-star, her ultimate goal and perennial paradigm for the organization of human society. This of course is why Catholicism's mortal enemies since the Enlightenment and the French Revolution have concentrated first and fore-most on destroying the Church's social and political power – on ejecting her from the public square. The secularization of politics can in fact be seen as the "original sin" of Western society since the eighteenth century – a sin which is now leading inexorably to a new era in which the right to RL of Christians themselves is being violated by anti-life and pro-homo-sexual intolerance on their left flank,[109] and creeping Islamic sharia law on their right.[110]

108 The duty of societies toward the true religion is treated in the *Catechism* (##2105–2109) in the section explaining the First Commandment: man's duty to love and honor God above all things.

109 It is now notorious that strong social, economic and legal pressures against any religious or moral criticism of homosexual activity, and even coercing believers to act against their religious convictions, are steadily mounting in many traditionally – even officially – Christian nations and states. Cf., for instance, A. Sears & C. Osten, *The Homosexual Agenda: Exposing the Principal Threat to Religious Freedom Today* (Nashville, TN: Broadman & Holman, 2003). And D.A. Wildmon, *Speechless: Silencing the Christians* (Richard Vigilante Books, 2009). At the time of writing, the "Manhattan Declaration," an ecumenical manifesto launched in the Fall of 2009 to denounce and resist these growing secularist assaults on the RL of Christians, has gained about half a million signatures. In his historic speech to British political and civic leaders in Westminster Hall on September 17, 2010, Pope Benedict XVI also voiced his concern about the "increasing marginalization of religion, especially of Christianity" in ostensibly tolerant Western society, and warned of the "worrying signs of a failure to appreciate not only the rights of believers to freedom of conscience and freedom of religion, but also the legitimate role of religion in the public square" (*L'Osservatore Romano* [English ed.], September 22, 2010, 12–13).

110 Cf., for instance, Robert Spencer, *Stealth Jihad: How Radical Islam Is Subverting America Without Guns or Bombs* (Washington, DC: Regnery Publishing, 2008);

61. Mr. Guminski chides me with confusing "public order" in this broad sense of a whole Christian socio-political scheme of things with "public order" in the narrower juridical sense intended by *DH*.[111] But in real life the two are inseparably linked. While anti-establishment propaganda might not, as such, threaten the "public peace" of a modern Catholic state, it would certainly endanger the other two components of the "just public order" specified in *DH* 7, namely, "public morality" and "the rights of all [other] citizens." How so?

62. As regards public morality, the post-Enlightenment reaction against Christendom makes it all too clear that where the Catholic Church is denied her rightful recognition in the political order as the unique authoritative interpreter of the natural moral law, basic norms of that natural law are themselves eventually discarded, and even indignantly rejected. Unchecked original sin, and the passions it unleashes, eventually blind people to the rational basis of certain naturally knowable ethical truths, especially those regarding the sanctity and transmission of human life, marriage, sexuality and the family. As a result, these truths come to be seen ever more widely as "irrational, oppressive and outdated religious dogmas."

63. Then, in regard to "the rights of all citizens," the abolition of the Church's rightful constitutional status, even when it has not resulted in outright totalitarian dictatorships, has also brought us that "culture of death" which jeopardizes the fundamental right to life itself, above all, the life of the very young (abortion and the destruction of embryos) and of the very old and infirm (the spread of legalized euthanasia). While the "pro-choice" feminists who chant, *"Keep your rosaries off my ovaries!"* may be philosophically challenged, they are politically astute. For they realize that the (now residual) influence of the Catholic Church over the laws and structures of Western nations still constitutes the biggest single obstacle to the achievement of their goals. Eliminating that influence also brings us the ongoing redefinition and debasement of marriage to include same-sex unions and (a little further down the road) polygamy and "polyamory." This ideological movement, trumpeting its concern for "human rights" and "diversity," is now deeply penetrating nearly all levels of power in Western society, including public education. As noted above, this gravely threatens the religious liberty of Christian citizens. It undermines their right as

Dinesh D'Souza, *The Enemy At Home: The Cultural Left and Its Responsibility for 9/11* (New York: Doubleday, 2007).
111 Cf. FR, #61.

parents to educate their own children according to their conscience (cf. *DH*, #4), free from a state-imposed code of sexual and "gender" ethics, and from harassment, discrimination and even persecution for "hate" and "bigotry," simply because they openly uphold traditional Christian morality.

64. The aforesaid dangers are now becoming more acute than ever before, as Benedict XVI pointed out with grave concern during his 2010 visit to Britain. This fact needs to be taken into account in considering an allocution of John Paul II that Mr. Guminski has appealed to,[112] which dates from 1995 – six years before 9/11 and five years before the world's first legislation recognizing same-sex "marriage." The late Pontiff then stressed that the Church seeks only freedom for the Gospel – for its preachers and hearers alike – and "neither seeks nor desires to seek any worldly power placed at the service of the truths she bears." This statement of contemporary Church policy does not conflict with my own reading of *DH*. For the few restrictions based on divine positive law that I claim the Declaration still allows for in the modern world would not be placed in civil law "at the service of" the Church's own "truths" as such. Rather, they would they would be there in order to safeguard human life and dignity itself, and indeed, that very freedom for Christians that John Paul was vindicating. For, as I have stressed above, these are values and truths which, while accessible to natural human reason *in principle*, cannot long be safeguarded *in practice* once the Church established by Christ the King is no longer socially and legally recognized as the authentic guardian and interpreter of the natural moral law. The resulting assaults on the religious freedom of traditional Christians are becoming more noticeable in Western society with every passing year of the new millennium. All this should serve to explain my claim that *DH* does not rule out a hypothetical modern Catholic country's decision to "set the bar for communal conduct higher" by disallowing public propaganda against the Church's rightful and unique constitutional position, as well as prohibiting – even on the part of non-Christian citizens – polygamy, divorce, and non-essential work and commerce on Sundays.[113]

---

112 Cf. CH, n52.

113 Mr. Guminski takes issue with my statement that the Declaration is "silent" about possible differences in its application "in Catholic, as distinct from non-Catholic, societies" (cf. FR, nn63–64). But *DH* #6.3, to which he appeals, does not address that issue. It simply says that in countries where a particular religion is established, "the right of all citizens and religious communities to religious freedom must at the same time be recognized and upheld." But recognizing and upholding *the right*

II. A regression to superseded Old Testament norms?

65. My adversary, however, goes so far as to assert that any such higher bar-setting is, according to *DH*, ruled out by "the new Law (i.e., the Law of the Gospel)."[114] But in appealing to the *Catechism* (#1972), Mr. Guminski assails only another straw man – a position I have neither stated nor implied. The *CCC* teaches here that the New Law of Christ "sets us free from the ritual and juridical observances of the Old Law [of Moses]." Indeed it does. But the norm of traditional doctrine which my critic thinks has been superseded by *DH* did not presuppose or imply any such return to the said "ritual and juridical observances." (Indeed, the Church both before and after Vatican II, in accordance with St. Paul's teaching, has always condemned as dangerous "judaizing" any tendency to present those sorts of Mosaic observances as being still binding on God's people after Calvary and Pentecost.[115])

66. My critic seems to be forgetting that not everything prescribed under the Old Covenant belonged to that body of merely "ritual and juridical" legislation that has been superseded by the Law of Christ.[116] The

itself in all countries by no means rules out differences between one country and another in regard to the specific limits which give it legal expression. Indeed, the *CCC* explicitly contemplates and approves such differences (cf. #2109). More specifically, *DH* #6.3, when it is "unpacked" in the light of #7.3, can be seen to teach that in countries where a particular religion is established, *civil authority must recognize and uphold the right of all citizens and religious communities to freedom in publicly carrying out those conscientious religion-related acts which do not objectively offend against public peace, public morality, or the rights of other citizens.*" And that proposition is indeed "silent" about whether, in countries where Catholicism, the *true* religion, is established, all public manifestations incompatible with Catholicism do in fact offend against one or more of those three fundamental components of the common good.

114 Cf. FR, #45.

115 The Council of Florence, for instance, declares: "All, therefore, who after [the promulgation of the Gospel] observe circumcision and the Sabbath and the other requirements of the [Mosaic] law, [are] alien to the Christian faith and not in the least fit to participate in eternal salvation unless they eventually repudiate these errors" (Dz 712 = DS 1348) (Tanner I: 576).

116 The "juridical" norms that Christians believe are now superseded are the *specific prescriptions and penalties* laid down in the Pentateuch for matters other than worship-related ("ritual") observances. For instance, Christian magistrates are not obliged by Deuteronomy and Leviticus to order the death penalty for all the offences for which it was prescribed in those books – and much less by the *means* they specified (e.g., stoning and even burning to death). But it does not follow from this that none of these offences may any longer be penalized *at all* by

Decalogue represents the most obvious example of perennially valid ethical teaching enshrined in the Pentateuch, but there are certainly many other instances. According to Mr. Guminski, Catholics should hold, on the authority of *DH,* that the legitimacy, under some circumstances, of repressing religious error as such ceased as soon as the New Law came into effect. Why? Because, he says, there was no longer any "divine positive law" authorizing it.[117] But if the legitimacy of such repression had suddenly ceased, the Church herself could scarcely have taken nearly two millennia to discover that fact. After all, the abrogation of a positive law, no less than its promulgation, is something which of its very nature needs to be made clear immediately by the legislator to those he expects to obey him. But Mr. Guminski points to no first-century-A.D. evidence for the abrogation by Christ of the right in principle of the People of God, once they are constituted as a civil society, to restrain the diffusion of religious error.

67. Understandably, there is no evidence for an abrogation that in fact never occurred. What clearly happened is that the early Church understood the repressive O.T. approach to religious error to have been simply carried over, *mutatis mutandis,* into the New Covenant, even though it was not reiterated in the New Testament books. Another example of such non-reiterated but uninterrupted covenant-spanning legislation would be the way in which the Third Commandment (also a precept of divine positive law) was carried over as a matter of course into Christian Tradition, even though it is not formally reaffirmed in the N.T. writings.[118] Soon after she emerged from the catacombs to acquire an extensive political influence that the New Testament authors had not anticipated (and so did not write about), it was natural that the Church, the "New Israel," should consult that part of her Scriptures – the Law of Moses – which *did* present guidance as to how the People of God might act when endowed with political power. So while the successors of the apostles did not urge the suppression of synagogues or Jewish worship, they quickly endorsed, without any noticeable intra-ecclesial controversy, the fourth-century imperial laws repressing the official and public exercise of the old pagan cults. Manifestly, they saw no incompatibility between these new civil laws and the Law of Christ.

Christian legislators and judges. (Cf. WD, n34 for some pertinent Old Testament references to penalties for religious infidelity – public and private.)

117 FR, #45.

118 Indeed, those writings do not even spell out the specific amendment to that commandment which is proper to the New Covenant – the replacement of the Seventh Day of the week by the First Day (now called *dies dominicus* – "the Lord's Day").

68. This eventually became explicit in the Church's formal teaching. Never did traditional Catholic doctrine present the New Law as disallowing all civil restrictions on public religious activity and propaganda except those which are "independently authorized by the natural moral law."[119] On the contrary, Leo XIII, who explicitly teaches that errors against both natural and divinely revealed truth should be kept in check by Christian rulers,[120] also declares that this and his other teachings on Church and State are (implicitly at least) "lessons taught by Christ," since they represent "the necessary growth of the teachings of the Gospel."[121] Blessed Pius IX, for his part, is no less explicit in *Quanta Cura*. In teaching the falsity of "QC3," Pius asserts that this liberal proposition is "contrary to the doctrine of Sacred Scripture (*contra sacrarum Litterarum . . . doctrinam*), of the Church, and of the holy Fathers."[122] So if Mr. Guminski were correct in asserting that in articles 9–12, *DH* "makes clear that the New Law . . . [does not authorize limits on RL] more than is independently authorized by the natural moral law," then not only would those articles of *DH* contradict the traditional doctrine; they would also thereby turn the Declaration into a self-contradictory, and so self-discrediting, document by virtue of contradicting the preamble (see section **B.II** above).

69. But is it true that articles 9–12 "make clear" the above proposition? Frankly, I am puzzled as to how my learned adversary can make such an implausible claim. For neither "the natural moral law" nor any equivalent expression occurs even once in that section of *DH* – or anywhere else in the Declaration, for that matter. Nor can the expressions "public order," "limits," or anything equivalent be found anywhere in articles 9–12. Indeed, article 9 itself, while making the rather general and uncontroversial statement that Christ's revelation fully "shows forth the dignity of the human person," admits that this revelation "does not expressly affirm the right to immunity from external coercion in religious matters." Indeed, the *relator* had to admit that this right cannot even be seen as a *consequence*

---

119 FR, #45.
120 Cf. Encyclical *Immortale Dei* (1885), #32, text accessible in *The Companion to the Catechism of the Catholic Church* (San Francisco: Ignatius Press, 1995) 682–683; Encyclical *Libertas* (1888) #26, (*Companion,* op. cit., 747).
121 *Immortale Dei, #2 (Companion*, op. cit., 675).
122 In Appendix B, n18, I have suggested the kind of reasoning that Pius IX and his advisers probably employed in order to reach this conclusion that QC3 is contrary to the Scriptures and the teaching of the Fathers – i.e., contrary to the New Law of Christ.

of the Gospel concept of freedom.[123] Much less does #9 make any claim that revelation (either expressly or implicitly) specifies natural law as being the *only* appropriate basis, under the Law of Christ, for determining legal limits to the said immunity. The most the Council does in this article is to emphasize "above all" that "religious freedom in society is in complete harmony with the freedom of the act of Christian faith."[124] But traditional doctrine did not deny that proposition: it never claimed that such freedom in society is *not* in complete harmony with the freedom of the act of faith.[125]

70. Nor do the three subsequent articles justify Mr. Guminski's appeal to them. Article 10 presents the teaching dating back to the Fathers that "nobody is to be forced to embrace the faith against his will." Article 11 proceeds to back this up with copious New Testament evidence to demonstrate that Christ himself, and then the Apostles he sent out as missionaries, always observed this teaching in practice: they preached, exhorted and admonished, but never tried to compel their listeners to accept the Gospel. But here the Declaration simply affirms what no "traditionalist" Catholic ever denied. It bypasses the main issue that divided the Council Fathers, namely, whether Christians, once they have attained the kind of political power that the Apostles themselves lacked, may in some circumstances restrict or repress the spread of religious error as such. Article 12

123 In response to a request from some Fathers that the declaration show more clearly the basis in divine revelation for the right to RL, the *relator* replied, "Together with many experts in Sacred Scripture we have examined all the sources again and again. If one looks into this question accurately, one must conclude that it is nowhere affirmed directly in the Scriptures that man has a right to [this] immunity from coercion in living together with his fellow man. Modern religious liberty cannot be seen as a juridical consequence of Gospel liberty (*Religiosa libertas moderna non potest considerari ut iuridica consequentia libertatis evangelicae*)" (*AS*, vol. IV, pt. I, p. 198).

124 " . . . *plene est cum libertate actus fidei christianae congrua.*" The widely used Flannery edition of the Vatican II documents mistranslates these words as "in complete harmony with the act of Christian faith," i.e., omitting "the freedom of" after "with."

125 When, in earlier historical circumstances, popes opposed the degree of religious freedom in Catholic countries that Vatican II implies is necessary in today's world, their opposition clearly did not arise from any fear that the diffusion in society of non-Catholic propaganda would *jeopardize* the freedom with which one should make acts of true Christian (i.e., Catholic) faith. Obviously, the diffusion of *non-*Catholic propaganda cannot ever make people feel pressured or coerced into becoming (or remaining) Catholic.

acknowledges that there have at times appeared among God's people coercive "forms of behavior" opposed to "the spirit of the Gospel." But this does not imply that any traditional Catholic *doctrine* was guilty of such opposition. Both conservative and liberal Fathers would no doubt have agreed that the Inquisition's torture of suspected heretics, the occasional massacres of civilians by crusaders, the forcible baptism of pagans in some parts of Europe, the pogroms and other indignities visited upon Jews, and other such deplorable events, were more than enough to amply justify this regretful historical admission in art. 12. But those sorts of injustices did not reflect what Catholics at the time were required to hold as doctrinal truth. Most of them were, on the contrary, *violations* of what the Church already taught about the treatment of non-Catholics and non-Christians.

71. In short, Mr. Guminski has in no way justified his contention that the part of preconciliar doctrine he considers to be "superseded" by *DH* embodied a regression to some already superseded part of the Old (Mosaic) Law. Nor has he adduced any plausible evidence for his claim that the New Law, as expounded in *DH,* ##9–12, approves only of those legal limitations on religion-related activity that can be justified by reference to the natural moral law alone.

III. The "objective moral order"

72. Mr. Guminski next returns to that issue which underlies all of our discussion in **C.I** and **C.II** above, namely, what Vatican II means by "the objective moral order."[126] Indeed, he considers this to be "the fundamental

---

126 Prior to embarking on his treatment of this issue, Mr. Guminski devotes a paragraph (#46) to part of a 1964 *relatio* which he says I have "apparently failed to notice." Since Bishop De Smedt's words, quoted here, add nothing of substance to what the text of the Declaration itself says in article 6, I am not sure why my critic feels it necessary to draw them to my attention. We read in *DH,* #6 that constitutional privileges for a particular majority religion in a given country are acceptable provided that "the right of all citizens and religious communities to religious freedom must be recognized and respected as well." As I have pointed out elsewhere in my writings on RL, this statement, in order to be compatible with traditional Catholic doctrine, has to be understood as premised on the *de facto* religious pluralism of the modern world that the Council is presupposing and addressing, and not as a purported "timeless" and "absolute" truth that would, as such, retroactively condemn all of the more repressive regimes endorsed by the Church in earlier times. And of course, #6 takes for granted, though it does not mention, those "due limits" on RL which are to be spelled out in the following article (#7), the meaning of which is precisely the main point at issue between Mr. Guminski and myself.

issue that divides us."[127] It will be remembered that in *DH,* #7 the Council affirms the said order to be the appropriate ethical yardstick for evaluating the justice or injustice of any restrictions that government, in the interests of public order, may seek to place on religion-related activity. And my adversary, of course, is claiming that "the objective moral order" must be taken to mean the natural moral law *exclusively.* I, on the other hand, would maintain that although the Council Fathers undoubtedly saw natural law as that aspect of the moral order which needed the most vigorous assertion in the Church's dealings with contemporary States,[128] they neither stated nor implied that divine positive law must be totally excluded in the modern world (and much less always and everywhere), as a criterion for determining the aforesaid legal restrictions. While considering my reply to this part of Mr. Guminski's critique, readers should keep in mind that, in my view, "the fundamental issue that divides us" is not this one, but that which I believe I have already resolved in section **B** of this essay.

73. Before we consider my opponent's specific arguments on this question, an important general point should be kept in mind. I have already recognized in my previous essay that what the Council means by the "objective moral order" in *DH,* #7 is "less than crystal-clear."[129] It's clearly a debatable point. Given this fact, the question arises as to who carries the burden of proof in the debate between Mr. Guminski and myself. Now, it is indisputable that in Catholic theology the term "objective moral order" *per se* – that is, by itself and prescinding from the varying contexts in which it might be used – must be understood to cover divine positive law as well as natural law. For all law coming from God himself is *ipso facto* objectively valid. I therefore submit that the burden of proof here plainly lies with my adversary. It is not I who must demonstrate that the term bears its normal *per se* meaning in *DH,* #7; it is he who must demonstrate that in this particular context it does not. In other words, the term must be *presumed* to encompass both divine positive law and natural law unless the contrary can be proven.

---

127 FR, #47.
128 It was then-Archbishop Karol Wojtyła, from Communist-dominated Poland, who urged that "the objective moral order" be specified in the text, especially in view of the threat posed by twentieth-century totalitarian regimes. Often in the name of "public order," these regimes repressed the exercise of many or all religions on the basis of tyrannical and arbitrary criteria that flouted even the natural moral law (cf. RLC, 98–99).
129 WD, #47.

1. Preliminary "difficulties"

74. Mr. Guminski begins his renewed discussion of "the objective moral order" by considering several related "difficulties," arising from my arguments, that first need resolution.

(a) Religious "discrimination": a necessary distinction

75. First, he says, my denial of his contention that admitting divine positive law as a limiting factor on religion-related activity would imply "authoriz[ing] repression of . . . violations of the Catholic religion, as such" is based on a misunderstanding of that contention.[130] (Indeed, we have already seen in **C.I** above that the expression "as such" can be taken in different ways.) His point seems to be that the concept of government having authority to "repress violations of the Catholic religion as such" does not necessarily imply (as I assumed it did) something as sweeping as a *"carte blanche* for the repression of *any and every* religious manifestation that conflicts with Catholic orthodoxy." Mr. Guminski's understanding of the said concept is, rather, that it also covers a more mitigated repressive power by which only *some* such un-Catholic manifestations would be prohibited – but *on the grounds* that they are un-Catholic. For instance, he says, a law which prohibited *unsolicited* mailings attacking specifically Catholic dogmas, but not *solicited* mailings of that sort, would still count as a law "repressing violations of the Catholic religion as such." And he claims that even this kind of mitigated repression – in effect, any legal disposition wherein government restrictions merely *discriminate* in favor of Catholicism – is also disapproved by *DH*. Well, *DH*, #6 certainly disapproves discrimination *among citizens* on religious grounds; but that does not *ipso facto* imply disapproval of restrictive laws which discriminate between *religions as such*.[131]

(b) "Moral legitimacy"

76. Secondly, in his paragraph 49, Mr. Guminski describes my "reasoning" regarding another issue as "radically defective." The problem here is actually just my wording, not my reasoning: it is my inappropriate choice of the term "moral legitimacy"[132] that has led him to misunderstand my position.[133] But I in turn think he should have used a more general word like

---

130 FR, 48.

131 Cf. my discussion of this point in *RLC*, 85–86, especially n4.

132 WD, #66.

133 I am of course well aware that traditional doctrine explicitly allowed that, even in predominantly Catholic countries, government can and should tolerate public non-

"illicitly," "wrongly" or "reprehensibly," instead of "unjustly," at the end of his #49.

(c) Natural rights and common-good rights

77. Mr. Guminski will probably reply that his third point, expounded in FR, #50, responds to this last criticism. Here he brings forth again his personally-minted terminology whereby "natural rights" are to be seen as a subset of "natural-law rights"; but he now explains that this subset consists only of those rights that are "*proximately* grounded upon the exigencies of human dignity." So I now understand him to be saying that there are some rights which are *neither* these basic (and universal) human rights that we call "natural rights," *nor* rights generated exclusively by the enacted will of a human legislator, but rights belonging to an intermediate category. These pertain on the one hand to the natural moral law (and so are "there" whether or not any human authority recognizes them); but on the other hand they arise not from human dignity *alone* (though that is their ultimate foundation), but proximately from an ensemble of contingent circumstances: for instance, in the civil sphere, rights generated by the objective requirements of the common good in a given society at a given time.

> Catholic manifestations under some circumstances. And insofar as "should" implies a moral duty to tolerate, repression will not, in those circumstances, be "morally legitimate." So let me clarify. These words from WD, #66 quoted by my critic: " . . . is *always and everywhere* a sufficient condition for the moral legitimacy of repressing all public manifestations of other religions," should be replaced by the following: ". . . will *always and everywhere* be sufficient to guarantee that legislation repressing all public non-Catholic religious manifestations will not, *per se*, violate any natural right of the non-Catholics concerned." My previous wording obscured the fact that the popes prior to Pius XI, even though they had not yet begun to develop explicitly any *DH*-type doctrine of a natural human right to RL, would by no means have held that such repressive legislation would always be "morally legitimate," even in Catholic countries. For instance, they would have held that if circumstances called for toleration in order to avoid a worse evil – for instance, serious civil disturbances, or even just widespread and counter-productive popular revulsion against a Church seen as "intolerant" and "persecuting" – then such repression would offend against the cardinal moral virtue of prudence. And if the tolerance was required because of the realistic prospect of achieving a greater good (e.g., facilitating the conversion of a benign, non-proselytizing religious minority by showing them forbearance and good will), then those earlier popes might well have considered such repressive legislation to contravene charity as well as prudence. Nevertheless, it by no means follows that they would have considered it *unjust*. After all, whose *rights* would they have thought it violated?

78. Now, I agree that there *can be* such "common-good" rights. For instance, one could reasonably claim that at least in all modern countries (and arguably everywhere since the invention of writing) there is an objective common-good right *to literacy* (i.e., to be taught to read and write); for this is just an application or development under present civilized circumstances of the more basic and generic natural right *to be educated*[134]). Again, one of the two major U.S. political parties currently maintains that under modern American circumstances there is a common-good right to universal health care, by government subsidies if necessary. Supposing this to be true, this right would be based on the more fundamental natural right to have one's life itself respected and protected by civil authority. However, Mr. Guminski wants to use this distinction between natural and common-good rights in support of his thesis that *DH* contradicts preconciliar doctrine. He is claiming that while Pius XII did implicitly allow in *Ci riesce* that under determined circumstances non-Catholics can have a more-than-merely-*civil* right to freedom in publicly manifesting their errors, this pope had in mind for those folks only a common-good right, not the natural right subsequently proclaimed by Vatican II. For we will "look in vain" in *Ci riesce*, says my critic, for anything suggesting that the public propagators of religious error in a predominantly Catholic country could ever enjoy a right to freedom based proximately on "the exigencies of human dignity." Well, even if that were true, it would also be in vain, logically speaking, for him to argue that *Ci riesce*'s mere *silence* about such a right puts this 1953 allocution in contradiction with *DH*'s affirmation of that right.

79. Quite apart from that, however, I do not concede that searching *Ci riesce* for a natural right to RL is as fruitless an exercise as my opponent says it is. Mr. Guminski seems to be assuming that if a legislator is under a common-good obligation to grant some benefit, B, this must be an obligation *in justice*, so that the potential recipients will have a corresponding common-good *right* to be granted B. But it will be a matter of justice only if this circumstances-generated duty to grant B also derives from a more basic *natural* right of the potential beneficiaries (for instance, the rights to life and education mentioned in the examples given above). So if our legislator denies that his present common-good duty to grant B derives ultimately from some *natural* right, then he should, logically, go on to deny that the potential beneficiaries have even a common-good *right* to be awarded B. For while the exigencies of prudence, charity, and certain other

134 cf. Vatican Council II, Decree on Christian Education, #1.

virtues can, like the exigencies of justice, generate *duties*, they cannot generate *rights*.[135] We could scarcely imagine a Catholic ruler and his country's bishops (assuming he and they are hard-line traditionalists who deny any *DH*-type natural right to RL) engaging in "reasoning" as bizarre as the following: "Hmm. Unfortunately it looks as if our Protestant dissidents now have a moral *right* to be granted the legal freedom to publicly manifest their heresies. That right arises from the fact that if we *don't* grant it, the Masonic-dominated media will be ever more merciless to us, our modernist-infected populace will be increasingly scandalized by our 'intolerance,' and so our Catholic church attendances will seriously decline." No, on those premises, such Catholics would of course see themselves as bound by a common-good duty based only on prudence, not justice, to grant the said legal freedom to religious dissidents.

80. These considerations should make it clear that if Pius XII had believed (as Mr. Guminski thinks he did) that the errant religionists he referred to in *Ci riesce* could never under any circumstances have a *natural* right to be left free to publicly manifest their false beliefs, he could not, logically, have recognized that they had even a *common-good* right to that freedom. But this pope clearly *did* imply that errant religionists could sometimes have a right to the aforesaid freedom.[136] And since he did not have in mind here a mere *civil* right freely created by human positive law, we must conclude by a process of elimination that the only kind of right he

135 To take a clear (and currently quite realistic) example: If prudence in the interests of the common good imposes on the civil authorities of a northern Mexican state a duty to tolerate a certain amount of drug trafficking, simply because trying to stamp it out altogether would predictably lead to a worse evil – to wit, full-scale warfare orchestrated by the powerful drug lords – then that duty certainly does not arise from any kind of *right* of the latter not to be prevented from engaging in this limited and currently tolerated drug peddling. It would be mere brutal sarcasm for a narco-baron to assert, "We have a *right* to be left free to sell these drugs, based on the fact that we will blow up your police station and all its occupants if you try to stop us!"

136 The Pope said that in determined circumstances, *God* would not grant human authority "any right" to repress certain forms of errant religious activity. That implies repression would be *unjust* in that situation even if civil law mandated it. Now, an unjust act by definition violates someone's rights. And whose rights, in this situation, would be violated by repression if not those of the repressed errant religionists themselves? For if *their* right was not being violated by the repressive legislation, *a fortiori* nobody else's right would be. *Ergo*, Pius XII implies in *Ci riesce* that there can in some circumstances be a God-given right to immunity from human coercion in publicly manifesting religious error.

could have been implying was a *natural* right – the kind *DH* was to affirm a few years later. I therefore agree with Msgr. Ocáriz that while the Church had never taught this explicitly before Vatican II, the conciliar affirmation was "something new that was already *implicitly* formulated by Pius XII [in *Ci riesce*]."[137] Indeed, as the Council Fathers themselves point out in a footnote, they propose to "develop" (i.e., harmoniously build upon) other teachings leading in the same direction enunciated by John XXIII and Pius XI as well as Pius XII.[138]

2. What does "the objective moral order" mean in *DH*, #7?

81. Hopefully the foregoing discussion has shed some light on these three preliminary "difficulties." I shall pass over Mr. Guminski's #52, wherein he waxes eloquent about how "odd," "bizarre," "far-fetched" and "implausible" my reading of the preconciliar doctrine is; for these very vigorous adjectives are based mainly on the serious misunderstanding and misrepresentation of my position that I have cleared up in **B.IV.2** above.[139] We can

137 ". . . *una novità già **implicitamente** formulata da Pio XII*" (op. cit., 90, emphasis in original).

138 Cf. the magisterial sources referred to in *DH* #2, n2, including another intervention of Pius XII (his radio broadcast of December 24, 1942). The note also has a reference to Leo XIII's 1888 encyclical *Libertas*. However this Leonine statement contains only a mere "germ" of *DH*'s doctrine, consisting in the fact that it mentions the subjectively upright and sincere *consciences* of Catholics, as well as their possession of objective religious truth, as being relevant to their claim to civil freedom. That may well have helped raise the question as to whether perhaps the upright consciences of sincere *non*-Catholics, even though erroneous, might also have some similar relevance.

139 To read Mr. Guminski's footnote to this paragraph (FR, n77), one would think I had already conceded that the postconciliar changes in Spanish law implied a reading of *DH* according to which it contradicts traditional Catholic doctrine. If I had made that concession, my denial that the said changes have any "probative value" for Mr. Guminski's claim that there is indeed such a contradiction would then be resting on nothing more than the fact (to which I drew readers' attention) that Spanish civil legislators enjoy no particular scholarly or juridical authority as interpreters of the Church's ecumenical councils (cf. WD, ##31–32). Evidently thinking that this is my only defense, my opponent thinks he has effectively countered it simply by pointing out that the legislative changes "were done only after governmental negotiations with and approval by the Holy See." But how strange it is that my learned adversary fails to see that I never conceded the aforesaid premise, upon which the "probative value" of his own argument depends! For the whole of my #32 is dedicated to my explicit *refusal* to concede that the "brief [Spanish] legal text itself" presupposes a Guminski-style interpretation of *DH* (i.e., one

now proceed to my critic's *ex professo* treatment of what we are to understand by "the objective moral order." Once again, however, readers should
keep in mind that even if Mr. Guminski should successfully discharge the
burden of proof which requires him to establish that the Council Fathers
meant by this term the natural moral law *alone*, this would not mean he has
proved his major claim in this dispute, namely, that there is a *doctrinal* contradiction between *DH* and traditional Catholic teaching (cf. **B.V** above).
However, even though Mr. Guminski has, as it were, lost the war, has he at
least won this particular battle? That is, do his arguments prove that the
Council has determined that, *at least under modern circumstances*, the natural moral law is the only acceptable ethical yardstick, in Catholic and non-
Catholic countries alike, for establishing and/or evaluating government
restrictions on religion-related activity?

(a) Why didn't the Fathers *spell out* "natural law"?
82. In support of his contention that natural moral law *alone* is intended in
DH, #7, Mr. Guminski, in FR, #54, appeals principally[140] to his

which reads the Declaration as reversing traditional doctrine by implicitly brand-
ing the restrictive provisions of the Holy See's own 1953 Concordat with Spain as
violations of immutable divine law). And since my critic offers not one word of
argument to buttress his assumption that the said legal text *does* presuppose such
a reading of *DH*, he would not have defeated my own argument even if he had
been able to point to a public, papally signed document (rather than just an unpub-
licized and "faceless" communiqué from the Vatican Secretariat of State) that
approved these postconciliar changes in Spanish law.

140 There is also a secondary argument in #54. I contended in my first response (cf.
WD, #48) that if the obligation to exclude divine positive law from all consideration in determining civil restrictions on religion-related activity were proposed by
Vatican II *as doctrine* (i.e., as a thesis valid always and everywhere under the New
Law), then it would not be a development of existing doctrine, but rather, a *brand-
new* doctrine – something Catholics believe cannot possibly be introduced after
revelation was completed in the first century A.D. Mr. Guminski objects that I
have cited as evidence of this impossibility only Vatican I's teaching that no new
revelation can ever be introduced after that point in history. So he claims that since
the admittedly novel doctrine which (in his view) was introduced by *DH* is not presented as divine revelation, but only as a norm of natural law, its introduction in
the twentieth century is not ruled out by this Vatican I teaching. I would reply that
since, as Mr. Guminski admits, Old Testament revelation (divine positive law)
allowed the repression of false religions in Israel, only another *revealed* norm
would suffice to prohibit under the Law of Christ the kind of repression that had
been allowed – indeed, prescribed – under the Law of Moses. But since any such
supposed revelation would be making its appearance nearly two millennia after the

interpretation of the preamble that I have already rebutted in **B.II.2** above. In the next paragraph he first addresses my question as to why, if the Fathers had wanted to present the natural moral law as the one and only acceptable yardstick, they did not save us all this confusion and trouble by simply saying so clearly. My critic's reply is, in effect, that their intention to exclude divine positive law altogether from any role in such deliberations was already so "plain" that they didn't *need* to spell it out!

83. The rhetorical boldness of this reply cannot compensate for its lack of substance. Mr. Guminski offers only one *reason* for claiming the aforesaid intention to be so transparently obvious: he says that the "plain meaning" of *DH*, Chapter I as a whole is to describe and define a right to religious freedom "in terms of the NML in a document addressed to all humanity, including non-Christians."[141] But only if the document had been addressed *exclusively* to non-Christian societies and states would it be obvious that divine positive law was completely off the table in this discussion. (It would indeed be quite unrealistic to expect avowedly secular and other non-Christian governments to obey the revealed Law of Christ in their legislation regarding public order.) Since Chapter 1 addresses both Christian and non-Christian states, the use of a generic term like "the objective moral order" fits in very well with an intention *not* to exclude divine positive law altogether as a criterion for determining legal restrictions. For the use of this term is entirely compatible with the thesis that while *all* governments are always bound to observe that basic part of the objective moral order which is the natural law, Christian and (especially) Catholic governments are entitled to enforce *in addition* certain points of the Law of Christ – no less "objective" than the natural law – in order to keep the bar for communal conduct set somewhat higher than could be expected in societies where the Gospel is less known and accepted.[142] It is

---

end of the apostolic age, it would indeed be ruled out as inauthentic by Vatican I's teaching. Cf. also section **C.II** *supra*.

141 FR, #55.

142 It seems worthwhile clarifying here that I am not suggesting *DH* allows for the idea that the natural right *itself* has different and more restrictive concrete implications for those living in Catholic countries than it does for those in other countries. As the *relator* told the Council Fathers, "It cannot be said that the requirements of the dignity of the human person, or the rights of man, are not the same in a so-called confessional state as they are in a 'pluralistic' society" (*AS*, IV, I, 192, #5, my translation). My position is that, in view of the sovereignty of Christ the King over all societies and states, Catholic and non-Catholic alike, there is no strict, God-given *right* of anyone, anywhere, to be left legally free by government

evident that this understanding of the document is in no way contrary to the passages of the *Catechism* that my opponent cites against me;[143] for

to violate these divine positive laws against divorce, polygamy, etc., that are (unlike most revealed truths) fundamental to God's revealed plan for the right ordering of human society as such, and are in fact necessary in practice for upholding respect for human dignity and the natural law itself. In other words, *DH* should be understood to mean the natural right to RL itself has (at least under modern circumstances) the same practical implications for the whole of humanity as regards what it would in principle be just or unjust for governments to permit or forbid in these areas of behavior; but only in Christian and Catholic countries will it be politically realistic to ask and expect governments to apply these few limitations which are derived from the Law of Christ rather than from natural law.

143 Cf. FR, #57. In this paragraph my critic also makes some secondary objections. Referring to WD, ##16, 39 and 47, he says I "quite frequently refer to the [natural moral law] alone, thus prescinding from supernatural revelation." Well, it is true that I do so in ##16 and 47 (not in #39), but not in a way that is inconsistent with my interpretation of *DH*, #7. At the beginning of my "imaginary codicil" (WD, #16) I say that Chapter I of *DH* "expounds the right to religious liberty from the standpoint of reason and natural law alone." But to read this chapter thus – i.e., as prescinding from revelation in establishing the reality of the right itself – is not inconsistent with claiming that the same chapter (in #7.3) allows that the legal *restrictions* placed on activity carried out in the name of that right might in some cases appropriately be drawn from revelation. Also in FR, #56, Mr. Guminski dismisses as a "desperate ploy" my saying that every violation of divine positive law *indirectly* violates natural law as well (cf. WD, #43). Such violation indeed occurs because an abundance of well-documented miracles over two millennia, along with other "signs of credibility," make the divine origin of the Christian religion (including, therefore, of its most basic affirmation, the existence of God) a truth accessible to natural human reason (cf. Vatican I, DS 3033, 3034). However, it is true, as my critic points out, that divinely revealed precepts cannot be "incorporated" into the natural moral law itself; so I concede that I overstated my case in saying that the latter, "known by the light of reason . . . *requires* individuals and societies . . . to *recognize* the truth of . . . what [the Church] proclaims as divine positive law" (emphasis added). For although natural reason can conclude that the Catholic Church is a credible bearer of a divinely revealed message, it "requires" the supernatural and freely accepted gift of faith to actually "recognize" (i.e., to believe) the content of that revelation (cf. DS, 3035). (Without self-contradiction – though perhaps not without ill will – one can admit that someone is a credible witness, and yet choose to believe he is lying or mistaken.) I should have limited myself to saying what Leo XIII taught (with implicit confirmation in *CCC*, #2105), namely, "Nature and reason . . . command" not only individuals, but also "the civil community," to "worship God in holiness . . . [according to] the religion which God enjoins, and which certain and most clear marks show to be the only one true religion" (*Immortale Dei*, 6, translation from *The Companion to the*

they simply emphasize what I have just acknowledged – that the natural law is indeed the indispensable *basis* for all human rights. And it would of course be begging the crucial question to assume, without textual evidence, that, according to the mind of the Council, *DH* intends to teach in Chapter 1 that every country on earth should adopt a single uniform ethical criterion for determining the requirements of public order.

(b) Do *Gaudium et Spes* and *Veritatis Splendor* support Guminski's position?

84. In my initial rejoinder I noted, but thought it unnecessary to refute, the claim that what the Council says in *Gaudium et Spes,* #16, and what John Paul II says in *Veritatis Splendor,* #53, constitute evidence that "the objective moral order" in *DH,* #7 should be read as excluding divine positive law altogether.[144] But since Mr. Guminski (still in FR, #55) now insists that these *GS* and *VS* texts do support his "exclusivist" reading of *DH,* #7, I had best explain why I think they do not.

85. First, *GS,* #16. My critic highlights two points made in this conciliar text: **(a)** man discovers through his conscience "a [moral] law which he has not laid upon himself," and which in fact is "inscribed by God" in his heart; and **(b)** "the more a correct conscience prevails," the more will people "abandon blind whims and work to conform to *the objective norms of morality*" (emphasis added by Guminski).[145] Now, even if Mr. Guminski were correct in claiming without qualification that "*Gaudium et Spes* is here referring to the natural law,"[146] i.e., to the natural law *alone*, what could we then conclude on the basis of **(a)** and **(b)**? Clearly, nothing more than that this (natural) "law" which man finds "inscribed in his heart" is not just some "blind whim," but an objectively valid moral standard. Of course, I do not dispute that. Is it really necessary to spell out that **(a)** and **(b)** in no way imply that the term "objective moral order" – as used in a different magisterial document and in connection with a very different

Catechism of the Catholic Church [San Francisco: Ignatius, Press, 1995], 676). I raised this point mainly in view of my claim that, even today, anti-establishment propaganda in an officially Catholic nation could, consistently with *DH*, be legally prohibited. For while the universal Kingship of Christ is itself a revealed truth, it is more directly and intimately linked to the natural-law duty of civic communities as well as individuals to recognize the credibility of Catholicism than are most of the other revealed truths.

144 Cf. CH, #32, WD, #41.
145 FR, #54.
146 Ibid.

issue – means natural law to the exclusion of divine positive law? Any such inference will be still more obviously invalid if *GS,* #16 itself includes divine positive law as well as natural law in that "law" which man discovers through his conscience. And indeed it does. Citing Jesus's summary of the *revealed* law of love (Mt. 22: 37–40 and Gal. 5: 14), the Council affirms here, "By conscience, in a wonderful way, that law is made known which is fulfilled in the love of God and of one's neighbor." Moreover, the sole magisterial document referenced in *GS,* #16 is a radio message of Pius XII about "forming the Christian conscience of youth." That the Pope did not have in mind natural law *alone* in this discourse is clear from his own words: "[F]orming the Christian conscience of children or of young people consists above all in illuminating their minds regarding *the will of Christ, his law, his way.*"[147]

86. In *VS,* #53, wherein John Paul II cites the words "objective norms of morality" from *GS,* #16, the only point he is making is that if natural law itself were not immutable, there would be no such "objective norms" valid for all men at all periods of history. It by no means follows from this that the Pope identifies the "objective norms of morality" in *GS,* #16 with the norms of "the natural moral law" *alone* – and much less that he is reading a similar identification into the words "objective moral order" in *DH,* #7.3. For what the Pope says here makes perfect sense on the assumption that he understands the norms of natural law to be, rather, that *subset* of all "objective norms of morality" which have been in principle accessible to all men at all periods of history. (The equally "objective" norms of divine positive law, under Old and New Covenants respectively, have been accessible only to some men at some periods of history.) Also, *pace* Mr. Guminski's implied claim in his initial critique,[148] the mere fact that RL is asserted in *DH* as a *natural* right by no means implies that divine positive law – a supernatural factor – may never be invoked in deciding what constitutes a punishable abuse of that right. (As we have seen,[149] my critic himself now recognizes that, consistently with our belief in the divine inspiration of the Old Testament, we "standard-orthodox" Catholics must acknowledge that divine positive law in the time of Moses *did in fact* restrict the exercise of the said natural right very severely.)

---

147 ". . . *formare la coscienza cristiana di un fanciullo o di un giovane consiste innanzi tutto nell'illuminare la loro mente circa* **la volontà di Cristo, la sua legge, la sua via**" (*AAS* 44 [1952], 272, emphasis added).

148 Cf. CH, #32, sentence beginning, "In the first place, ..."

149 Cf. section **B.V** *supra.*

(c) *DH*, #3 and the "divine and eternal law"

87. Mr. Guminski next expresses regret that he did not previously cite, as further evidence against my position, the passage at the beginning of *DH,* #3 that speaks of the divine and eternal law as the "supreme rule of life," and as an "unchanging truth" that people "are able . . . increasingly to recognize" under "the gentle guidance of God's providence."[150] But again, even supposing it to be true that the Council is referring here to natural law exclusively,[151] that would by no means prove that the same exclusive meaning must be ascribed to the term "objective moral order" in article 7. In fact, the Fathers' purpose in drawing attention to the eternal law in article 3 is quite different, and is made clear in the sentence following the one cited by my opponent: "For this reason everybody has the duty and consequently the right to seek the truth in religious matters, so that, through the use of appropriate means, he may prudently form judgments of conscience which are sincere and true." By "the truth in religious matters" the Council manifestly means what is revealed as well as what is naturally knowable. The Fathers go on to affirm in the next paragraph of #3 that this "search"

---

150 Cf. FR, #55, citation over n79.

151 In fact, such an interpretation of *DH* 3 seems too restrictive, despite Prof. William E. May's apparent reading of this text in that sense. (Cf. references to May's writings in FR, n80.) Catholic doctrine regards *every* kind of just law, not only natural law, as coming under the over-arching and immutable divine plan for creation that is called the eternal law (cf. *CCC,* #1952). (Divine positive law is also "immutable," both in the sense that by an immutable decree of the eternal law the Mosaic Law was destined to be replaced at the appropriate moment of human history by the Law of Christ, and also in the sense that the latter, ever since its promulgation at Pentecost, remains immutable until the end of the world.) In the three passages from the *Summa Theologiae* cited in the (original) text of *DH* 3, the first (Ia IIae, 91, 1) simply establishes that there *is* an eternal law, while the third (Ia IIae, 93, 3) argues that every other law, human and divine, is derived from this eternal law. Only in the second cited passage (Ia IIae, 93, 2) does St. Thomas even mention natural law. And he does so in the context of arguing that all men are capable of knowing the *eternal* law, though in widely varying degrees: everyone, he says, can at least understand "the general principles of the natural law" (*principia communia legis naturalis*). But Aquinas by no means suggests here that man's knowledge of the eternal law is *restricted* to what he can know of the natural law. Indeed, any such suggestion would of course be heretical by virtue of denying the knowability of revealed (divine positive) law (cf. Vatican I's definitions, DS 3027, 3028). If the Council Fathers had wanted to give unique or exclusive emphasis to natural law in *DH,* #3, they would presumably have referenced only Ia IIae, 91, 2, which is dedicated to establishing that *there is* a natural moral law binding on all men.

for truth must be carried out in a way appropriate to human nature and dignity, namely, by free inquiry, dialogue, etc. Now, this requirement in no way rules out the handful of legal restrictions based on divine positive law that I maintain could still today, consistently with *DH,* be applied to religion-related activity in any country where this would be politically feasible. For an officially Catholic nation's legislation against divorce, polygamy, anti-establishment propaganda and certain activities on Sundays and major Feast Days will clearly not present any obstacles to the free and untrammeled search for religious truth on the part of that nation's non-Catholic minorities.

(d) Do May and Finnis support Guminski?

88. According to Mr. Guminski, the respected moral theologian William E. May also "argues that this passage" of *DH, #3,* in the light of its references to Aquinas, and together with the already cited passages of *GS* and *VS,* "discloses that *the objective moral order* is indeed the [natural moral law] alone."[152] My critic thus leaves readers with the impression – especially in view of his italicization of the pertinent term from *DH, #7* – that May, in the writings referred to here,[153] has in mind article 7 as well as article 3. But in fact May does not discuss article 7 on any page of either the book or the online article referenced in Mr. Guminski's footnote. Indeed, the term "objective moral order" itself appears nowhere in either of those publications. (Professor May has personally confirmed[154] that he has never argued that in *DH, #7* the said term means the natural moral law *alone,* and that in fact he disagrees with such a reading of the conciliar text.)

89. Mr. Guminski also refers us to an essay[155] by Professor John Finnis of Oxford University about the Council's teaching on natural law and objective morality. But no more than May does Finnis suggest here that "the objective moral order" in *DH, #7* means natural law exclusively. Indeed, in commenting on the passage of *DH, #3* under discussion, Finnis says that when the Council Fathers affirm, "It is through his conscience that man sees and recognizes the dictates of the divine law," they mean to "*include* the requirements of the natural law"[156] – i.e., they do not mean the natural law *alone.* Finnis thus reads the Council as implying that this

152 FR, #56, emphasis in original.
153 Cf. references to May's book and article in FR, n80.
154 This was in an e-mail message to the present writer of September 13, 2010.
155 See FR, n80, for publication details.
156 Finnis, 116 (my emphasis).

"divine law" which "man sees and recognizes" through his conscience includes both the revealed Law of Christ and the natural law. (That of course is the orthodox doctrine we would expect the Pope and bishops to teach, in line with Pius XII's radio message which they referenced in *GS*, #16.[157])

(e) The *relatio* of November 1964

90. Mr. Guminski goes on, "Finally, as to the meaning of *objective moral order*, I refer the reader to the relatio in which it was stated: . . . [followed by citation]."[158] But here again, my critic's italicization and choice of words tend to insinuate something false without actually stating it – in this case that the *relator*, in the passage cited, was explaining part of a draft that included the term "objective moral order." In fact, that term was not introduced into the conciliar text until the final session, nearly a year after this *relatio* was presented to the Fathers.

91. This point of chronology raises an important hermeneutical question: Are all official *relationes* of equal relevance for establishing the true meaning of a promulgated conciliar document? Clearly they are not, for a given *relatio* may come to be superseded by another as the text of the schema itself is amended during the drafting process. This was especially true in regard to the RL schema, since its doctrinal content became less and less liberal in each of the five successive drafts, as the Commission sought to win more votes from tradition-conscious Fathers.[159] For instance, the *relator*'s word "gravely," in the first sentence cited here by Mr. Guminski, subsequently became obsolete, as it were, when the words "*grave damnum*" were deleted from the final draft of article 7. (The Council thus opted *not* to teach that the threat to public order arising from any given religion-related activity must be "grave" before government may prohibit it.[160])

92. More importantly, at the time this *relatio* was delivered the schema still strongly reflected John Courtney Murray's very un-traditional position that the State is incompetent to make any judgments on religion as such.[161]

---

157 Cf. text accompanying n147 *supra*.
158 FR, #57, emphasis in original.
159 Cf. discussion in *RLC*, 64–68.
160 Cf. *RLC*, 99–100.
161 The original (1963) draft of the RL schema was quite dogmatic about this, claiming that "it is manifest that the State . . . is not qualified (*ineptam esse*) to make judgments of truth in religious matters" (*AS*, vol. III/pt. VIII, 442, my translation).

And the *relator*, Bishop Emil De Smedt, strongly endorsed this view – at least at that time. For during this same 1964 session he also stated emphatically, "If everything is to proceed correctly, it must be held that the State, or government, is quite incapable of making judgments of truth in matters of religion."[162] The second draft (*textus emendatus*) then under consideration stated that "Civil authority must . . . be considered as going beyond its proper limits if it involves itself (*sese immisceat*) in those things that concern man's orientation to God. . . . [It should] restrict itself to the things of this world (*sese ad res huius saeculi restringendo*)."[163] So it is understandable that De Smedt, in explaining *this* text, laid down the naturalistic restrictions on State intervention which Mr. Guminski cites against me, and that he grounded them on the premise that "the coercive action of the public power" may not "operat[e] in the order of religion as such."

93. However, this "Murrayite" insistence in the second and third drafts on a strict juridical naturalism on the part of the State was sharply criticized by conservative Fathers and proved incapable of winning the desired consensus of votes. It was replaced in the fourth draft (*textus recognitus*) by a more traditional statement, and by a still more traditional one in the finally approved version (*textus denuo recognitus*), as follows:

> Therefore the civil power, whose distinctive purpose is to care for the common temporal good (*cuius finis proprius est bonum commune temporal curare*), must recognize and favor the religious life of citizens; but it must be seen as exceeding its limits if it presumes either to hinder or to take charge of religious activity.[164]

As I have commented elsewhere on this amendment,

> This was much more in accordance with the traditional position. The temporal good is now the *distinctive* purpose of civil authority – that which distinguishes it from ecclesiastical authority – but it is no longer said to be the *only* purpose. Civil authority

---

Readers will recall that the only kind of constitutional "establishment" of religion Murray would allow was one that had no juridical effects and was limited to the sociological observation that such-and-such a religion is the prevailing one among citizens.

162 "*[U]t omnia autem recte procedant, tenendum est quod a Statu vel gubernio nulla possidetur capacitas ad iudicia de veritate circa rem religiosam ferenda*" (comments of September 23, 1964, *AS*, vol. III/pt. II, 352, my translation).

163 This wording was retained in the *textus reemendatus*: AS, vol. IV, pt. V, 81.

164 *DH*, #3, last section.

should keep in mind the transcendent destiny of man, and should order temporal affairs so as to help, rather than hinder, the attainment of that destiny.[165]

94. It was also in this final version, of course, that the passage we have discussed at length in **B.II.2** above was introduced into the Preamble – that which reaffirmed the "traditional Catholic doctrine regarding the moral duty of men and societies [toward Catholicism]." Since that "traditional" doctrine makes it very clear that the public power has not only the capacity, but the duty, to make the religious "judgment of truth" that Roman Catholicism is the true religion, it is incompatible with Murray's opinion, which was still embedded in the *textus emendatus* that De Smedt was expounding in the *relatio* cited by Mr. Guminski.

95. In view of these subsequent and very substantial changes in the text of *DH* itself, this 1964 *relatio* must be seen as superseded and obsolete – at least as regards any force it might otherwise have had in countering my contention that the term "objective moral order" bears its normal Catholic sense in *DH*, #7, covering both natural law and divine positive law. When the passage containing this term was introduced into the fourth draft during the 1965 session, the *relator's* explanation did not suggest that it meant natural law *alone*. This is all he said:

> This is an addition of great importance. It has been introduced in accord with the thinking of many Fathers who ask that, in the assessment of public order, there must be taken into account not only historical situations (*non solum . . . historicas situationes*), but also, and above all, those things that are required by the objective moral order (*sed etiam et in primis . . . ea quae morali ordine obiectivo postulantur*).[166]

(f) Authoritative postconciliar statements

96. It is clear that the chief signatory to *DH*, Pope Paul VI, cannot have not understood "the objective moral order" in #7.3 to mean natural law *alone*. The corollary to this restrictive reading of the conciliar text is, in Mr.

---

165 *RLC*, 67–68. The word *proprius* does not mean "proper" in the modern English sense of "appropriate," "right" or "correct." It designates what is exclusively or at least especially *one's own,* in contrast to something one shares equally in common with others. This Latin-derived usage is conserved in the distinction between "proper" and "common" texts in Catholic liturgical books.

166 *AS*, vol. IV, pt. V, 154 (*relatio* of October 25, 1965).

Guminski's words, that "it is inadmissible to juridically presuppose the truth of Catholicism as a supernatural religion."[167] But less than five years after promulgating the Declaration, the Pontiff taught the opposite of this, affirming that divine positive law not only could, but should in principle, be reflected in the "juridical norms" of civil society. Pope Paul exhorted the participants in an international congress of civil lawyers as follows:

> If [as Cicero taught] justice "is the mistress and queen of all the virtues," your activity . . . should be inspired constantly by those ethical principles which are solidly based on the objective order of the divine law, natural *and positive*, as well as on the subjective conscience, and which confer upon *juridical norms* their stability and their social value, over and above their legal character as such.[168]

97. Finally, we have the *Catechism of the Catholic Church*. No more than the actual text of *DH*, the relevant 1965 *relationes*, or Pope Paul VI, does it suggest that the juridical requirements of public order must today be determined everywhere in accord with natural law exclusively. On the contrary, it teaches that public order must not be "conceived in a 'positivistic' or 'naturalistic' manner."[169] Now, according to Mr. Guminski, this statement "appears [to be a warning] against any interpretation of 'public order' that would preclude the promotion of religious life or subvert the freedom of the Church."[170] True, but that is not the only thing it is warning against. Indeed, the footnote to this statement confirms the impression already left by the text itself, namely, that in censuring "naturalistic," as well as "positivistic," concepts of public order, the *Catechism* includes within this censure precisely that understanding of public order which my opponent

---

167 FR, #58.

168 *"Se la giustizia 'omnium est domina et regina virtutum,' come già arrivò a concepirla la sapienza pagana (CICER., De Officiis, 3, 6), la vostra attività . . . dovrà ispirarsi costantemente a quei principi etici, aventi nell'ordine obiettivo della legge divina, naturale e positiva, non meno che nella coscienza soggettiva, la loro consistenza, e che conferiscono alla norma giuridica, oltre che la sua 'ratio iuris,' la sua stabilità e il suo valore sociale"* (Paul VI, allocution to VIII International Congress of Young Lawyers, September 24, 1970, *AAS* 62 [1970], 614, emphasis added). The allocution is also accessible at: www.vatican.va/ holy_father/paul_vi/speeches/1970/documents/hf_p-vi_spe_19700924_avvocati_it.html .

169 *CCC*, #2109, my emphasis.

170 CH, n96.

attributes to *DH,* #7 – and which, as we have seen, bears within itself the potential to "subvert the freedom of the Church."[171] For the footnote refers to the passage of *Quanta Cura* wherein Blessed Pius IX affirms:

> And, since where *religion has been removed from civil society*, and the doctrine *and authority of divine revelation repudiated*, the genuine notion of justice and human rights is darkened and lost, and the place of true justice and legitimate right is supplied by material force, thence it appears why it is that some, utterly neglecting and disregarding the surest principles of sound reason, dare to proclaim that "the people's will, manifested by what is called public opinion or in some other way, constitutes a supreme law, free from all divine and human control . . ." But who does not see and clearly perceive that *human society, when set loose from the bonds of religion* and true justice (*religionis ac verae iustitiae vinculis solutum*) can have, in truth, no other end than the purpose of obtaining and amassing wealth, and that (society under such circumstances) follows no other law in its actions, except the unchastened desire of ministering to its own pleasure and interests?[172]

98. The passages italicized above highlight the fact that Pius IX – and therefore the contemporary Catholic Church which here confirms his teaching – is insisting that the "divine revelation" and "the bonds of religion" (meaning here, of course, the Catholic religion) should in principle be part of those legal and juridical norms that guard public order in civil society.

99. I began this section (**C.III**) by pointing out that the burden of proof lay with Mr. Guminski to show that the term "objective moral order" does not, in the context of *Dignitatis Humanae*, bear the inclusive meaning that accrues to it, normally and *per se*, on the basis of orthodox Catholic theology. I now conclude **C.III** by submitting, on the basis of the foregoing argumentation: **(1)** that my opponent has altogether failed to demonstrate that the term, as used in *DH* 7, means the natural moral law exclusively; and **(2)** that, on the contrary, the evidence abundantly supports my contention that it should be taken to include *in principle* divine positive law as

---

171 Cf. discussion in the last pages of section **C.I** *supra*.
172 DS 2890. The above translation is that given in *The Companion to the Catechism of the Catholic Church* (San Francisco: Ignatius, Press, 1995), 759–760, emphasis added. The definitive Latin version of the *Catechism*, in its n37 to #2109, gives this Denzinger reference, whereas the footnote in the earlier English version simply referred to "*Quanta Cura* 3."

well, even though the latter will in practice be inevitably disregarded in the legislation and jurisprudence of the great majority of States, and (given the clearly implied judgment of the Council about the degree of freedom required *universally* under modern circumstances[173]), will be of only quite limited applicability even in officially Catholic States. Indeed, the *Catechism*'s explicit censure of "naturalistic" concepts of public order can, especially in the light of its footnoted grounding in *Quanta Cura* at that point, be taken as an authentic magisterial interpretation of *DH, #7* that rules out Mr. Guminski's "natural-law-alone" reading.

100. This in turn implies that section **C** as a whole can now end with the following corollary to the above conclusion, in answer to the question we posed at the outset of **C**: Mr. Guminski is quite wrong in ascribing to *DH* the novel doctrine that when civil authorities (past, present and future) are determining the "due limits" to be placed on activity carried out in the name of religious freedom, "the truth of Catholicism [must be] deemed not juridically relevant in determining what constitutes a just public order."

D. "Important Remaining Points"

101. I believe I have now replied sufficiently to the principal arguments put forward in Mr. Guminski's second critique. His concluding paragraphs 59–64 deal with some "important remaining points,"[174] and I shall now briefly respond to those among them that I have not already addressed.[175]

---

173 In his final paragraph on the "objective moral order," my opponent insists that, according to *DH*, this order cannot be considered as being violated by "public non-Catholic propaganda and manifestations" which would "subject [Catholics] to temptations against their faith" (FR, #58). Of course, I have consistently acknowledged in all my publications on this topic, beginning with *RLC* (at 143), that the Council implicitly judges this to be the case *under modern circumstances*. For practically any public denial of any Catholic doctrine would *ipso facto* qualify as a "temptation" of that sort in countries with many Catholics; and *DH* is clearly implying that, even in such countries, such denials may not *as such* – i.e., when there is no additional aggravating factor – be repressed as offences against public order. Of course, Mr. Guminski's central claim, expressed in Proposition Z, is that *DH* is not referring here only to modern circumstances, but is teaching, as Catholic doctrine, that such repression has (at least since the New Law of Christ came into effect) always and everywhere violated the natural right to RL of those affected. Section **B** of this essay, building on my previous rejoinder to Mr. Guminski, is my rebuttal of this claim.

174 FR, #58.

175 I have replied to the third of Mr. Guminski's "remaining points" (FR, #61) in the last four paragraphs of section **C.I** *supra*, and to the last of them (FR, #64) at the

I. "Moral rights" vs. "juridical rights"?

102. In the first of these (FR, #59) my opponent describes as "captious" the argument at the end of section II of my previous essay. However, I think that word applies more aptly to his own quite pedantic objection.[176] Moreover, on looking more closely at the two pertinent paragraphs of *DH,* #7.2 and #7.3, I now think I conceded too much to my adversary in accepting his premise that they embody a distinction between two different kinds of rights, only one of which may be guarded by legal sanctions. For while #7.2 emphasizes a certain "moral principle" and a corresponding "moral obligation," it says nothing about "moral rights" (or anything equivalent). Nor does #7.3 speak of "legal (or juridical) rights." In none of the three occurrences of the word "rights" (*iurium* and *iuribus*) in these two paragraphs, is it accompanied by any qualifying adjective. So it seems gratuitous to assert that one sort of right is meant in #7.2 and another in #7.3, even though my adversary can claim the support of a highly placed conciliar *peritus*, Father (later Cardinal) Jérôme Hamer, in reading the text in that

end of **B.V** above (cf. n100 and accompanying text). I shall deal with FR, #62 here in this footnote, because this objection seems to be based on nothing more than a simple misreading of what I said. Mr. Guminski protests that he "make[s] no claim that 'the Church was always wrong'" in her more repressive judgments of earlier times. But, as is patent from his own quotation of my words here, I never said that he (or anyone else in particular) was in fact making that claim. All I said was that it would beg the vital question to read *DH* as though *Paul VI and the Council Fathers* were making such a claim. (In this dispute Mr. Guminski has set himself the limited task of arguing only that a traditional Catholic doctrine has been contradicted by *DH*, not that the former was "wrong" – although of course, like non-Catholics in general, he thinks it certainly *was* wrong.) As for my adversary's brief critical allusion in #62 to my understanding of "objective moral order," cf. section **IIIg** (##39–43) of my previous essay and **C.III** of this one.

176 Mr. Guminski is in effect insisting that when I (and by implication, the Council's *relator*) wanted to speak of people who transgress just *legal* limits in the first way specified in #7.3, we should not have said that such folks violate the rights "of other citizens," but rather – following the precise wording of #7.3 – the rights "of *all* citizens." But of course, the latter term is confusing and stylistically awkward in a context where the *violators* of those rights are being spoken of. My opponent grounds this insistence on the equally captious claim that since the text of #7.2, in discussing merely "moral (or quasi-moral) rights," happens to attribute them to "others" rather than to "all," it follows that the terms "rights of others" (or "rights of other citizens") must always – at least in commentaries on *DH* – be assumed to mean *only* those kinds of rights, and never the "legal (or juridical) rights" referred to in #7.3. (Cf. CH, #12, cited in WD, #10.)

sense.[177] A further reason for my disagreement with them is the fact that the *relator* never said anything to suggest that article 7 contained a distinction between legally enforceable and legally unenforceable rights. So there is no reason to suppose that the Fathers intended the text to make that distinction, especially since ##7.2 and 7.3, taken together, make perfect sense without it. The former stresses our moral obligation to respect the rights of others in exercising our own liberties; the latter then points out that those who fail to do so can and should be restrained by civil authority, according to appropriate juridical norms.

103. This *quaestio disputata* has practical relevance especially in connection with certain methods of religious proselytism that *DH* says amount to a "violation of the right of others" (#4.4). To what extent is the Council teaching that these may be repressed by law? Only to a very limited extent, say Hamer and Guminski, appealing to the distinction supposedly found in article 7.[178] I would dispute their opinion not only on the basis of my above comments on that article, but also in the light of the redaction history of article 4. It was already obvious in the penultimate draft of the RL schema that *some forms* of these "coercive, dishonest, or otherwise 'unworthy' types of persuasion" were to be understood as meriting legal prohibition; for, of course, the worst types of such behavior would *ipso facto* violate the public order norms already spelled out in article 7. Now, the problem with reading the promulgated text as do Hamer and Guminski, who imply that it allows for no more legal restrictions on proselytism than the penultimate draft did, is that this reading renders virtually superfluous the insertion into the final draft of the last sentence in #4.4. In effect, it reduces this strongly worded assertion to an additional bit of literary finger-wagging – a verbal wrist-slap with no practical civil implications. The sentence, inserted straight after the existing reprobation of the aforesaid types of proselytism, reads, "That kind of behavior must be considered an abuse of one's own right and a violation of the right of others."[179] Especially since these last-minute amendments to *DH* were motivated mainly by the pressing need to win additional votes from the more conservative Fathers, this inserted sentence should be understood as clarifying that the aforesaid reprehensible proselytizing methods constitute *as such* – that is, not only in their more

---

177 Cf. CH, n27. Hamer is quoted here from a book published in 1967, six years before his episcopal ordination.

178 Cf. ibid.

179 *"Talis modus agendi ut abusus iuris proprii et laesio iuris aliorum considerari debet."*

extreme forms – the rights-violation that #7.3 sees as a punishable offence against public order. I therefore stand by the contention of my book that even today, consistently with *DH*, both blasphemy and "the more virulent forms of Protestant and other propaganda against the Catholic Church (e.g., those that demonstrably misrepresent the content of Catholic doctrine or the facts of Church history) could certainly be legally banned."[180] This ongoing ecclesial recognition of the State's right to prohibit that sort of material helps us to see the underlying doctrinal continuity between *DH* and the nineteenth-century encyclicals that urged legal sanctions against "violators of the Catholic religion" (*QC*) and "lying opinions that corrupt the mind and heart."[181]

II. Rights, past and present

104. In FR, #60, Mr. Guminski defends those passages of his first critique in which, by the use of present-tense verbs, he left the false impression that I had, in my book, interpreted *DH* as teaching that Catholics *still today* have an effective "right" to be protected by law from the temptations to their faith constituted by public manifestations of anti-Catholic doctrine *as such* (i.e., not just the "virulent forms" thereof mentioned in **D. I** above). He now says I have "only [my]self to blame" for what he ascribed to me, and cites as evidence p. 142 of my book, where, referring to the contemporary world, I speak of a "right of Catholics not to be 'led into temptation' . . . [by] the diffusion of false religious ideas."

105. Very well, *mea culpa*. I should have used in that context a term like "claim," or "putative right," rather than simply "right." Nevertheless, I insist that my critic's earlier statements seriously misrepresented my position. Why? Because he did not tell our readers in his first critique what he acknowledges in the second, to wit, that in the same breath wherein I spoke of the above "right" in connection with today's world I also said that this "right" was now (according to the Holy See's interpretation of *DH*

180 Cf. *RLC*, 110–111. In these times when Koran-burners, anti-homosexual funeral disrupters and other over-zealous religious militants are exacerbating inter-religious tensions, it would seem quite appropriate for Catholic governments also to prohibit equally "unworthy" forms of attacking religions other than Catholicism.

181 Leo XIII, Encyclical *Libertas* (June 20, 1888), #23. Also, Encyclical *Immortale Dei* (November 1, 1885), #32: "[T]he State is acting against the laws and dictates of nature whenever it permits the license of opinion and action to lead minds astray from truth and souls away from the practice of virtue." Cf. *The Companion to the Catechism of the Catholic Church* (San Francisco: Ignatius, Press, 1995), 682–683 and 746.

manifested in concordat revisions) *trumped* by "the right of at least the more moderate and upright non-Catholic groups to immunity from government interference" in publicly diffusing their beliefs. Of course, if a specific "right" A is everywhere trumped from now on by another right B, then A is, *in effect,* a right that no longer exists. So my basic complaint still stands: to read Mr. Guminski's comments in his first essay, without reading *all* my observations on p. 142 of *RLC* and my clear affirmation on p. 88 (cited in WD, #12 at n. 31), one would wrongly think that in my book I had offered an indefensibly "traditionalist" reading of *DH.* That is, one would think I had implausibly ascribed to the Council the judgment that Catholic governments could still today *justly* (even if perhaps not *prudently*) repress all public manifestations of non-Catholic religions.

III. "Common good" vs. "public order"

106. Finally, in FR, #63, we find a case of *ignoratio elenchi.* My critic, citing a 1964 *relatio,* insists on something I was not denying, namely, that after the first draft of *DH,* "common good" was replaced by "public order" because the former term was so broad in meaning as to give governments a pretext for introducing or maintaining the kinds of legal restrictions that the Council wanted to censure as infringements of religious freedom. But I had already acknowledged that the substitution was made for that reason:[182] I explicitly recognized that "common good" was understood to mean the ensemble of *all* valued social conditions (VSCs),[183] while "public order" was defined more narrowly as the "fundamental part" of the common good, i.e., as that subset of VSCs which society sees as essential or fundamental to its ordered existence, not merely beneficial or advantageous.[184] But by focusing on the respective definitions (meanings) of these two terms, that is – to use the terminology of classical Logic – on their *comprehension,* my critic has missed the new point I was making, which has to do with their *extension* (that is, with the question of which specific VSCs are to be understood as included under one term rather than the other).

182 It was not, however, made *only* for that reason: cf. WD, n40.

183 Cf. WD, ##18–19.

184 Cf. WD, #18, especially the last sentence. This paragraph also clearly exposes the falsity of my critic's claim that, according to my reading of *DH,* the term *public order* is being used as "just another name for the traditional notion [of] the *common good*" (#63). I have always explicitly recognized the obvious fact that the Council does not use these two terms as synonyms.

107. This evidently needs a little more explanation. I am claiming that the Council's decision to replace "common good" by "public order" in *DH* has not made nearly as much difference in the Church's doctrinal teaching as both the conservative minority (who wanted to retain the former term) and the more liberal majority (who insisted on the latter) thought it would. Like Mr. Guminski, Fathers on both sides appeared to assume that the undoubted difference in *comprehension* between those two terms would flow over into a real doctrinal difference, depending on which one the Council adopted. But this focus on comprehension seems to have deflected their attention from the more pertinent fact that while earlier theologians and Church authorities appealed to what they called the "common good" in order to justify legal restrictions on anti-Catholic manifestations as such, they nevertheless saw these restrictions – duly based on the "objective moral order" of natural and divine positive law, and not on arbitrary or ideological prejudices[185] – as protecting pretty much the same specific VSCs that come under the *extension* of the term "public order" as this is explained in *DH,* #7.3. That is, those earlier Catholic authorities certainly saw anti-Catholic propaganda *per se* as a threat to one or more of the three VSCs which together, according to the Council, constitute "public order," namely, public peace, public morality, and the protection of the rights of all citizens.[186]

108. Hence, especially in the light of the final revision of article 7,[187] it now matters little whether we use "common good" or "public order" in expressing contemporary Catholic teaching on the appropriate legal limits to RL. (That is probably why the *Catechism*, to Mr. Guminski's puzzlement,[188] uses both terms together in #1738.) Both are useful as shorthand, but the said teaching can be expressed accurately and unambiguously only in longhand, omitting both terms and listing what Vatican II says are the components of the latter. For example, **"Civil authority has the right, using juridical norms based on the objective moral order, to restrain activity carried out in the name of religious freedom when this threatens public morality, public peace, or the rights of other citizens."**

---

185 Cf. *DH,* #7.3.
186 Cf. WD, n34, as to why public peace and the religious freedom of Catholics themselves were more directly threatened by such propaganda in earlier centuries than they are at present.
187 Cf. WD, #19.

Conclusion

109. There have been two main issues discussed in this final reply to Mr. Guminski. Section **B** deals with the central one in our debate. I have argued there that he has failed in his overall objective, namely, to show that *DH* contradicts traditional Catholic doctrine, concerning which Propositions **X, Y** and **Z** were used to elucidate the state of the question at the beginning of my first essay. My opponent has concentrated his main efforts on trying to prove that, according to the conciliar Declaration, "the truth of Catholicism [must be] deemed not juridically relevant" by governments in determining what legal limits may justly be placed on religion-related activity in the interests of public order. But he has forgotten that even if *DH* did say or imply this thesis, it would not in itself amount to a contradiction of traditional Catholic *doctrine*. For in order for such a contradiction to occur, the Council would have had to teach that such exclusion of revealed (supernatural) truth from juridical relevance is not only an objective requirement of justice under modern socio-political circumstances, but has *always and everywhere* been such a requirement.[189] And Mr. Guminski, far from demonstrating that the Council made a universal and retroactive judgment of that sort, has scarcely even attempted to argue that it did so.

110. An indeed it did not. In fact, as we saw in section **C**, the Council does not require the complete exclusion of supernatural truth (divine positive law) from the aforesaid juridical determinations even in contemporary society – much less throughout the whole earth from Pentecost until Doomsday. For the "objective moral order," which article 7 presents as the ethical yardstick for deciding and evaluating legal limitations on religion-related activity, can still today, according to *DH* and the postconciliar magisterium, be taken to include aspects of divine positive law as well as the natural moral law which is its foundation.

111. A few final words about our respective personal attitudes to the RL issue may be appropriate after all our clinically dispassionate dissections of the Vatican II text. Mr. Guminski finds incongruous my own lack of discomfort or embarrassment with the less tolerant approach taken by the Church in earlier times. For one who "so intellectually thrives and profits from controversy," he writes, "Father Harrison . . . has a rather crabbed view of the value of free public discussion and enquiry in religious

---

188 Cf. CH, #65. I agree with Mr. Guminski, however, that the *Catechism*'s wording is confusing. One suspects that "or" rather than "and" should have been the word connecting the two terms in #1738.

189 Except, that is, in ancient Israel (cf. n181 supra).

matters."[190] My critic also denounces old Christendom as a "poisoned tree,"[191] given that its gradual establishment, not just its continuance, often involved restrictions on free public discussion and enquiry.

112. Now, while not in any way justifying the real abuses by Christians against human dignity admitted and deplored in *DH,* #12,[192] I find anachronistic (as J. C. Murray did) this kind of censorious application of modern Western standards – liberal, democratic and individualistic – to past ecclesial policies worked out for largely illiterate (and often tribally organized) cultures. With the exception of a few anti-Christian zealots like Richard Dawkins, secular Westerners even today see no violation of "human rights" in the religiously unilateral upbringing "imposed" on children by their believing parents, who routinely shield them from propaganda understood to endanger their eternal salvation. (Indeed, these same secularists usually shield their own offspring from exposure to religious "superstition" and "dogmatism.") But for most of human history, most adults in most cultures have shared relevant similarities with children: a lack of sufficient education to engage competently in philosophical and theological inquiry; an unreflective acceptance of authoritarian, paternalistic governance; and a communally rather than individually oriented social structure that took it for granted that major decisions, including those such as the replacement of pagan cults by baptism and Christian observance, should be taken by chiefs, elders or princes on behalf of the whole tribe or civic community, whose members would all then be expected to "follow the leader." Even in regard to the modern world, the Vatican II *relator* clarified that mere "social pressure" to conform to other people's religious expectations does not constitute that "coercion" which the Council says violates human dignity.[193]

113. Given his reference to a seeming inconsistency in my own attitude to the subject of our debate, Mr. Guminski will perhaps not object too much if I reciprocate with a similar brief personal observation. I confess that his resolute indignation at the Church's former severity toward religious dissent – accompanied by his own confidently proposed scheme of RL rights, neatly divided into "hard-core" and "soft-core" varieties[194] – strikes me as quite incongruous, coming as it does from a professed non-believer. For the high

---

190 FR, n68.
191 FR, n41.
192 Cf. second-last paragraph in section **C.II.**
193 *"Ceterum coercitio non est idem ac 'pressio' socialis"* (*AS*, vol. IV, pt. VI, 733).
194 Cf. FR, ##66–67.

concept of human dignity upon which he bases these ethical judgments never arose historically in pagan or Islamic cultures; it depends fundamentally on the Judaeo-Christian doctrine that each human being is made in the image of God himself. Nor has it ever survived for long in societies that have turned their back on that doctrine. How can humanity hope to find an objectively valid and generally discernible body of moral law if (with no transcendent Lawgiver in heaven and no spiritual souls on earth) all ethical beliefs are ultimately nothing more than by-products of a blind process of evolution, determined by varying forms of social indoctrination, and indeed, by trillions of neural reactions in our cerebral cortex?[195]

114. In any case, I once again thank Mr. Guminski for his penetrating scrutiny of my writings on *Dignitatis Humanae*. It is the most serious challenge I have had to confront, during a quarter-century of intermittent controversy on this topic, to the claim – made by the Church herself,[196] not just by individuals such as myself – that there is no contradiction between traditional doctrine and that of Vatican II regarding RL.

115. Not least among my adversary's merits is that, by not letting us Catholics forget the repression of religious error frequently urged upon

---

195 Contemporary champions of unbelief (Dawkins, Christopher Hitchens, *et al.*) are understandably anxious to dissociate the massive and brutal contempt for human life and liberty displayed by Nazi and Communist rulers from their rejection of Judaeo-Christian belief. These apologists for atheism insist there is no logical connection between the unbelief of those regimes and their barbaric tyranny, which of course was historically unprecedented in its ruthlessness and genocidal magnitude. But even if unbelief does not itself logically imply a totalitarian ideology, it certainly helps pave the way for totalitarian regimes, not only by excising the fear of Hell from the hearts of those power-hungry Machiavellians who most need it, but by undermining the intellectual cogency and objectivity of any *alternate* social or political philosophy that makes specific ethical claims. Being logically compatible with the whole spectrum of (non-theistic) views of man and human rights, ranging from the heights of Guminskian personalism to the depths of Stalinist cynicism, atheism – especially its most common and most consistent form, materialism – effectively relativizes all these views, reducing them to a series of rival subjective preferences. Thus, as that inconveniently and remorselessly consistent atheist, Nietzsche, realized, the "death" of God opens the way for sheer will – the will of the strongest individual or group – to impose its own decisions as to how we shall live. For a good exposition of the indebtedness of secular Western liberalism to the Christian world-view it rejects, and of its own increasing fragility as a result of that rejection, see David Bentley Hart, *Atheist Delusions: The Christian Revolution and Its Fashionable Enemies* (New Haven & London: Yale University Press, 2009).

196 Cf. section **B.II** *supra*.

civil rulers by the Church's *universal and ordinary* magisterium from the foundation of Christendom onwards, he has exposed the inadequacy of certain attempts to reconcile the conciliar and preconciliar doctrines that have pretty much equated the latter with the content of several nineteenth-century papal encyclicals and the 1864 *Syllabus*. (If the Church's doctrine were embodied *only* in the Creeds and the formal teaching documents of popes and councils, she would have taught hardly any ethical doctrine at all for many centuries after Christ!) Moreover, these attempts have often "harmonized" *DH* with the said nineteenth-century papal documents only by blunting the cutting edges of the latter.[197] They leave the impression that, in regard to the State's treatment of religious minorities, the Church's traditional *doctrine* – which they wrongly try to isolate completely from her diplomatic *practice* – never in any case endorsed legal restrictions much more extensive than those which *DH* has judged appropriate for today's pluralistic and democratically-conscious "global village." But since that impression is false, the defender of doctrinal continuity faces a more demanding and complex task than these authors have realized. Readers can judge for themselves whether I have successfully accomplished this task in these pages.

---

197 Some have portrayed these documents as containing, at the doctrinal level, nothing more illiberal than a censure of certain secularist ideologies (e.g., indifferentism, rationalism and laicism). Others have given them an abstract, minimalist reading that deems hermeneutically irrelevant their historical context (e.g., the repressive concordat provisions that still implemented them in a few countries until after Vatican II). As examples of attempted harmonization which I think are inadequate in such ways, cf. William G. Most, "Religious Liberty: What the Texts Demand," *Faith & Reason*, IX, 3, Fall 1983, 196–209; William. H. Marshner, *"Dignitatis Humanae* and Traditional Teaching on Church and State," ibid., 222–248; Kenneth D. Whitehead, "Summarizing the Controversy," *Catholic Dossier*, vol. 6, no. 2, March-April 2000, 6–13; and Regis Scanlon, O.F.M. Cap, "Did Vatican II reverse the Church's teaching on religious liberty?", *Homiletic & Pastoral Review*, January 2011, 61–68.

Appendix A:
The Scope and the Limits of the Church's Inherent Coercive Power*
Arnold T. Guminski with Brian W. Harrison, O. S.

Introduction

1. Fr. Harrison and I have hitherto been almost completely focused on the issue of the consistency of preconciliar doctrine with that of *Dignitatis Humanae* concerning religious freedom insofar as it pertains to the public manifestation and propagation of beliefs in religious matters.[1] Until now we had not thought it necessary to extensively discuss the private manifestation and propagation of beliefs in religious matters because we had agreed that the doctrine of *DH* concerning the freedom of the act of faith and the Church's inherent coercive power precludes reliance upon temporal penalties typical of civil authority only.[2] Thus, as Fr. Harrison wrote in his *RLC*, "people should not be coerced [by way of physical compulsion] by governments [or the Church] for wanting to opt out of the church by

---

*   The title of this essay is abbreviated throughout this book as "AppA." Although Mr. Guminski is the principal author, nevertheless this essay is largely the result of a collaborative effort with Fr. Harrison. He endorses the theses of this essay as chiefly set forth in paragraphs 4 and 16 *infra*, and concurs in almost, but not quite all, of the argumentation. Some differences of opinion are disclosed in what follows.

1   See Guminski, CH, n10. Nevertheless, Fr. Harrison and I have since 1998 intermittently discussed in considerable detail the Church's inherent coercive power and its relation to *DH* in our ongoing correspondence.

2   Neither I nor Fr. Harrison intends that the expression *public propagation or manifestation of beliefs in religious matters* should be understood as including all expressions of beliefs in public places or places open the public (e.g., engaging in a conversation on religious matters with a few other persons). On the other hand, propagation or manifestations of beliefs in religious matters is not private just because it occurs on privately owned property open to the public or a considerable number of persons (e.g., a church, temple, or other place open to members of a religious community for public worship, public meeting hall).

private acts of heresy, schism or apostasy."[3] In his first essay, Fr. Harrison amply confirms this opinion.[4]

2. However, it now behooves me to address at length the issue of the Church's inherent coercive power (especially with respect to acts of apostasy, heresy, and schism, and cognate offenses) since both Fr. Harrison and I are quite aware that some SOCs (i.e., Standard-Orthodox Catholics) as well as others wonder how one can show that *DH* is consistent with preconciliar doctrine with respect to freedom of the act of faith insofar as it pertains to remaining in the faith, and also generally with respect to the temporal aspects of the Church's coercive power. And, to be sure, there are those who question and even deny that such consistency obtains. Fr. Harrison and I believe it would therefore be useful to explore this subject in sufficient detail, and thereby make available references to some source material that might not otherwise be readily available to most readers.

A. The Nature of the Church's Inherent Coercive Power

3. In this appendix I use the term the *Church's inherent coercive power* to refer to such coercive power that Church has as a religious community by virtue of the natural moral law and supernatural revelation.[5] The *Church's*

---

3   Harrison, *RLC*, 125. See also ibid., 64. Inclusion of the bracketed matter more fully states the view expressed by Fr. Harrison in the paragraph that includes the quoted matter. Fr. Harrison thought that the relevant doctrine of *DH* (i.e., that the freedom of the act of faith also pertained to retaining it) is a legitimate development of traditional doctrine and, therefore did not contradict it. Ibid. On the other hand, I had opined in my first essay (CH, n90) that Pius XII had already "used language concerning the act of faith broad enough to mean that the freedom also pertains to remaining in the faith" – citing the pontiff's encyclical *Mystici Corporis* (1946), #104, and his Allocution to the Sacred Roman Rota (October 6, 1946) 38 AAS (1946) 392 (trans, *Catholic Mind* (March 1947), XLV: 129–33."

4   WD, #13; cf. #29. Fr. Harrison has pointed out in his book that, given the lessons of history and experience learned through the centuries, there should be a domain of social and civil liberty within the limits of a just public order for *some* public manifestations and propagation of *some* non-Catholic beliefs in religious matters in order that the freedom of the act of faith for Catholic and non-Catholics would obtain as a practical reality. See *RLC*, 125–26; cf. WD, #13.

5   In note 9 to my first essay I announced that I was using the term "*coercive power*, as used in [that] essay, to mean the power to impose penalties of the kind typically imposed by civil authority only involving the use, or the threat of the use, of physical force by an agent of that authority, as distinguished from the kind typically imposed by ecclesiastical authority, i.e., spiritual and such temporal penalties as are not typical of civil authorities."

acquired coercive power, whatever or wherever it may have existed, obtained solely by virtue of: (a) the *jus publicum* of Catholic Christendom in the medieval era and for some time thereafter, (b) the discretionary delegation or grant of power by the secular authority; or (c) customary law by which the Church acted as civil authority because of exigencies that arose during a period of severe political and social disorder;[6] or (d) because of some erroneous theory, based upon the power of the keys,[7] of what constitutes the Church's inherent power over temporal matters in a Catholic State – an inherent power that would include as a component that the Church had the power to either directly impose temporal penalties typical of civil authority only and/or to indirectly do so by requiring under penalty of ecclesiastical sanction (i.e., excommunication, deposition of the offending civil ruler or release of subjects from their duty of allegiance) the *secular arm* to do in religious matters what would otherwise not be within its power in a non-Catholic State.[8]

6 As to items (a) and (b), see such classical works as: Joseph Fessler, *The True and the False Infallibility of the Popes: A Controversial Reply to Dr. Shulte* (New York: Burns and Oates, 1875), 103–10: Jean-Edmé-Auguste Gosselin, *The Power of the Popes during the Middle Ages: or an historical Inquiry into the Origin of the Temporal Power of the Holy See and the Constitutional Laws of the Middle Ages* (trans. M. Kelly) (London: C. Dolman. 1853), 1: 60–61, 149–72; [Cardinal] Joseph Hergenröther, *Catholic Church and Christian State: A Series of Essays on the Relation of the Church to the Civil Power* (London: Burnes & Oates, 1876), 1: 62–64, 2:301–39.

7 *Mt.*16: 19 ("I will give you [i.e., Simon Peter] the keys of the kingdom of heaven, and whatever you bind on earth shall be bound in heaven, and whatever you loose on earth shall be loosed in heaven"). In *Mt* 18:18, the same power is given to all the apostles.

8 See Joseph Lecler, S.J., *The Two Sovereignties: A Study of the Relationship Between Church and State* (London: Burns Oates & Washbourne, 1952) 13–84, for a succinct account of the several direct and indirect theories of the temporal powers of the Pope and the Church based upon the power of the keys. For more comprehensive accounts of the theories in question, see (Gaston Glez.) "Pouvoir du Pape en Matière Temporale," *Dictionnaire de Théologie Catholique* (Paris: Letouzey et Ané, 1937) 12: 2704–72; Fred. J. Moulart, *L'Église et L'État ou Les Deux Puissances* (Louvain-Paris, 3rd ed. 1887), 156–234. Moulart discussed at length the theory that the power in temporal matters of the Pope as supreme head of Catholic Christendom insofar as it constituted a political commonwealth (which included the power to depose rulers and release subjects from their duty of allegiance because of the failure of such rulers to comply with a constitutional duty to maintain and protect the Catholic Church and religion), did not exist by divine right but rather by virtue of the public law of the times. He characterized this particular historical theory as theologically legitimate since it was based on

4. In this appendix, my aim is to argue for five related theses concerning the Church's inherent coercive power.

(a) The Church has neither definitively nor even authoritatively taught the doctrine that its inherent coercive power encompasses temporal powers typical of civil authority only, and thus ultimately finding their sanction in the use of physical force or the threat thereof. The key for a proper appreciation of this assertion is that it is crucial to make a distinction between temporal penalties that are typical of civil authority only, and those that are not. Temporal penalties typical of civil authority chiefly include the deprivation of: (a) goods pertaining to property (e.g., fines, confiscations of property); (b) goods pertaining to the body (e.g., imprisonment, detention, and other restraints on liberty of movement or habitation, scourging, capital punishment); (c) goods pertaining to political, social and economic entitlements, privileges, or benefits; (d) goods pertaining to honor and reputation (e.g., mandatory wearing of badges and stigmatizing articles of clothing in public places or places open to the public for the necessities and conveniences of life).

(b) The Church certainly legislated for centuries upon the premise that it had the power to impose temporal penalties typical of civil authority only or to require rulers of Catholic States to do so,[9] and this premise

grave reasons and supported by respected authorities. Ibid., 209–10. Almost needless to say, no theory of the kind mentioned in the accompanying text can now be rightly considered as being the received opinion of the Church today. See *Gaudium et Spes* #76 (the pastoral constitution on the church of the world of today) (December 7, 1965).

9   Lest any reader doubt that the Church legislated on the basis provided by this theory, it suffices to cite canon 3 (on heretics) of the Fourth Lateran Council. This canon provided: "Let secular authorities, whatever offices they may be discharging, be advised and urged and if necessary be compelled by ecclesiastical censure, ... to take publicly an oath for the defence of the faith to the effect that they will seek, in so far as they can, to expel [exterminare] from the lands subject to their jurisdiction all heretics designated by the [C]hurch in good faith.... If however a temporal lord, required and instructed by the [C]hurch, neglects to cleanse his territory of this heretical filth, he shall be bound with the bond of excommunication... If he refuses to give satisfaction within a year, this will be reported to the supreme pontiff so that he may declare his vassals absolved from their fealty...." Norman P. Tanner, S.J., ed. (trans. G. Alberigo et al.), *Decrees of the Ecumenical Councils* (Washington DC: Georgetown Univ. Press, 1990) (hereafter Tanner) II: 234. Canon 68 of the same council decreed that Jews and Saracens (i.e., Muslims) "in every [C]hristian province and at all times are to be distinguished in public from other people by the character of their dress." Tanner II: 266. Of compelling interest too is the decree on Jews and neophytes, September 7, 1434, of the

had been the common opinion of theologians and canonists during medieval times and until even well into the last century.[10]

(c) Some Church doctrinal teachings are arguably open to the interpretation that the Church had the power in question before the publication of Pius XII's encyclical *Mystici Corporis* in 1943. Nevertheless, these doctrines were even then patently open to the theologically admissible interpretation that it did not have this power by virtue of the natural moral or divine positive law but instead had been acquired over the course of time due to the concession of rulers or customary law in Catholic Christendom.

(d) The Church's inherent coercive power encompasses the following kinds of temporal penalties not typical of civil authority only: **(i)** the exercise of its *household rights* to control access to and use of her property and facilities, and participation in her activities, primarily devoted to religious purposes and associated cultural, social, education, and charitable activities engaged in by the Church and its sponsored societies by virtue of being a religious community;[11] **(ii)** its power to punish with spiritual penalties (e.g., major excommunication) that have temporal aspects (e.g. Church-mandated shunning in profane matters, denial of Christian burial, denial of privilege of being baptismal sponsor); **(iii)** its authority to

Council of Basile which, according to the received opinion, is to be regarded as a legitimate decree of an ecumenical council. (See H.J. Schroeder, *Disciplinary Decrees of the General Councils* (St. Louis: B. Herder, 1937), 472.) The decree commanded that "[Jews and other infidels] of both sexes who have reached the age of discretion … attend [conversion] sermons under pain both of being excluded from business dealings with the faithful and of other apposite penalties." (Tanner I: 483.)

10 That the common theological opinion in question, which served as the basis of Church repressive legislation respecting apostates and heretics, remained widespread until well into the twentieth century, see *Catholic Encyclopedia,* "Apostasy" (A. Van Hove), I: 624–25 (http://www.newadvent.org/ cathen/01624b.htm); "Heresy" (J. Welhelm), III: 260–62 (http://www. newadvent.org/cathen/07256b.htm); "Inquisition" (J. Blötzer), VIII: 26–38 (http://www.newadvent.org/cathen/08026a.htm); "Persecution" (J. Bridge), XI: 703–04 (http://www.newadvent.org/cathen/11703a.htm). The Church's legislation, still officially "on the books" (albeit in duesetude for some decades) until the Code of Canon Law of 1917 went into effect on May 19, 1918, authorized the infliction by the Church or by its secular arm of temporal penalties not typical of civil authority only.

11 See paragraph 16 *infra* for a listing of some components of the Church's household rights.

impose temporal penalties as a condition for or in satisfaction of penitential absolution from sin; **(iv)** its authority to impose temporal penalties
(e.g., restraints on liberty of habitation, travel, or association) compliance
with which has its ultimate sanction in excommunication, interdiction, or
suspension.

(e) The Church's inherent coercive power, as defined and described in
this appendix, is fully consistent with the doctrine of *DH* concerning religious freedom, provided that any exercise of this power is within the limits of a just public order.

5. The Church's inherent coercive power pertains to both its members
and non-members. Who are and are not members of the Church were identified by Pius XII in his encyclical *Mystici Corporis* #22;[12]

> Actually only those are to be included as members of the Church
> who have been baptized and profess the true faith, and who have
> not been so unfortunate as to separate themselves from the unity
> of the Body, or been excluded by legitimate authority for grave
> faults committed. "For in one spirit," says the Apostle, "were we
> all baptized into one Body, whether Jews or Gentiles, whether
> bond or free."[I *Cor.*, XII, 13] As therefore in the true Christian
> community there is only one Body, one Spirit, one Lord, and one
> Baptism, so there can be only one faith.[Cf. *Eph.*, IV, 5] And there-
> fore, if a man refuse to hear the Church, let him be considered –
> so the Lord commands – as a heathen and a publican. [Cf. *Matth.*,
> XVIII, 17] It follows that those who are divided in faith or govern-
> ment cannot be living in the unity of such a Body, nor can they be
> living the life of its one Divine Spirit.

12 The encyclical is accessible at http://www.vatican.va/holy_father/
pius_xii/encyclicals/documents/hf_p-xii_enc_29061943_mystici-corporis-
christi_en.html. Given the development of doctrine initiated by Vatican Council II,
the meaning of *members of the Church* must be understood to mean those baptized
Christians who "are fully incorporated into the society of the [C]hurch who, possessing the spirit of Christ, accept its whole structure and all the means of salvation that have been established within it, and within its visible framework are united with Christ, who governs it through the supreme pontiff and the bishops, by the
bonds of profession of faith, the sacraments, ecclesiastical government and communion." *Lumen Gentium* (Dogmatic Constitution of the Church) (1964) #14.2
(Tanner II: 860). Those baptized Christians, not "fully incorporated into the society of the [C]hurch," are nevertheless "in some kind of communion with the
[C]atholic [C]hurch, even though this communion is imperfect." *Unitatis redintegratio* (Decree on ecumenism) (1964) # 3.1 (Tanner II: 910).

B. The Meaning of Coercion in *Dignitatis Humanae*

6. Before specifically addressing what was the preconciliar doctrine concerning the Church's inherent coercive power, I shall first expound what I believe is the relevant teaching of *DH*.[13] *DH* #2.1 defines religious freedom as "such immunity from coercion by individuals, or by groups, or by any human power, that no one should be forced to act against his conscience in religious matters, nor prevented from acting according to his conscience, whether in private or in public, whether alone or in association with others, within due limits." (*DH* #2.1.)

7. The question arises whether the term *coercion*, within the meaning of *DH* # 2.1, was understood by those council fathers approving *DH* as not encompassing the then extant ecclesiastical penalties, especially major excommunication and its codified temporal effects, and those other temporal penalties fashioned to vindicate her household rights with respect to members and non-members, within the limits of a just public order.[14] The legislative history of the Council clearly indicates that this was the intent of the framers of *DH*. Among the detailed responses provided to the Council Fathers by the Secretariat for the Promotion of Christian Unity to objections made to the final draft of *DH* (the *Textus denuo recognitus*) is the following:[15]

13 The text of *DH* (in Latin and English) appears in Tanner II: 1001–11.

14 Fr. Harrison kindly sent me the following in an e-mail (October 4, 2010): "Moreover, there had been a request from some Fathers to delete from the key text of the whole declaration (#2, par. 1) the reference to coercion on the part of 'social groups' (*sive coetuum socialium*), on the grounds that 'nobody is capable of isolating himself from social *pressure*' [*quia nemo potest sese subtrahere a <<pressione>> sociali*]. In responding negatively to this request, the *relator* explained as follows the Commission's decision to leave the above three words in the text: 'Coercion on the part of social groups is also to be rejected. Besides, coercion is not the same thing as social *pressure* [*Etiam coercitio proveniens ex parte coetuum socialium reicienda est. Ceterum coercitio on est idem ac <<pressio>> socialis*].'" *Acta Synodalia Sacrosancti Concilii Oecumenici Vaticanii II* (1978), vol. IV/pt. VI, 733. In my view, *coercion* as used in *DH* does not encompass social pressures incident to moderate shunning in the domestic and other equivalent social domains based upon religious grounds that arise sua sponte, that is as a matter of personal choice. The case of ecclesially mandated socio-economic shunning of groups or individuals (i.e., shunning in so-called profane matters) based upon religious grounds is quite a different matter. The critical issue, in my opinion, is whether such organized shunning in profane matters constitutes a kind of coercion foreclosed by *DH*.

15 Ibid., 725. Translation provided by Professor John Finnis to the participants of the Notre Dame symposium on *DH* (November 13–15, 1998).

....The same father affirms ... "the plenary power of the magisterium and government of the Church, and its power of applying spiritual penalties to its subjects should be admitted."

R. – These are all sufficiently proposed in the text, so far as they concern the Declaration's scope/objective [*scopum*]. Cf. n. 1, 10, 13 and 14. Moreover, it should be observed that the approved text affirms a right whose object is immunity from coercion, and not the content of some religion....

The Secretariat also explained elsewhere:[16]

Moreover, coercion of adults, both in society and in the state, in religious matters in the sense articulated in the first part of this Declaration, is intrinsically unjust. Ecclesiastical penalties for wrongful acts are from the Church's coercive power over its members, but are not coercion.

Almost needless to say, the second sentence vividly discloses that *coercion* is a very ambiguous term. And it can also be plausibly said, with all due respect, that the Secretariat engaged in a bit of confusing double-talk.

8. The Council Fathers overwhelmingly approved the final draft thereby arguably endorsing the foregoing and similar responses submitted by the Secretariat.[17] Therefore, the term *coercion* in *DH*, it can also be argued, was used as a term of art and thus understood by the Council Fathers approving *DH* as not encompassing those exercises of the Church's coercive power of the kind as were in force circa 1965. To properly assess why the Secretariat favored this all-much-too-easy semantic solution of our problem, we should advert to the fact that Code of Canon Law of 1917 was still in force in 1965 and remained so until the Code of Canon Law of 1983 was promulgated by John Paul II. The relevant canons from the 1917 code provided: all penalties, whether spiritual or temporal, that the Code does not mention are to be taken as abrogated (can. 6, n.5); no one is to be compelled to embrace the Faith against his will (can.1351); independently of all human authority, the Church has the right, inherent and proper to her nature, to inflict penalties, whether they be spiritual or even temporal, on her delinquent subjects (can. 2214, n.1). Canon 2257, n.1 defined excommunication as a censure by which someone is excluded from the communion of the faithful, with the effects enumerated in the following canons

16 Ibid., 761,
17 Ibid., 779–80 (November 19, 1965).

(i.e., canons 2258–67). Canon 2258, n.1 distinguished between those who are to be tolerated (the *tolerati*) and those to be shunned (the *vitandi*). Canon 2258, n2 included among the *vitandi* persons excommunicated by the Holy See, publicly denounced as such, explicitly declared *vitandi* in a decree or sentence of excommunication, or had assaulted the Pope.[18] The 1917 code did not recognize *minor excommunication*, which is constituted by simply being prohibited from receiving the sacraments.[19] Although the 1917 code only recognized major excommunication (i.e., a censure entailing loss of all rights which a member of the Church as such possesses besides a prohibition from receiving the sacraments), there were some differences between members of various classes of the excommunicated, depending upon whether they were among the *tolerati* or the *vitandi*. Canon 2267 provided that the faithful must avoid relations in profane matters with *vitandi*, other than spouses, parents, infants, domestics, subordinate, and in general, without a reasonable excuse.[20] Canon 2259, n.1 deprived every excommunicate of the right to actively or passively assist at divine offices (e.g., assistance at Mass, processions, funerals). According to Canon 2259, n.2, the *tolerati* who passively assisted at a religious service were not to be expelled. However, the *vitandi* were to be expelled unless this was practically impossible; in which case the service was to cease unless it would have been gravely inconvenient to do so. On the other hand, the *vitandi*, other persons excommunicated after a declaratory sentence or condemnation, or those whose excommunicated status was notorious were to be prevented from actively assisting at a divine office. It is incredible that the Council Fathers approving *DH* believed that the Declaration was inconsistent with the extant canon law concerning the coercive power of Church to impose temporal penalties not typical of civil authority only.

9. We should also take into account that the now-defunct legislation

18 For the text of the 1917 Code, see Edward N. Peters, *The 1917 Pio-Benedictine Code of Canon Law* (San Francisco: Ignatius Press, 2001).

19 Minor excommunication was understood as ceasing to exist after the promulgation of *Apostolicae Sedis* in 1869 by Pius IX, and this understanding was ratified by the Holy Office in 1884. (A. Boudinhon) "Excommunication," *Catholic Encyclopedia, supra* (1909), 5: 680 (http://www.newadvent.org/cathen/05678a.htm).

20 However, as Henry Davis, S.J., noted in his *Moral and Pastoral Theology* (London: Sheed and Ward, 1945), 3: 461: "Practically a reasonable cause will nowadays exist in nearly every case in a normal community, but this fact does not abrogate the law."

of the Church, authorizing or requiring temporal penalties typical of civil authority only with respect to apostasy, heresy, schism, and cognate offenses, had fallen into desuetude well before the adoption of the Code of Canon Law of 1917, which formally abolished the ecclesiastical law in question. Thus, for example, one theologian, Clément Marc, in his *Institutiones morales* declared that as of 1889, the date of the publication of his work, canonical penalties of the temporal order against apostates had fallen into desuetude and, for that reason, should be considered as abrogated.[21] No doubt all Council Church Fathers were aware, or should have been aware, that Church legislation authorizing or requiring the temporal penalties typical of civil authority only for apostates and heretics had been in desuetude and later formally abrogated during at least eight decades before 1965.

10. However, the framers' intent concerning the term *coercion*, as previously suggested, may strike some people as an exercise in confusing double-talk. What, it may well be asked, is the effect of the exercise of the Church's coercive power but *coercion*? It seems very likely, it might be argued, that an astute, well-informed person (but without special expertise) studying the text of *DH* would think that major excommunication with respect to *vitandi* involves a coercive component, i.e., ecclesiastically mandated shunning in profane matters (i.e., social and economic shunning unrelated to Church activities and functions).[22] It might be noted that

---

21 *Institutiones morales* (Rome, 1889), 1: 301, n442; approvingly cited in (Auguste Beugnet) "Apostasie," *Dictionnaire de Théologie Catholique*, supra (1909)1: 608. See also (J. Wilhelm) "Heresy," *Catholic Encyclopedia* (1910), 8: 200: "The present-day [Church] legislation against heresy has lost nothing of its ancient severity; but the penalties on heretics are now only of the spiritual order; all the punishments which require the intervention of the secular arm have fallen into abeyance. Even in countries where the cleavage between the spiritual and secular powers does not amount to hostility or complete severance, the death penalty, confiscation of goods, imprisonment, etc., are no longer inflicted on heretics." Cardinal Hergenröther in his *Catholic Church* (note 6 *supra*), 1: 63, declared that (circa 1876, the date of the publication of his book): "It was known at Rome as well as elsewhere than modern States and Governments no longer recognize any civil and political consequences as attached to excommunication."

22 Here Fr. Harrison "would question whether ecclesially mandated shunning in 'social' matters should be included here as something most people would see as 'coercive'" – unlike ecclesially mandated shunning in economic matters. He believes that "in the light of the subsequently released *Acta*, the inclusion of merely *social* shunning is scarcely a penalty typically only used by civil authorities." In Mr. Guminski's opinion, the fact that ecclesially mandated shunning in social mat-

although *DH* was promulgated on December 7, 1965, the relevant part of the *Acta Syndolia Sacrosancti Concili Oecumenici Vaticani II* (i.e., vol. IV/pt. VI) was not published until 1978. Thus it might plausibly be argued that while legislative history might be helpful for understanding the Declaration, it is nevertheless the objective meaning of the actual text of the Declaration, with its accompanying notes, that provides the best evidence of how propositions proposed for belief by the faithful as Catholic doctrine are to be interpreted; and not the content of some explanation of the text by its framers made publicly available only well after the promulgation of the Declaration.[23] Taking this view, it readily appears the major excommunication insofar as it entails ecclesially mandated shunning of the *vitandi* in profane matters would be understood by some persons as being an instance of *coercion* within the meaning of *DH*. It might be further urged that *DH* was intended to be widely read and understood by non-Catholics of many differing persuasions on religious matters, to persuade them of the commitment of the Church to ecumenism and religious freedom as a universal human right based upon the natural moral law – something capable of being understood by any intelligent person without theological expertise.[24]

ters unrelated to church activities and functions constitutes coercion does not entail that the Church, or any religious community, is necessarily acting outside the limits of a just public order whenever it requires its members to engage in such shunning.

23 Fr. Harrison, on the other hand, is of the opinion "that the 13–year delay in publishing the *Acta* with the *relator's* official explanations to the Fathers is not an adequate reason for interpreting the document in a way that prescinds from them. I think the intention of the Fathers – the way *they* understood the document they promulgated – definitely trumps, as a hermeneutical criterion, the presumed immediate public impression made by the text on outside readers."

24 The natural moral law, as the *Catechism of the Catholic* Church, #1956 tells us, is "present in the heart of each man and established by reason, [and] is universal in its precepts and its authority extends to all men.... [e]xpresses the dignity of the person and determines the basis for all fundamental rights and duties." However, as Fr. Harrison well observes, #1960 of the *Catechism* states that "[t]he precepts of natural law are not perceived by everyone clearly and immediately," and he remarks in the same message that "an awareness of the natural right to [RF[... wasn't always in the heart of most 'intelligent person[s] without theological expertise.' Indeed, until the twentieth century, the vast majority of persons even *with* theological expertise – in whatever world religion – had little idea of this right, at least in its recently developed form." Indeed, as *DH* #9 explains: "The statements made by this Vatican synod on the right of people to religious freedom have their basis in the dignity of the person, the demands of which have come to

C. The Legitimacy of Some Temporal Penalties according to *DH*

11. Fortunately, we need not here adjudicate the technical question whether *DH* should be taken to mean that the possible exercises of the Church's coercive power not involving temporal penalties typical of civil authority only constitutes *coercion* within the meaning of *DH*. This is the case because Fr. Harrison and Mr. Guminski agree that: (a) the exercises of the Church's inherent coercive power do not encompass temporal penalties typical of civil authority only; and (2) the Church, as well as any other religious communities, is not foreclosed by *DH* from imposing any of the temporal penalties of the kinds described in paragraphs 4(d) and 16 of this appendix, provided it is within the limits of a just public order. Let us therefore examine the text of *DH*, fairly construed in terms of the purposes of the approving Council Fathers, with respect to the issue of the Church's inherent coercive power. In this inquiry we should bear in mind that "all the freedom of action [the Church] needs to care for the salvation of humanity" (*DH* #13.1) is in "harmony ... [with] that religious liberty which should be accorded as a right to all individuals and communities." (Ibid., #13.3.)

12. The Church, in the view of *DH* insofar as it pertains to the natural moral law, is a religious community equally entitled with other religious communities, whether Christian or not, to religious freedom.[25] But the Church, just as any other religious community, is also subject to the injunction that "in the use of their rights individuals and social groups are bound by the moral law to have regard to the rights of others, to their own duties towards others and to the common good of all [*DH* #7.2]." But even a particular moral abuse of the right of freedom in religious matters may nevertheless be within the scope of religious freedom if that abuse *per accidens* does not offend the just public order. This is the case because *DH* #7.3 defines the notion of a *just public order* (that is *within due limits*) as providing the juridical limits of freedom in religious matters as a fundamental right (i.e., *religious freedom ? freedom in religious matters within the limits of a just public order* [df.]). Thus the Church, just as any other religious community, is both an active and passive subject of the rights

be more fully known to human reason from the experience of centuries." (Tanner II: 1006.)

25 Besides being entitled to religious freedom in view of the doctrine of the freedom of the Church, *DH* #13.2 proclaims: "The [C]hurch further claims freedom in that it is a human association enjoying the right to live in civil society according to the requirements of [C]hristian faith." (Tanner II: 1009.)

embraced by *DH* # 2.1 because religious freedom is defined here as immunity within due limits from coercion in religious matters "by individuals, or by groups, or by any human power."[26]

13. Some persons have urged that the Church does not fall within the ambit of *DH* #2.1 as a "human power" since it is not a "merely human power." The term "merely human power" only appears in #3.3, which reads: "The practice of religion of its very nature consists principally in internal acts that are voluntary and free, in which one relates oneself to God directly; and these can neither be commanded nor prohibited by any merely human power." However, I believe the objection in question is without merit because it is very arguable, to say the least, that an SOC is likely to hold that the Church, divinely founded as it is, has the authority to command or prevent internal acts in religious matters upon penalty of sin. For instance, she is understood to have the authority to command assent to her magisterial decisions. He *should* conform to these commands, as well as others bearing upon his spiritual life, because of the dictates of an upright conscience, and not because he is apprehensive that he might suffer any temporal penalties, whether imposed by the Church or civil authority were he to fail to do so. It is in view of the foregoing that *merely* is used to qualify *human power* only in *DH* #3.3, and not in #2.1.[27]

14. Not every exercise of coercive power with temporal aspects is forbidden to the Church and other religious communities by *DH*. Here *DH* # 4 is especially relevant. *DH* # 4.2 affirms: "[Religious] communities, as long as they do not disturb the proper requirements of public order, are entitled to due freedom [in governing themselves according to their own norms[28]] ..., in developing institutions in which their members can cooperate in ordering their lives according to their own religious tenets."

15. Since religious communities are free within due limits to govern themselves according to their own norms, they not only may make rules

26 Fr. Harrison, in his e-mail message of October 4, 2010 called my attention to how the *relatio* concerning the final draft discloses the intent of the Secretariat that the Church is also bound by the injunction of *DH* concerning religious freedom. See n15 *supra*.

27 Bishop De Smedt, in his *relatio* of November 19, 1965, concerning *DH* #3.3, explained: "The words 'merely human' have been deliberately used so as not to prejudice the disputed question regarding the power of the Church to command internal acts." (AS [1978] vol. IV/pt. VI, 730) (trans. by Fr. Harrison).

28 I have inserted the bracketed phrase to replace that provided in Tanner (i.e., "conducting their affairs in their own way") because the former constitutes a more apt translation of the Latin "secundum proprias normas sese regant." Tanner II: 1004.

and regulations but may provide for their enforcement by authorizing punishment of violators with appropriate penalties. Note that *DH* #4.3 also includes as components of the religious freedom of religious communities "the right not to be prevented [within due limits] by the state by legal or administrative measures from choosing, training, appointing and transferring their own ministers, ... from constructing buildings for religious purposes, or from acquiring and using appropriate property." *DH* #4.4 provides that "religious communities are entitled to each and give witness to their faith in speech and writing without hindrance"; and #4.5 affirms "the right of those who are stirred by religious ideals freely to hold meetings and to form associations for educative, cultural, charitable and social purposes."

16. Thus, reading the text of *DH* in light of a common understanding of the members of theologically conservative Christian churches, the right of religious communities to a due freedom, within the limits of a just public order, to regulate their affairs according to their own norms (as well as to establish their own internal government and religious institutions for its members, to own and operate real property, to propagate their faith, and to form associations for religious, social, educational, and charitable purposes), entails that whatever coercive power each community has by virtue of its own constitution and by-laws may legitimately encompass temporal penalties *not* ordinarily understood to be typical of only civil authority. These component coercive powers, that any religious community has with respect to members and other persons deemed to have violated its rules and regulations, include but are not limited to:

(a) depriving a person of membership or depriving him of some of the rights and privileges of members in good standing;

(b) excluding participation by a member, former member, or non-member in, or attendance at, some or all its public or quasi-public religious rites, ceremonies, and other exercises, either as a just penalty for some specified violation of its rule or regulations or for some other reason deemed just by the community;

(c) depriving a member or former member of the privilege of belonging to some or all organizations composed of its members and formed for religious, social, cultural, educational or charitable purposes, or of participating or attending their social and other functions of the organization (except those open to the general public on public grounds such as public street or park fairs or festivals);

(d) depriving a member or former member of the privilege of entering its structures and adjacent grounds devoted to religious, social, cultural, educational or charitable purposes;

(e) depriving-a member or former member of the privilege of using some or all of its facilities to address by the spoken or written word the public or a quasi-public;

(f) (partially or totally) depriving a member or former member of the privilege of being employed by the religious community with respect to its religious, social, cultural, educational or charitable purposes.

17. A particular exercise of any such component power may perhaps constitute a moral abuse without also constituting a violation of the just public order. It may also be the case that any particular exercise may be counter-productive to greater or lesser extent. It would be a grave error to think that a religious community exceeds the limits of a just public order just because it exercises any of the foregoing component powers for the purpose of pressuring a person to reform his behavior or belief-system (or to retrain or regain the status of membership), rather than merely enforcing an understood condition for entitlement to a right or privilege. Thus what may be legitimately possible for a religious community to do under the aegis of religious freedom may be very well beyond what is legitimate for the civil authority to do because the body politic is not a religious community. Civil authority, let the SOC recall, is a *merely human power*. (See *DH* #3.3.) On the other hand, a religious community (including the Church) would not be acting within the limits of a just public order were it to coerce its members or other persons by the use or threatened use of temporal penalties typical of only civil authority.

18. The due freedom of religious communities includes a component right to be free within the limits of a just public order to require under penalty of sin or ecclesiastical sanction that some or all excommunicated or expelled members be shunned as to profane matters to some extent by its members in good standing. It was commonly understood that the exercise of this right is to reform behavior or to induce a change of mind of the offender.[29] It would be very strange indeed were the council fathers, and

---

29 St. Thomas Aquinas has explained how "the Church by passing sentence of excommunication imitates the judgment of God. For by severing a man from the communion of the faithful that he may blush with shame, she imitates the judgment whereby God chastises man with stripes; and by depriving him of prayers and other spiritual things, she imitates the judgment of God in leaving man to himself, in order that by humility he may learn to know himself and return to God." *Summa Theologiae*, Supp. q. 21, art. 2.

other theologically conservative Christians, to have understood religious freedom to be inconsistent with the clear teaching of the New Testament about the coercive power of the apostolic church with respect to shunning in profane matters.[30] See, inter alia: I *Cor.* 5: 11 ("But rather I wrote to you not to associate with anyone who bears the name of brother if he is guilty of immorality or greed, or is an idolater, eviler, drunkard, or robber – not even to eat with such a one"); II *Thess.* 3: 14–15 ("If anyone refuses to

---

30   Some have argued that the apostolic church as such also had coercive powers involving physical penalties, citing the sudden deaths of Ananias and Saphira following their confrontations with Peter (*Acts*: 5: 1–11), and the striking with blindness of Elymas the magician who sought to turn away the proconsul Sergius Paulus from the faith expounded by Paul (ibid., 13: 7–12). But, as Aquinas explained: "As regards Peter, he did not put Ananias and Saphira to death by his own authority or with his own hand, but published their death sentence pronounced by God." *Summa Theologiae* II.II. q. 64, art. 4, ad 1. A similar conclusion obviously applies in the case of Elymas. (See André Bride, "Peines Ecclésiastiques," *Dictionnaire de Théologie Catholique*, supra, 12: 633.) It has also been argued physically coercive action was involved in Paul's judgment requiring the delivery of the incestuous sinner to Satan for the destruction of the flesh (I *Cor.* 5: 3–5) and the similar delivery to Satan of Hymenaeus and Alexander, who had made shipwreck of their faith, so that they might learn not to blaspheme (I *Tim.* 1: 19–20). But Thomas Aquinas commented that a permissible interpretation of what is meant by the *delivery to Satan* is the following: "To deliver this man [i.e., the incestuous sinner] to Satan can also be understood as referring to the sentence of excommunicating by which a person is cut off from the community of believers and from partaking of the sacraments and is deprived of the blessings of the Church.... For the destruction of the flesh would mean that, being cut off from the Church and exposed to the temptations of the devil, he might more easily fall into sin.... Hence he calls mortal sins the destruction of the flesh, because 'He who sows to his own flesh will from the flesh reap corruption' (*Gal.* 6:8)." *Commentary to the First Epistle to the Corinthians* (trans. Fabian Larcher) (987–1046 by Daniel Keating) (Html-edited by Joseph Kenny, O.P.) (http://*DH*spriory.org/thomas/SS1Cor.htm#51). Finally, perhaps the SOC may find it very plausible to suppose that the Apostles were each possessed of charisma proper to them as personal prerogatives. (See H. Coppieters, S.V., "Apostles," *Catholic Encyclopedia*, supra (1909) 1:628 [http://www.newadvent.org/cathen/01626c.htm.]) Thus (later) Cardinal Journet remarked: "[s]ome commentators believe [e.g. Ferdinand Pratt, S.J., *The Theology of St. Paul* (trans. J.L. Stoddard) (Westminster Md.: Newman Bookshop, 1926), 1: 101] . . . that just as the Lord left the Apostles the privilege of casting out devils, so He left them the power to compel the devils to chastise sinners, and that St. Paul ordered the Church at Corinth to deliver the shameless one to Satan's vexations." [Cardinal] Charles Journet, *The Church of the Word Incarnate vol. I: The Apostolic Hierarchy* (trans. A.H.C. Downes) (New York; Sheed and Ward, 1955), 265.

240

obey what we say in this letter, note that man, and have nothing to do with him, that he may be ashamed. Do not look on him as an enemy, but warn him as a brother"); *Tit.* 3: 10–11 ("As for a man who is factious, after admonishing him once or twice, have nothing more to do with him, knowing that such a person is perverted and sinful; he is self-condemned"); 2 *Jn.* 9–11 ("Anyone who goes ahead and does not abide in the doctrine of Christ does not have God; he who abides in the doctrine has both the Father and the Son. If any one comes to you and does not bring this doctrine, do not receive him into the house or give him any greeting; for he who greets him shares his wicked work").[31]

19. Some readers might contend that the text of *DH* itself precludes any argument that the religious freedom of religious communities includes any coercive power, even those temporal penalties not typical of civil authority only, to limit the freedom of its members or former members in religious matters. These readers might rely upon such passages in *DH* as the following: #1.3 ("religious liberty ... concerns freedom from compulsion in civil society"; #3.3 ("People .... must therefore not be forced to act against their conscience. Nor must they be prevented from acting according to it, especially in religious matters"); #10 ("It is therefore entirely in accord with the nature of faith that every kind of human coercion should be excluded from religion"); #12.2 ("in religious matters this dignity [i.e., the dignity of the human person] must be preserved intact in society from every kind of human coercion"). However, in the first place, the very text of *DH* (##2.1, 3.4, 4.2, 7.3) makes clear that religious freedom is freedom from coercion in religious matters within due limits (i.e., within the limits of a just public order). The relevant passages in *DH*, where the terms

---

31 In his treatise *La Liberté Religieuse et la Tradition Catholique* (Le Barroux FR.: Abbaye Sainte-Madeleine, 2nd ed. 1998) IA: 239–30, Fr. Basile comments as follows about 2 *John* 10 and also the *Apocalypse* (2, 6: 14–15, 18–23) (my trans.): "2 *Jn* 10 suggests non-visiting, certainly not as to pagans, but as to those who trouble others [i.e., believers] by making believe that they are Christian, all this by teaching false doctrines. Besides, there is a suggestion to guard oneself from them, but not to invoke civil coercion against them. As to the *Apocalypse* [2: 2, 6, 14–15, 18–23] the bishops are there exhorted there to expel heretics. But religious freedom does not at all contradict the right of the Church to 'put outside' (if need by force, just as all associations may do, especially a perfect society) those who sow trouble within its bosom. On one hand, this has nothing to do with impeding heretics from leaving the Church thereby renouncing the faith; on the other hand, the heretics are dangerous precisely because they do not wish to leave, and remain in the community sowing their errors."

"within due limits" (or an equivalent expression) are omitted, should be understood as implicitly qualified by that term. Second, it is not necessarily the case that general terms are to be understood as necessarily without exception. Verbally unqualified general terms are often used hyperbolically to emphasize some point, or because some exceptions are ordinarily understood to apply to the general term.[32]

D. The Consistency of Preconciliar Doctrine concerning the Church's Inherent Coercive Power with the Doctrine of *DH*

20. The crucial question for us is whether the doctrine of *DH*, concerning such coercive inherent powers of religious communities consistent with religious freedom, is also consistent with preconciliar doctrine. My conclusion is that preconciliar doctrine extant circa 1965, and for some time before that date, was certainly consistent with the doctrine of *DH* in question for the following reasons.

(a) Leo XIII in his encyclical *Immortale Dei* #36 (November 1, 1885) affirmed that "the Church is wont to take earnest heed [the custom of the Church is to take great care] that no one shall be forced to embrace the Catholic faith against his will, for, as St. Augustine wisely reminds us, 'Man cannot believe otherwise than of his own will.'"[33] In this passage the pontiff makes an immediate inference from the point that "[m]an cannot believe otherwise than of his own will" to the bar against being "forced to embrace the Catholic faith against his will." There is no intimation here that this proposition concerns only those who have never been Catholics since the justifying principle equally applies to them. Yet it must be admitted that the pontiff did not say that he is stating Catholic doctrine, especially because he is explicitly referring to the custom of the Church in taking great care ["[a]tque illud quoque magnopere career"]. Nevertheless, as we

---

32 The New Testament itself provides examples of apparently unqualified terms or expressions with understood exceptions. Thus, for example, see the passages in the *Gospel According to St. Matthew* in which Simon Peter and then all the apostles are given in unqualified terms the power of the keys, and of binding and loosing. *Mt.* 16: 19, 18: 18. But surely Peter and the other apostles could not, for example, rightly claim a power to bind and loose contrary to the natural moral law or the divine positive law.

33 http://www.vatican.va/holy_father/leo_xiii/encyclicals/documents/hf_l-xiii_enc_01111885_immortale-dei_en.html. The Latin text reads: "Atque illud quoque magnopere cavare Ecclesia solet ut ad amplexandam fidem catholicam nemo invitus cogatur, quia, quod sapienter Augustinus monet, *credere non potest homo nisi volens.*"

shall see, this text from *Immortale Dei* was thereafter taken by the magisterium to have far-reaching doctrinal import.

(b) The Code of Canon Law of 1917 went into force on May 19, 1918. Canon 6 n5 provided that all spiritual or temporal penalties that the Code does not mention are abrogated. This provision served to abolish all the then extant Church legislation authorizing or requiring temporal penalties typical of civil authority only.[34] Canon 1351 codified the injunction stated in *Immortale Dei* that no one shall be forced to embrace the Catholic faith against his will.

(c) Most importantly, Pius XII in his encyclical *Mystici Corporis* #104 (June 29, 1943) declared:[35]

> Though We desire this unceasing prayer to rise to God from the whole Mystical Body in common, that all the straying sheep may hasten to enter the one fold of Jesus Christ, yet We recognize that this must be done of their own free will; for no one believes unless he wills to believe. [n.198: Cf. August., *In Ioann. Ev. tract.*, XXVI, 2: Migne, P.L. XXX, 1607] Hence they are most certainly not genuine Christians [n.199: Cf. August., *ibidem.*] who against their belief are forced to go into a church, to approach the altar and to receive the Sacraments; for the "faith without which it is impossible to please God" [n.200: *Hebr.*, XI, 6] is an entirely free "submission of intellect and will."[n.201: Vat. Counc. *Const. de fide Cath.*, Cap. 3.] Therefore, whenever it happens, despite the constant teaching of this Apostolic See, [n.202: Cf. Leo XIII, *Immortale Dei:* A.S.S., XVIII, pp. 174–175; *Cod. Iur. Can.*, c. 1351] that anyone is compelled to embrace the Catholic faith against his will, Our sense of duty demands that We condemn the act. For men must be effectively drawn to the truth by the Father

---

34 Canon 2198, however, provided that offenses against the law of the Church alone are, of their nature, within the cognizance of the ecclesiastical authority alone, which, if it judges it necessary or prudent, can claim the help of the secular arm [*auxilio brachii saecularis*]. But this canon does not require the secular arm to accede to the Church's claim for help. In any event, it appears by hindsight that this canon was only a relic and a nod to the past since it was in virtually complete desuetude from the time the Code went into force in 1918. See René. Laprat, "Bras Séculier," *Dictionnaire de Droit Canonique* (Paris: Letouzey et Ané, 1937), 2: 1059.

35 http://www.vatican.va/holy_father/pius_xii/encyclicals/documents/hf_p-xii_enc_29061943_mystici-corporis-christi_en.html.

of light through the spirit of His beloved Son, because, endowed as they are with free will, they can misuse their freedom under the impulse of mental agitation and base desires. Unfortunately many are still wandering far from the Catholic truth, being unwilling to follow the inspirations of divine grace, because neither they [n. 205: Cf. Aust., *ibidem*] nor the faithful pray to God with sufficient fervor for this intention. Again and again We beg all [who] ardently love the Church to follow the example of the Divine Redeemer and to give themselves constantly to such prayer.

The preceding paragraphs ##101–103 of this encyclical appear to indicate that lapsed or former Catholics are among the *straying sheep*. There is no indication that the act of embracing the faith refers only to the act of the convert who embraces the faith for the first time. On the contrary, the pontiff strongly disapproves of forcing any persons, against their belief, to go into a church, approach the altar and receive the sacraments. For the faith without which it is impossible to please God is an entirely free submission of intellect and will. This rationale precluding the coercion of those who embrace the faith for the first time applies equally to the possible re-embracing of the faith by persons who had abandoned it – whether or not they had formally or notoriously left the Church. The reference by the pontiff to faith as being "an entirely free submission of intellect and will" should be read in the light of the teaching of the First Vatican Council:[36]

> [I]n order that the submission of our faith should be in accordance with reason, it was God's will that there should be linked to the internal assistance of the holy Spirit outward indications of his revelation, that is to say divine acts, the first and foremost miracles and prophecies, which clearly demonstrating as they do the omnipotence and infinite knowledge of God, are the most certain signs of revelation and are suited to the understanding of all.[37]

36 Vatican Council I, ch. 3 (De fide) (Tanner II: 807).
37 Fr. Harrison agrees that Pius XII, being aware of this quoted passage, would think that if lapsed or former Catholics are to return to the fold then their assent too must be as free. Thus he is not suggesting that Pius XII was deliberately leaving room in *Mystici Corporis* for the use of coercion (by means typical of civil authority only) to force lapsed or former Catholics back to the practice of the faith. However, Fr. Harrison does not think it likely that the Pope was including such persons among the "straying sheep" he mentions in *MC*, ##104, basing this opinion on the preceding context (##101–104), which he sees as clearly envisaging the two great blocs (baptized and unbaptized) of those who have hitherto been non-

(d) In his Allocution to the Sacred Roman Rota, October 6, 1946,[38] Pius XII spoke as follows of the freedom of the act of faith:[39]

> The Church herself, in Canon 1351 of the Code of Canon Law, has given legal effect to the maxim: *Ad amplexandam fidem Catholicam nemo invitus cogatur* (Let no one be compelled to embrace the Catholic faith against his will). This canon is couched in the very words of our great Predecessor Leo XIII in the encyclical, *Immortale Dei*, issued November 1, 1885. It is a faithful echo of the doctrine taught by the Church since the very earliest years of Christianity. Let it suffice US to quote the testimony of Lactantius, written between the years 305 and 310:
>
>> There is no need of violence or injustice. Religion cannot be imposed by force. To obtain what we desire, words, not blows should be used. That is why we keep no one who does not wish to stay with us.... The man without loyalty and faith is useless before God.... There is nothing so voluntary as religion. When the spirit is lacking in him who offers sacrifice, religion itself has already disappeared; it is already dead. (*Divinae institutions*, t. 5, c. 19 [...].)
>
> Whereas, consequently, a few days ago, according to newspaper reports, it was officially stated, in the course of a scandalous trial, that the Pope also had approved "the said forced conversions" ... We have the right and duty to deny so false an accusation. And to support Our assertion with serious documentary proof, We think it opportune to read to you a memorandum from our Secretariat of State, dated January 25, 1942, in answer to an inquiry addressed to the Holy See by the Yugoslav legation touching the circumstances of these conversions. [Sentence omitted.] Here, then, is the text of Our memorandum:

Catholics or non-Christian. Fr. Harrison also maintains that the terms "enter the one fold" and "embrace the Catholic faith," which the Pope uses in #104, are in standard Catholic parlance used when referring to persons who have never previously been Catholics.

38 *Catholic Mind* (March, 1947) 45: 129–36.

39 Ibid., 131–32.

> [Paragraph omitted.] **According to the principles of Catholic teaching, conversion should be the result not of coercion from without but of sincere interior assent to the truths taught by the Catholic Church. That is why the Catholic Church grants admission to those adults desired to be received or to return to her only on condition that they are fully conscious of the meaning and effect of the action they propose to take.** [Paragraph omitted. Bold emphasis added.]
>
> Far from according official approval, either explicitly or implicitly, to the situation of fact, the [Croatian] bishops made it a matter of duty to remind the interested parties explicitly that dissidents must be guaranteed entire freedom of choice in the matter of their return to the Faith. [Further text omitted.]

.... [A] member of the Church may not without fault deny or repudiate the Catholic truth he has once known and accepted. And when the church, having certain proof of the fact of heresy or apostasy, punishes the guilty party by excluding him from communion with the faithful, she remains strictly within the field of her competence, and acts, so to speak, as guardian of her household rights.

Note that Pius XII endorsed the teaching of Lactantius: "Religion cannot be imposed by force. To obtain what we desire, words, not blows should be used. That is why we keep no one who does not wish to stay with us." Especially note that the above quoted paragraph with added bold emphasis ("According ... take") pertains "to those adults desired to be received *or to return* [to the Church]" (emphasis added).

(e) To fully appreciate the doctrinal significance of the foregoing quoted passages from *Mystici Corporis* and the Pius XII's 1946 allocution, we turn next to *DH* #10 – which declares (Tanner II: 1006–07, emphasis added):

> One of the chief [C]atholic teachings, found in the word of God and repeatedly preached by the fathers of the [C]hurch, [n.8] is that the response to God in faith should be voluntary; so no one must be forced to embrace the faith against her or his will. [n.9]

246

Indeed, the act of faith is by its very nature voluntary. Human beings, redeemed by Christ their savior and called to adoptive sonship through Jesus Christ, [n.10] can only respond to God as he reveals himself if, with the Father drawing them, [n.11] they give to God a *free and rational allegiance of faith.* It is therefore entirely in accord with the nature of faith that every kind of human coercion should be excluded from religion.

Note 8 provides citations to various statements "by the fathers of the church." Note 9 provides the following citation: "See CIC, canon 1351; Pius XII, Allocution to the prelate auditors and other officials and administrators of the Roman Rota, 6 Oct. 1946: AAS 38 (1946), p. 394; Idem, Encyclical *Mystici Corporis*, 29 June 1943: AAS (1943), p. 243." (Tanner II: 1007–08.) However, in the last draft of *DH* (the *Textus denuo recognitus*) (November 17, 1965), the above-quoted text was accompanied by only one note (i.e., n. 13), and this was placed at the conclusion of the sentence quoted above. This note includes not only the citations in notes 8 and 9 of the final and approved text of *DH*, but also what were deemed by the Secretariat to be relevant quotations to which the citations pertain. The quotation selected from *Mystici Corporis* consisted entirely of #104, quoted in subparagraph c) above. The quotation selected for the Allocution consisted of the first paragraph ("According....take") (bold emphasis added in subparagraph (d) above) from the letter of the Holy See to the Yugoslav Legation. The pages cited in note 9 of the final, approved text of *DH* include the quotations from *Mystici Corporis* and the 1946 allocution found in note 13 of the draft text. The foregoing considerations compel the conclusion that *Mystici Corporis* and the 1946 Allocution are best to be understood as teaching that the freedom of the act of faith applies to Catholics who want to opt out or have already opted out of the Church, as well as baptized non-Catholics who culpably fail to become her members. Indeed, a person can only once enter the Church; but he can return to her as many times as he has left her. A person can only once for the first time embrace the faith; but he can embrace it anew as many times as he has abandoned the faith whether openly or not.

21. The Catholic doctrine concerning the freedom of the act of faith, understood as encompassing those who want to opt out of the Church or have already done so, is found according to *DH* "in the word of God and repeatedly preached by fathers of the church."[40] Among the relevant texts from the

40   *DH* #11 is devoted to an exposition of several texts in the New Testament bearing on the freedom of the act of faith.

New Testament supportive of the doctrine of *DH* #10 are the following: *Jn.* 18: 36 ("Jesus answered: 'My kingship is not of this world; if my kingship were of this world, my servants would fight, that I might not be handed over to the Jews; but my kingship is not from the world'"); *Matt.* 22: 21 ("Then he said to them, 'Render therefore to Caesar the things that are Caesar's, and to God the things that are God's'"); *Matt.* 18: 17 ("If he refuses to listen even to the church, let him be to you as a Gentile and a tax collector"); 2 *Cor.* 10: 3–4 ("For though we live in the world we are not carrying on a worldly war, for the weapons of our warfare are not worldly but have divine power to destroy strongholds").[41] These texts are highly relevant not only as to doctrine of the freedom of the act of faith but also with respect to the question of whether the Church's inherent coercive power includes the authority to inflict the kinds of temporal penalties that are typically used only by civil authority. So too are the teachings of the early fathers of the Church before her establishment by the Roman imperial power in the fourth century. Thus, for example besides the declaration of Lactantius that "we keep no one who does not wish to stay with us" (endorsed by Pius XII in his 1945 allocution), is that of Tertullian who (in 212) explained in a letter addressed to the pro-consul Scapula: "It is a law of mankind and the natural right that each individual worship what he thinks proper."[42] St. Cyprian, bishop of Carthage, cogently explained (circa 246–58) how the inherent coercive power of the Church differed from that of the priests under the Old Law. He wrote:[43]

41 But see the parable of the great banquet of *Luke* 14: 23–24, with its controversial passage: "And the master said to the servant, 'Go out to the highways and hedges, and compel people to come in, that my house may be filled." (Ibid., 23.) St. Augustine of Hippo made much of this passage in arguing for temporal penalties to physically coerce apostates and heretics, albeit by civil authorities, to return to the Church. See, inter alia, Augustine, Epistle 93 (to Vincentius) #5 (http://www.catholicculture.org/culture/library/fathers/view.cfm?recnum=3240). The admittedly puzzling nature of this passage from *Luke* is enhanced because those invited to the feast were not compelled to enter despite their all having refused the invitation. In any event, a legitimate interpretation of this passage is to the effect that what is meant in the passage is *moral* compulsion by persuasive zealous preaching rather than compelling persons by force or the threat of force to attend conversion sermons or instruction. (See, e.g., Arthur Vermeersch, S.J., *Tolerance* (New York: Benzinger Bros., 1913) 196; Fr. Basile, *La Liberté Religieuse* (*supra* note 31), IA: 280n1344.)

42 "To Scapula," *Tertullian: Apologetical Works and Minucius Felix Octavius* (trans. R. Arbesmann et al.) (New York: Fathers of the Church, 1950), 152

43 Epistle 64 (to Pomponius) #4 (http://www.catholicculture.org/culture/library/fathers/view.cfm?recnum=1778). The probative value of the witness of Cyprian

God commanded those who did not obey His priests to be slain, and those who did not hearken to His judges who were appointed for the time. And then indeed they were slain with the sword, when the circumcision of the flesh was yet in force; but now that circumcision has begun to be of the spirit among God's faithful servants, the proud and contumacious are slain with the sword of the Spirit, in that they are cast out of the Church.

22. The foregoing account shows that the extant preconciliar doctrine as of 1965 concerning the Church's inherent coercive power (as not including the infliction of temporal penalties typical of civil authority) is not only consistent with that of *DH* but substantially identical with it. This conclusion provides the basis for an explanation of a fact adverted to by a learned scholar in private correspondence, namely, that for quite some time (let us say following the pontificate of Pius XII) before, during, and after the Council proceedings, there appears to have been a general consensus (including even among those strongly opposed to adoption by the Council of the doctrine of *DH* concerning religious freedom pertaining to the public manifestation or propagation of beliefs in religious matters) that preconciliar Catholic doctrine precluded coercing people to enter, remain in, or return to the Church by the use of temporal penalties typical of civil authority only.[44] On the other hand, to affirm that the Church's inherent

concerning the Church's inherent coercive power is enhanced given that he immediately adds: "For they cannot live out of it, since the house of God is one, and there can be no salvation to any except in the Church."

44 See, for example, the preparatory draft text, "De Ecclesia" for the schema "De Relationibus Inter Ecclesiam et Statum Necnon de Tolerantia Religiosa," proposed by the preparatory theological commission, chaired by Cardinal Alfredo Ottaviani, for the Council (June 19–20, 1962). (*Acta et Documenta Concilio Oecumenico Vaticano II Apparando* (Typis Polyglottis Vaticanis, 1968: s.II/vol.II/pt.IV, 657–672. An English translation is provided in Appendix V at pages 295–302 (less the copious notes), in Michael Davies, *The Second Vatican Council and Religious Liberty* (Long Prairie, Minn.: Neumann Press, 1992). With respect to the Catholic City, the draft declared: "Nevertheless, even in those fortunate conditions, the civil Authority is not permitted in any way to compel consciences to accept the faith revealed by God. Indeed the faith is essentially free and cannot be the object of any constraint, as the Church teaches by saying, 'That no one be compelled to embrace the Catholic Faith unwillingly'" (Davies, at 300). Of significance is that the draft thereafter only concerned itself with what the civil authority could legitimately do by itself, i.e., "regulate and moderate the public manifestations of other cults and defend its citizens against the spreading of false doctrines which, in the judgment of the Church, put their eternal salvation at risk." (Ibid.) Davies, who

coercive power does not encompass temporal penalties typical of civil authority only is consistent with the doctrine that the Church has jurisdiction over all baptized persons, including apostates (whether from Catholicism or, more globally, from Christianity), with respect to matters of canon law concerning sacramental, disciplinary, and related issues.[45]

23. *DH* #12.1 recites that throughout the centuries, despite "there hav[ing] been ways of acting hardly in tune with the spirit of the gospel, indeed contrary to it, nevertheless the [C]hurch's teaching that no one's faith should be coerced has held firm." I do not propose to discuss in this appendix whether prior of *Mystici Corporis* in 1953, there actually was any teaching about the matter that can justly be called *Catholic doctrine* (i.e., a teaching by the Church which the faithful are bound to give at least a presumptive albeit defeasible assent) that is identical with that of *Mystici Corporis* and *DH*. But, on the other hand, I propose to show, first, that no relevant statements of preconciliar doctrine preclude a reasonable,

professed himself unable to see how preconciliar doctrine could be squared with that of *DH* about the public manifestations and propagation of non-Catholic religions, himself endorsed the view that no one should be forced to act, as to religious matters, against his conscience in private and public, and that no one should be prevented from acting in accordance with his conscience in private unless harm is thereby done to the public welfare. Davies agreed that this is in accord with "the traditional papal teaching, as expounded by the representative authors in the approved manuals." Ibid., 44. The "learned scholar" mentioned in the accompanying text is Thomas Pink, professor of philosophy at King's College, London, who has written an interesting essay to be included in a Festschrift volume in honor of John Finnis entitled "What is the Catholic doctrine of religious liberty?" A draft of this paper is currently accessible on-line (that is, as of June 23, 2011) at http://kcl.academia.edu/ThomasPink. I believe that Appendix A anticipates the substance of Professor Pink's essay.

45 Benedict XVI's Motu Proprio, *Omnium in Mentum* (October 26, 2009) (available on-line at http://www.vatican.va/holy_father/benedict_xvi/apost_letters/documents/hf_ben-xvi_apl_20091026_codex-iuris-canonici_en.html) furnishes us with a recent example of the exercise of this jurisdictional authority of the Church over all persons who have been validly baptized. Canon 11 of the 1983 Code of Canon Law provides: "Merely ecclesiastical laws bind those baptized in the Catholic Church or received into it and who enjoy the sufficient use of reason and, unless the law expressly provides otherwise, have completed seven years of age." Before the changes made by *Omnium in Mentum*, "[t]he *Code of Canon Law* nonetheless prescribe[d] that the faithful who have left the Church "by a formal act" are not bound by the ecclesiastical laws regarding the canonical form of marriage (cf. can. 1117), dispensation from the impediment of disparity of cult (cf. can. 1086) and the need for permission in the case of mixed marriages (cf. can. 1124)." The Motu Proprio of October 26, 2009, abolished these exceptions.

legitimate interpretation consistent with the doctrine of *Mystici Corporis* and *DH* in question; and, second, there were reputable, orthodox theologians who adhered to that interpretation during the pre-*Mystici Corporis* preconciliar period.

24. Let us initially consider whether there was any *definitive* (i.e., infallible) doctrine inconsistent with the doctrine of *Mystici Corporis* and *DH* in question. The most plausible candidate is canon 14 of the first decree (on the sacraments) of session 7 of the Council of Trent (March 3, 1547). The canon reads:[46]

> If anyone says that, when they grow up [cum adoleverint i.e., when they are adults], those baptised as little children should be asked whether they wish to ratify what their godparents promised in their name when they were baptised; and that, when they reply that they have no such wish, they should be left to their own decision and not, in the meantime, coerced by any penalty into the [C]hristian way of life, except that they be barred from the reception of the eucharist and other sacraments, until they have a change of heart: let him be anathema.

Let us assume (for argument's sake at least[47]) that the contradictory of the proposition condemned in canon 14 constitutes a definitive doctrine. Now what is forbidden by canon 14 is to assert a proposition of the general form: **if A** (when they grow up ... were baptized) **and B** (and that, when ... wish) **then C** (they should be left ... change of heart). We note that canon 14 characterizes the barring of the defiant adults in question from the reception of the Eucharist and the other sacraments (i.e., minor excommunication) as being one of those penalties (albeit the mildest of them) that are *coercive* in nature. Therefore the imposition of *major* excommunication upon the defiant adult described in canon 14, or the deprivation of some of the rights and privileges of membership in the Church (even were a major excommunication not imposed), would *a fortiori* constitute a "coercive" penalty within the meaning of canon 14. But since these more burdensome ecclesiastical penalties are still milder than the kinds of coercion typically used only by civil authorities, someone who says that the former, but not the latter, may legitimately be imposed upon the defiant persons under discussion will not fall under the *anathema* of canon 14. Thus understood, the Tridentine canon does not conflict with the teaching of

---

46   Sess. 7 (3 March 15457), Canons on the Sacrament of Baptism (Tanner II: 686).
47   Fr. Harrison holds that this assumption is certainly true.

DH, which has in mind the severer penalties typically imposed only by civil authorities when it reprobates *coercion* in religious matters.

25. In compelling confirmation of what I submit is the true meaning of canon 14, I call the reader's attention to the constitution *Licet iuxta doctrinum* (October 23, 1327) of Pope John XXII, in which he condemned the doctrines of Marsilius of Padua, including the proposition that (the pope or) the Church taken as a whole may not punish a man (whatsoever villain he may be) by a coercive punishment, unless the emperor has given them the power.[48] John XXII, after affirming the Church's inherent coercive power, declared that, since major excommunication not only deprives the excommunicated of reception of the sacraments but excludes him from the communion of the faithful, bodily coercion is something that Christ has permitted to his Church.[49] It follows therefore that a legitimate interpretation of canon 14, consistent with our reading of *DH*, entails that there are possible temporal penalties not typical of civil authority only that the Church may inflict on the wayward adult described in the canon and which could also be well within the limits of a just public order.

48 (Henricus Denzinger-Adolfus Schönmetzer, *Enchiridion Symbolorum Definitionum et Declarationum de Rebus Fidei et Morum* (33rd ed., 1978), 290, #945.) This proposition is among those censured by John XXII as follows: "We declare as Our sentence that it is to be made manifest and known to all that the aforesaid articles are contrary to Sacred Scripture and inimical to the Catholic faith, heretical, or erroneous and savoring of heresy; and also that the aforesaid Marsilius and John are heretics, and indeed, heresiarchs." (Trans. by Fr. Harrison) (ibid., #946.)

49 As Fr, Harrison well notes, the choice by John XXII of *corporalis* is actually quite appropriate here, because in major excommunication, *exclusion from communion* means physically removing the excommunicated person from a Church service if he refuses to leave voluntarily, as stipulated right up to the 1983 Code in the case of (say) an excommunicated deacon, lector, Eucharistic minister or usher who might insist on exercising his ministry at Mass.

The complete relevant passage from *Licet* reads (with John XXII developing his thought based on the text of *Matthew* 18: 17): "*Adhuc* constat, sicut ibi legitur in Matthaeo, quod si aliquis damnum alicui indebite dederit, illudque ad mandatum Ecclesiae noluerit emendare, quod Ecclesia per potestatem a Christo sibi concessam, ipsum ad hoc per excommunicationis sententiam compellere potest, quae quidem potestas est utique coactiva. Circa quod est animadvertendum, quod cum excommunicatio major nedum excommunicatum a perceptione sacramentorum removeat, sed etiam a communione fidelium ipsum excommunicatum excludat, corporalis est a Christo coactio Ecclesiae permisssa." (N. Iung & R. Naz) "Contrainte," *Dictionnaire de Droit Canonique* (Paris: Letouzey et Ané, 1949), 4: 500.

26. Let us briefly review other doctrinal documents of the Church relevant to our inquiry.

(a) The ecumenical Council of Constance in 1415 condemned the following proposition (#14) attributed to John Hus:[50]

> Doctors who state that anybody subjected to ecclesiastical censure, if he refuses to be corrected, should be handed over to the judgment of the secular authority, are undoubtedly following in this the chief priests, scribes and the pharisees who handed over to the secular authority Christ himself, since he was unwilling to obey them in all things, saying, *It is not lawful for us to put any man to death* [*Jn.* 18:31]; these gave him to the civil judge, so that such men are greater murderers than Pilate.

However there is no indication whatever that this proposition was itself condemned as being contrary to any definitive or authoritative doctrine of the Church. Rather, in the sentence against him, the Council had only globally declared (Tanner I: 427):

> [Hus] ha[d] asserted and published certain articles listed below. . . . This most holy synod of Constance therefore declares and defines that the articles listed below .... are not catholic and should not be taught to be such but rather many of them are erroneous, others scandalous, others offensive to the ears of the devout, many of them are rash and seditious, and some of them are notoriously heretical and have long been rejected and condemned by holy fathers and by general councils.

As Fr. Harrison notes, the character of being *scandalous* or *offensive to the ears of the devout* might well have consisted above all in casting Church authority in the role of the "bad guys" (i.e., the chief priests, scribes, and Pharisees who handed over Christ to secular authority), and likening the heretic or rebel to Christ himself.

(b) Pope Martin V, on February 22, 1418, addressed to the hierarchy and to the inquisitors a questionnaire targeted for Wycliffites and Hussites, which directed that anyone suspected of holding any of the proscribed articles or who affirmed them must be interrogated according to the questionnaire. Item 32 required the subject be asked if he believed that, in the circumstances of increasing disobedience or revolt on the part of

50   Sess. 15 (July 6, 1415), Condemned Articles of John Hus (Tanner I: 430).

excommunicated persons, prelates or their vicars have the power to impose a penalty or to increase a penalty on excommunicates, to lay an interdict, and to appeal to the secular arm, and that the subjects must be made to obey the censures.[51] This document is not a statement of Catholic doctrine but rather a disciplinary decree. Hence a negative answer to the question posed in item #32 could have been censured only as being scandalous, offensive to the ears of the devout, or rash and seditious.

(c) In his constitution *Exsurge Domine* (June 15, 1520), Pope Leo X condemned forty-one theses attributed to Martin Luther. Item 33 asserted that the burning of heretics is contrary to the will of the Holy Spirit. However, here again there is no indication whatsoever that this proposition is condemned as being contrary to any definitive or even authoritative doctrine of the Church. Indeed the constitution globally condemned the propositions set forth in the bull as being heretical, or scandalous, or false, or as offensive to pious ears, or inducing error in simple souls, and opposed to Catholic truth.[52] Hence the condemned proposition might just be one offensive to pious ears or as inducing error in simple souls.

(d) Pius VI, in the constitution *Auctorem Fidei* of August 28, 1794, condemned the fourth proposition of the synod of Pistoia (1786), as heretical insofar as it is asserted that it was an abuse of authority for the Church to use coercion with respect to her subjects if *coercion* is understood to mean the external discipline used by the Apostles. Moreover, the condemned proposition leads to heresy if it is understood to mean that the Church has not received from God the power, other than that to direct by counsel and exhortation, to command by laws and to restrain and to curb

51 Denzinger-Schönmetzer (*supra* note 47), 326–29, ##1246–79. Fr. Harrison thinks that this item appears to be more a matter of the coercive power of the State, not of the Church itself, because the Church is not appealing here to a putative power of her own to use coercive measures typically used only by civil authority. The item, he maintains, clearly says it will be the "secular arm," not ecclesiastical authorities and their own agents, who will inflict those coercive penalties after being duly requested to do so by said authorities. Moreover, some of these rebellious excommunicates could well have been a threat to a just public order (within the meaning of *DH*). Mr. Guminski thinks that item 32 also encompasses the exercise of coercive power by the Church involving temporal penalties typical of civil authority if rebellious excommunicates were or subject to being in the physical custody of the Church for the imposition or increase of penalties prior to delivery to the secular arm. (In any case, any interrogated person would be in the physical custody of the Church.) Furthermore, the item pertained also to some cases in which there was no threat to a just public order (within the meaning of *DH*).
52 Ibid., 361–62, ##1485, 1492.

by external judgments and salutary penalties those who disobey her.[53] There is nothing here that is facially inconsistent with the views that are advocated in this appendix since the term *salutary penalties* is more vague that *temporal penalties*.[54]

(e) In the encyclical *Quanta Cura* (December 8, 1864) #5, Pius IX condemned the proposition that affirmed "that the Church has no right of restraining by temporal punishments those who violate her laws."[55] In the accompanying, even more famous, *Syllabus*, the condemned proposition #24 stated that the Church has no power of employing force [Ecclesia vis inferendae potestatem non habet], nor has she any temporal power direct or indirect.[56] In neither item is there a sufficient basis for concluding that the condemnation applies to someone who claims that the Church has the

---

53 Ibid., 519–20, ##2604–05.

54 Fr. Basile has remarked that it is likely that Pius VI thought [songeait], without formally teaching, of a physical coercion exercised immediately by the Church and mediately by the State at the demand of the Church. Basile, *La Liberté Religieuse* (*supra* note 31), IA: 367. Earlier, Pius IX, in his decretal letter **Quod Aliquantum of March 10, 1791** addressed to the French hierarchy (French version accessible on-line at http://www.laportelatine.org/bibliotheque/encycliques/PieVI/Quod_Aliquantum.php), criticized in (unnumbered) paragraph 13 the failure of the French National Assembly to take account of the difference between those who are strangers to the Church (such as infidels and Jews) and those who by the regeneration of baptism are subject to her laws. The first, he declared, are not subject to the obedience prescribed for Catholics; but for the latter, obedience is a duty. The pontiff in support cited Aquinas, *ST* 2a2ae, q.10, a.8 (which endorses in effect coercion involving temporal penalties typical of only civil authority) because Aquinas proves this difference with his ordinary cogency. What Pius IX complained was that "[t]his equality, this liberty so exalted by the National Assembly therefore leads only to the overthrow of the Catholic religion, and thus this is why [the assembly] has refused to declare [the said religion] *dominant* in the kingdom, which status had hitherto always belonged to [the Church]" [Cette égalité, cette liberté si exaltées par l'Assemblée nationale, n'aboutissent donc qu'à renverser la religion catholique, et voilà pourquoi elle a refusé de la déclarer *dominante* dans le royaume, quoique ce titre lui ait toujours appartenu]. However the papal letter of Pius VI, just as his constitution *Auctorem Fidei*, does not itself formally teach (whether explicitly or implicitly) as Catholic doctrine that the Church's inherent coercive power includes the power to inflict temporal penalties typical of only civil authority.

55 http://www.papalencyclicals.net/Pius09/p9quanta.htm.

56 Denzinger-Schönmetzer, 579, #1724. In his *Church of the Word Incarnate, supra*, 270n3, Cardinal Journet wrote of the first clause of proposition 24 of the *Syllabus* that it "undoubtedly refers to the coercive powers; but it does not say whether intrinsically temporal or simply moral penalties are envisaged."

inherent coercive power to impose only those temporal penalties not typical of civil authority. For that claim is quite consistent with readily acknowledging that agents of the Church are free, within due limits and subject to reasonable regulation by civil authority, to use physical force or the threat thereof, directly by themselves or with the assistance of law enforcement officers, to protect the property and kindred rights that the Church possesses under the civil law, including the prevention of trespasses and disturbances of religious ceremonies.[57]

(f) In his encyclical, *Immortale Dei* #11 (1885) Leo XIII declared: "In very truth, Jesus Christ gave to His Apostles unrestrained authority in regard to things sacred, together with the genuine and most true power of making laws, as also with the twofold right of judging and of punishing, which flow from that power." Canon 2214 n1, of the Code of Canon Law of 1917, provided that the Church, independently of all human authority, has the proper and inherent right to inflict spiritual or temporal penalties on delinquent subjects. But the only temporal penalties that the 1917 Code encompasses are those not typical of civil authority. Canon 1311 of the present code simply declares: "The Church has an innate and proper right to coerce offending members of the Christian faithful by means of penal sanctions."

E. Pre-*Mystici Corporis* Theological Opinion that the Church's Inherent Coercive Power Does Not Encompass Temporal Penalties Typical of Civil Authority Only

27. The foregoing authorities discussed in paragraphs ##20–26, concerning the Church's inherent coercive power, collectively establish and confirm what must certainly be regarded as Catholic doctrine. It should be noted that nothing in these authorities clearly says or implies that temporal penalties typical of civil authority only are within the Church's inherent coercive power. Notwithstanding the pre-*Mystici Corporis* common theological opinion to the contrary,[58] I shall now show that there also coexisted a legitimate, well-founded probable theological opinion, according to

---

57 See, for example, canon 1331 §2 n.1, of the Code of Canon Law of 1983, which provides that an excommunicated person wishing to have any ministerial participation in celebrating any ceremony whatsoever of public worship "is to be prevented from doing so or the liturgical action is to stop unless a serious cause intervenes."

58 Among the authorities supporting this opinion were such theologians and canonists as Louis Choupin, *Valeur des Décisions Doctrinales et Disciplinaires du Saint-Siège* (Paris: Gabriel Beauchesne, 3d ed. 1928), 260–79, 525–26; (A.

which the Church's inherent coercive power does not include the infliction of temporal penalties typical of civil authority only.

28. The following is a selection of those authorities.

(a) Of great probative value is the fact that on February 2, 1865, Mgr. Jacques-Marie-Achille Ginoulhiac, then bishop of Grenoble, wrote a circular letter that defended *Quanta Cura* and the *Syllabus*, and in which he commented upon the condemned proposition concerning temporal penalties for violators of the Church's laws set forth in *Quanta Cura*.[59] The prelate asserted that it is true that the words "temporal penalties," taken in their general sense, embrace or can be taken to embrace all sorts of penalties, from the most minute fines to the most terrible afflictive and injurious penalties. But, as he remarked, it is also true that this word may well only designate a certain order of these penalties.[60] The bishop maintained that evidently the words "temporal penalties" only signify a simple deprivation of temporal goods, like the deprivation of the enjoyment or the usage of properties that the Church possesses and which she freely administers. Additionally, he explained, every day in the penitential tribunal the Church requires almsgiving as a penalty and expiation of sins; and that, since her origin, she imposes on-certain days the obligation of fasting, abstinence, and almsgiving. Bishop Ginoulhiac vehemently protested against the charge that Pius IX wished to re-establish the tribunal of the inquisition.[61]

(b) Fr. Arthur Vermeersch, an important moral theologian and canonist, in his book *Tolerance* (1913)[62] distinguished between what he called the *original* and the *derivative* coercive power of the Church. The former was given by God as something permanent and essential. The latter was conferred by

---

Bride), "Peines Ecclésiastiques," in *Dictionnaire de Théologie Catholique*, XII: 630–37; Ferd. J. Moulart, *L'Église et L'État*, supra, 441–48.

59 *L'Encyclique et L'Épiscopat Français: Recueil Complet* (Paris: Gaiguet et Pougeois, 1865) 326–81. Mgr. Ginoulhiac, who despite his being a leading inopportunist against the pending definition of the dogma of papal infallibility at Vatican Council I in 1870, was nevertheless made archbishop of Lyons, the primatial see of France, during the Council. He absented himself from Rome during the session when the dogma was defined in the public session of July 18; but communicated his adhesion to the dogma in mid-August of the same year. Dom. Cuthbert Butler, *The Vatican Council 1869–1870* (ed. C. Butler) (Fontana Library, 1962), 116, 175, 408, 418.

60 *L'Encyclique et L'Épiscopat Français, supra*, 352.

61 Ibid., 353–54.

62 *Tolerance, supra* note 41. Vermeersch played a major role in the drafting of Pius XI's famous encyclical *Casti Connubii* (1931) concerning (inter alia) abortion and birth control

men, according to the age, the country, and the actual constitution of society.[63] After an extensive inquiry, he concluded: "But if we confine our attention to the inherent power of the Church, that power which she possesses
always and everywhere, we consider that her power is limited to those penalties, spiritual or temporal, which find their last sanction in the supreme penalty of excommunication."[64] However, as we have already argued, the Church's
inherent coercive power also extends to temporal penalties not typical of civil
authority only independently of the sanction of excommunication.

(c) Cardinal Thomas-Marie-Joseph Gousset (1792–1866)[65] wrote in
his celebrated treatise on dogmatic theology as follows:[66]

> The Church ... has received from God the power not only to direct
> by her counsel and by persuasion, but moreover to command by
> laws, and to compel obedience to her laws by an exterior judgment

63 Ibid., 59.
64 Ibid., 102. Earlier in his book, Vermeersch had already remarked: "According to
    one interpretation, which, though minimalistic, is admissible, the error dealt with
    in the Encyclical *Quanta cura* is avoided by attributing to the Church the right of
    inflicting temporal punishments in the sense that we have called 'conditional.'
    Expressly or implicitly the judgment takes this form: 'Under pain of suspension,
    or interdict, or excommunication, the accused person is ordered to pay such and
    such a fine, or to reside in such and such a place.'" Ibid., 60. Nevertheless,
    Vermeersch also asserted: "we recognize in [the Church] the right to claim the
    assistance of the State for the application of those temporal punishments which, in
    view of her spiritual end, she considers it proper in certain circumstances to pre-
    scribe or inflict." Ibid., 102. But Vermeersch thus thought that the theoretical basis
    of the right is based upon positive or customary human law. The probative value
    of Vermeersch's judgment about the Church's inherent coercive power should (for
    some readers who might be initially skeptical about his thesis) be somewhat
    enhanced given that he held: "[i]n a Catholic society [where] the true religion will
    be publicly honoured and protected.... [T]he civil power may declare that any pub-
    lic contradiction of the faith or the propagation of heterodox doctrines is an
    offence, and may inflict reasonable punishment for it." Ibid., 250–51.
65 Gousset became bishop of Périgueux in 1836 and thereafter archbishop of Reims
    in 1840. He was made cardinal in 1850. He was a renowned theologian, a moder-
    ate Gallican concerning the issue of the yet to be defined dogma of papal infalli-
    bility. He repudiated the doctrine embodied in the first of the Four Gallican
    Articles of 1852 insofar as it could be construed as a denial that the popes had an
    indirect power, with respect to temporal and civil matters, to use the Church's spir-
    itual penalties to punish rulers for violations of the moral law. *Théologie
    Dogmatique: ou Exposition des Preuves et des Dogmes de la Religion Catholique*
    (9th ed., Paris, 1861) 1: 733–34 (§ 1203).
66 Ibid., 1: 673–74 (§1109) (my trans.).

and by salutary penalties. The contrary proposition was condemned by the bull *Auctorem fidei* in 1794 as leading to heresy. Thus, the power of the Church is a coercive power, a power of coercion in the moral order. Confiscation of goods, disinheritance, and afflictive and corporal penalties, are not directly within the Church's competence; an ecclesiastical law may not inflict a penalty of that nature without the concurrence of the temporal power. But the Church may punish those who rebel against her authority by excommunication, suspension, interdiction, deprivation of a spiritual office, of a benefice, sacred factions, discharge, deposition, degradation, which are so many ecclesiastical penalties. The coercive power, being necessary to all government, belongs to the Church as it does to all other societies: it properly belongs to her, it is inherent in her constitution; it is, consequently, independent of the secular power.

The Cardinal's statement of the scope of the Church's inherent coercive power as encompassing some temporal aspects nevertheless is not as expressly broad as the view taken in this appendix since the cardinal omitted any mention of the Church's power to forbid members or former members access to its property and functions chiefly devoted to religious and other purposes incident to its status as a religious community.[67] But then the cardinal's "laundry list" of ecclesiastical sanctions was not intended by him to be exhaustive; and the "laundry list" does not include temporal penalties typical of civil authority only.

(d) The Belgian philosopher and theologian, Nicole-Joseph Laforêt (1823–72), wrote in his treatise on dogmatic theology[68] that the Church's coercive power may be only exercised within the limits of the moral and religious domain, and that the penalties she may inflict are, by themselves, only spiritual penalties. Here he approvingly cited and quoted most of the passage from Cardinal Gousset's treatise, the same quoted in subparagraph (c) above.[69] Laforêt quite obviously used the term *spiritual penalties* as

---

67 However, Gousset (in discussing the first of the four Gallican articles) favorably referred to how Saint Ambrose, bishop of Milan, forbade the Roman emperor Theodosius I from entering churches and required him to undergo a public penance for having ordered the Thessalonian massacre of 390. *Théologie Dogmatique*, supra, 1: 734 (§1109).

68 *Les Dogmes Catholiques: Exposés, Prouvés et Vengés des Attaques de l'Hérésie et de l'Incrédulité* (2nd ed., Paris/Tournai, 1860) 3 88–89.

69 The part of the passage quoted by Laforêt begins with "The confiscation [La confiscation]" and concludes with "ecclesiastical penalties [peines ecclésiastiques]."

encompassing some temporal aspects such as those incident to major excommunication.

(e) Jean-Edmé-Auguste Gosselin (1787–1858), the French ecclesiastical historian and theologian, wrote in his influential treatise about the temporal power of the popes.[70] He described "[e]xcommunication [as] a spiritual punishment, inflicted by a spiritual superior, or by the laws of the Church, which deprives a Christian of all or some spiritual benefits enjoyed by members of the Church, such as the participation of the sacraments, public prayers, &."[71] He explained:[72]

> From the establishment of Christianity, excommunication, according to the institution of Jesus Christ and of his apostles, deprived the Christian not only of the spiritual goods peculiar to members of the Church, but also of some acts of civil intercourse dependent on the will of private persons, and from which they abstain without violating any right; such, for instance, are many ordinary marks of civility or friendship, such as sitting at the same table, familiar conversations, mutual salutations, &.

Gosselin approvingly quoted the following passage from a treatise by Bishop Jacques-Bénigne Bossuet (1627–1704):[73]

70 *The Power of the Pope* (*supra* note 2), 80–83.
71 Ibid., 81n3.
72 Ibid., 82.
73 Ibid., 83. Bossuet was bishop of Meaux, a French court preacher, theologian and controversialist. The passage quoted was from Bossuet's posthumously published *Defensio Declarationis Conventis Cleri Gallicani*, lib. I, sect. II, cap. xxii, p. 345. In this work Bossuet defended the theological Gallicanism, a theory concerning the constitution of the Church and its relations with secular authority that were codified in the famous Four Articles of 1682 of the Church in France. These articles were declared null and void by papal decree; but nevertheless Catholics were free to adhere to the tolerated opinions embodied in the Four Articles since they were without theological censure. (See Gousset, *Théologie Dogmatique, supra*, 729–30 §1197.) The propositions embodied in the second, third, and fourth articles, pertaining to the constitution of the Church, papal primacy and infallibility, however, were definitively condemned by the dogmatic definitions of Vatican Council I (1869–70). The first article rejected the deposing power of the Pope, his authority to release subjects from their oath of fealty to their rulers, and denied that the Pope or any ecclesiastical authority had the power, direct or indirect, in civil and temporal affairs. The proposition embodied in the first article became erroneous by virtue of the condemnation of proposition 24 of the *Syllabus* in 1864. It can be safely said that virtually no theologian today accepts the notion of the direct temporal power of the pope. And there were differing opinions about what

According to the testimony of the Gospel and of the apostles, an excommunicated person is outlawed from human society, so far as human society regards good morals; but he retains all his civil rights, unless the law has ordained otherwise. If in the course of time, excommunicated persons were declared infamous, incapable of making a will, and deprived from certain functions of civil life, until they returned to their duty; this arose from the fact, that princes made their laws as conformable as possible to the laws of morality, and to the discipline of the Gospel, and not because excommunication of itself entails the loss of any temporal right, or any temporal property.

29. The reader should bear in mind that Bossuet, Laforêt, Gosselin, and Gousset wrote before the publication of *Quanta Cura* and the accompanying *Syllabus* in 1864. Although these four writers verbally limited the Church's inherent coercive power to what they call spiritual penalties, some of these penalties had temporal aspects (e.g., denial of Christian burial, mandated shunning in some profane matters). In any event, it appears to be much more probable than not that had they been aware of *Quanta Cura* and the *Syllabus*, and later *DH*, they would have amended their theories so as to be consistent with the view that the Church's inherent coercive power does not encompass temporal penalties typical of civil authority only.

Conclusion

30. I submit that I have sustained the burden of establishing the theses set forth in paragraph 4 and 16 above. I have made every effort to ensure that nothing contained herein favors or disfavors my opinions or those of Fr. Harrison concerning religious freedom as it pertains to the public manifestation or propagation of beliefs in religious matters. This dispute with Fr. Harrison about the meaning of the doctrine of *DH* on religious freedom

constitutes the true doctrine about indirect temporal power of the pope. But a pre-*Mystici Corporis* Catholic could have safely held as a well-founded probable opinion that the pope, and the Church generally, only has the limited power to declare as morally null and void those laws, regulations, and orders of civil authority contrary to divine positive or natural law. (G. Glez., "Pouvoir du Pape en Matière Temporale," *Dictionnaire de Théologie Catholique*, 12: 2264–72; Lecler, *The Two Sovereignties, supra,* 71–84.) This moderate theory of the Pope's indirect power in temporal matters does not imply that the Church's inherent coercive power encompasses temporal penalties typical of civil authority only. See note 8 *supra.*

would be full of sound and fury, but signifying nothing, unless we both substantially concurred in the theses set forth in this appendix. For the kind of *coercion* from which, according to *DH*, the human person has a natural right to immunity in religious matters must be understood as the kind of coercion typically used by civil authorities only: imprisonment, fines, deportation, capital punishment, etc. (cf. paragraph #4(a) *supra*). But this purported *natural* right to religious freedom would certainly seem rather hollow if it ruled out the use of those sorts of coercion on the part of the State, but allowed in principle for the Catholic Church and her agents to impose them, by her independent authority, on her own disobedient members and former members. Needless to say, if this were the correct interpretation of *DH* (as some have claimed it is), then the Declaration's promulgation by the Church would rightly appear hypocritical in the eyes of the world. How credible would her loudly trumpeted proclamation of a *right of the human person to immunity from coercion in religious matters* sound if she had quietly stipulated in the "fine print" that while everyone else on earth is morally bound to respect and grant that immunity, the Church herself is not? Thus *DH* cannot legitimately be read as tacitly retaining a putative older doctrine to the effect that the Church and her agents have their own inherent authority to repress religious dissent by means of the same kind of coercive measures that are typically used only by civil authorities. Thus it is very gratifying that, despite our profound differences about many issues concerning *Dignitatis Humanae,* Fr. Harrison and I substantially agree about the scope and limits of the Church's inherent coercive power.

Appendix B:
Are the Condemnations
in *Quanta Cura* Definitive?*
Brian W. Harrison, O.S.

1. The most important thesis that I affirm, and Arnold Guminski denies, to have been taught definitively by Bl. Pope Pius IX is the *falsity* of the following proposition (which he refers to as "QC3"): **"The best condition of society is that in which there is not recognized as incumbent upon civil authority any duty to restrain violators of the Catholic religion by enacted penalties, except so far as the public peace may require."**[1] The reader may at this point wish to refer back to the last lines of FR, #11 for Mr. Guminski's citation of the "operative declaration" near the end of *QC* by which Pius IX condemned this and several other theses.

2. Mr. Guminski first remarks that, while qualifying them as "evil," "depraved," "erroneous," "false and perverse," "Pius IX does not otherwise characterize these condemned propositions with any customary theological censure."[2] My critic then clarifies this observation by pointing out, correctly, that when the Pope in *QC* repeatedly reprobates these opinions collectively as being (among other things) "errors," he is using this word not in its technical sense – i.e., as a specific censure applied to certain disapproved doctrines that are less gravely unorthodox than heresy – but in a broad sense denoting proscribed doctrines of any degree of gravity.[3] But is

---

*   The title of this essay is abbreviated throughout this book as "AppB."
1   Cf. FR, ##9–10 (my translation of QC3). The original text, taken from P. Gaspari (ed.), *Codicis Iuris Canonici Fontes* (Rome: Vatican Press, 1924), vol. II, 995, is: *"optimam esse condicionem societatis, in qua Imperio non agnoscitur officium coercendi sancitis poenis violatores catholicae religionis, nisi quatenus pax publica postulet."*
2   FR, #12 (emphasis added).
3   Cf. FR, #14. However, when Pius IX singles out one particular compound thesis – that which Mr. Guminski refers to as QC4–5 (cf. FR, #10) – as being an "erroneous opinion" (*erroneam . . . opinionem*), there seems no reason to doubt that he is using *erroneam* as the censure referred to above. But whether or not this is rel-

the inclusion of a specific theological note or censure in a doctrinal definition essential for it to qualify as an exercise of papal infallibility? In his
final *relatio* of July 16, 1870, Bishop Vincent Gasser authoritatively clarified for the assembled Fathers that the verb "defines," in the Council's formula of papal infallibility, was to be taken as meaning that the Pope, in
words of his own choosing,

> directly and conclusively pronounces his sentence about a doctrine
> which concerns matters of faith or morals, and does so in such a
> way that each one of the faithful can be certain of the mind of the
> Apostolic See, of the mind of the Roman Pontiff; in such a way,
> indeed, that he or she knows for certain that such-and-such a doc-
> trine is held to be heretical, proximate to heresy, certain *or* erro-
> neous, etc., by the Roman Pontiff.[4]

3. However, Gasser effectively ruled out the view that any such "customary" terminology is a necessary feature of an *ex cathedra* definition.
Some bishops at Vatican I wanted such a condition to be included: they
asked that "the form to be used by the Pontiff" in exercising his infallibility be determined and spelled out in the dogmatic formula they were
preparing. But in his main *relatio* of July 11, Gasser insisted that "this proposal simply cannot be accepted, because we are not dealing with something new here."[5] His point was that popes have *always* had the charism of
infallibility, and have handed down many definitive judgments over nearly
two millennia using a variety of formulae. Trying to insist on one or more
of the precise theological notes that had gradually become "customary" in
theology since, say, the Renaissance or Counter-Reformation period would
wrongly rule out *a priori* the infallibility of any papal intervention prior to
that period.[6] So the *relator*'s key words in his (already cited) July 16

evant to the infallibility or otherwise of this particular condemnation is a moot
point for present purposes, given that my opponent accepts that QC4–5 "is actually consistent with *DH*" (ibid.).

4   James T. O'Connor (ed. and transl.), *The Gift of Infallibility: the Official Relatio
on Infallibility of Bishop Vincent Gasser at Vatican Council I* (Boston: St. Paul
Editions, 1986), 74 (emphasis added).

5   O'Connor, op. cit., 47.

6   Cf. ibid. It is true that, in the last lines cited over n4 above, Gasser's terminology
includes, as we have already noted, several specific theological notes which for
several centuries had become quite "customary." But he was presenting those only
as examples of terms that popes *might* use in defining doctrine, and was certainly
not implying that they *must* use one or other of those terms every time they want-

clarification are those giving us this relatively simple criterion: the Pope, in *defining* something, "directly and conclusively pronounces his sentence" regarding a doctrine of faith and morals; and he does so "in such a way that each one of the faithful can be certain of the mind of . . . the Roman Pontiff."[7]

4. Now, in the case of proposition QC3, it is already plain from what has been said that Pius IX has "directly . . . pronounced his sentence" *as to its falsity* in such a way that "each one of the faithful" can easily "be certain of [his] mind" in that regard. For he brands it as not only as "evil" and "false and perverse," but as "contrary to the doctrine of Sacred Scripture (*contra sacrarum Litterarum . . . doctrinam*), of the Church, and of the holy Fathers."[8] So, going by Gasser's criteria for identifying infallible definitions (the only *official* criteria so far given to us outside of Vatican I's *Pastor Aeternus* itself), the only remaining question is whether it is equally certain that the Pontiff has also spoken "conclusively" in handing down this sentence. Some have held that a pope must pronounce an *anathema* against dissidents, or otherwise make it clear that they are outside the Church, in order for his sentence to bear the finality or conclusiveness that

ed to issue a recognizable *ex cathedra* definition. This is clear, first, from Gasser's use of a casual, almost dismissive, "etc." This would have been totally inappropriate and insufficient if his intention had been to tell the Fathers that there is a specific, determined set of now "customary" terms which popes must choose from every time they wish to *define* a doctrine. In that case the *relator* would of course have had to spell out and justify each and every one of those supposedly privileged terms. Secondly, and more importantly, any such intention on the part of Gasser would have been in flagrant contradiction with his own *relatio* of only five days earlier, in which, as we have seen here (cf. citation over n5 *supra*), he had firmly rejected the proposal of some other Fathers who thought the Council could and should specify the precise formula or vocabulary popes need to use in making *ex cathedra* definitions.

7 Cf. n3 *supra*.

8 Mr. Guminski raises a red herring here, citing this last expression but claiming it is irrelevant to whether QC3 is being condemned definitively (cf. FR, #13). However, he seems to be misunderstanding the "axiomatic" theological norm that he cites in support of this claim, namely, that "a solemn definition does not as such include arguments or incidental statements," since "only the doctrine itself, to which those arguments lead and which these *obiter dicta* illustrate, is to be considered as infallibly defined" (cf. FR, n17). Of course that norm is a valid one; but it has no relevance here, because neither I nor any other theologian is *claiming* that anything other than the "doctrine itself" that we are referring to as QC3 (reproduced in bold type in the first paragraph of this Appendix) "is to be considered as infallibly defined" – defined here, of course, as being false rather than true.

is necessary for an *ex cathedra* definition. But the *relator* suggests no such requirement. And in any case, such automatic exclusion from Church membership would apply only to dissidents from a *dogmatically* defined (i.e., revealed) truth, not from a defined truth of the second order ("necessarily connected to divine revelation").[9]

5. As regards *conclusiveness*, the key word in what Mr. Guminski calls the "operative declaration" of QC is undoubtedly *omnino*. Let us look at the whole sentence again:

> Therefore, by our Apostolic authority, we reprobate, proscribe, and condemn all and singular the evil opinions and doctrines severally mentioned in this letter, and will and command that they be thoroughly (*omnino*) held by all children of the Catholic Church as reprobated, proscribed and condemned.[10]

This appears to be the most common translation, but the English is poor, stilted and unclear at key points. We never speak of "thoroughly holding" that something is the case (as I am sure most readers will thoroughly agree). And when was the last time you heard anyone refer to a series of propositions or things with the expression "all and singular"?[11] Nevertheless, Mr. Guminski assures us that *omnino* "is best to be translated as *thoroughly* or *entirely*, in the quantitative sense of *without exception*."[12]

6. Now this is a patently indefensible understanding of what *omnino* means here, for several independent reasons. *First*, even supposing that we translate it – awkwardly – by either of the two words my adversary recommends, the resulting sentence would still never be used by any competent English speaker to express a "quantitative sense." In the sentence, "*I thoroughly/entirely hold that the above propositions A, B, C, D, and E are*

9   John Paul II, Apostolic Letter Motu Proprio, *Ad Tuendam Fidem* #3). And these "necessarily connected" truths are of course those which, as the 1998 document itself makes clear (cf. *Nota Doctrinalis* ##6–7, referenced at DHFR, n23 supra), are the object of definitive (infallible) teaching of the second category, as specified in the official 1989 Profession of Faith and in the *Code of Canon Law* as amended in 1998. They, no less than revealed truth itself, require from faithful Catholics an assent which is "full and irrevocable" (ibid., #8).

10 "*Itaque omnes et singulas pravas opiniones ac doctrinas singillatim hisce litteris commemorates auctoritate Nostra Apostolica reprobamus, proscribimus atque damnamus, easque ab ómnibus catholicae Ecclesiae filiis veluti reprobatas, proscriptas atque damnatas omnino haberi volumus et mandamus*" (DS 2896).

11 This is a slavishly literal rendition of the Latin "*omnes et singulas*" (see n9 *supra*).

12 FR, #12 (emphasis in original).

reprobated," who would ever guess that the adverb is supposed to mean "without exception"? Indeed, if it *did* mean that, the syntax would then be atrocious, because that adverbial phrase ("without exception") would be qualifying the wrong word, namely, "hold" instead of "reprobated." Correct English for the kind of "quantitative" affirmation that would support Mr. Guminski's case would of course be, "*I hold that the above propositions A, B, C, D, and E are, without exception, reprobated.*" But *omnino*, in the text of *QC*, plainly qualifies "be held" (*haberi*) and not *reprobatas*. Ergo. *Second*, Mr. Guminski offers no lexicographical evidence that *omnino* ever *can* mean "without exception." In almost a full column of tiny print dealing with this word, Lewis and Short's authoritative dictionary does give a couple of secondary senses that could be described as "quantitative," but not this.[13] *Third*, the only reason Mr. Guminski gives for favoring a quantitative sense of *omnino* over the primary qualitative sense is that "the pontiff wanted to make clear that every proposition condemned in *QC* was intended by him to be regarded . . . as reprobated, proscribed, and condemned."[14] But this makes *omnino* repetitious and superfluous; for Pius IX has already made that quantitative aspect of his intention abundantly clear earlier in the same sentence, where he says he is hereby reprobating, proscribing and condemning "each and every one (*omnes et singulas*) of the evil opinions mentioned one by one (*singillatim*) in this Letter." *Fourth,* the accepted translations of *QC* in other languages confirm that *omnino* is to be understood here in the first and most common sense given by Lewis and Short, which is qualitative rather than quantitative: "altogether, wholly, entirely, utterly." According to their dictionary, the word in this sense is a synonym for *penitus* (= "deeply," "through and through," "completely") and *prorsus* (= "by all means," "certainly," "truly," "absolutely"). In fact, the alternate quantitative sense of *omnino* seems to have disappeared from ecclesiastical Latin. In Aquinas's writings, for instance, the word is only used to mean "altogether, wholly, entirely, absolutely, utterly."[15] Now, to

---

13 The closest, near the end of the dictionary entry, is an admittedly "quantitative" usage sometimes found in classical Latin wherein *omnino* means "in general, generally, universally." But "in general" is still not a synonym for "without exception." Lewis and Short do give another quantitative sense of the word in classical Latin, but in this usage it accompanies a specific numeral, which it indicates as the total of a number of items being counted: "*omnino quinque,*" for instance, means "five in all" or "a total of five."

14 FR, #12.

15 Roy J. Deferrari, *A Latin-English Dictionary of St. Thomas Aquinas* (Boston: St. Paul Editions, 1986), 724. Indeed, in *QC* itself, Pius IX twice uses *omnino* in at

qualify a verb like "hold," the most idiomatic of these various vernacular alternatives would be "absolutely." And the following common translations in Spanish, Italian and French bear this out (emphasis added in each case):

". . . *queremos y mandamos que por todos los hijos de la Iglesia católica [las mismas] sean **absolutamente tenidas** por reprobadas, proscritas y condenadas.*"[16]

". . . *e vogliamo e comandiamo, che da tutti i figli della Chiesa cattolica s'**abbiano affatto** come riprovate, proscritte e condannate.*"[17]

". . . *et Nous voulons et ordonnons que tous les fils de l'Église catholique les **tiennent absolument** pour réprouvées, proscrites et condamnées.*"[18]

7. Now, to hold something "absolutely" is of course to hold it without reservations – without any element of tentativeness, uncertainty, or openness to possible correction. In other words, definitively, *conclusively*. So, judging by what the Vatican I *relator* has told us, nothing more can reasonably be asked for in order for "each one of the faithful [to] be certain" that Pius IX has intended to condemn definitively and infallibly QC3 and the other "evil" opinions enclosed by quotation marks in the encyclical. The Pontiff does not go so far as to condemn any of them as *heretical* – that is, as being directly opposed to some revealed truth. So we must conclude that he intended to define them as being contrary to certain secondary doctrines that are "to be held definitively," as truths that at least have a necessary connection to the revealed deposit.[19]

least two other places in this sense. The proposition condemned just prior to QC3 is that "the best constitution of public society and (also) civil progress **altogether** (or **absolutely**) require (*omnino requirere*) that human society be conducted and governed without regard being had to religion any more than if it did not exist; or, at least, without any distinction being made between the true religion and false ones." And QC3 itself is branded as an "**absolutely** (*or* **totally**) false (*omnino falsa*) idea of social government." Cf. Gaspari (ed.), op. cit., 994–995.

16   www.filosofia.org/mfa/far864a.htm
17   web.tiscali.it/pionono/quanta_cura.htm
18   www.salve-regina.com/Magistere/PIE_IX_quanta_cura.htm
19   In condemning QC3 as "contrary to the doctrine of Sacred Scripture" Pius IX and his theologians would not have had in mind a *direct* contradiction of something unequivocally revealed in the Bible. For that would have merited the censure "heretical," and in any case no such biblical text exists. What the Pope clearly had in mind is that QC3 is *indirectly* contrary to Scripture, i.e., that the truth opposed to QC3 is a theological conclusion reached by *reasoning from* the Bible. One suspects that the argument behind this appeal to Sacred Scripture would have been

8. Finally, it is worth pointing out that since Vatican II the magisterium itself, not just theologians and a conciliar *relatio,* has taught ever more explicitly that *non-revealed* doctrines can also be taught definitively. The 1917 *Code of Canon Law* had laid it down that "no doctrine is to be understood as dogmatically defined unless this is manifestly the case."[20] This was misleading, since, by omitting all reference to definitions other than those of *dogmas* (revealed truths to be held with "divine and Catholic faith"), the *Code* left the impression that the existence of any other kind of definition was uncertain. The 1983 *Code* has corrected this, replacing "dogmatically" by the broader term "infallibly."[21] This clearly makes room for definitions of secondary (necessarily connected) truths – definitions such as are found in *QC.* Their reality has been made still more explicit in the *Catechism of the Catholic Church*[22] as well as in the 1998 Motu Proprio *Ad Tuendam Fidem,* which amended the *Code* to this effect, together with the CDF's accompanying "Doctrinal Note." Indeed, this last document adds yet another type of magisterial teaching that expresses definitive doctrine (of either primary or secondary truths) when it states that the Pope can formally "confirm or reaffirm" doctrines already taught infallibly by the ordinary magisterium (as John Paul II had recently done regarding abortion and euthanasia in the Encyclical *Evangelium Vitae*).[23] Mr. Guminski mentions a number of Catholic theologians and canonists who did not recognize *QC* as containing infallible definitions.[24] However, as he notes, they all wrote "[w]ell before Vatican II." One suspects that if those scholars were able to re-evaluate Blessed Pius IX's *QC* condemnations now, in the light of *Lumen Gentium* and the postconciliar canonical and

along the following lines: first, God's law for Israel revealed in the Old Testament penalized "violators of the [true] religion" with the greatest severity (cf. WD, n33); second, the Catholic Church, the new Israel, is now the teacher of the true religion; and third, the "holy Fathers" and other Catholic popes and bishops have found nothing in the New Testament implying that in a Christian state the earlier Mosaic repression of religious unorthodoxy would have to be mitigated to the point of penalizing *only* those dissidents whose activity reaches the point of threatening "public peace." *Ergo.*

20 C. 1323 §1.
21 *"Infallibiliter definita nulla intellegitur doctrina, nisi id manifesto constiterit"* (c. 749 §3).
22 Cf. *CCC,* #2035, with its references to Vatican II (*LG* 25) and the 1973 CDF Instruction *Mysterium Ecclesiae,* #3.
23 Cf. *Nota Doctrinalis,* op.cit., 547–548, #9.
24 Cf. FR, n21.

magisterial developments we have just mentioned, most of them might join Blessed John Henry Newman (among many others) in concluding that the Pope's "infallible teaching voice" is heard "so [i.e., very] distinctly" in *QC*,[25] or that he was at the very least "confirming" there certain secondary doctrines already taught definitively by the ordinary and universal magisterium.[26]

25 Cf. WD, n20 for reference. In the authoritative *Dictionnaire de Théologie Catholique*, Edmond Dublanchy includes *QC* as the most recent example in a list of papal documents from the fifth to the nineteenth centuries that are "customarily, or quite customarily, considered to contain an infallible definition" ("Infaillibilité du Pape," t. VII, c. 1703). Dublanchy quotes Lucien Choupin, an expert on the respective degrees of authority of different kinds of magisterial interventions, as follows: "Many theologians and canonists would gladly add [to *Ineffabilis Deus*, i.e., as a second infallible document coming from Pope Pius IX] the celebrated encyclical *Quanta Cura* (*Beaucoup de théologiens et canonistes y ajouteraient volontiers la célèbre encyclique* Quanta cura)" (ibid., c. 1704). Among these theologians are Henri Hello, *Le Syllabus au XXme siècle* (Paris: Retaux, 1906) at 30–31, and J. M. Hervé, *Manuale Theologiae Dogmaticae*, vol. 1 (Paris: Berche & Pagis, 1962) at 481. Hervé here claims, as I do, that the infallible character of the *QC* condemnations "is obvious from the very words of the conclusion (*patet ex ipsis verbis conclusionis*)." By the "conclusion" he means the words Mr. Guminski has called the "Operative Declaration" (OD).

26 Fr. J. C. Fenton's changing views on this issue seem worthy of comment. Mr. Guminski quotes him as writing in 1947, "The teaching of the [*QC*] cannot, of course, be classified as a solemn definition of the Sovereign Pontiff, in the technical sense in which the Bull *Ineffabilis Deus* had contained a definition. Nevertheless the [*QC*] was and remains very obviously a tremendously important document of the ordinary *magisterium* of the Church" (FR, n21). Now, is Fenton implying here that *QC*, as well as containing no "solemn," i.e., dogmatic, definition of revealed truth (the primary object of infallibility), also contains no ex *cathedra* definitions pertaining to the secondary object – i.e., of truths necessarily connected to revelation? Most readers are likely to spontaneously answer "Yes" to this question, given that Fenton here classifies *QC* as part of the "ordinary" magisterium. For it is widely assumed that *ex cathedra* definitions are always exercises of the *extraordinary* magisterium, even when they involve the secondary object. But Fenton thought otherwise. Not long after publishing the comments cited by Mr. Guminski, he wrote: "[T]here has been an unfortunate inclination on the part of some authors to imagine that the Council's definition of papal infallibility applied only to the Sovereign Pontiff's solemn and extraordinary utterances, as distinguished from what is called his ordinary pronouncements" ("The Doctrinal Authority of Papal Encyclicals," Part II, *American Ecclesiastical Review*, (1949) vol. 121, at 211). Fenton thus understood 'non-solemn' *ex cathedra* definitions (i.e., those of 'secondary' truths) to be part of the *ordinary* papal magisterium. He also claimed that these could occur in papal encyclicals, not only

in the more august documents (Bulls and Apostolic Constitutions) used for "solemn and extraordinary utterances." So if, as seems quite likely, Fenton had already arrived at – or was arriving at – this position by the time he wrote his 1947 essay, his statement in that year that *QC* is part of the ordinary magisterium would not necessarily have implied a denial that its condemnations are *ex cathedra* (i.e., infallible *per se*).

Regardless of who is right about the meaning of "ordinary" and "extraordinary," Fenton's disagreement with the "inclination" he mentioned in 1949 shows he agreed by then with my contention that those pre-Vatican II authors were wrong who supposed that Vatican I's definition regards as "*ex cathedra*" only those papal utterances which either define dogmas (the "primary," *de fide* truths) or condemn opinions directly opposed to dogmas (i.e., heresies). Fenton (although he does not acknowledge this in his 1949 essay) had himself initially shared that same "inclination," which he finally came to recognize as "unfortunate." This undue limitation of the scope of papal infallibility – at odds, as we have seen, with Gasser's authoritative *relatio* at the Council itself – is the position clearly taken by Fenton in his 1941 book *The Concept of Sacred Theology* (cf. FR, n19) at 116–121 and 126.

271

Select Bibliography with Citations to Notes

Albornoz, A.F. Carrillo de. *Religious Liberty* (New York: Sheed and Ward, 1967): CH, n. 27.

_____. "Religious Freedom: Intrinsic or Fortuitous?" *Christian Century* 82 (September 15, 1965): 1122–1126: DH, n. 12.

Aquinas, St. Thomas. *Summa Theologiae,* (trans. Fathers of the English Dominican Province, 2nd & Rev'd ed., 1920) (http://www.sacred-texts.com/chr/aquinas/summa/index.htm): WD, n. 54; FR, nn. 31, 65, 67, 79; DHFR, n. 151; AppA, nn. 29–30.

_____. *Commentary to the First Epistle to the Corinthians* (trans. Fabian Larcher) (987–1046 by Daniel Keating) (Html-edited by Joseph Kenny, O.P.) (http://dhspriory.org/thomas/SS1Cor.htm#51): AppA, n. 30.

Augustine of Hippo, St. *Epistle 93* (to Vincentius) #5 (http://www.catholic-culture.org/culture/library/fathers/view.cfm?recnum=3240): AppA, n. 41.

Basile [Valuet], O.S.B., Fr. *La Liberté Religieuse et la Tradition Catholique* (2nd ed.) (Le Barroux FR.: Abbaye Sainte-Madeleine, 1998): FR, nn. 16, 59; WD, n. 33; DHFR, nn. 17–18, 48; AppA, nn. 31, 41, 54.

_____. *Le droit à la liberté religieuse dans la tradition de L'Église* (Le Barroux: Éditions Sainte-Madeleine, 2005): FR, nn. 16, 59; DHFR, n. 18.

Bea, S.J., [Cardinal] Augustin. *La Parola de Dio e l'Umanità: la dottrina del Concilio sulla rivelazione* (Assisi: Citadella Editrice, 1967): DH, n. 33.

Bernard, Edmond D. "The Doctrinal Value of the Ordinary Teaching of the Holy Father in View of *Humani Generis*," *Proceedings of the Sixth Annual Convention* (1951) (Catholic Theological Society of America), 78–121: FR, n. 27.

Bouscaren, T. Lincoln. *Catholic Law Digest: Officially Published Documents Affecting the Code of Canon Law* 1942–1953 (Milwaukee: Bruce Pub. Co.): FR, 75.

Butler, Cuthbert. *The Vatican Council 1869–1870* (ed. C. Butler) (Fontana Library, 1962): AppA, n. 58.

Carbone, Vincenzo. "Il ruolo di Paolo VI nell'evoluzione e nella redazione della dichiarazione 'Dignitatis Humanae'," in *Paolo VI e il rapporto Chiesa-mondo al Concilio* (Brescia: Istituto Paolo VI, 1991), 126–173: WD, nn. 60, 62, 89).

Cartechini, S. J., Sixtus. *De valore notarum theologicarum et de criteriis ad eas dignoscendas (ad usum auditorum,* (Rome: Pontificia Universitas Gregoriana, 1951) : FR, n. 27.

Choupin, Lucien. *Valeur des Décisions Doctrinales et Disciplinaires du Saint-Siège* (Paris: Gabriel Beauchesne, 3d ed. 1928): FR, n. 27; AppA, n. 58; AppB, n. 25.

Cyprian of Carthage, St. *Epistle* 64 (to Pomponius) #4 (http://www.catholicculture.org/culture/library/fathers/view.cfm?recnum=1778): AppA, n. 43.

Davies, Michael. *The Second Vatican Council and Religious Liberty* (Long Prairie: Neumann Press, 1992): CH, nn. 7, 54, 63, 77, 81; WD, nn. 106–107, 109; FR, nn. 75, 84; AppA, n. 44.

_____. *Apologia Pro Marcel Lefebvre*, [Dickinson, TX: Angelus Press, 1983] vol. II: DH, n. 26.

_____. *I Am With You Always* (Long Prairie, Minnesota: 1997): WD, n. 111.

Davis, S.J., Henry. *Moral and Pastoral Theology* (London: Sheed and Ward, 1945): FR, n. 67; AppA, n. 20.

Deferrari, Roy J. *A Latin-English Dictionary of St. Thomas Aquinas* (Boston: St. Paul Editions, 1986): AppB, n. 15.

D'Souza, Dinesh. *The Enemy At Home: The Cultural Left and Its Responsibility for 9/11* (New York: Doubleday, 2007): DHFR, n. 110.

Dulles, S. J., [Cardinal] Avery. *Magisterium: Teacher and Guardian of the Faith* (Naples FL: Sapiente Press, 2007): FRFR, nn. 9, 32.

_____. "*Dignitatis Humanae* and the development of Catholic Doctrine," in K.L. Grasso and R.P. Hunt (eds.), *Catholicism and Religious Freedom: Contemporary Reflections on Vatican II's Declaration on Religious Liberty* (Lanham, MD: Rowman & Littlefield, 2006), 43–67: DHFR, n. 14.

Fenton, Joseph Clifford. *The Concept of Sacred Theology* (Milwaukee: Bruce Publishing Co., 1941): FR, n. 19: AppB, n. 26.

_____. "The Theology of the Church and the State," *Proceedings of the Catholic Theological Society of America*, 2–46 (1947): FRFR, n. 21; DHFR, n. 25.

_____. "The Doctrinal Authority of Papal Encyclicals," Part II, 121 *American Ecclesiastical Review*, (1949) 210–20: AppB, n. 26.

_____. "The Religious Assent Due to the Teachings of Papal Encyclicals," 123 *American Ecclesiastical Review* (1950) 59–67: FR, n. 19.

_____. "Principles Underlying Traditional Church-State Doctrine," *American Ecclesiastical Review,* 126 (1952), 452–462: WD, n. 100; FR, n. 47; DHFR, n. 54.

_____. "The Question of Ecclesiastical Faith," 128 *American Ecclesiastical Review* (1953) 287–301: FR, n. 19.

Fessler, Joseph. *The True and the False Infallibility of the Popes: A Controversial Reply to Dr. Shulte* (New York: Catholic Publication Soc., 1875): FR, n. 41: AppA, n. 6.

Finnis, John. *Aquinas* (New York: Oxford University Press, 1998): FR, n. 3.

_____. "The Natural Law, Objective Morality, and Vatican Council II," in William E. May, ed., *Principles of Catholic Moral Life* (Chicago: Franciscan Herald Press, 1981), 113–150: FR, n. 80; DHFR, nn. 155–156.

Flannery, S.J., Kevin. "*Dignitatis Humanae* and the Development of Doctrine," *Catholic Dossier,* 6 (no. 2, March-April 2000), 31–35: DHFR, n. 16.

Gosselin, Jean-Edmé-Auguste. *The Power of the Popes during the Middle Ages or an Historical Inquiry into the Origin of the Temporal Power of the Holy See and the Constitutional Laws of the Middle Ages* (trans. M. Kelly) (London: C. Dolman. 1853): FR, 41, AppA, nn. 6, 70–73.

Gousset, [Cardinal] Thomas-Marie-Joseph. *Théologie Dogmatique: ou Exposition des Preuves et des Dogmes de la Religion Catholique* (9th ed., Paris, 1861): AppA, nn. 65–67.

Grisez, Germain. *The Way of the Lord Jesus, vol. I: Christian Moral Principles* (Chicago: Franciscan Herald Press, 1983): CH, n. 49; FR, n. 11.

_____. *The Way of the Lord Jesus, vol. II: Living a Christian Life* (Quincy IL: Franciscan Press, 1993): FR, n. 11.

Guminski, Arnold T. *The Constitutional Rights, Privileges, and Immunities of the American People: The Selective Incorporation of the Bill of Rights, the Refined Incorporation Model of Akhil Reed Amar, Dred Scott, National Citizenship and Its Implied Privileges and Immunities, the Second Amendment Right, and Much More* (Bloomington IN: iUniverse, 2009): FR, n. 1.

_____. *"Contra Harrison in Re Libertate Religiosa*: On the Meaning of *Dignitatis Humanae" Faith & Reason* 26 (2001): 39–83. [CH as published in this book slightly differs in several details from the version published in *Faith & Reason*]: WD, n. 1; FR, n. 2.

_____. "With How Great Care: The Authentic Meaning of the Doctrine of Pius IX's *Quanta Cura* and the *Syllabus of Errors* Concerning Freedom in Religious Matters" (Forthcoming): FR, n. 58.

Hamer, [Cardinal] Jérome. *La libertá religiosa nel Vaticano II* (Torino-Leumann, Elle Di Ci, 2nd. Ed., 1967): WD, n. 92.

Harrison, O.S., Brian W. *Religious Liberty and Contraception* (Melbourne: John XXIII Fellowship Co-Op. Ltd, 1988.) (referred to in this book as *RLC*) : *passim.*

_____. "Heresy – An Uncommitable Sin?" *Faith & Reason* 13 (1987), 9–27: FR, n. 78.

_____. "Vatican II and Religious Liberty: Contradiction or Continuity?" (*Catholic Dossier*, vol. 6, no. 2, March-April, 2000, 21–30) *Social Justice Review,* July/August 1989, 104–112 [referred to in this book as "*SJR89*"]: CH, nn. 2, 66–67, 69, 71; WD, nn. 71–72, 75; FR, n. 24; DHFR, n. 105.

_____. "The Church, Archbishop Lefebvre, and Religious Tolerance," *Fidelity,* October 1989, 38–44 [referred to in this book as "F89"] CH, nn. 2, 72, 76, 91.

_____. "The Second Vatican Council and Religious Liberty by Michael Davies," *Living Tradition,* No. 44, January 1993, 4–12 [also published in *Fidelity* (May 1993, 39–47), as "Did the Church Change Her Teaching on Religious Liberty?"]: CH. nn. 2, 78–87, 90; WD, nn. 101, 108, 113; FR, nn. 71, 74–75.

_____. "The Ex Cathedra Status of the Encyclical *Humanae Vitae*," in *Faith & Reason,* vol. XIX, no. 1. Spring 1993. 25–78: CH, n. 1; AppB, n. 3.

_____. "Roma Locuta Est, Causa Finita Est," in *For the Glory of God and the Salvation of the World (Proceedings of the 26th Annual National Wanderer Forum September 24th–26th, 1993)* (The Wanderer Forum Foundation), 39–48 (http://www.rtforum.org/lt/lt57.html) referred to in this book as "Roma ... Est"]: CH, nn. 2, 98–104; FR, nn. 7, 13, 26, 33, 89.

_____. "John Courtney Murray: A Reliable Interpreter of *Dignitatis Humanae?*" in *We Hold These Truths and More: Further Reflections on the American Proposition,* eds. Donald J. D'Elia & Stephen M. Krason (Steubenville: Franciscan Univ. Press, 1993), 134–165: CH, n. 2; WD, nn. 13, 17; FR, n. 46.

_____. "The 'Secondary Object' of Papal Infallibility: A Reply to Frank Mobbs," *Irish Theological Quarterly,* 65 (2000): 319–334: FR, n. 14.

_____. "Skeletons in the Conciliar Closet," *The Remnant* (2004) (http://ourworldcompuserve.com/homepages/remnant/skel.htm): FR, n. 25.

_____. "What Does *Dignitatis Humanae* Mean? A Reply to Arnold Guminski" *Faith & Reason* 30 (2005), 243–295 [WD as published in this book slightly differs in several details from the version published in *Faith & Reason*]: FR, n. 2.

Hart, David Bentley. *Atheist Delusions: The Christian Revolution and Its Fashionable Enemies* (New Haven & London: Yale University Press, 2009): DHFR, n. 195.

Hello, Henri. *Le Syllabus au XXme siècle* (Paris: Retaux, 1906: AppB, n. 25.

Hergenröther, [Cardinal] Joseph. *Catholic Church and Christian State: A Series of Essays on the Relation of the Church to the Civil Power* (London: Burnes & Oates, 1876): FR, nn. 18–19, 27, 41; AppA, nn. 6, 21.

Hervé, J.M. *Manuale Theologiae Dogmaticae,* vol. I (Westminster, Maryland: Newman Bookshop, 1946): WD, n. 111; AppB, n. 25.

Hittinger, F. Russell. "The Declaration on Religious Freedom, *Dignitatis Humanae*" in M.L. Lamb and M. Levering (eds.), *Vatican II: Renewal Within Tradition* (Oxford University Press, 2008), 359–382: DHFR, n. 18.

Hughey, Jr., John David. *Religious Freedom in Spain: Its Ebb and Flow* (Nashville, Tenn: Broadman Press, 1955): FR, nn. 55, 58–59, 77.

Iung, Nicolas. *Le Droit Public de L'Église* (Paris: Procure Générale Du Clergé, 1948): FR, n. 21.

Jiménez-Urresti, Teodoro. "Religious Freedom in a Catholic Country: The Case of Spain," in *Religious Freedom* (*Concilium* volume 18) (New York: Paulist Press, 1966), 91–108: FR, n. 77.

Journet, [Cardinal] Charles. *The Church of the Word Incarnate vol. I: The Apostolic Hierarchy* (trans. A.H.C. Downes) (New York; Sheed and Ward, 1955): AppA, nn. 30, 57.

Koch, Anthony – Preuss, Arthur. *A Handbook of Moral Theology* (St. Louis: B. Herder Book Co.. 1919–1924): CH, n. 49; FR, n. 67.

Laforêt, Nicole-Joseph. *Les Dogmes Catholiques: Exposés, Prouvés et Vengés des Attaques de l'Hérésie et de l'Incrédulité* (2nd ed., Paris/Tournai, 1860): AppA, nn. 68–69.

Lamont, John R.T. "Determination of the Content and Degree of Authority of Church Teachings," 72 *The Thomist* (2008): 371–407: DHFR, n. 25.

LeGuillou, Louis & Marie-Joseph. *La condemnation de Lamennais* (Paris: Beauchesne, 1982): FR, n. 19.

Lercher, S.J., Ludovicus. *Institutiones Theologiae Dogmaticae*, 5th ed. (Barcelona: Herder, 1951): WD, n. 111–112.

Lecler, S.J., Joseph. *Toleration and the Reformation* (trans. T.L. Westow) (London: Longmans, 1960): FR, n. 41.

_____. *The Two Sovereignties: A Study of the Relationship Between Church and State* (London: Burns Oates & Washbourne, 1952): AppA, nn. 8, 73.

Levada, [Cardinal] William J. *Infallible Church Magisterium and the Natural Moral Law: Excerta ex dissertatione ad lauream in Facultate Theologiae Pontificiae Universitatis Gregorianae* (Roma: Pontificia Universitas Gregoriana, 1971): FR, n. 32.

Lucien, Bernard. *Révelation et Tradition: Les lieux médiateurs de la Révelation divine publique, du depot de la foi au Magistère vivant de l'Église* (Brannay FR: Editions Nuntiavit, 2009): FR, n. 19.

Marc, Clément. *Institutiones morales* (Rome, 1889): AppA, n. 21.

Margerie, S.J., Bernard de. *Liberté religieuse et règne du Christ* (Paris: Ed. du Cerf, 1988): DHFR, n. 15.

Marshner, William. H. "*Dignitatis Humanae* and Traditional Teaching on Church and State," *Faith & Reason,* 9: Fall 1983), 222–248): DHFR, n. 196.

Martin, Thomas Owen. "Theodosius' Laws on Heretics," *The American Ecclesiastical Review* 123 (Aug. 1950), 117–136: FR. N. 41.

Mattei, Roberto de. *L'Italia Cattolica e il Nuovo Concordato* (Rome: Centro Culturale Lepanto, 1985): WD, n. 98.

May, William E. *An Introduction to Moral Theology* (Huntington, IN: Our Sunday Visitor Publishing Division, 2nd ed. 2003): FR, nn. 79–80.

_____. "The Church's Moral Teaching, Holiness, and Personal Vocation" (May 2003), (www.christendom-awake.org/pages/holiness.htm): FR, n. 80; DHFR, nn. 151, 153.

Minnerath, Roland. *L'Église et Les États Concordataires (1846–1981)* (Paris: Les Éditions du Cerf, 1983): CH, n. 54.

Mobbs, Frank. *Beyond Its Authority: The Magisterium & Matters of Natural Law* (Morehouse Pub. Co., 1997): FR, n. 8.

Most, William. "Religious Liberty: What the Texts Demand," *Faith & Reason,* 9 (1983), 196–209: CH, n.105; DHFR, n. 197.

Moulart, Fred. J. *L'Église et L'État ou Les Deux Puissances* (Louvain-Paris, 3rd ed. 1887): AppA, nn. 8, 58.

Murray, John Courtney. "The Problem of Religious Freedom," in (ed. J.L. Hooper), *Religious Liberty: Catholic Struggles With Pluralism* (Louisville, KY: Westminster/John Knox Press, 1993) (originally published in *Theological Studies* 25 [1964]: 503–575): WD, 15: DH, nn. 10–11; DHFR, nn. 10–11.

Newman, [Cardinal] John Henry. "Letter to the Duke of Norfolk," in *Certain Difficulties Felt by Anglicans in Catholic Teaching Considered* (London: Longmans, Green, 1920): WD, n. 20.

O'Connor, James T. (ed. and transl.), *The Gift of Infallibility: the Official Relatio on Infallibility of Bishop Vincent Gasser at Vatican Council I* (Boston: St. Paul Editions, 1986): AppB, nn. 3–5.

Ocariz, Fernando. "Sulla libertà religiosa: continuità del Vaticano II con il magistero precedente," *Annales Theologici,* 3 (June 1989), 71–97: DHFR, nn. 13, 19, 47, 66.

Orsy, S. J., Ladislas. *Receiving the Council: Theological and Canonical Insights and Debates* (Collegeville MN: Liturgical Press, 2009): FR, n. 9.

Ott, Ludwig. *Fundamentals of Catholic Dogma* (Rockford, IL: TAN Books, 1974): FR, n. 19; AppB, 3.

Pavan, [Cardinal] Pietro. "Declaration on Religious Freedom," in 4 *Commentary on the Documents of Vatican II,* ed. Herbert Vorgrimler (New York: Herder and Herder, 1969), 49–86: CH, nn. 25, 35.

Pavlischek, Keith J. *John Courtney Murray and the Dilemma of Religious Toleration* (Kirksville, Missouri: Thomas Jefferson University Press, 1994): WD, nn. 99–100; DHFR, n. 12.

Pratt, S.J., Ferdinand. *The Theology of St. Paul* (trans. J.L. Stoddard) (Westminster Md.: Newman Bookshop, 1926): AppA, n. 30.

Rodríguez, O.P., Victorino. "Estudio histórico-doctrinal de la declaración sobre libertad religiosa del Concilio Vaticano II," *La Ciencia Tomista,* 93 (1966), 193–339: DHFR, nn. 18, 47.

Scanlon, O.F.M. Cap, Regis. "Did Vatican II Reverse the Church's Teaching on religious liberty?," *Homiletic & Pastoral Review,* January 2011, 61–68: DHFR, n. 197.

Schroeder, H. J. *Disciplinary Decrees of the General Councils* (St. Louis: B. Herder, 1937): AppA, n. 9.

Sears, A. & Osten, C. *The Homosexual Agenda: Exposing the Principal Threat to Religious Freedom Today* (Nashville, TN: Broadman & Holman, 2003): WD, n. 97, DHFR, n. 109.

Spencer, Robert. *Stealth Jihad: How Radical Islam Is Subverting America Without Guns or Bombs* (Washington, DC: Regnery Publishing, 2008): DHFR, n. 110.

Sungenis, Robert A. *Galileo Was Wrong: the Church Was Right,* 4th ed. (Stateline, Pennsylvania: Catholic Apologetics International Publishing, Inc., 2008): DHFR, n. 3.

Suarez, Francisco. *De Triplici Virtute Theologica, Fide, Spe, et Charitate* (1621), in Gwaldys L. Williams, ed., *Selections from Three Works of Francisco Suarez, S.J.,* (Oxford: Clarendon Press, 1944): FR, n. 83.

Tertullian. "To Scapula" [212], *Tertullian: Apologetical Works and Minucius Felix Octavius* (trans. R. Arbesmann et al.) (New York: Fathers of the Church, 1950): AppA, n. 42.

Vacandard, Elphège. "La Nature Du Pouvoir Coercitif De L'Église," in *Études De Critique Et D'Histoire Religieuse (Deuxième Série)* (Paris: Librarie Victor Lecoffre, 1914), 219–243: FR, n. 21.

Vermeersch, S.J., Arthur. *Tolerance* (New York: Benzinger Bros., 1913): AppA, n. 41, 62–64.

Ward, William George. *Essays on the Church's Doctrinal Authority* (London: Burns & Oates, 1880): FR, n. 61.

Wernz, S.J., Franz Xavier. *Jus Decretalium* (Rome, 1905), I: FR, n. 21.

Whitehead, Kenneth D. "Summarizing the Controversy," *Catholic* Dossier, 6 (2000). 6–13: DHFR, n. 196.

Wildmon, Donald A. *Speechless: Silencing the Christians* (Richard Vigilante Books, 2009): DHFR, n. 109.

Wogaman, Philip. *Protestant Faith and Religious Liberty* (Nashville: Abingdon Press, 1967): DHFR, n. 12.

ENCYCLOPEDIAS

The Catholic Encyclopedia (Robert Appleton Co. – Encyclopedia Press, 1907–1914) (http://oce.catholic.com/volumes.php], [http://www. catholicity.com/encyclopedia], or [http://www.newadvent.org/cathen/index.html]):

Blötzer, Joseph. s.v. "Inquisition," (1910) vol. 8: 26–38: AppA, n.10.

Boudinhon, Auguste. s.v. "Excommunication," (1909) vol. 5: 678–91: AppA, n. 19.

Bridge, James. s.v. "Persecution," (1911) vol. 11: 703–04: AppA, n. 10.

Coppieters, Honoré. s.v. "Apostles," (1907) vol. 1: 626–29: AppA, n. 30.

Fox, James J. s.v. "Natural Law," (1910) vol. 9: 76–79: CH, n. 49; FR, n. 38.

_____. s.v. "Slavery," (1912) vol. 14: 36–41: CH, n. 49.

Harty, John H. s.v. "Definition, Theological," (1911) vol. 4: 675–76: FR, n. 17.

Van Hove, Alphonse. s.v. "Apostasy," (1907) vol. 1: 624–26: AppA, n. 10.

Wilhelm, Joseph. s.v. "Heresy," (1911) vol. 7: 257–62 : AppA, nn. 10, 21.

Dictionnaire de Théologie Catholique (Paris: Letouzey et Ané, 1909–1950).

Breugnet, Auguste. s.v. "Apostasie," (1909) vol.1: cc. 213–72: AppA, n. 21.

Bride, André. s.v. "Peines Ecclésiastiques," (1933) vol. 12: cc. 624–59: AppA, nn. 30, 58.

Dublanchy, Edmond. s.v. "Église," (sec.IV) (1911) vol. 4: cc. 2185–2186: WD, nn. 111–112.

_____. s.v. "Infaillibilité du Pape," (1927) vol. 7: cc. 1637–1718: AppB, n. 25.

Glez, Gaston. s.v. "Pouvoir du Pape en Matière Temporale," (1933) vol. 12: cc. 2670–2772: AppA, nn. 8, 73.

Mangenot, Joseph-Eugène. s.v. "Encycliques," (1924) vol. 5: cc. 14–16: FR, n. 21.

Dictionnaire de Droit Canonique (Paris: Letouzey et Ané, 1935–1965).

Iung, Nicholas & Naz, R. s.v. "Contrainte," (1949) vol. 4: cc. 498–505: AppA, n. 49.

Laprat, René. s.v. "Bras Séculier (Livraison au)," (1937) vol. 2: cc. 981–1060: AppA, n. 34.

CHURCH DOCUMENTS WITH PAGE CITATIONS
ENCYCLICALS AND OTHER PAPAL DOCUMENTS

John XXII:
[Constitution] *Licut iuxta doctrinum* (1327): AppA, n. 48.

Pius VI:
[Brief] *Quod Aliquantum* (1791) (http://www.laportelatine.org/biblio-theque/encycliques/PieVI/Quod_Aliquantum.php): CH, n. 96; AppA, n. 54.

Gregory XVI:
[Encyclical] *Mirari Vos* (August 15, 1832), (http://www.papalencyclicals.net/Greg16/g16mirar.htm): CH, nn. 6, 87; WD, n. 105; FR, nn. 27, 59: DHFR, n. 77.

[Encyclical] *Singulari Nos* (June 25, 1834) (http://www.papalencyclicals.net/Greg16/g16singu.htm: FR, n. 27.

Pius IX:
[Encyclical] *Quanta Cura* (December 8, 1864) *Dublin Review* (n.s.) 4

(April 1865): 500–513) (http://www.papalencyclicals.net/
Pius09/p9quanta.htm): CH, nn. 6, 61, 87, 96, 104; WD. nn. 20; FR, nn.
14–16, 18, 21, 58, 60–61; DHFR, nn. 66–67, 103, 172; AppB, nn. 1,
7, 9–10, 14.

_____. *Syllabus of Errors* (December 8, 1864) *Dublin Review* (n.s.) 4
(April 1865): 5: 513–529) (http://www.papalencyclicals.
net/Pius09/p9syll.htm): CH, n. 6; WD, nn. 20, 77; FR, nn. 14, 18, 58,
61; DHFR, 77; AppA, n. 55.

_____, Allocution] *Quibus Luctuosissimis* (September 15, 1851): FR, n. 59.

Leo XIII:
[Encyclical] *Immortale Dei* (November 1, 1885)
(http://www.vatican.va/holy_father/leo_xiii/encyclicals/documents/hf
_l-xiii_enc_01111885_immortale-dei_en.html): CH, n. 6; WD, nn. 69,
83; FR, nn. 35, 61; DHFR, nn. 120–121, 143, 181; AppA, nn. 33

[Encyclical] *Libertas Praestantissimum* (June 20, 1888) (http://www.vati-
can.va/holy_father/leo_xiii/encyclicals/documents/hf_l-
xiii_enc_20061888_libertas_en.html): CH, n. 6, 61; WD, n. 93; FR,
nn. 34–35; DHFR, nn. 120–121, 138, 178, 181.

[Encyclical] *Longinqua Oceani* (January 6, 1895) (http://www.vatican.va/
holy_father/leo_xiii/encyclicals/documents/hf_l-
xiii_enc_06011895_longinqua_en.html); FR, n. 50.

Pius XI
[Encyclical] *Quas Primas* (December 11, 1925) (http://www.
vatican.va/holy_father/pius_xi/encyclicals/documents/hf_p-
xi_enc_11121925_quas-primas_en.html): WD, n. 93; FR, nn. 33.

Pius XII:
[Encyclical] *Mystici Corporis* (June 29, 1943) (http://www.
vatican.va/holy_father/pius_xii/encyclicals/documents/hf_p-
xii_enc_29061943_mystici-corporis-christi_en.html): CH, n. 89;
AppA, nn. 3, 12, 35, 37.

Ecco che già un anno, Allocution to the Sacred Roman Rota (October 6,
1946) (*Catholic Mind* 45 [March 1947] 129–33): CH, n. 89; FR, n. 75;
AppA, nn. 3, 38–39.

Ci Riesce, Allocution to Catholic Italian Jurists (December 6, 1953) (*Catholic Mind,* 52 [April, 1954]: 244–251) (http://www.ewtn.com/library/papaldoc/p12ciri.htm): CH, nn. 6, 61; WD, nn. 107, 109; FR, n. 75; DHFR, nn. 136–137.

John XXIII:
[Encyclical] *Pacem in Terris* (11 April 1963) (http://www.vatican.va/holy_father/john_xxiii/encyclicals/documents/hf_j-xxiii_enc_11041963_pacem_en.html): CH, nn. 13, 89.

Paul VI
Allocution to VIII International Congress of Young Lawyers, September 24, 1970) (www.vatican.va/holy_father/paul_vi/speeches/1970/documents/hf_p-vi_spe_19700924_avvocati_it.html): DHFR, n. 165.

John Paul II:
[Encyclical] *Redemptor Hominis* (March 4, 1979) (http://www.vatican.va/edocs/ENG0218/_INDEX.HTM): FR, 90.

[Encyclical] *Veritatis Splendor* (August 6, 1993) (http://www.vatican.va/edocs/ENG0222/_INDEX.HTM): CH, nn. 49, 51–52, 60; FR, nn. 37.

[Motu Propio] *Ad Tuendam Fidem* (May 18, 1998) (http://www.vatican.va/holy_father/john_paul_ii/motu_proprio/documents/hf_jp-ii_motu-proprio_30061998_ad-tuendam-fidem_en.html); FR: nn. 9, 18–19, 20; DHFR, n. 22; AppB, n. 9.

[Apostolic Letter] *Tertio Millennio Adveniente* (November 10, 1994) (*AAS* 87/1 [January 2, 1995]. 5–41) (http://www.vatican.va/holy_father/john_paul_ii/apost_letters/documents/hf_jp-ii_apl_10111994_tertio-millennio-adveniente_en.html) : CH, nn. 51–52; WD, nn. 50–51; FR, n. 39.

[Apostolic Letter] *Ecclesia Dei* (July 2, 1988) (http://www.vatican.va/holy_father/john_paul_ii/motu_proprio/documents/hf_jp-ii_motu-proprio_02071988_ecclesia-dei_en.html): CH, 73.

[Apostolic Exhortation] *Pastores Dabo Vobis* http://www.vatican.va/holy_father/john_paul_ii/apost_exhortations/documents/hf_jp-ii_exh_25031992_pastores-dabo-vobis_en.html: DHFR, n. 42.

Address to the Participants in the Congress on Secularism and Religious Freedom marking the Thirtieth Anniversary of [*DH*] (December 7, 1995) (http://www.vatican.va/holy_father/john_paul_ii/speeches /index.htm): CH. n. 52, 96.

Message for the XXIV World Day of Peace for January 1, 1991 (December 8, 1990) (http://www.vatican.va/holy_father/john_paul_ii/messages/ peace/documents/hf_jp-ii_mes_08121990_xxiv-world-day-for-peace_en.html): CH, n. 89.

Message for the XXXI World Day of Peace for January 1, 1999 (December 8, 1998) (http://www.vatican.va/holy_father/john_paul_ii/messages/ peace/documents/hf_jp-ii_mes_14121998_xxxii-world-day-for-peace_en.html): CH, n. 89.

Address to the European Parliament of Strasbourg (October 11, 1988) (http://www.vatican.va/holy_father/john_paul_ii/speeches/1988/october/documents/hf_jp-ii_spe_19881011_european-parliament_fr.html): FR, n. 41.

Homily and the Prayers of the Faithful during the Day of Pardon Mass (12 March 2000), (*The Pope Speaks* 45: 242–248) (http://www.vatican.va/holy_father/john_paul_ii/homilies/2000/documents/hf_jp-ii_hom_20000312_pardon_en.html): CH, n. 52.

The Pope's Catechesis of 1 September 1999, 45 *The Pope Speaks* 49–50: CH, n. 52.

Benedict XVI

[Encyclical] *Sacerdotii Nostri Primordia* (1 August 1959) (http://www.vatican.va/holy_father/john_xxiii/encyclicals/documents/hf_j-xxiii_enc_19590801_sacerdotii_en.html): DHFR, n. 41.

Motu Proprio, *Omnium in Mentum* (October 26, 2009) (http://www.vatican.va/holy_father/benedict_xvi/apost_letters/documents/hf_ben-xvi_apl_20091026_codex-iuris-canonici_en.html): AppA, n. 45.

Address to the Roman Curia (December 22, 2005) (http://www.vatican.va/holy_father/benedict_xvi/speeches/2005/december/documents/hf_ben_xvi_spe_20051222_roman-curia_en.html): FR, nn. 28–29; DHFR, n. 3.

Address to Representatives of British Society at Westminster Hall, September 17, 2010) (http://www.vatican.va/holy_father/

benedict_xvi/speeches/2010/september/documents/hf_ben-xvi_spe_20100917_societa-civile_en.html) (*L'Osservatore Romano* [Eng. ed.], September 22, 2010, 12–13: DHFR, n. 109.

Address to the Members of the Diplomatic Corps, January 10, 2011(http://www.vatican.va/holy_father/benedict_xvi/speeches/2011/january/documents/hf_ben-xvi_spe_20110110_diplomatic-corps_en.html): CH, n. 96.

Message for the World Day of Peace , January 1, 2011 (http://www.vatican.va/holy_father/benedict_xvi/messages/peace/documents/hf_ben-xvi_mes_20101208_xliv-world-day-peace_en.html): CH, n. 96.

CONGREGATION FOR THE DOCTRINE OF THE FAITH [CDF]

Declaration *Mysterium Ecclesiae* (June 24, 1973) (http://www.vatican.va/roman_curia/congregations/cfaith/documents/rc_con_cfaith_doc_19730705_mysterium-ecclesiae_en.html): FR, n. 9; AppB, n. 22.

Donum Veritas: Instruction on Ecclesial Vocation of the Theologian (May 24, 1990) (Boston: St. Paul Books & Media, n.d.) http://www.vatican.va/roman_curia/congregations/cfaith/documents/rc_con_cfaith_doc_19900524_theologian-vocation_en.html: CH, n. 49; FR, nn. 9–10, 29, 32, 37; DHFR, n. 27; AppB, n. 3.

Doctrinal Commentary on the Concluding Formula of the "Professio fidei" (June 29, 1998) http://www.vatican.va/roman_curia/congregations/cfaith/documents/rc_con_cfaith_doc_1998_professio-fidei_en.html (see FR n9) : FR, nn. 9, 18, 20; DHFR, nn. 23–24, AppB, nn. 3, 23.

DOCUMENTS OF ECUMENICAL COUNCILS

Fourth Lateran Council (1215): Tanner I: 230–271.

[Constitution] *Firmiter*: CH, n. 89; AppA, n. 9.

Council of Basile (1431–1438): Tanner I: 455–513).

Decrees on Jews and Neophytes (1434): AppA, n. 9.

Council of Constance (1414–1418): Tanner I: 405–450.

Condemned Articles of John Hus: AppA, n. 50.

Council of Florence (1439–1443): Tanner I: 523–582).
Bull of Union with the Copts (1442): DHFR, n. 115.

Council of Trent (1545–1563): Tanner II: 660–799.
Decretum primum [De sacramentis] (1547): AppA, nn. 46.

Vatican Council I (1869–1870): Tanner II: 802–816.
De Fide: WD, n. 69; AppA, 36.
Dei Filius: FR, n. 9.
Dei Verbum: WD, n. 33.
Pastor Aeternis: WD, nn. 20, 74; FR, n. 9.

Vatican Council II (1962–1965): Tanner II: 820–1135.
Dei Verbum [Dogmatic Constitution on Divine Revelation] (November 18, 1965): FR, n. 36.

Dignitatis Humanae [Declaration on Religious Liberty] (December 7, 1965) passim.

Gaudium et Spes [Pastoral Constitution on the Church in the World of Today] (December 7, 1965): CH, n. 59; FR, n. 51; DHFR, n. 28; AppA, #76.

Gravissimum Educationis [Declaration on Christian Education] (October 28, 1965): WD, n. 78; DHFR, n 134.

Lumen Gentium (Dogmatic Constitution of the Church) (November 21, 1964); FR, n. 9; DHFR, n. 26; AppA, n. 12.

Unitatis Redintegratio (Decree on Ecumenism) (November 21, 1964): AppA, n. 12.

MISCELLANEOUS AUTHORITIES

[Schema on the Church: On the Relations between the Church and State and on Religious Tolerance] Schema De Ecclesia, caput IX, De Relationibus Inter Ecclesium et Statum Necnon de Tolerantia Religiosa (*Acta et Documenta Concilio Oecumenico Vaticano II Apparando* (Typic Polyglottis Vaticanis, 1968): s. II/vol. II/pt. IV/ 657–672 [Eng. trans., less notes, in M. Davies, *The Second Vatican Council and Religious Liberty, supra*, at 295–302]: CH, nn. 25, 63, 81; WD, n. 106, FR, nn, 75, 83; AppA, 44.

Acta Synodalia Sacrosancti Concilii Oecumenici Vaticani (Vatican City: Typis Polyglottis Vaticanis) (1970–1986): CH, nn. 25, 34; WD, nn. 26, 37, 39, 41, 61, 85, 87; FR, nn. 23, 49, 69, 81, 88; DHFR, nn. 50, 123, 142, 161–163, 166, 193: AppA, nn.14–17, 27.

Catechism of the Catholic Church (2nd ed.) (Vatican City: Libreria Editrice Vaticana, 1997): CH, nn. 71, 93–96, 102; WD, nn. 52, 69, 76–77, 93, 113; FR, nn. 1, 9, 20, 45, 53–54, 81; DHFR, at nn. 4, 29, 61–62, 82, 102, 108, 113, 143, 152, 169, 172.

The Companion to the Catechism of the Catholic Church (San Francisco: Ignatius, Press, 1995): FR, n. 16; DHFR, nn. 120–121, 143, 172, 181.

Code of Canon Law: Latin-English Edition (Washington DC: Canon Law Society of America, 1983): FR, nn. 55, 68; AppA, nn. 45, 57; AppB, nn. 9, 20–222.

Codicis Iuris Canonici Fontes, P. Gaspari, ed. (Rome: Vatican Press, 1924), vol II: AppB, n. 1.

Decrees of the Ecumenical Councils, Norman P. Tanner, ed. (trans. G. Alberigo et al,), (Washington DC: Georgetown Univ. Press, 1990): passim.

Enchiridion Symbolorum Definition et Declarationum de Rebus Fidei et Morum (Henricus Denzinger – Adolfus Schönmetzer) 33rd ed., 1978): AppA, nn. 48–49, 51–53, 56.

L'Encyclique et L'Episcopat Français: Recueil Complet (Paris; Gaiguet et Pougeois, 1865): AppA, nn. 59–61.

The 1917 Pio-Benedictine Code of Canon Law (Peters, Edward N., ed.) (San Francisco: Ignatius Press, 2001): AppA, nn. 18, 34; AppB, n. 21

The Papal Encyclicals 1740–1878, ed. Claudia Carlin, IHM (Ann Arbor: Perian Press, 1990): FR, n. 16.

About the Authors

Arnold T. Guminski received his BA in history and philosophy from the University of Buffalo in 1952, and his juris doctorate from the University of California at Los Angeles School of Law in 1956. Admitted to the California State Bar in 1957, he was on active duty in the US Army 1957–1963 including service as a JAGC officer in France (1930–1963). He was a deputy district attorney for Los Angeles County, 1963–1993, with extensive appellate practice which included twice appearing before the United States Supreme Court. He is now retired and resides with his wife, Annegret, in Boulder, Colorado. Guminski is an independent scholar. He has authored the book *The Constitutional Rights, Privileges, and Immunities of the American People: The Selective Incorporation of the Bill of Rights, the Refined Incorporation Model of Akhil Reed Amar, Dred Scott, National Citizenship and its Implied Privileges and Immunities, the Second Amendment Right, and Much More* (Bloomington, Ind.: Universe, Inc., 2009); and has also written essays published in the journals *Whittier Law Review*, *Philo*, and *Philosophia Christi*, as well as on the Secular Web.

Brian W. Harrison, O.S., a priest of the Society of the Oblates of Wisdom, is an emeritus Professor of Theology of the Pontifical Catholic University of Puerto Rico. He was born in Australia and, after being raised a Presbyterian, converted to the Catholic faith in 1972. After completing his Licentiate in Theology at the 'Angelicum' university in Rome, he was ordained as a priest in 1985 by Pope John Paul II. In 1997 he gained his doctorate in Systematic Theology, *summa cum laude*, from Rome's Pontifical Athenæum (now University) of the Holy Cross. Since 2007 Fr. Harrison, who is well-known as a speaker and writer, has been scholar-in-residence at the Oblates of Wisdom Study Center in St. Louis, Missouri. He is the author of two books and over 120 articles in Catholic books, journals and periodicals in the U.S.A., Australia, Britain, France, Spain and Puerto Rico. His special interest in theological and liturgical matters, in keeping with the charism of the Oblates of Wisdom, is upholding a 'hermeneutic of continuity' between the teachings of Vatican Council II and the bimillennial heritage of Catholic Tradition.